THE MONEY SAVING WEALTH BUILDING GUIDE FOR THE NEW ECONOMY

By Glenn H. Petry, PhD
Finance and International Economics

www.financejock.com

This publication was written to provide authoritative information with regard to the material covered. It is sold with the understanding that the author and publisher are not engaged in offering accounting, legal, automotive, financial, construction, travel, educational, and other professional services in this publication. If such services are needed, then a competent professor should be hired.

While the author has made every effort to provide current information at the time of publication, some information may change. The author and publisher specifically disclaim any liability for any implied warranties or errors, lack of completeness, losses, or damages (including consequential, special, incidental, or any other) that occur from any use of information in this book. The advice contained herein may not be suitable for your situation.

Published by
Grand Avenue Press
Bend, Oregon
Portland, Oregon
email: info@grandavenuepress.com
website: www.GrandAvenuePress.com

Dr. Petry's website: http://www.financejock.com

Copyright © 2010
ISBN: 978-0-692-01043-3
Cover Design and Book Layout by:
Vicki Grayson Liden, www.graysondesign.net

Printed in the United States of America

WHY YOU SHOULD BUY THIS BOOK

Most people buying this book want advice on securing their financial future because they are spending too much and saving and investing too little. Here are 16 reasons why you should read my financial advice. I have

- *Refined these techniques over more than four decades.*
- *Saved money and built wealth so I am both a teacher and a doer.*
- *Grown up dirt poor and earned my money the hard way.*
- *Authored or coauthored over 60 publications.*
- *Finished my B.S., M.B.A., and PhD from four different major universities in 5 ½ years despite having three different undergraduate majors while working my way through college.*
- *Spent over 5,000 hours in researching and writing this book.*
- *Taught basic finance courses to 14,000, often financially challenged, students so I know how to communicate at the basic level.*
- *Been a consultant for many entities including Fortune 500 companies, banks, state and U.S. Governments including NASA and NOAA.*
- *Been an expert witness in federal and state court and before Congress.*
- *Been the Director of the Executive-in-Residence Program at Washington State University for 20 years.*
- *Started and run numerous businesses.*
- *A broad array of experiences in large and small businesses.*
- *Been a real estate developer and/or general contractor for 23 of my projects.*
- *Been a landlord for 34 years.*
- *Owned both residential and commercial real estate.*
- *Never defaulted on any debts.*

For many people, this book will fundamentally change their philosophy of investing, saving, and spending. I am an entrepreneur not only in the sense of making money in business but also in life and in education. I am truly **"The Everyday Everywhere Entrepreneur"** (which was the original title of this book). I am always on the look-out for deals, **Everyday, Everywhere**.

This book would be a superb gift for everyone from high school and college graduates to families or retirees. It contains a vast amount of information and guidance for the unsophisticated to those who "know everything." This book will truly surprise you with its insights and wisdom. I believe you will love this book. If you do, tell both your friends and your enemies. If you hate it, then just tell your enemies you love it and don't mention it to your friends.

I should advise you that I do like to make people smile with a funny story or joke.

If you were impressed with the previous list of my business credentials, I should tell you that I am world renowned, not for those business activities, but for pheasant hunting. Yes, I said, "Pheasant hunting, bird hunting." You see, I regularly get my limit of pheasants without ever firing even one shot. Using my skills learned as a professor, I lecture to the pheasants and bore them to death.

I came from an educationally and economically impoverished background with virtually no role models for making money. Before me, none of my known family had ever gone to college, and we would have ranked in the bottom 20% of the U.S. in income and assets. I learned most business things by the "**seat of my own pants**." During my early life, I suffered from a severe case of EW or NM Syndrome, i.e., "Empty Wallet" or "No Money Syndrome."

As people age, particularly by age 55, they start to think about getting dementia, the most common form being Alzheimer's disease. This book, which was started at age 60, is my rebellion against this mind robbing disease. I believe that vigorous mental and physical activities, combined with a healthy attitude and eating practices are important for delaying it.

ACKNOWLEDGEMENTS

I wish to thank the following people who contributed to the successful completion of my book: Dave Christy (insurance agent/expert), Sean Coyle (editorial assistant), Dr. Russell Fuller (author, investments expert, and President and founder of Fuller & Thayer Asset Management, Inc.), Vicki Grayson Liden (see page 2), Michael Lortz (C.P.A., tax expert), Bill Love (author, newspaper columnist, and automotive expert), David Root (insurance agent/expert), and Richard Sias (Gary P. Brinson Chair of Investment Management, Washington State University) and four family members. Opinions expressed herein represent my own and not necessarily those of my reviewers.   —Dr. Glenn Petry

CONTENTS

CHAPTER 1
Important Ideas for Survival and Creating Wealth

As we go through life we make tens of thousands of financial decisions about the three big Ws: namely, **what, where**, and **when** to spend our money. Before wealth is accumulated, most cash flow will be spent on our basic needs. The hardest part of wealth creation, along with making the right choices, is getting the initial capital to make investments. Most of us don't have the mentoring or the wealthy parents named Rockefeller, Trump, Carnegie, or Gates. However, this book will help you bridge that knowledge and wealth gap.

I started out with a negative net worth and built considerable wealth. Most of my initial nest egg and asset accumulation are attributable to the ideas and activities discussed in this book. They also helped set the tone of saving and investing for my family.

Most multi-millionaires didn't win the lottery, inherit their wealth (though some did), or suddenly come up with a brilliant idea that made them rich. Most started modestly and earned, saved, spent, and invested a few bucks at a time. As their asset pot grew, they became smarter. **Their accumulated wealth was the result of thousands of small and a few large decisions.**

A Penny Saved is More Than a Penny Earned

Ben Franklin's famous quotation "A penny saved is a penny earned" was mostly right for his time, but a penny saved now is worth more than a penny earned because of high taxes on those earnings. Using an average tax burden of 40%, a typical person needs to make $167 (and more if you are self employed) before taxes to pay $100 for a good or service.

Depending upon which state you live in and your individual tax situation, your tax rate may be higher or lower. However, most people pay some taxes so nearly everyone makes out better by saving money than earning it. This book is about finding ways to save you money. If I can save you $1,000, that is the same as making $1,670 for the average worker.

Save and Invest

The cardinal rule (which is a variant of Gloria Vanderbilt's politically incorrect famous saying, "You can never be too rich or too thin.") is:

"You can almost never save too much or start too early."

That means start today, not tomorrow or next week or next year. For extreme procrastinators, the "next year" never comes, and they are facing retirement with only social security and at best, a small nest egg to live on. Of course, you don't need to go to the extreme. I remember one couple whose financials I was reviewing about 25 years ago. Their net worth then was $15,000,000, but they were advising their grown children to buy Christmas gifts at yard sales.

A second cardinal rule is:

"Save more in good times than in bad times."

Unfortunately, people often do the opposite, figuring that the good times will go on forever. If you are currently not saving, then set a modest goal of saving 5% of after tax income in the first year. Check your progress every month. Tell the family about your successes and failures. If you are successful, then raise the "bar" to 8-10% for the second year. The ultimate goal should be 15-20%.

Recognize the Trade-off of Saving Versus Spending

Some people have the attitude as reflected by an acquaintance of mine who said, "If I have a nickel in my pocket at the end of the day, I've wasted the day." His second comment to me was, "In my lifetime, I have spent a lot of money on whiskey and women and the rest I've wasted." He will never save much money. His spending will always be based on his current earnings and eventually just social security.

It is clear that one must sacrifice some current spending in order to save for the future. If you follow my suggestions, you will have extra money to save and spend.

Another principle is:

> **"The more you save and invest in the present, the more you will have to spend in the future, in part because the savings will generate higher earnings.**

Learn Smarter, Faster, and Cheaper

There are times that you just want to kick back and enjoy life at a slow pace. However, the American dream and the higher standard of living we enjoy was built on the "smarter, faster, and cheaper" concept. Economists call it "productivity increases." In the early years of our country, the most common occupation was farming, but now relatively few pursue that occupation because they learned this concept. Look for opportunities to pursue your own productivity increases.

Don't Fret Unduly about the Future of the United States or the Availability of Jobs

The U.S. is one of the most vital countries in the world. There will always be job losses here as other countries learn "smarter, faster, and cheaper" or what economists refer to as having a "competitive advantage" in making products and providing services. This competitive process is good because it forces businesses to increase productivity, and this raises the standard of living and keeps inflation down. As a result, new industries and new technologies are created. To maintain this creative and evolving process, the U.S. and the world need open markets, consistent and fair laws, and growth not burdened by harsh regulations and high taxes.

It is easy in the current environment to be pessimistic, but the long run prospects for U.S. job growth look good according to a recent study by MetLife Foundation and Civic Ventures, a San Francisco based think tank. They analyzed in-migration, births, deaths, and retirement and concluded that 15.3 million jobs would be created by 2018 with 3.3-4.0 million vacant jobs. The success of this forecast depends upon an improving economy and higher stock market and real estate prices. However, immigration and the export of many types of jobs will likely erase lasting vacancies.

Learn to Do Minor Repairs on Your Own

There are a number of easy repairs that most people can do with a little guidance. You can find free repair information at the hardware store or on the internet. If you want to replace a toilet, type in "replacing a toilet," and you can see how to do it at doityourself.com. Type "replacing a battery" and go to eHow.com. Other self help sources include Wonder-HowTo.com and Howcast.com.

Ask a Friend to Help

Another approach is to ask a friend how to fix something. Most neighbors and friends are delighted to be asked for advice. Giving advice strokes their ego while asking them to fix it may be pushing the envelope for some people. However, the friend may volunteer to fix it once there.

Two good gift ideas are to give a "fix-it" book or a personal gift certificate for fixing something. The former would make a great house-warming gift. In our family, the kids often gave a ticket book instead of buying a present, hopefully for work not normally done. The kids would put items like "serve breakfast in bed," "give a back rub," etc. However, one could put "fix-it" activities on the card.

Trade Work

Another option is to trade with someone. For example, you could trade someone a lunch, gardening, or housecleaning for some plumbing work. A lunch out could cost $25 while the plumbing bill is $75 or more.

Live Within Your Means

The following observation is almost universally true:

> **"If you live within your means, you will be happier and healthier than if you are constantly stressed out trying to live a more upscale but unaffordable life."**

Learn to Distinguish Needs from Wants

Unfortunately, advertising and the media have changed a lot of things that are simply "wants" into perceived "needs." This not only includes things like fancy clothes, electronics, and expensive cars, but even drugs that we really don't need. Our needs include **basic levels** of food, water, clothing, sunshine, some medical care, exercise, transportation, and human interaction. Almost everything else is a want which has caused the financial ruin of many people.

Control Your Expenses by Developing a Budget

The next 10 steps are very important in developing a sense of control in your life and reducing anxiety from the feeling of financial helplessness. It is no secret that many people spend more than their income. If you commit your budget, priorities, and plan to paper, you are much more likely to be successful in achieving those goals.

1. Find out where you spend your money. This information helps to solve your financial problems. This is the same principle as driving somewhere only after you know where you are.

For credit card purchases and checks, it is easy to track past and current expenditures which should be done for 12 months (could be every other month). Then calculate a total for each of following categories and a grand total:

- Grocery store food
- Grocery/convenience store alcohol and tobacco
- Fast food restaurants (including coffee shops)
- Non-fast food restaurants
- Entertainment
- Household repairs
- Utilities
- Rent or mortgage payments
- Other loan payments (except credit cards)
- Credit card payments
- Vehicle expenses
- Investments (including savings accounts)
- Travel/vacation (excluding your vehicle)
- Charitable contributions (including religious)
- Special services (maid, lawn, etc.)
- Clothing
- Daycare
- Electronics & DVDs/CDs
- Insurance
- Medical bills
- Other (gifts, coin-op laundry, etc.)

Cash purchases need to be included in the above. You should then compute the percentage of each expenditure category to the total. For example, if you spent $8,500 on grocery store food out of a total $60,000 spent for all categories, then 8500/65000 or 14.2% was spent on that one item.

2. Make a list of priorities. Now that you know where the money is being spent, sit down with your family members and decide which categories to increase or decrease. The opinion(s) of the parent(s) carry the most weight because they generally earn the money, better understand their financial situation, and hopefully can distinguish needs from wants. List priorities in order of importance and more than one can have the same priority. Here is a sample list with the number designating each priority:

1. Pay off the credit card debt with the highest interest rate.
1. Put money into my IRA.
2. Fund a bank account for emergencies.
3. Cut vacation expenses.
3. Save for college.
4. Reduce car expenses.
5. Downsize entertainment.
6. Cut utility bills.
6. Trim clothes budget.
7. Reduce the food bill.

The list of priorities will vary for every family and likely will change annually if not sooner. If you are having financial difficulties, this should be an exercise of **"tough love."**

3. Develop a budget. Divide each category of annual expenditures by 12 to get a monthly average. Put those historical averages on either a computer generated or hand drawn spreadsheet. Then using your priority list, decide on changes to each budget category. Some categories are fixed and easy. You need to pay your mortgage. Other categories may vary on a monthly basis based upon emergencies, your vacation months, clothing sales, etc. Ideally, you should keep a running total by category and not worry about month to month variations unless they are severe and unexpected.

It is important to update this monthly as people seem to have difficulty looking at the long range. Leona Tam of Old Dominion University and Utpal Dholakia of Rice University found that people saved dramatically more when they planned month by month than those who planned ahead in four month intervals. This finding probably shows people's procrastination tendencies when they are not regularly held accountable.

4. Generate strategies for balancing your budget. Now develop a specific design for achieving your budget. For example, if you cut last year's vacation budget by $2,000, then you will have that money to use in other categories or to make up for a drop in income. You could reduce your food expenses by substituting store or generic brands for name brands, buying only at sales and/or used clothing, and by cooking more.

5. Be disciplined. You won't be successful without discipline which often means making unpopular decisions.

6. Lead by example. If your kids or significant other are complaining about their sacrifices, show them what you are giving up.

7. Associate with people whose wealth and spending don't make you feel uncomfortable. To keep up and avoid feeling inferior, you may spend too much.

8. Don't buy a house in the very best neighborhood you can currently afford. The reality is that besides committing yourself to a higher mortgage, you will be among people that spend more on almost everything than those from a less pricey neighborhood.

9. When your financial situation deteriorates or you see dark clouds coming, quickly circle the wagons to preserve cash. Some people react in the wrong way by digging a deeper hole. They go buy a new wardrobe, car, or something they can do without, or take an expensive vacation so they "feel' better. That solution gives you a temporary "high" and a long term headache.

10. Read this book carefully. It will help you save thousands of dollars.

Get a Shopping Make-over

There are 13 types of shoppers who can be detrimental to the family finances including:

- **Compulsive** (they must regularly shop)

- **Impulsive** (must buy what they see)

- **Bored** (need shopping to keep life interesting)

- **Trendsetter** (must have the latest fashions)

- **Oscar Wilde devotees** (He said, "I have the simplest of tastes; I am always satisfied with the best" and inherently most expensive)

- **Gadget people** (got to have the latest "whatchimacallit")

- **Status seekers** (possessions define their importance)

- **Wonderlusters** (must see the world, work can wait)

- **The unsatisfied** (must keep buying and selling- unfortunately he loses money on every sale)

- **The gourmet** (always eat out since he never cooks)

- **No resistance to salespersons** (she buys stuff not needed just because it is on sale)

- **The friend seeker** (he must treat others to gain friends)

- **The budget buster** (budgets are for other people)

A combination of these (herein called the Multiple Personality Shopping Disorder or MPSD) can be deadly for wealth accumulation and the family budget. Such people are also less likely to wait for sales. They may need to give up their credit cards and only leave home with cash, strictly adhere to a budget and a shopping list, and go with someone who has no more than one of the 13 MPSDs.

Understand that Good Returns Mostly Involve Some Risks

Some people have a difficult time with accepting risks, but we all face them every day of our lives from the supermarket or restaurant that sells us food, the doctor who treats us, the mechanic who works on our car, etc. Uncertainty is everywhere and is inescapable to living. The only thing about uncertainty is that it is certain. You must accept risk to secure your future from the risk of minimal existence, especially in your old age. These are often called the golden years but they wouldn't be golden without some golden investments.

There is an old saying about risk and reward that is so true today.

"Wealth is created by small efforts with big pay-offs; poverty is created by big efforts with small returns."

An example of small returns would be a low paying job or investing in short term debt such as money market funds or savings accounts. These types of accounts do not provide much wealth building and after income taxes, the returns usually do not even keep up with inflation.

Calculate Your Marginal Tax Rate and Use it for Financial Decisions

One of the most importance financial activities a person can do is to estimate her marginal tax rate, the rate at which your last dollar in taxable income is taxed or your tax savings if you take a deduction (like donations to charity). If you have your taxes prepared, your tax preparer can tell you what it is.

If your marginal rate is 40%, then a charitable donation of $100 will cost you only $60 because you will save $40 in taxes. By the same token, if you make $100, you will only have $60 after taxes.

How to Calculate it. First, find your taxable income and filing status (such as single, married filing jointly, etc.) on your tax return. Now look at the "Tax Rate Schedule" for your filing status in the tax booklet. Suppose you are single and have a taxable income of $52,000. You would find your marginal bracket from Schedule X, a portion of which is reproduced below. The schedule (which changes every year) shows taxable income and marginal tax rates.

Taxable Income			Of the
Over	But not over	The tax is	amount over
$33,950	$82,250	$4,675 + 25%	$33,950

You will note that your taxable income falls between $33,950 (column 1) and $82,250 (column 2). Your tax is then $4,675 plus 25% of the amount over $33,950.

Your marginal federal tax rate is 25%, but 25% should be viewed as simply an estimate to guide in making decisions. Your exact marginal tax rate is affected by what decisions you make as well as many tax rules. Furthermore, one should recognize that one's rate may change from year to year and that a large deduction or addition to income could shift you into another tax bracket. These complexities should be ignored except possibly for large transactions for which you should seek professional help.

The next step is to add your state marginal tax rate (if any) to the federal rate to estimate your total marginal tax rate. If, in the above example, your state income tax rate is 6%, then your total marginal rate is 25% plus 6% or 31% (if you itemize and are not subject to the AMT or loss of deductions, the actual rate is 29.5%). If income subject to social security is involved, then the marginal rate jumps to about 37% or more (if you are self employed or don't itemize).

Hire Others to Do Tax Deductible Work First Before Hiring Anyone for Work Not Deductible

If you have two repair jobs and don't have time to do both, hire someone to do the tax deductible one first. For example, for two plumbing repairs, one in a rental and the other in your home, do the home repair yourself and hire someone to do the tax deductible rental work.

Become a Specialist

Diversification is good in stocks but not when you are running a business. The most profitable entrepreneurs are those who find a field, learn it forward and backward, and then make smart investments. The old saying about "sticking to your knitting" applies. During the 1960s and 1970s, many companies (called conglomerates) bought other firms in fields unrelated to their core businesses. These executives thought that such diversification would provide steadier earnings and raise their stock prices. The results were a disaster.

Give Proper Incentives

To motivate people, proper incentives must be provided such as awards, plaques, titles, raises, promotions, etc. Back in the 1970s, I was an assistant scoutmaster of teenage boys for the Boy Scouts of America. They funded their activities by several events including selling concessions in the bleachers at Washington State University's football games. The scouts received a percentage of the gross sales. To spur participation, I offered unlimited ice cream at the end of the season and a certificate designating any scout selling over $100 as a "Super Hawker." The incentives, unfortunately, had no effect on participation or sales. The second year, I raised the rewards by offering a first, second, and third prize for each game and a grand prize. The prizes included fishing rods, knives, compasses, and a backpack. The results were spectacular with the amount of concessions sold increasing by 400%. The grand prize winner is now an emergency room surgeon so potential shows up early.

Take All Legal Steps to Minimize Your Taxes

One of the most important aspects of wealth accumulation is to legally reduce your tax burden where possible. You may be paying too much in taxes because you don't understand the laws, are very conservative, or are investing in assets that don't offer tax shelters (which isn't always necessarily bad). However, much of wealth accumulation is simply deferring taxes and the extra money allows one to make more investments with the tax sheltered money. This, in my opinion, is one of the two key advantages to real estate. The other is the leverage allowed. Tax issues will be discussed more fully in Chapter 17.

Establish Credit Early

Some financial advisers say that a person should tear up his/her credit cards. For those people who run up large credit card debts at high interest rates and don't pay off in full each month, I agree. For such people, credit cards are almost seen as fake or free money, and they spend more than if they paid in cash. Money spent on consumer goods is money unavailable for investment and retirement. My credit card rule is:

> **"Never buy anything with a credit card that you wouldn't buy with cash."**

However, for those with the self discipline who can pay in full every month, then credit cards are a great way to raise their credit scores. This is especially important when you have little loan history. Low credit scores can raise interest rates on consumer loans, lower success in job applications, and even raise insurance company rates. Techniques for raising your credit score are discussed in Chapter 6.

Use Other People's Money

Wealth is increased by charging on credit cards or using zero interest loans such as for furniture, as long as you pay in full before the interest bearing period begins. My personal rule is:

> **"Any purchase over $20 will be charged to my credit card."**

This gives me a high credit rating which allows me to borrow money more cheaply, gives me airline or gift points or cash, saves interest charges, and allows me to use someone else's credit.

The credit card purchase has a double value if paid in full every month. First, you get an interest free loan for probably an average of 25-30 days depending upon when the bills were incurred and paid. The second part is the cash back or the value of what is received for the points.

The combined value of the interest free loan and the award is usually at least 2%. For a $1,000 purchase, 2% is worth $20.00. If the cardholder pays in full every month, the $20 is worth 24% or more annually, a fantastic bargain for a tax free and risk free investment.

Interest free installment loans can sometimes cause headaches. I had a bad experience with a computer purchased via the phone. I paid in full before the six month deadline to start accruing interest and my canceled check verified it. In any case, the company attempted to collect about $160 after the six month period ended. My wife wrote to the President and founder and talked with one of company's attorneys, but no one would give us an explanation for the extra charges. Finally, we started hearing from a collection agency in India. Eventually we paid it after late charges were added.

When you receive no explanation for charges, a red flag goes up. We assumed that it was an attempt to falsely collect interest charges or for an optional service contract that may not have been ordered. That computer purchase was later part of a class action lawsuit for sales taxes collected on the optional service contract. I actually tried to interest the class action attorney in our case, but the statute of limitations had run out.

Always take cash discounts from those few businesses that offer them. Cash discounts are usually in the form of giving a 1% or 2% discount if paid by the 10th of the month with the full price at the end of 30 days. I had a doctor who allowed me to deduct 5% and then charge it on my credit card for paying at the time of visit. The combined discount value was about 7% or 84% on an annual basis.

Pay Off the Most Costly Debt First and Use it Last

The interest on some debts (like a mortgage or business debt) is tax deductible while others (such as personal credit cards) aren't. The tax deduction reduces the cost of the debt. If a person is in the 40% total marginal tax bracket, her after tax cost is 60% of the interest rate. The following cases illustrate this tax effect:

Type of Debt	Annual interest rate	Interest deductible	annual after tax cost
Credit card (personal)	14%	No	14%
Credit card (business)	14%	Yes	8.4%
Car loan (non business)	7%	No	7%
Business loan	9%	Yes	5.4%
Personal family loan	4%	No	4%
Mortgage	6%	Yes	3.6%

Thus, the personal credit cards costing 14% annually would be paid off first and used last and the mortgage would be paid off last and used first, except in special circumstances. Of course, if you carry a balance on your credit cards, always carry it on any business cards instead of personal cards because of the interest deduction.

Get Advice and Mentoring

Some advice is to be taken as a grain of salt, diluted in a gallon of water, and used only as a gargle. That being said, I highly recommend that novice investors and employees find a mentor. The best investment mentor would be someone who has a track record in actually making money. The best executive is one who has risen in the type of organization of interest. The intensity and nature of politics varies among companies and different types of organizations.

Generally, the more successful a person is in her field, the more likely that advice is to be useful. The downside is that such people are likely to be more in demand. You may need to craft a unique appeal, but usually you will find some assistance. Probably the most accessible and willing executives or entrepreneurs are those who have retired.

In general, it takes much longer to accumulate wealth and get promotions without a mentor. In my own case, I was hindered by having zero capital to start, some school debt, and living in a small community.

Allow Failure to be an Option

I have heard the motto "Failure isn't an option." That may be fine for a goal, but it is totally unrealistic and may actually cause people to hesitate because of their fear of failure. Failure certainly can result in economic losses and cause one to "lose face." However, readers need to recognize that even the biggest companies in business and finance, managed by the smartest brains, frequently make bad investments or even go bankrupt. You only need to look at the casualty list of General Motors, Chrysler, Lehman Brothers, Merrill Lynch, Enron, Bear Sterns, Countrywide Financial, Washington Mutual, and the hundreds of other bank failures.

Part of the big business problem is that many top executives are empire builders who have a conflict of interest. If a company becomes larger, but not necessarily more profitable per dollar of investment, the executives will receive greater income, stock options, prestige, and power.

Accept a few losers as part of the cost of doing business and learning. What you want to avoid is having a series of one or more big losses that financially wipe you out. The best way to avoid that is to ask questions, do your research, be patient (at first at least) in choosing investments, find a mentor (such as me), and understand the parameters of your investments.

Start an Emergency Fund

There is a lot of discussion about how much to keep in emergency funds which are easily accessed assets like savings accounts, short term CDs, lines of credit, or checking accounts. It simply varies with each person or family. You can have lesser amounts if:

- You have a senior position and your company lays off by seniority.
- Your employer is highly profitable.
- You have well off relatives or friends who will come to your rescue.
- You have a large home equity line of credit.
- You work in a less cyclical industry like food production or sales, education, government, or the utility sector.
- You have investments (like stocks, commercial or Treasury paper, and bonds not in a retirement fund) which can be quickly converted into cash.
- You have low expenses relative to your income.
- You have skills which allow you to get a new job easily.
- You have two or more wage earners in the household and you

don't spend it all.
- You have lots of discretionary purchases which can be quickly stopped.
- You have friends or relatives who would let you live with them.
- You pay off your credit cards in full every month.
- Your house is paid off.
- You have adequate insurance including life insurance.
- You have disability insurance if you are still working.

Most people should have three months extra cash and maybe more, but those who qualify for some of the above may be safe with less. For example, if you have a $50,000 untapped line of credit on your house, pay off your credit cards every month, and have a secure job, you likely need a very small emergency fund, maybe one month's worth.

One important principle is:

"You should pay off high interest credit cards before you put money into an emergency fund."

The reason is that your credit card's interest paid (which isn't deductible for personal cards) is far higher than the net interest on the savings account after tax . There is one caveat, namely, if you are stretched thin and the credit card limit might be lowered or the card canceled if paid in full, one could make a short run case for not paying off the credit card.

Pets are Partly an Economic Decision

I currently have three cats and a dog and have had pets most of the last 40 years. Pets provide unremitting love and affection. They don't care if we are the scum of the earth and for many people, they are like family. All of our animals sleep in our bed.

However, as much as we love our pets, their vet and food bills can be quite expensive. We spend about $5,000 per year or about $1,250 per pet. Just like humans, the end of life care can be very expensive if one tries to extend a pet's life. They also absorb our time and may require us to go outside in inclement weather.

Before getting a pet, a person needs to think about these monetary and time costs. Obviously, if the pet is fed really inexpensive food, the owner skimps on pet shots (which you can buy and administer yourself), and the animal gets minimal vet care, most of which is not recommended, the costs will be much lower. Outdoor pets, especially cats (even if neutered), are likely to be more expensive as they get into fights and often don't live as long. Unfortunately, most cat wounds seem to get infected.

Children are Partly an Economic Decision

Ideally, one should know the costs of raising a child in advance of having one. Indeed, if you go to cnpp.usda.gov, the site of the Center for Nutrition Policy and Promotion (a division of the U.S. Department of Agriculture), you can see a cost calculator. Click "Expenditure on Children by Families," "Cost of Raising a Child Calculator," and then "Click Here to Start."

You need to fill in the information specific to your family situation. Basically, you provide the age of each child, whether you are single or married, your location, and your income before taxes. The average cost to raise a child from birth through age 17 is $221,190 (2008 dollars) for an average income family. The costs rise and fall with income and the estimated unadjusted (actual) cost is $291,570. The totals exclude college and birth expenses.

Basically, the calculator apparently assumes that you buy a bigger house and car when children are born; don't buy at yard sales or second hand stores or get gifts; children don't share rooms or "hand me downs;" and ignores tax savings from write-offs for taxes, interest, an extra exemption, various tax credits, and eating out less often, etc. It also ignores rising income. I would think that with consumer tips from this book, frugality, gifts, sharing, and tax savings, one might reduce the cost to $100,000 per child or less.

Housing costs represent 32% of the total cost; food, 16%; and child care/education, 16%. Thus, if one parent stayed home and cooked a lot, you didn't get a larger house and car or have much daycare or private schooling, you could pare those costs dramatically.

Write a Will, Power of Attorney, and a Medical Directive

Wills are a must for everyone because the assets of those dying without one are distributed based upon state law. Do you want your sister who hasn't seen you in 30 years to receive some of your inheritance? What about Uncle Charlie who is in jail for embezzling money from your church? If you have children, they need to be cared for and someone designated as a care giver. You also don't want your children fighting with your step-children. Your will should be updated periodically to take into account changes in beneficiaries as a result of divorces, deaths, births, financial circumstances, and other important events. Many beneficiary changes can be made on-line.

Do not depend upon the goodwill of others to fulfill verbal wishes. Estate battles often end up in court and the more detailed and specific your instructions, the less likely that will occur. Making wills is not expensive and can be done through LegalZoom.com, Suze Orman's Will and Trust Kit, Quicken's Willmaker Plus, or We the People (a storefront franchise that helps people fill out legal forms). For those making decisions for you or your estate, provide detailed information and instructions about all loans, bank accounts, insurance policies, tax returns, litigation, contracts, retirement funds, investments, bills, safe combinations, and other important documents.

In addition, all adults should have a "durable power of attorney," a "living will," and a "medical power of attorney" so that medical and other decisions can be made in case of incapacitation. If there is little hope of survival, most people do not want their assets depleted for unneeded medical care, especially since health care providers do not want to make medical decisions in our litigious society. Living wills specify the desired kinds of care and life support and a health care agent. Aging with Dignity offers one copy for $5 or 25 for $25 at agingwithdignity.org or call 1-888-594-7437.

If you have special circumstances or a large estate, consider establishing a trust. There are a number of sites that provide useful trust information including savewealth.com, laweasy.com, pueblo.gsa.gov (Federal Citizen Information Center- type "trusts" in search box), and estateretirementplanning.com. After becoming knowledgeable, then hire an attorney to set up the trust. There are options besides trusts which can reduce estate taxes and the expense of trusts such as annual and lifetime gifts, buying an annuity for a beneficiary, transferring partial ownership of a business whose value is discounted, and having someone else own your insurance policy.

CHAPTER 2

The Keys to Success and Happiness

Many decisions and behaviors that are keys to success and happiness may not be viewed as financial. However, your ability to achieve them can make you more productive and therefore, have a great bearing on your income and wealth accumulation. In the next sections, I will discuss them.

Accept Your Lot and Take Responsibility

It does little good to constantly blame others. It only puts you in a depressed mood. Once you accept your circumstances, try to improve on them. Develop a plan and goals. Even simple and easily achievable goals such as "I won't charge any more on my credit card this week" are a good start. After you achieve simple goals, it will make you feel good and you can move to more difficult ones.

Don't Panic when Times are Tough

First of all, if you plan ahead, the rough spots will cause less stress and likely won't be as severe. However, people often panic more than they should. Problems don't get solved by panic. That reaction only causes you to act "like a deer in the headlights." An example of financial panic would be cashing in your 401(k) and paying taxes on it and possibly a penalty or selling all of your family heirlooms. These actions ultimately may be necessary, but people planning ahead are less likely to suffer these consequences.

When Things Get Tough, the Tough Get Going (and Quickly)

If you receive a layoff notice or are fairly sure of a bad financial event, quickly decide what is most important and act on it within **days, if not hours.** Then **cash should be king.** Start making contacts and applying for jobs, tighten up your finances, cancel that vacation, stop remodeling plans, apply for unemployment, get your medical work done (especially if you still have insurance), have an emergency family meeting and tell them, not ask them, to tighten their belts, start buying food in bulk, buy mostly at sales, do repairs yourself, stop eating out or entertaining others (except cheaply at home), don't lend money to others in trouble (you probably won't get it back and you need it), stop buying gifts for non-family, bring your lunch to work, suspend contributions to college funds, don't sign car leases or buy a new car, etc.

If you are still employed, consider trying to get a home equity loan (HEL). HELs are relatively low cost and allow a tax deduction for the interest for the first $100,000. A home equity loan allows you to borrow on short notice and repay what you don't need. Consider refinancing your mortgage if it will lower your monthly payment. Try to keep up your 401(k) contributions, especially if you have employer matching.

Watch the Small Stuff

Warren Buffett likes to invest in companies in which the top executive counts the sheets in a roll of toilet paper. That means he would love me. If you pay attention to the small things, you are more likely to look at the big things and in addition, the small stuff adds up.

R.A.N. There are three things that I do on a regular basis. It doesn't mean that I run from bad opportunities although there are a few I should have "RAN" from. R.A.N. stands for **Read, Ask**, and **Negotiate.**

Read, Read, Read. I read an average of three hours every day. Some reading is purely for pleasure but much is focused on economic issues or increasing my breadth of knowledge. My subscriptions have included *The Wall Street Journal, Business Week, Financial Times of London, Fortune, Barron's, U.S. News and World Report, Time, Kiplinger's, Newsweek, Smart Money, Money, AARP Bulletin, AAII Journal, AAA Magazine*, two daily newspapers, and a number of other magazines, including *Multifamily Executive, Building*, environmental publications, trade publications, etc.

I also watch five channels regularly including CNBC, CNN, MSNBC, Fox, and Bloomberg, plus the some local and national news programs. My reading and viewing habits should put me into the top 1% nationally. However, extensive reading won't put money in your and my pockets unless we use the information and take some risks. Unfortunately, some of the information will point in conflicting directions. For example, rising material prices would suggest higher inflation but lower job creations would suggest a lessening. The fact that decisions are usually not always clear cut and risky is what creates opportunities for making money.

What you read will depend upon how much time and money you want to devote to the effort and your focus. I always recommend reading your local newspaper, but that can take a half hour or more per day. I would add one publication at a time to see if you actually read and benefit from them. In my personal opinion, a person that wants to be knowledgeable and a good decision maker should read at least one hour per day.

For those with limited budgets and time, I would suggest starting with one or more of the following: *Smart Money, Money, AARP magazine (for those 50 and over), AAII Journal, or Kiplinger.* The cost of each subscription is mostly less than $25 per year and they are published usually no more than once a month. It might be good to rotate subscriptions as each publication has areas of interest though all are relatively broad. With more time and a higher budget, I would add *The Wall Street Journal, BusinessWeek, U.S. News and World Report, Fortune,* or some other publications of interest. You can find information about them at most of the publication's websites or check them out at newsstands. However, you don't want to regularly pay newsstand prices since subscription prices are much cheaper than cover prices.

In your reading, **be cautious of get rich schemes.** I saw one newsletter in which the writer was touting the buying of government bonds with the highest interest rates. What the writer didn't say was that those high rates probably indicate an abnormal risk of default, massive deficits, and/or great currency risk (remember Greece in 2010). The old saying applies, "There is no such thing as a free lunch."

Ask, Ask, Ask. Over the years, I have picked up a lot of information regarding financial decisions and investment opportunities by asking questions of my bankers, contractors, friends, neighbors, workers, accountants, lawyers, competitors, colleagues, store employees, etc. A curious mind is important to wealth creation. One should look for important information that will:

- Help find better deals
- Solve problems
- Locate the best workers
- Assist in planning
- Reduce and understand risk
- Reduce costs
- Finish on time

- Understand tax, legal, and regulatory statutes
- Make good decisions
- Understand your competition

Negotiate, Negotiate, Negotiate. You obviously can't negotiate with everyone in all cases, but the idea of negotiating for goods and services should be in the back of your mind at all times. Some people feel more comfortable with this approach than others. In most situations, the worst outcome is usually that they will decline to give you a discount.

In only one instance in thousands of my requests was there ever a really irritated response. About 20 years ago, there was an auctioneer who sold some consigned goods for me. I asked him for a reduced rate if the amount auctioned hit a certain target. He was very annoyed and told me to take my business elsewhere in the future. However, when my wife approached him about some work several years later, he agreed to do it.

Be Determined and Persistent

History is full of stories of successful people who failed early in their career or were told they weren't good enough including the Beatles, Michael Jordan, J.K. Rowlings, Steve Jobs, and Thomas Edison. In fact, probably 99% of highly successful people can share similar stories.

Being persistent usually pays off as long as you don't offend the person you are trying to influence. If you start off with a statement like," Your company is the sleaziest business on the planet," you may not get any results. Let me illustrate with a less dramatic and more typical example. My wife and I were on a cruise from Lima, Peru to Los Angeles, California. Overall, I liked the ship and had a great time.

Cruises often have shore excursions which are over hyped. However, the ones in Esmerelda Chile, in opinion, were so misadvertised and so far below the normal standards of planning and cleanliness that I protested to the ship's cruise director and asked for a full refund.

The only apparent reason that the ship stopped in Esmerelda was to pick up passengers who departed in Lima to visit the famous ruins at Machu Picchu. The experiences of most passengers on these excursions would suggest that no one from the cruise line had actually visited Esmerelda before scheduling the on-shore trips.

The cruise director gave me a paltry discount of 25%. When I arrived home, I wrote to the complaint office and got a full refund. The letter took about 30 minutes to write and resulted in an additional refund of about $90 so it was worth about $180 per hour. With a total marginal tax rate of 40%, my hourly earnings before taxes were about $300 per hour.

Sometimes we can do things that truly amaze us if we are determined. Back in 1972, I took my oldest daughter, then two years and two months old, camping. We parked at 9500 feet in altitude and hiked two miles to an elevation of over 11,000 feet. I never carried her on any portion of the rough trail though we did stop for a nap and snacks. I wonder how many five year olds would make the trek.

This next story could fit under a number of headings, but it is funny. In 1969, I quit my job in Los Angeles and moved to Denver where I was briefly unemployed. In between looking for work, I heard a radio station offering $5 (worth $29 today) plus a gift certificate to Arby's for winning a contest called "Spot a Sticker Sweepstakes." The station sent a driver out each day at 10am and his first stop was about ½ mile from my apartment. You would win if you spotted the Arby's logo on his car. After I won six times in one week, the radio station driver would drive off when he saw me coming.

Be Adaptable

Your family, employer, civic and church groups will all value you more highly if you meet challenges head-on and bend but not break.

Go Around or Over Roadblocks

In 1972, I had applied for financial aid at the University of Colorado and was turned down because of about $5,000 in liquid assets. So I used the money to buy a house in Boulder, and this allowed me to qualify for a student loan with a zero interest rate during school and a 3% rate that started six months after graduation. The money was to be paid back in ten years. Furthermore, if you went into teaching as I did, the payments for the first five years were forgiven.

The house purchase was interesting because I wasn't eligible for a new home loan but was allowed to assume one with an interest rate of 5%.

We sold it the following year for a net gain of 22%, allowing us to buy a larger house.

In the words of John Wooden, the UCLA basketball coach with an unprecedented 10 NCAA national men's championships, "Don't let what you can't do interfere with what you can do."

Lead Often, Don't Always Follow

Sometimes, you have to follow, but show leadership as often as possible. The world values leaders, both financially and socially.

Try to Exceed the Minimum

Having hired more than 600 employees and subcontractors and taught more than 15,000 students, I place people in the upper half of the adult dependability scale if they can:

1. Follow directions. Ask questions if they don't understand. Write it down.
2. Show up on time.
3. Have a good attitude about their work. If they don't like it, find another job.
4. Work the hours expected in a productive manner.
5. Communicate regularly with their boss.
6. Be honest.
7. Don't abuse substances.

Frankly, some of my most disappointing experiences are with college students. I have hired hundreds of students for maintenance and cleaning at my apartments, paying well above the minimum wage. The results were disappointing. At most, 30% seemed reliable enough to show up and regularly work part-time for a 30 day period during the summer. Parents need to give their kids more jobs to develop a sense of responsibility while growing up. By the time the students graduate from college, most had matured and were more responsible, but they should be that way upon entering college.

I think the above seven behaviors will help you keep most jobs except when severe downsizing occurs. However, these represent the minimum. If you want to advance, you need to show creativity, leadership, initiative and a survivor instinct. One of my former department chairmen once told me that "If there is a nuclear war, I want to be with Glenn because he will be a survivor."

Probably, the individual with the most memorable attitude toward work that I ever met was my boss Joe Fallon, the chief accountant of the manufacturing division at Hughes Aircraft Company in Culver City, California where I worked in 1968. His resume's primary stated goal was, "To contribute to the profit-making ability of a company." That is the kind of attitude that gets a job applicant noticed.

Think Before You React

When people are angry, they have a tendency to do things without thinking about the issues or the ramifications. I once had a boss whose wife wrote this really vicious and demeaning letter to a relative. It was unwarranted, untrue, "out of the blue," and created a very uncomfortable situation for me. My options were to confront the boss, go to his boss, ignore it, write an "in-kind" letter back, or write a nice letter back. We chose the latter of the five options. However, if the problem had persisted, I would have gone to his boss.

This is one of those cases where you may want to delay your response for a few days. If you write a letter, don't send it quickly. Think about it. In most cases, you will at least modify your comments.

Don't Waste Your Time or Worry Much About Things Beyond Your Control

You will notice that I used the word "much" in the heading since it is inevitable that some effort will be placed in areas that are probably a waste of time. However, successful people "separate the wheat from the chaff" and concentrate on the former.

Determine Your Strengths and Weaknesses

This is the first step in trying to set goals. In my case, I was always fascinated with numbers and would ask my parents how many stars were in the sky or grains of sand in the ocean. When I was in 2nd grade, my teacher sent me up to the 6th grade class where I was paired against the best math student. We doubled numbers (1,2,4,8, etc.) in our head, and I was able to go into the millions. Another trait that stood out was writing skills. My high school teachers were very positive about that aspect (one said I wrote like humorist Robert Benchley). In a business writing class at The Pennsylvania State University, my professor who taught there for 20 years said my two reports were the best he had ever seen. When I became a professor of finance at a research university where writing was important, I obviously combined the two talents (writing and math) that my teachers noticed.

One of my professor's assignments was especially noteworthy and probably wouldn't be given today. The task was to write to several businesses complaining about their products. I was stumped until my roommate, whose religion required him to forego alcohol consumption, asked me to write to candy manufacturers and inquire about their use of alcohol as an ingredient. The responses were hilarious. One executive wrote telling me that I would need to consume 50 pounds of candy in a short period of time to get drunk. Another admitted to the use of alcohol, but reminded me of the amount dispensed into the air from automobile radiators; with an inference that maybe I should stop breathing to avoid inhaling it.

Ask your teachers, professors, friends, family, counselors, and yourself to identify your strengths and weaknesses. Hopefully that will mesh with your interests as it did for me. A reviewer of this book asked what my weaknesses are– well that's another book.

Be Objective

When it comes to ourselves and our family, this desirable trait often fails us. Some leaders lack it. However, on average, you will be more successful and respected if you score high on objectivity.

Set Goals

Many people simply react to events and what happens in their life. You are likely to be more successful and happier if you "take the bull by the horns" and shape your life by setting some goals. Goal setting should start early with children, but should not be so intrusive that they lose their "growing up" time. These goals could be as simple as my child needs to have one hour of exercise every day or 9 hours of sleep. You will find much information in this book that will aid in goal setting.

Goals, of course, will change for different periods of our life to include such things as grades, time to graduate, retirement funds, second homes, college preferences, house purchases, marriage, etc. **Most people accomplish things faster when they have goals, strategies, and timetables and write them down.** Then, look at them regularly and share them with others including their family and/or friends. Realistically, some goals are not met either because the goal were too high, some adverse event happened, or it became less important. However, the most important causes of failure are not identifying the problems related to an idea and not putting forth enough effort. That said, don't beat yourself up if you don't attain everything.

In any case, one's goals must be realistic. I wouldn't set my sights on making the Olympic ski team (not enough ability) or becoming President of the United States (I am not interested in politics).

Identify Multiple Ways to Solve a Problem

The most successful people do this. If you are planning a trip, you have choices regarding the method of travel and the routes to take. If you are looking at a piece of land to buy, you have alternatives for what to build on the property and how to arrange the parking. Each of these choices will have a different payback or rate of return, different costs, and advantages and disadvantages. Identifying multiple solutions is an important creative process that is highly valued and will lead to higher rates of return, wealth, and promotions.

The same creative process is important for building wealth and financial security. For some people, the pathway may involve ascending the career ladder of a company. For others, it may involve starting their own business or making substantial real estate or stock market investments or a combination of these. In my case, my job created a stable income that allowed me to make investments and take risks on the side.

Act Before an Idea Becomes Apparent

Early starters have more risk and potentially greater rewards. It is natural to wait until others have tested the waters so as to reduce risk, but that is often not the best route. I have my own share of such missed opportunities. Some of them turned out to be not so great, but others had golden returns.

Playing is Almost as Important as Work

I put a heavy emphasis on having fun. Except for my college periods, I regularly took several vacations per year. To me, it doesn't make a lot of sense to accumulate money and not enjoy it. The 2009 Vacation Deprivation Study found that 34% of Americans took an average of three less vacation days than their allotted number.

One should not wait for retirement to pursue hobbies or traveling that you enjoy. When our four children were growing up, we traveled extensively to Europe, Caribbean, Mexico, Canada, Hawaii, Alaska, and the continental U.S. We traveled on the low budget plan but the kids were exposed to many cultures.

Get an Education

A college degree is a sound investment but frankly not everyone wants to take the time, has the aptitude, or wants to borrow the funds to get a degree. For those others, they should at least finish high school and learn a craft such as a plumber, electrician, welder, lab technician, beautician, etc. Of course the most money will come from owning your own successful business.

If You Marry, Marry Well and Carefully

There are few events that will destroy or delay wealth building more than a divorce. You will need two households instead of one. There are attorney fees and possibly support payments. Your credit score may suffer a hit which impedes wealth building. The stress will affect your concentration in your job. Tiger Woods is a good example of that problem. It may cost you promotions at least until things are more settled. You are likely to pass up investment opportunities for years because of the need to heal yourself, to get over the trauma, to feel like risk taking, and to put your finances in order.

The U.S. has one of the highest divorce rates in the world. Depending upon whose numbers one uses, the rate is 50-55%. However, the rate is highest for people aged 24 and under, and the rate drops off dramatically after age 29. The risk of break-up peaks at 4 ½ years of marriage.

College educated and higher income partners are much less likely to divorce than uneducated and poor people. Depending upon the source, the divorce rate for first marriages is 41-50%, for second marriages, 60-67%, and for third marriages, 73-74% (divorcerate.org). **The definition of a second or third marriage is the triumph of hope over experience.**

When I got married, it was common to "tie the knot" at 20-22. Now marriage is being delayed and for the good. There are enormous changes in people from high school graduation until the ages of 25-26 when you start to have a better understanding of yourself and others. Later marriages also allow you to see the good and bad choices of some of your friends. The downside of later marriage is having children late in life when you have less energy, more difficulty getting pregnant, and a greater chance of birth defects. If a woman has children later and their offspring are born later, then she could be 70 years or older before grandchildren are born.

To reduce your chances of divorce, it would also be a good idea to take a course about marriage and relationships which is often offered by junior colleges, churches, etc. The same principles that apply in marriage apply in all long term committed relationships. The reason that college graduates have lower divorce rates is that they are older, have more income, learn problem solving, and have a certain commitment and "stick-to-itiveness."

I would never suggest that someone marry for money. In fact, you couldn't get much poorer than my wife and I and we certainly married for love. That said, the career and background of your mate will affect your wealth building. If a potential mate has a good job or future potential and parents who could help out and possibly leave an inheritance, you will be far ahead. That said, I would also not tell someone to choose careers that they hate just to make money or marry someone they don't love.

I would also counsel that you look at a potential spouse's handling of money. Does she/he carry a lot of credit card debt and is he/she living at or above his/her means? What kind of track record do the parents have? What is the attitude about saving versus spending? Will he accept a budget? Do you agree on the number and spacing of children? Are religion and a particular faith important?

People often have the misguided idea that love will always change undesirable characteristics in a potential mate. You may be able to effect some changes, but it is risky to assume so. Such changes are most likely to occur if you have a loving and mutually respectful relationship and the change is not coerced.

You should pass on questionable mates and look for less risky spousal investments. **Yes, spouses or significant others should in one aspect be viewed as investments.**

I also recommend that you avoid splurging on dates with potential long term mates except for special occasions. Excessive spending suggests that you have plenty of money or that you don't care about saving. This might attract the wrong mate, i.e., one who is not very frugal. Such a hook-up can be detrimental to your mental health, your bank account, and your retirement.

Try to Avoid Divorce or Make it Less Costly

As you watch the failure rate rise after the first and subsequent marriages, it seems that counseling and personal reassessment are due. Since divorce is so costly, try a marriage counselor first. Choose one whose goal is to try to make a marriage survive. Every married couple has its share of rough patches. The couples who stayed together learned how to respond positively, to listen carefully, and to show respect and love.

In the end, you may find that you and/or your spouse are simply not good marriage material because of too much baggage, a demanding nature, selfishness, bad habits, or unreliability. Others may be making the same bad choices as their parents. In any case, before taking the marriage plunge again, a person should solicit advice from a counselor, church worker, and/or friends and try to fix her problems.

Despite good intentions, planning, and attempts to hold a marriage together, many will still not last. In that case, I recommend trying to work out as many issues on your own before and after you hire an attorney. You don't have to have attorneys at all meetings. Get guidance from them, work on the issues, and then get more guidance. You could easily be paying $600-800 an hour for two dueling attorneys to resolve issues. The issues are obviously more complex when children or significant assets are involved. You and your partner might even consider having a paid facilitator or mediator try to resolve differences before hiring two attorneys. Facilitators are often retired judges and attorneys, who charge about the same or even less than one attorney.

Be Honest

There is an old saying, "If you always tell the truth, you don't have to remember as much." I am, of course, excluding little white lies that spare someone's feelings. Being honest doesn't necessarily involve volunteering information that might prove detrimental to you or that people will always speak well of you. In fact, not being criticized is impossible unless perhaps for a never discovered hermit in a cave with no relatives.

Despite the original success of some infamous frauds involving Michael Milken, Charles Ponzi, Bernie Madoff, Kenneth Lay, and Jeffery Skilling, most people who are consistently dishonest will eventually suffer financially and socially (as they did).

Be an Optimist

While you should carefully analyze potential investments and new business ventures, it helps to be a "cautious or moderate optimist." People who are perennial pessimists see the glass as "half empty." A little bit of Obama's "Yes, we can" is in order. On the other hand, extreme optimists tend to have higher debts and overspend. Perhaps, like Voltaire's *Candide*, they feel, "All is for the best in the world."

It is also important to be an "educated cautious optimist." Although a college education helps, I am thinking more about the experience from the "college of hard knocks" and being "street-wise." Successful executives and entrepreneurs develop a "sixth" sense that helps them limit bad decisions. Finally, males are more likely to be optimists if they don't have real low levels of testosterone.

Assume Good Intentions and Behavior

People don't always have good intentions, but I am convinced that the majority of people do. It is easy to interpret situations the wrong way. Until you find out otherwise, give people the "benefit of the doubt." If you start off with the notion that a person is "guilty until proven innocent" and you are wrong, it could poison your relationship for quite awhile. On the other hand, if you assume honesty and good intentions, you have risked much less and can reverse directions quickly.

Trust but Cut the Cards

Please don't be misled by the positive tone in this book. It is important to monitor and audit people and reduce their exposure to temptation. I have been surprised (well, maybe not) at the number of embezzlers in the news that steal even from small, charitable non-profit organizations. In an educational division in which I once worked, a woman that everyone would have trusted with their family fortune and was the "go to" financial expert, embezzled. Characteristics of employees like having long term employment, expertise, an honest face, religious values, and good family are no guarantee against fraud.

Be Happy

A "happiness" study, done by researchers from the Universities of Illinois, Virginia, and Michigan State, was published in *Perspectives on Psychological Science* using data from the World Values Survey. The worldwide survey included students and had a 1-10 point scale on which people reported their "life satisfaction score" as well as many other variables.

Compared to other rated individuals, the moderately satisfied or happy people rated 8-9 were more likely to get and stay married, to volunteer, to be rated highly by their supervisor, and have the highest levels of income, education, and political participation. The 8-9 rated students also had the highest grade point averages, class room attendance, and conscientiousness.

The 10s were lower than the 8-9s except for gregariousness, close friendships, self confidence, energy, and time spent dating. Thus, being moderately happy may offer the best combination of success and happiness, though I would rather be a 10 than a six or less.

One of the daily activities that causes the most unhappiness is commuting so try to live close to work. Back when $5,000 was a lot of money, Bernard Baruch said that "Enough money is always $5,000 more than I am making." People mistakenly think that money buys happiness, but after reaching a certain level of income ($50-60,000 or so), additional amounts don't increase happiness very much. In fact, people winning the lottery often aren't very happy because they are overwhelmed and many lose it quickly. People are likely to be happiest if they have a reasonable income, treat others well, live in a safe neighborhood, are honest, have good relationships, and/or a close knit family.

Laugh Often

Laughter really is the best medicine. A few years ago, I was on an ocean cruise that went from Los Angeles to Sidney, and the ship crossed the International Date Line. The ship's crew had a special ceremony marking the event with many passengers participating in the "crossing the line" ceremony. I overheard one wife commenting to her husband, "You don't need to participate in that because you "cross the line" every time you open your mouth."

On another cruise, I was talking with a couple that I had met playing "Team Trivia" on the ship. They had been married for 47 years and obviously were much in love. I inquired as to their secret for happiness. The husband replied instantly, "Sex." The wife, almost as quickly replied, "Stupidity."

Be Generous

I think a generous person is happier. You don't have to give lots of money. You can donate your time in raising funds for charity, doing something like "Meals on Wheels," or canvassing your neighbors on behalf of organizations like the American Cancer Society or the American Heart Association. You can give your good new or used items to charity (including locks of hair to Locks of Love) and take a tax deduction if you itemize. You can also bequeath part of your fortune that you accumulate by reading this book.

Though poor, my parents were extremely generous to their children and others. I remember my mother saying this about my father, "If he had one pair of pants and you wanted to wear it, he would stay in bed."

Avoid Greed

Greed causes us to over invest in the stock market, real estate, or other assets. It causes bubbles and encourages us to invest in things that are "too good to be true." The first recorded and most famous bubble is the crash in 1637 of the Holland tulip bulb market. At the peak, the rarest tulip bulbs sold for 6-10 times a workman's annual salary. Warren Buffett famously said that he "Buys when people are fearful and sells when they are greedy."

Develop Self Discipline

If I were to identify a list of reasons that put families and individuals into financial trouble, "weak willpower" and "lack of discipline" would be near the top.

Being Rude is Sometimes Okay

I generally try to be nice to people and will occasionally slip into the "gruff" or "tough mode," but a few times in my life, I have really become rude. About 20 years ago, I was renting a five bedroom duplex unit in Pullman Washington, a mostly college town. Five bedroom units must be rented during February or March because there is a limited demand for them.

At the time, I had five guys living there, and I reluctantly gave them until the end of April to re-rent. They all finally did, including one kid who was flunking out and who didn't bother to tell his parents, me, or his roommates. He left for the summer and didn't show up in August. Eventually, he called his roommates and said he wasn't returning though he was committed to a year's lease and had a $125 deposit. I used the deposit money for advertising, subletting fees, trash disposal, cleaning, and work time ($62 was given to his roommates).

After his roommates found a replacement, I released the tenant from the $14,000 liability in lease payments and a sent a list of charges to him. His father, who was extremely upset about losing the $125 deposit and whom I will refer to as Mr. Jones, called me at home while I was sitting in a hot-tub. His call ruined a perfectly lovely day, especially after he began to accuse me of coercing his son into signing the lease (even though the tenants were given an extra month). Then he went on to tell me what a lousy professor I was for taking advantage of naïve students. When I refused to budge on refunding the money, his last comment crossed the line. He said that he was going to complain to my boss's boss, Dr. Samuel Smith, President of Washington State University (WSU).

I said, "Mr. Jones, when you speak with President Smith, I want you to tell him something." He indignantly asked, "What's that?" Even though I normally don't use profanity, I exclaimed in a loud voice, "Tell him that it's none of his &#$!* business." Well, he did call President Smith's office and it was passed down to my department chairman. He called me in and explained that the incident had been shuttled to him. I listened; then stood up and as I was leaving, said, "It's none of your business either," but left out the &#$!.

It is not Okay to be Incredibly Stupid

In my basic finance class at WSU, I gave three exams with the last one given two weeks before finals. The date was listed in the syllabus and I announced it during the last six classes. A student's grade was based upon his highest two scores. One particular student, who apparently didn't read the syllabus or attend the last six classes (at least in a conscious state), showed up at my office about 10 days after missing the last exam.

I didn't want to make up a special test for him so I gave him three days to study for an oral exam. He failed that just like the first two written exams. However, I wanted to turn in my grades so I offered him a "D" after explaining that he had failed. At first he accepted, but later became upset that he was the only student given an oral (he was also the only one who missed the final exam). Thereupon, I offered to write another exam on the condition that if he failed that, he would get an "F." He accepted and predictably, failed that exam too. The real surprise was the letter that he wrote to my department chairman. He explained that it was inappropriate for me to offer him a "D" when he failed the oral, and he wanted to know why WSU would employ a professor who would do that. If I saw him again, I would have told him his "D" was for "dopey" or "dumb."

Think Ahead and be Prepared

People get into a lot of problems by not planning ahead or thinking about the worst case scenarios. For example, if you are riding in a small boat and can't swim or the water is cold enough to cause hyperthermia, then you should wear a life jacket at all times. If you are hiking in an unfamiliar place, you should carry a map and/or GPS. If you are riding with people and they end up getting drunk, you should have another way to get home. As my own example, when I was young, I couldn't afford a four wheel drive for elk hunting in the high Blue Mountains of southeast Washington so I carried a long tow chain. Twice I was rescued; once when the car was about to slide off a cliff and another time when I was caught in a blizzard.

Accept Life's Unexpected Events

If something very unusual or scary happens, accept that such things happen. I could tell many interesting tales, but four are particularly noteworthy. In my basic finance class, I had a 50 year old student who sat in the front row and asked excellent questions. Though I didn't give extra credit for participation, I was considering his case to be the one exception because his class involvement was the best out of the 14,000 students who had ever taken this class. About an hour before the second exam, he called and said that he wanted a make-up because he had a headache. I explained my policy of not giving make-up exams and that he should drop that test as the grade was based upon the best two of three exams.

About a half hour later, he called back and angrily and emphatically stated, "This is Phil Abrams (made up name); remember my name. You are going to regret your decision!" I called the campus police and it turns out that he had served time for murdering a child. The incident didn't make the newspaper as I didn't press charges, and he got a B- for the class. Interestingly, during the same semester, a failed Ph.D. student was arrested for trying to murder another professor. I should point out that Pullman is comparatively safe and that many people never lock their doors during the day.

The importance of this next story must be understood in the context of its time. During the 1960s, there was great turmoil in the United States with opposition to the Vietnam War and rising racial tensions especially between black and white Americans. Such groups as the Black Panthers and the Students for a Democratic Society became forces. There were important events including the assassinations of John and Robert Kennedy and Martin Luther King, the Los Angeles Watts riots (34 people killed and 1032 injured), the Selma to Montgomery civil rights marches, the Chicago riots during the Democratic National Convention, and the passage of the Civil Rights Act of 1964 and the Voting Rights Act of 1965. The following event occurred in 1965 near the peak of racial tensions. By the way, I had 12 black Americans read this story, and all of them approved of it and wanted it included.

During breaks while at Penn State, I drove to New Jersey and worked for Manpower, Inc., the temporary employment agency. This episode might be titled, "It is better to make friends than enemies." Anyway, I was always given a job because I was sober, dependable, and had a vehicle." Most of my fellow temps were high school drop-outs, and many had a substance abuse problem. During a job of unloading freight cars, I met "Ace the Great," a 6'6" African American, who weighed about 350 pounds and claimed to be a professional wrestler. We were unloading 100 pound bags containing a charcoal-like product, and Ace wondered if a scrawny 140 pound kid would be able to finish the job. Well, I did and went on to work another nine hours. One vivid memory of that job was coughing up black dust for three days. It was my first understanding of miner's black lung disease.

I worked several more jobs with Ace and grew to like him because he worked hard, was dependable, didn't come to work smelling of alcohol, and was quite the story teller. His favorite topics were wrestling and his many girlfriends. On one occasion, we were rehabbing metal forms used to lay concrete, and I mentioned to the group that I had a better and faster method for doing our job. Thereupon, one disgruntled worker picked up a metal pipe and started toward me shouting the words, "No f__ing Joe College student is going to tell me what to do!" Within seconds, Ace picked up a beam weighing more than 125 pounds like it was a baseball bat and shouted to my assailant, "You touch my buddy and you will die!" I know there is a special place in Heaven for "Ace the Great."

In 1972, during the hippie era, I was pursuing my Ph.D. in Boulder Colorado and was working 14-16 hour days. During that summer, I would try to hike the Rocky Mountains in areas with no trails. On one occasion, I found a wrecked single engine airplane above the tree line (about 12,000 feet). The only thing missing were the bodies and the radio. So I called the Federal Aviation Administration to inquire about whether I might remove some usable equipment. Apparently, the wreck belonged to the insurance company. In any case, I went back three days later and the plane was stripped.

During another trip, I found a particularly inviting stream with no road access. It was crystal clear and with polarized glasses, you could spot the inhabitants. The fishing was fantastic, and there was a nice breeze blowing during a blue sky day. Several times, I sat down and on my final rest stop, I smoked my "once a month cigar." Two years later, after I found myself getting addicted, I quit for good.

As I rounded a bend in the creek during my last half hour of fishing, I stumbled upon a woman in the buff sitting on a rock and breast feeding a baby. As she was reading a book and pretending not to notice me, I wondered what the etiquette rules were in such a case. Finally, I treated her as another fisherman and stayed 25 feet away on either side of her. As I fished down the stream, I glanced up and saw two more similarly attired people. My curiosity nearly got the best of me, but having lived in Los Angeles during the 1969 Charles Manson murder spree, I decided not to engage the three, who were likely part of a hippie commune.

Think About Winning All or Most of the Time

This trait has served me well. You will see some of it in this book and the writing of this book is a good example. Some people were often not too encouraging with comments like, "Don't quit your day job" and "Do you realize how many books are written every year that flop?" The number published is about 800,000 annually in the U.S. with few making money.

Use Declarative Words

Instead of saying, "I think I can do it," say, "I can do it" though be realistic about it.

Avoid Illegal Drugs

This seems obvious but is worth stating. If you are caught, you may do jail time, have a criminal record, and pay a lot of attorney fees. You may lose your job and your family, and having a criminal record is one of the surest ways to destroy your future and your finances. Your credit is likely to be affected and having good credit is critical to building wealth.

Use Moderation in Drinking Alcohol

Though there have been a number of studies showing the medicinal value of a small daily amount of alcohol, there are obviously huge societal costs from accidents, medical and family problems, criminal activities, and lost work. It goes without saying that excessive consumption will reduce your wealth accumulation.

If Possible, Give up Smoking

Though quitting smoking is a struggle for most people, the lifetime cost of smoking is huge, amounting to more than the average retiree has saved. The actual cost of smoking will keep going up because of inflation, lawsuits, and taxes. Assuming a two pack a day habit for 50 years at $5 per pack, the cost in today's dollars of just the cigarettes will be $182,500 (assumes costs rise as fast as inflation). Using a typical overall tax rate of 35%, the average person would need to earn about $281,000 to pay for them. Putting that $10 per day into a retirement fund that grew two percent faster than inflation would grow to over $491,000 (today's dollars) in 50 years.

The secondary effects include lost wages due to more illness, shorter life spans, and the ill health and associated costs to other people exposed to the smoke. Your employment prospects are lessened if you smoke, and many insurance companies will charge higher premiums. Your marital/ partner prospects are more limited because many people will not marry/ date a smoker. Some landlords will not rent to you. The combination of these factors will have strong negative effects on accumulating money.

Parents can have an important impact on keeping their children from smoking. Studies have shown that when parents talk with their children candidly at an early age, they are less likely to smoke. The biggest reasons for keeping them from smoking are to improve their health and future financial situation. From a purely selfish standpoint, parents often need physical and financial assistance as they age. Non-smoking children are likely to be wealthier, healthier, live longer, and able to provide that assistance.

Smoking has had a direct effect on me. My father was a closet smoker who died about 30 years younger than his non-smoking relatives.

If Overweight, Try to Slim Down

I don't underestimate the difficulty of losing weight especially if caused by medicine being taken, low wages (making it more difficult to purchase healthy foods), metabolism issues, etc. However, a very high percentage of weight and health problems are due to inactivity and eating patterns.

It is now becoming clear that health care costs are much higher for an obese person than a normal weight person. After analyzing anonymous data from nine large corporations involving 54,000 employees, Thomson Healthcare has provided some startling numbers (BusinessWeek). A severely obese employee has an annual healthcare cost of $5,695 (probably based upon 2006 and earlier) which is $2381 or 75% more than a normal weight employee. The differential for moderately obese is 20%. The obese persons had more injuries, back pain, arthritis, and three times more circulatory and metabolic diseases such as diabetes. Thus, we may see subtle forms of discrimination in terms of persons not being hired for a position or job requirements that limit an obese person's ability to get a job.

Don't Worry if You Aren't the Best Looking Person

Tall, macho men and gorgeous women usually have more friends because it is people's nature to want to be with them. However, most people can find some friends, and it is important to cherish these friendships with love and support. Be aware that intelligence is more highly regarded than looks when it comes to making money. According to a study in the *Journal of Applied Psychology*, people with the highest intelligence scores have higher lifetime earnings and have less financial strain than people with high beauty scores.

Love and Support Your Children

This may seem like a strange category for a personal finance book. However, children who experience a loving home and support will be more confident individuals who are less likely to end up in jail, pregnant, or on drugs. They are more likely to go to college, develop good relationships, be less financially dependent upon their parents, and have the confidence to be entrepreneurs. If a parent is constantly distracted by the negative behavior of their children (having raised four, there will always be some problems), he/she will have less energy, time, and extra funds to devote to building his/her nest egg.

Poor parenting is usually passed on from one generation to the next. To break this cycle, parents, especially new ones, should consider taking a parenting class that is often available through community or governmental organizations, hospitals, community colleges, and for profit companies. Free classes are often offered through child and family services. Look on the internet under your city or county or in the blue pages in the front of the phone directory.

Teach Your Children Good Values and a Work Ethic

My wife and I began at an early age to build our children's independence and stress the importance of contributing their share to the family and community. They had household duties starting about the age of three, a good age to give kids a large clear piggy bank so they can see their savings progress.

By the age of eight, our children were required to cook one complete dinner for the family each week. Within a year or two, their duties were expanded to include working at our rental apartments doing maintenance work.

With some tasks, I spent more time supervising my children than the amount of time required to do them myself. They were shown how to unclog drains and toilets, do roofing, change oil and tires, and do miscellaneous repairs. My kids often did not like the work, and there was no differentiation between the sexes except activities requiring strong arms. By the age of 12, each child was given the task of balancing the family checking account and helping with income taxes. In order for the kids to have time for sports, homework, and work, we did limit their TV exposure.

This level of activity seems to be more than most parents are giving their children as reflected in a recent study by the Maryland Population Research Center at the University of Maryland. Children spend only 24 minutes a day doing housework, a decline of 12% from 1997 and 25% less than 1981. Since modern women, especially those working outside the home, want their husbands to materially participate in domestic activities, this trend is not encouraging since girls and women still do more housework than boys and men. Furthermore, both sexes are likely to be better mates and have better marriages if they take early responsibility (*American Journal of Sociology*).

I did make one monetary mistake with my children. In exchange for paying most of their college expenses, they were not paid much for their family and other work, except a small allowance until age 16 when it went to zero. This meant that they had to take on a side job while in high school. It tended to build resentment since they wanted money to buy things. A better plan would have been to pay them slightly more than they could make in other part time work and offer to match any savings invested for college.

I do think that children, if feasible, should be paid an allowance. A typical guideline is to pay them a $1 per week for each year of age so that a 10 year old would get $10 per week. I actually received an allowance of 25 cents during only one year of my life. The kids should be expected to buy some gifts from the allowance, and that would need to be adjusted for the income levels of your social circle and the amount of work done. You should set up rules as to what the child would be expected to buy with the allowance and the parents should certainly monitor the expenditures. If they are expected to buy clothes, then the amount may need to be adjusted. Budgeting, saving, and spending are important lessons to be learned by children.

One thing that occurred to me years after the children were raised was how their activities meshed with the state child labor laws at the time. I always felt they were well supervised and did less risky work than farm children. However, readers considering hiring anyone under 18 including their own should probably investigate their state rules especially about what constitutes dangerous or prohibited work. In some states, minors are not allowed near demolition sites and heavy equipment. In any case, there may be a difference between work at your home and work for your business.

The time spent with them definitely was worthwhile despite their occasional resistance. It gave me great pleasure to hear several of my daughters tell how the tasks built their self confidence and how they accepted challenges other females would not, especially in the area of repairing items or hiring contractors. All of my children finished college within the normal times of their respective majors and all worked during college, in part because we expected that of them. That brings to mind another axiom:

The less you expect of children, the less you will get.

Avoid Unusual Names that may Harm a Child

My last name (Petry) was a source of frequent teasing as I grew up. My family pronounced it "pee tree" so you can image the crude variations starting with "pee." Anyway, after graduating from Penn State, I changed the pronunciation to "pet tree" to successfully spare my kids from some of the razzing. Johnnie Cash's song a "Boy Named Sue" captures some of the feelings caused by an unusual name (though in this case it was to make a strong man out of a boy).

A recent study suggests that parents should be careful in naming their children. Professors David Kalist and Daniel Lee (*Social Science Quarterly*) analyzed 15,000 names of boys and found the more uncommon the name, the more likely the boy was to become a juvenile delinquent. Constant name calling, teasing, and discrimination may cause a child to become bitter and result in destructive behavior. The situation is likely acerbated if the child is less attractive, frail, overweight, or has some disability.

To find the popularity of names, go to babycenter.com. The average ranking of the top 10 "bad boy" names in the Kalist/Lee study was 871 with the popularity ranging from 38th to 5157th. By the way, "Sue" as a boy's name was ranked $10,126^{th}$ while my name (Glenn) was ranked 813th, right up there with the average "bad boys." One can find very successful people whose names are uncommon such as "Glenn" for a female (ranked $18,754^{th}$) as in Glenn Close.

Please look at the popularity of names, the various spellings of each one, and commonality of the same name in the opposite sex. You may want to avoid the very most popular names so five kids in your child's class don't have the same first name. Also think carefully about a name that is bound to cause teasing like Blossom or Rainbow or whose initials are undesirable such as Babycenter's example of Zachary Ian Thomas (ZIT). Some names are just too bizarre like "Can't." In any case, the site gives tips on the naming of babies and includes 100,000 names.

Grandparents Make Great Caregivers

Children aged 30-33 months suffered the most injuries that required medical attention when they did not live with their fathers or where the parents were not married and the least accidents when cared for by the grandparents. The study, covering 3,449 children, was conducted at Bloomberg School of Health at Johns Hopkins University.

Silence is Golden

As you become more and more successful, people including your neighbors, friends, and especially your co-workers, will begin to talk about you. When I was building a considerable number of apartments in Pullman, WA, I had some people refer to me as owning half of Pullman. Such comments do not reflect reality but only people's curiosity and jealousy.

On one occasion, a female faculty member came up to me and said, "A group of us were talking about you, and we concluded you are not nearly as wealthy as we thought you were." One could spend quite a while pondering that comment. To avoid jealousy and gossip, I rarely discussed outside activities with my colleagues. Another reason to be guarded is that you may receive lower raises (as I did). However, when talking with lenders, my strategy was the opposite since I wanted to convince them of my successes.

Watch the Petry Puffery Index

I developed the Petry Puffery Index (PPI) in the 1970s because of an unwise professor in my department who had a strong, mostly wrong, opinion on everything. The faculty and staff didn't like him because he was always "right." He seemed to have a much higher opinion of himself than others did. This is an intuitive index defined as follows:

Petry Puffery Index = Your opinion of yourself divided by others' opinion of you

The ideal would probably be close to one. Individuals that are too high on this list may be domineering and overbearing and want you to do everything their way. They often dominate conversations and could be hazardous to your wealth and health. They may overlook or dismiss others' views which may be better than their own.

Someone too low on the index could lack the confidence to move ahead with an investment or take risks. To them, Chicken Little was right, "The sky is falling." The PPI is meant to be fun, but you will undoubtedly recognize people that are high or low on the list. You are likely wondering where the author stands on this list. That is probably like asking a car salesman if his price is good. Naturally, I'm a "one" or slightly below as others recognize what a "gem" I am.

One should not confuse this PPI with the Producer Price Index or the CPI, the Consumer Price Index. These indexes are subject to their own problems of quantification and confusion though they are more widely used than my PPI. Hopefully there will be enough copies of this book sold that it will become a household phrase.

Can you imagine a conversation between two business executives. Mary, who is on the board of a large company, complains to a cohort about the CEO who has a PPI of two. "Phil, can you recommend anyone with a PPI of .8 to 1.2? We need a new CEO who is more receptive to our ideas." "Mary," Phil says, "We are using the new standardized PPI test that was developed by PPS (Princeton Puffery Screeners), and we have some great candidates in that range. Please don't tell anyone as it is controversial. It allegedly discriminates against movie stars, pro athletes, politicians, talk show hosts, and Santa Claus, who score high on the index and nuns and monks who score low. Can you imagine the lawsuits that would result from our actions?"

Learn from Your Mistakes

Individuals with a high PPI are less likely to acknowledge and learn from their mistakes though many successful people have high and low PPIs. It's just that you will be more productive if the extreme PPIs are avoided, especially the high ones.

Try not to focus on less significant mistakes. Everyone makes minor gaffs. I saw a billboard in front of a restaurant called "India 40" in Portland, Oregon which humorously portrays this notion. It said, "Don't sweat the petty stuff. Don't pet the sweaty stuff."

CHAPTER 3

Is Luck Important for Success?

Some really successful people say that luck wasn't very important to their success. **My response is nonsense.** Everybody has some degree of luck, especially **earned luck.** Some people have the good fortune (or misfortune) of being born wealthy or having some unusual athletic, theatrical, intellectual, or creative talent. Most of us are somewhere in the broad middle range of talent or heritage, and we need to earn our luck by aggressively pursuing new courses of action. These actions aren't just in the business sense but things that occur in everyday life. In fact, this chapter features non business aspects of luck.

Ben Franklin once said, "I'm **a firm believer in luck; I find the harder I work, the more I have of it**."

There is random luck which just happens. It can be good, bad, or neutral. An example of random bad luck happened to me about 20 years ago while walking on a street in Pullman, WA. It was a cold day. I was all bundled up, the wind was blowing, and I was not very aware of my surroundings. I had, in fact, walked this way hundreds of times because it led past three of my duplexes.

Suddenly, there was a loud gunshot like boom. Having hunted most of my life, I instinctively froze thinking that someone was shooting a gun. Within a few seconds, I was hit on the head by a falling squirrel. I was concealed on the right by a concrete wall with a high hedge on top and was convinced that someone had shot the squirrel from an open window of a nearby fraternity.

After a brief moment, it dawned on me that the squirrel had the misfortune of shorting out an electrical transformer on the electric pole beside me. What are the odds of being hit on the head by a falling electrocuted squirrel? Certainly, it is rarer than being struck with lightning, an incredibly unlikely event. If only I had used my once in a million lifetimes event to win a $200 million lottery. When anyone notices any of my odd behavior, I simply invoke the Falling Squirrel Syndrome.

An example of my random good luck (not earned) occurred one day when I was about five years of age. Four of us kids were retrieving golf balls from a golf course pond. The golfers kept signaling for us to move but at 200 yards, their intent was not clear. One fellow hit a drive that brushed my hair just above my right ear. At my age, I likely would have been killed if struck about two inches or so to the left.

You can benefit from earned good luck if you are out there aggressively pursuing opportunities. The luck may take many forms such a promotion, a raise, investment opportunities, a new idea, new friends, or a new career. Unfortunately, we are often stuck in such a rut of work, family, and play that we don't allow our creative side any room to maneuver.

Of course, the more new venues pursued the more chances of experiencing bad luck. With more experience, you will learn to discern those situations which provide better odds of a positive outcome. Again, a mentor, even a book mentor like me, is very important.

Let me further illustrate the importance of pursuing new adventures or ventures with an example. At the age of 44, I decided that it would be fun to play slow pitch softball. With my very modest athletic ability, I opted to play in the coed leagues and was selected by a newly formed team expected to finish last. Though all of my previous experience was as an outfielder in sandlot baseball 30 years ago, I wanted to pitch and promoted myself for that position. To hone my skills, I threw hundreds of pitches into a low cut box which was the size of a home plate.

I was chosen as the starter, pitched every game up to the last one of the regular season, and had the top record in the league. Our last game was with our arch rivals for the league lead. Anyway, my coach let this young male hotshot from the college pitch. We were ahead until the last inning when all "hell broke loose." The opponents scored three runs, loaded the bases with one out and were just one run down. The coach approached me and said, "Glenn, I want you to pitch."

Though the outcome would not affect my livelihood, the tension was high, and I agreed to relieve the young fellow. My first two pitches were balls and I had this sinking feeling that I would walk in the tying run and the winning run would score on any ground ball. My third pitch was another ball but the hitter swung anyway and grounded into our only double play of the season.

On the next day, tournament play started. I pitched and the team won the first game. The new pitcher started the second game and after our opponents scored 7 runs in the first inning, I replaced him. I won both that one and the next game, giving us the tournament victory. This is an example of boldly pursuing your dreams even if it was only in a softball league. There is an element of both random good luck (especially the double play) and earned luck because I practiced hard and took some chances. Despite the fact that playing softball did not put any money in my pocket, I have often looked back on this success to boost my spirits when feeling blue.

CHAPTER 4

Be Bold and Stand Up for Your Principles

I think that it is important to stand up for what you feel is right and take bold steps. Having written many newspaper editorials, letters to representatives of Congress, and attended many hearings before city officials, I know that most people do not take the time to make a difference. Decisions are often made by the vocal few, who often do not represent the majority.

This first episode of my boldness is included partly because it was funny and there are some interesting facets to it. During my academic year of 1964-5 at Penn State, my abode was a dormitory named "Butternut." Other dormitory names included "Hickory," Chestnut," and "Walnut." Our "house" was planning a spring party up at a lake in the Nittany Mountains so I needed a date.

The problem was that there were 2 ½ guys for every gal and there were 67 national fraternities or houses collectively competing for the few women. I was also "dirt" poor. This was indeed my first understanding of the law of supply and demand. My dilemma was do you settle for any date or do you, to quote the snowboarders, **"Go big or go home?"**

Well the "Go big" option was pursued. Unfortunately, there were only two women that met my criteria. The first was a gal in my cafeteria who had a warmth and stunning beauty about her (as much as could be told from a distance of 1000 feet). At 19, I had a fear of talking with beautiful women. If this gal knew me at all, it would be the guy who stared at her from afar, all the while pretending not to stare.

The other alternative was this sorority gal who was in my accounting class. She might actually know my face since our seats were about 10 feet apart. However, she was a "knock-out" and pursued by 5,000 fraternity guys. Jackpot lottery odds looked better than my chances. This was David against Goliath. I had to be really creative to compete.

So I called sorority gal on the phone and identified myself by the location of my classroom seat. After a brief introduction, I explained that our "house" was having a party at the lake and asked if she would like to go. She immediately agreed and then asked the dreaded question, "What house do you belong to?" I hesitated for what was probably a millisecond but seemed like forever and then answered weakly, "Butternut." There was a pause which seemed like 10 eternities while I waited for her to withdraw her acceptance. Her commitment to our first date never wavered, and we had a ducky time rowing around the lake.

About a week later, I invited her on another date. Much to my disappointment, she was busy but indicated that she had a date on another night and would cancel it to go out with me. To me, it showed a lack of integrity to accept a date and then break it to go out with someone else. I turned her down and told her that this ended our short relationship because I did not approve of hurting a guy like that. You be the judge-integrity or stupidity?

Here are two more instances of sticking up for your principles. Back in 1977 before I had tenure at Washington State University (WSU), there was growing support in the state of Washington for a massive new irrigation project that would draw water from the Columbia River. It was backed by Tom Foley of Washington state, then Speaker of the U. S. House of Representatives. Being avidly interested in salmon and steelhead, I was not thrilled to see large amounts of additional water drawn out of the river.

Upon investigation, I learned that the U.S. Bureau of Reclamation, which had conducted the benefit/cost study, had omitted the value of the hydropower generation lost from the 11 downstream dams from their cost calculations. Their study had shown significantly greater benefits than costs. However, when the lost hydropower was included, the benefits were only about 25 cents per dollar in cost. It was clearly a big waste of taxpayer money.

After I conducted my research, I waited until my tenure (generally a lifetime appointment) was granted in 1978 to publish my findings. At that time, I sent a summary of my work to all of the major newspapers in Washington, Idaho, and Oregon. It was published on the front page of the daily *Seattle Post Intelligencer* and appeared in most other Northwest newspapers and *Newsweek* magazine.

The effect was much greater that I could have ever realized. The farming, irrigation equipment, and banking industries in central Washington went berserk. They wrote to Dr. Glenn Terrell, President of WSU, questioning all of my funding and other research. They wanted me and another professor in agricultural economics fired or at least our work stifled. Much to the credit of Dr. Terrell, he stuck up for us. The project was never finished.

The other episode involved the building of apartments in Pullman, Washington by WSU. During the early 1970s, there were a number of bankrupt developers in Pullman, and the banks repossessed many properties because of over development. Much of the problem was created by WSU's building apartments on its own property.

To allay the fears of the banking and real estate community, the next WSU president, Dr. Sam Smith, wrote them a letter promising not to build housing unless there was a shortage of family housing. WSU was on the verge of breaking that pledge when I wrote to remind Dr. Smith (my boss) of the negative consequences of an institution of higher education breaking a pledge like that. The press would have had a field day with the issue highlighting that broken promise. It seems like no one but me was willing to hold WSU accountable. The project was put on hold and the land was eventually sold.

CHAPTER 5

How to Protect Against Fraud and Theft

You have to realize that stealing from the American consumer is big business. According to a 2005 Federal Trade Commission (FTC) survey, 30.5 million U.S. consumers were victims of marketing frauds during the prior year. The most common fraud was bogus weight loss products with the second being foreign lottery schemes.

It appears to be legally acceptable to make outrageous claims and then in a footnote disclaim them. I clicked on one internet ad from "News 6 Reports" that was a purported story by a health and fitness writer. The banner headline said "Lose 47 lbs. in The Next 10 Days (Without Exercise or Dieting?)." The ad's banner listed various news media with the following caption "As seen on MSNBC, CNN, ABC, 60 Minutes, and BBC." One would infer (probably incorrectly) that this claim was proven on those networks.

Maybe the "?" was the key to being able to make an outlandish assertion. I looked at the "Terms and Conditions" at the end of the ad which stated, "This website, and any page on this website, is based loosely off a true story, but has been modified in multiple ways including but not limited to: the story, the photos, and the comments. This blog and any page on this website, are not to be taken literally or as a non-fiction story."

This brings up the regularly over used phrase: **If it seems too good to be true, it probably is (too good to be true).**

Theft of Consumer and Business Records

Another more serious problem is the theft of consumer and business records involving numbers for social security, driver's licenses, accounts, or health records which could result in identity theft on a massive scale. A total of 355 million records have been breached from January, 2005 to May 15th, 2010, according to an average of the websites **privacyrights. org** and the **idtheftcenter.org,** though the actual number may be greater than 600,000,000. According to the Identity Theft Resource Center

(ITRC), 52% of businesses with publicly reported breaches in 2009 didn't report the number of records, and many others don't even report the theft.

Some people's records are breached more than once so the number of records is more than the number of individuals affected. The ITRC claims that less than 3% of the breaches involve encrypted data and less than 9% had password protection (which it considers inadequate) so the consumer is poorly protected. The breaches were caused by the following:

- Data on the move (stolen after it has left its main storage location, usually the company database)

- Accidental exposure

- Insider theft

- Subcontractors

- Hacking

For 2009, the highlights of ITRC findings were as follows:

- Paper breaches account for 26% of the records (an increase of 46% over 2008). This is inexcusable. State laws need to require shredding of sensitive documents.

- Business sector breaches climbed from 21% to 41% between 2006 and 2009.

- Malicious attacks now exceed human error. The criminals have become more sophisticated.

The biggest breaches involved the TJX Companies, Inc.(2007), Heartland Payment System (2009), and the U.S. military (2009). These breaches reportedly included the following number of records: 70,000,000 (U.S. military), 100,000,000 (TJX), and 130,000,000 (Heartland).

According to Javelin Strategy & Research, nearly 10 million U.S. adults, or 4.32% of the population were, victims of identity theft in 2008, up from 3.58% in 2007. Obviously, the majority of breached records do not result in a loss. You can obtain free emails on the latest breaches by sending an email to dataloss-subscribe@datalossdb.org.

Every place that records are stored is a potential source of identity theft. These include your doctor's office, employer, financial institutions, government agencies, home, car, computer, your mailbox, credit card companies, purse/wallet, trash, and retail establishments.

Phone Scams

1. The first rule to avoid phone scams is "Don't respond to any solicitation in which you don't know the caller or its organization." I personally go further than that as I don't respond to any calls even from the 20 organizations receiving my support. My reasons go beyond avoiding scams. I simply don't want to be bothered.

2. The second rule is "Wait a day and call them back if you are still interested." You should also find their phone number on your own as opposed to using one that the caller provides.

3. Avoid "slamming." Slamming occurs when your long distance carrier is changed without your knowledge or by a caller asking misleading questions or misrepresenting themselves. This actually happened to one of my businesses when one of my staffers was duped into changing carriers.

4. Don't fall for phishing. "Phishing" occurs when the calls really aren't legitimate, and the caller often pretends to represent a legitimate business. The perpetrator needs more information to scam you. I have had several calls stating that there was a problem with my ___ Bank credit card. I suspected something was amiss because the phone number on the recording was different than the one on my credit card, but I wanted information for this book. Actually, one call appeared to have originated in Florida and another one was from Indonesia. **However, technology now exists that allows the caller to show any number and name he wants on your caller ID.**

Upon calling back to the Florida number, I gave them my name (which they already had) and informed them that I was calling about the ___ Bank card. The agent asked for my credit card number so I inquired as to what other information they needed. They wanted my date of birth, social security number, and the small security code to "verify" my identity. This was a two pronged scam. The first was to use my card for purchases and the second was to open new accounts under my name.

It is common practice for card issuers to ask for the last four digits of your social security number, your address, and phone number. For stock brokers and mutual funds, they commonly ask for your entire social security number. However, **you should only give this information out when you initiate the call using the phone number on your card or statement.**

5. Sign up for the "do not call" registry. You can sign up for five years by going on line to donotcall.gov (you need a working email) or calling 1-888-382-1222 or TTY (1-866-290-4326) from the phone you wish to register. Despite being on the list, many groups or businesses can call you. The political parties are the worst offenders. One political party has probably called my home 30 times in the past five years despite my repeated pleas to take me off its phone lists. That may be a good reason to not give to any political party or to get an unlisted number. Others that can call include non-profits, companies from whom you have purchased a product or made a payment to within the last 18 months, or a company to which you asked about a product or service or submitted an application in the past three months.

If telemarketers call you anyway, you can sue them in small claims court for $500 and that can be raised to $1,500 if they knowingly broke the law. If you have caller ID, take a picture of the call information.

Ponzi Schemes

This scam is named after the Italian immigrant, Charles Ponzi. During 1919-20, Ponzi promised investors a 40% return in 90 days by investing in international reply coupons (IRC). IRCs can be exchanged for postage in a foreign country. Ponzi hoped to take advantage of differing postal rates between countries and was able to get millions of dollars from investors. It seems that every year, another alleged Ponzi scheme is uncovered, the latest two involving Bernard Madoff and Allen Stanford.

These schemes are most likely to occur in privately owned businesses where there is less scrutiny. Doing your own due diligence helps, but clever con artists can fool even seasoned veterans. The unfortunate thing is that in the Madoff and Stanford cases, authorities failed to heed many warning signs. The most important "red flags" are probably consistently high returns in good and bad times and promises of abnormally high returns of 30-40% or more annually. If one invested $100,000 in Ponzi's scheme, an investor would amass $70 billion in 10 years (ignoring taxes and realizing a 40% return every 90 days).

Job Scams

With the rise of the internet, job scams are proliferating. Many people are desperate for work and want to believe an opportunity is legitimate. A lot of job scams look real and can be very elaborate. Here are the things that these scams have in common or actions to take (*Equifax.com*):

1. Sensitive personal information such as your Social Security number, driver's license number, bank account numbers, and PINs is requested up front. Criminals seek this information supposedly for a background check. I have hired several people on Craigslist and eventually asked for Social Security numbers and a copy of their driver's license to do such checks. However, before I asked, we exchanged information about the job location, duties, preliminary contract, starting dates, references, and a number of phone and in-person interviews. The background check was the last item to be done with one or two finalists.

2. Spelling and grammatical errors and job offers from developing countries are common red flags. Obviously some real jobs come from developing countries.

3. Always research the firm to which you are applying thoroughly. Check the company's website, the Better Business Bureau, and type the company's name on the internet and see what pops up. Some scammers may not actually work for the firm so find the firm's main number and call the person. If there is no such person there, it is likely a scam. You don't even need to talk with the person; simply ask the receptionist if he works there. For direct line numbers, block your caller ID by pushing *67 before dialing the number. If the person answers, simply say "Sorry, wrong number," maybe in a disguised voice. However, the direct line doesn't guarantee that the person works at a specific company, but at least the number is genuine.

4. Avoid positions such as "Accounts Receivable Clerk" and "Payment Representative" except for the most reputable companies. A number of "money mule" scams employ unsuspecting victims to launder illegally obtained money from selling narcotics or evading taxes. Such victims could end up charged with crimes.

5. Consider opening an email account solely for job applications and resume submission. This consolidates your information and reduces the incidence of spam and phishing.

6. Be especially wary of jobs like data entry, on line ad posting, envelope stuffing, coupon selling, and assembly work. For some of these "jobs," the scammer simply sends information about placing ads to find new people to pay for information about placing ads. Others may be trying to obtain your social security and driver's license numbers.

7. Be cautious of jobs that don't include an address and phone number.

Marketing Scams

Personally, I have stopped buying most products directly from television. The products have been mostly inferior, over-priced, and/or involve high pressure sales tactics or phony billing. Several times, I have called a company offering "free" products if I paid shipping and handling, only to be told that I still had to buy some to get the free samples. In one case, I declined and it appeared on my credit card anyway. A favorite tactic is to put you on hold and make you decline repeatedly to stop double orders or being sent other products.

The abuses are so common that they have caught the attention of state regulators, the Federal Trade Commission, and the Better Business Bureau. Assume that all telemarketer calls are recorded and avoid saying "yes." They can alter tapes which imply that you agreed to something. In most cases, I simply hang up on telemarketers if they call me, but if they ask if this is "Glenn Petry," I simply ask, "Who's calling?" or say "That's me."

On Line Gaming Problems

Many people, including lots of children, play games on line. This attracts predators, identity thieves, and cyber bullies. You should instruct your child to play only with those people known in real life, to not engage in cyber bullying and to report it when it occurs, and to not give out personal information such as their school, address, age, gender, vacation plans, phone number, and social security number. There was a recent scandal involving on-line poker in which scammers had written the computer code to make themselves win.

Secret Shopper Scams

People are supposedly hired to be a "secret shopper" and shop at stores and write a review (*Equifax.com*). The hiring company may provide fake Better Business Bureau ID numbers and appear legitimate. The scam usually involves money transfers. The scammer sends a check to the victim and asks him to deposit it with a portion kept for his services with the rest to be wired back to the company. By the time the scammer's deposited check bounces, the company is long gone. If you are asked to wire money back to the company, it is definitely a scam.

Charity Scams

When there is a natural disaster like the Haitian earthquake or the tidal wave that hit Indonesia or at holiday times, the scammers come out. Here are some tips (some from scambusters.org) to avoid scams:

- Unless the charity is a local one that you recognize, check out national and some regional charities at give.org, which is the site of the Better Business Bureau's Wise Giving Alliance, which has over 100 years experience in evaluating charities. The best ones carry the Alliance's National Charity Seal.

- Another useful source for checking charities is CharityNavigator. org which rates charities and shows how they spend their money. Check out the percentage of funds that go to fundraising and administration. High percentage charities should be avoided. A minimum of 60% should go to the people, animals, species, or causes they serve, not to the administrators or fund raising.

- Be cautious about email requests, especially if you have never donated to them before. Cyber begging is becoming big business through such sites as Craigslist, DonateMoney2Me.com, Cyber-Beg, and Begslist.

- Write a check to the charity, instead of giving cash.

- Don't make any checks out to an individual.

- Ask for a receipt with the name, address, and phone number of the charity on it.

- Scammers may falsely claim to be affiliated with a specific charity so you may wish to call them to verify the legitimacy of the person and the appeal.

- Be wary of charities that claim to be raising money for the local police or firefighters. At CharityNavigator.org, when I typed in "police" and "firefighters," 21 of the 33 charities were rated 0-1 stars and only nine were rated 3-4 stars. Before donating to this charitable category, you need to ask a lot of questions about use of funds and who benefits.

- Decide on the amounts and charities to support and contact **them**.

- Avoid the "suggested" donations. Your ability to contribute could vary from year to year, and suggested donations are often last year's amount plus something additional.

Mortgage Scams

There are many housing or mortgage scams as follows (some from occ.treas.gov):

1. **Foreclosure "Rescue" and Refinance Fraud.** The scammer guarantees to save your house by negotiating with your lender. You may be asked to stop making mortgage payments and pay him instead along with hefty fees. He likely will not pay the lender, you will be stuck with late fees, and it may push you into foreclosure.

2. **Reverse Mortgages Scam.** For many seniors, their house is often their most valuable asset. When short of cash, many take out a reverse mortgage which converts home equity into cash as explained in Chapter 19. The problem occurs when the senior doesn't receive the money or any benefit such as paying off his debts. The best solution is to have an attorney (who is not part of the senior's estate planning) handle the closing and distribution of funds.

3. **Fake Government Modification Program.** The scammer appears to be representing or approved by the U.S. Government and uses words that suggest this connection such as "federal," "HOPE," "TARP," etc. The scammer may even have an official looking website.

4. **Leaseback/Rent-to-Buy Scheme.** The scammer asks you to transfer the property's title to him in order to obtain better financing. You are supposedly allowed to stay in the home as a renter and then buy it back later. Transferring the title does not change your payment obligations unless the bank agrees to it and the scammer assumes the mortgage.

5. **Bankruptcy Fraud.** The scammer may claim that bankruptcy will stop a foreclosure. While it does temporarily, the bank still must be paid and it will eventually foreclose.

6. **Mortgage Debt Elimination Scheme.** The scammer claims to know of "secret laws" and legal arguments that allow a person to forego mortgage payments and eliminate debt.

7. **Sale of or Loans on Your House.** Scammers will forge paperwork, your signature, or ID cards or sell your house or get a loan on it. The elderly are often the target because they are more likely to have no mortgage. If you receive a payment book or other strange documents regarding your house, call the company who sent it and check with a title company or your county clerk to see if the title to your house has been transferred.

Don't fall for any of that. The best advice is to:

• Check with the Better Business Bureau about a business.

• Investigate suspicious activity by contacting trusted friends, lawyers, bankers, government agencies, non-profit or government websites, and advisers.

• Avoid paying up front fees.

• Contact your lender first.

• Understand what you are signing (get advice if needed).

• Use established financial institutions.

• Be cautious about having an unknown third party work with your lender (do it yourself).

• Get promises in writing.

- Don't sign over your deed without consulting **your** lawyer.

- Make all payments to your lender, not a third party.

- Take your time; rash decisions are often bad.

- Beware of exaggerated claims.

- Stop dealing with anyone employing high pressure sales tactics or that asks you to do anything illegal like using falsely inflated appraisals or overstating your income.

- Don't borrow more than you can repay.

- Don't refinance unless there is a clear benefit to you.

Senior Citizen Scams

Some senior citizens become too trusting or are mentally incapable of handling their affairs. A significant percentage of those preying on seniors are friends, relatives, caretakers, financial advisers, or supposedly trusted individuals. The following scams affect the elderly more because they are home more, may be lonely and polite, have money, and often have had people help them so they may be more generous or trusting.

Door to Door Salespersons or Solicitors. They may claim to be selling magazines, religious products, cleaning supplies, yard services, repairs (like recoating your roof or driveway), etc. to pay for some seemingly worthwhile activity. In fact, they may not be selling anything, the price may be grossly inflated, or they may be planning to commit a crime either on the spot or are "casing" your home for a latter crime.

Of course, there are legitimate people that go door to door. However, it is risky to let such people in your house. We all make some allowances for people we know and others such as girl scouts. My advice is to engage them only through a locked front door, but at the very least, through a locked screen. You could even ask them for a driver's license or other ID and copy the number down.

These individuals are often part of organized crime families that roam the U.S. looking for victims and they may even rob, rape, or assault you. They often have out-of-state license plates. You are advised to call police if you are suspicious. If fraud is suspected, you can contact the following agencies:

Better Business Bureau: 816-421-7800

PhoneBusters: 888-495-8501

Federal Trade Commisssion: 877-382-4357

National Fraud Information Center: 800-876-7060

U.S. Housing and Urban Development (HUD): 1-800-569-4287

HUD Hope Program: 1-888-995-4673

Free Lunch Seminars. First, not all of them are scams, but many involve a lot of high pressure tactics and follow-up phone calls and letters. I attended one just to get information for this book. Frankly, unless you are familiar with the business or individual presenting the seminar, I would likely avoid it. The dangers are that you will be pressured into buying something that you don't understand, whose risks are not well understood, that is just a scam, is illiquid, or that involves a "leap of faith."

Investment Fraud. Seniors age 60 and over account for about half of the complaints received by state security regulators (*North American Securities Administrators Association*). According to a National Association of Security Dealers Investor Education Foundation study, those senior victims are more likely to be married men who are better educated and financially more literate than non fraud victims. They are often reluctant to admit to being a victim and may have recently suffered a serious health problem or loss of a job.

For more information about investment fraud, go to the Securities and Exchange Commission's website called investor.gov. While it has a section "Protect Your Money" that applies to everyone, it also has one specifically "For Seniors." The Federal Bureau of Investigation also has a site about many crimes at fbi.gov.

This doesn't necessarily involve seniors, but one investment scam involves dividing 1,000 investors into two groups and telling one group that a stock will go up and the other one that it will go down. Then the 500 winners are divided into two more groups with the same trick, but with another stock. After three advisories, one group of 125 investors has had three winning stock picks in a row and another 125 have been advised about three losing stocks. These two groups are now convinced of the scammer's wisdom and are ripe for a big scam.

Lottery Scam. The victims are told they have won a lottery or sweepstakes (particularly a foreign one), and they need to send in money to cover taxes or bank fees. They often receive a bogus check and are asked to deposit it and send some of the balance. They are more likely to be women, less wealthy, and less educated than investment fraud victims.

To guard against the above problems, relatives and guardians need to advise people of these scams and monitor people who fit a vulnerable profile.

ATM Thefts and Scams

ATMs can be among your more vulnerable spots for thefts and scams. Here are some tips from the American Bankers Association.

- Look carefully at your surroundings, especially at night. If you observe suspicious circumstances or persons, don't use the ATM. Look for hidden cameras.

- At night, go to a store or bring a friend.

- Never divulge your PIN to anyone, not even family or friends.

- Have your card in hand as you approach the ATM machine.

- Don't visually display the money and pocket it immediately. Count it later.

- If you are using a drive-up, be sure that passenger windows are rolled up and doors locked. If you leave your car to go to the ATM, lock your car.

- Shield the keyboard with your body as you enter your PIN. Enter your numbers quickly.

Other Scams

Many of the following scams involve the same pattern of trying to get sensitive personal information. They try to scare you into thinking that you will lose some important service; your card will be cancelled; you will face some serious fines or jail time; or someone is trying to steal your identity. Of course, the latter is true as they are trying to do it. Many of these are from the IRTC or fraud.org.

Old Account Scam. The statute of limitations (SOL) limits the time a creditor has to sue to collect a bill. Sometimes creditors will try to collect bills years after the SOL runs out. The SOL varies by state, the type of obligation, and whether it is written or oral. It is usually 3-6 years. If a collection agency goes beyond that SOL, they can be sued and shut down. If the amount is large, you may wish to consult an attorney. If small, you could challenge the collection agency to provide your state's SOL for your type of account. Another possibility is to contact "Legal Aid" (for low income people) or contact your state attorney general's office.

Sponsorship Scam. You are invited to invest in a business with a big pay-off of say 50% a year. If you invested $10,000 and got that rate of return, you would have $33 million in 20 years (ignoring taxes). Obviously, such returns are not realistic.

Hitman Scheme. Someone claims to be a hitman hired to kill the recipient. The purpose, of course, is to extort money. These are coming from overseas, and IRTC experts advise recipients to not even make a crime report.

Nigerian Scam. I actually received one of these in the mail. The recipient receives a notice from a supposed wife of a political prisoner who has a large sum of money that just needs a little capital to free the jackpot.

Advanced Fee Scam. Scammers from Canada, using the names and locations of reputable companies, are asking for advanced fees to secure a loan. Such fees are illegal in both the U.S. and Canada and the loan non-existent.

Security Alert Scam. Credit card or bank customers are asked to provide information at a website to update security measures. The request usually has the bank's logo. Banks generally don't ask for sensitive information via email. There is one exception. Personal bankers with whom you have a relationship sometimes do, but any information is only sent to them.

Jury Duty Scam. The caller claims to work for the local court and that you have failed to report for jury duty. The scammer then asks for confidential information for verification.

Western Union Scam. The scammer supposedly deposits some amount as a credit on your credit card, and you pay them a portion of that amount by Western Union.

EBay, Paypal, or Yahoo Scam. The scammers will generally ask for important credit information and may threaten to close your account.

EBay Sales Scam. Find information to avoid fraudulent sales by going to ebay.com/help.

IRS or Bank Scams. Contacts claim to be needing information for an audit or other purposes. The IRS never sends emails to taxpayers.

Car Part Scam. Many repair shops charge for a new part without actually replacing it or replacing it with another used part. To guard against the former, mark oil filters, spark plugs, alternators, air filters, and other accessible parts with a permanent magic marker and then ask to see them.

Work at Home Scam. The unemployed or stay at home parents are often sucked into this type of fraud. You receive useless literature that tells you to place ads to recruit more victims. There are legitimate work at home jobs so be cautious.

Other Fake Check Scams. This is similar to the "secret shopper" and "lottery scams" in which you receive a bad check for something you have advertised or for work to be done at home, and you are asked to send a portion of the money to usually a third world country. The check is for more than you are owed so you send the extra to them. For the work at home, you may be told you are processing money for their clients or that the extra money was a mistake. By the time the "certified" fake bank check bounces, the thief is long gone, and you are responsible for replacing the bank's funds. Just because the bank deposits the check doesn't mean it is good.

Apartment Rental Scam. Apartments are advertised for rent and pictures may be included. Unfortunately, the scammers don't own the property and may be in another country. They offer to send the keys or have someone meet you after the rent and deposit are received. However, neither event happens. Don't ever rent an apartment without seeing it or at least being in contact with a rental company.

Chimney Scam. A chimney sweep tells you that some expensive repairs are needed to your chimney because your chimney has a few loose bricks or cracks. The same thing can happen if you need to replace a furnace, and you are told the code has changed and you need a special chimney liner. The latter situation happened to me. In those cases, you may wish to hire an independent house inspector, other heating contractors, or consult with the city or county building inspector.

Inheritance Scam. A relative supposedly has left you an inheritance so you need to pay some taxes or fees for attorneys, banks, documentation, processing, etc. in order to get the inheritance.

Insurance Scam. Scammers are using the new health care legislation to peddle phony insurance policies. Sometimes, a policy is termed "ObamaCare Insurance" to suggest federal government involvement that doesn't exist.

Other scams include order or gift confirmations (that never happened), scammers posing as employees from the government (welfare offices, Social Security Administration, Medicare, etc.), a utility company, or a hospital, "get out of debt" emails, false credit card cancellation notices, and money requests for free social security services.

Internet Security

Here are my suggestions (some of the latter ones from fraud.org):

1. Consider an Apple computer as that brand has much less virus and spyware problems than the Microsoft based systems. It also scores higher on consumer surveys, is reliable, and boots faster than most PCs. Among the drawbacks for Apple systems are greater expense, fewer varieties, and less available software options. I personally use both Microsoft and April, but the constant security issues of Microsoft based software is annoying and takes some of my time.

2. Netbooks need the same type of security as laptops.

3. People are often tricked into opening malicious software at some holiday like Halloween or Christmas. Christmas greetings or Halloween spooks are often the teaser.

4. Make sure your spam filters, firewall, anti-virus, and spyware protection are up to date.

5. Don't use your social security or driver's license number as your password. Use more complex passwords with at least eight characters including numbers, letters, and symbols and **keep it to yourself.**

6. Never enter personal information on pop-up screens. Follow your gut instincts when asked for information.

7. Don't shop at on-line stores without a privacy policy and opt out of information sharing.

8. Never use a debit card online. They often don't have the same on-line protections as credit cards. A theft could wipe out your entire checking and savings accounts.

9. Check to see whether the Better Business Bureau approves the site.

10. Use only secure websites that show a padlock at the bottom of the browser window or have "https" in the address bar. The sites are likely to be encrypted to protect your information.

11. Use a different password for Web mail accounts than you use on the most sensitive accounts like bank accounts.

12. Only use a wireless router with strong encryption features. The most secure type of encryption is WPA2. For more detailed information, see "Protect Your Computer from Viruses, Hackers, and Spies" at scsa. ca.gov (California State and Consumer Services Agency).

13. Be very careful when file sharing. You could download viruses or spyware, allow others to copy your files without permission, connect your modem to a foreign telephone number resulting in expensive telephone charges, and you might even break the law.

14. Assume that everything you do at a wireless service in a public place is unencrypted. Furthermore, someone can set up a bogus wi-fi that appears to be supported by a business. An ad-hoc wi-fi connection is a common scam and often shows up as an icon with two computers. Lifehacker.com advises public Wi-Fi users to turn off their file and printer sharing and remote log-in, make sure your firewall is turned on, log off unless you see "https" (note the "s"), and turn off Wi-Fi when not using the internet.

15. Business travelers should ask their employers to use Virtual Pri-

vate Network (VPN) connections for their computers. VPN ensures complete encryption of all traffic.

16. Make sure your children understand how to use the internet and protect your family and computer. Kids need to be 13 years of age in order to use YouTube, Facebook, and MySpace. Be aware that some kids will lie about their age. If your kids want to use the social network sites, have them discuss what will be placed on the sites and how important it is at all times to guard personal information such as addresses, ages, birth dates, interests, names, and numbers such as phones, social security, driver's license, and accounts.

Be aware that social networking sites are the latest and perhaps easiest place for planting viruses and hacking because people tend to open attachments from their friends. Never open any attachments. Facebook accounts contain an enormous amount of information about you, your family, and friends. Hackers can send believable requests for money that appear to be coming from or supported by you. Also, mobile services such as FourSquare, Latitude, and Loopt have become popular for broadcasting one's location so friends can join you. Doing this is risky as it also shows your location to thieves.

17. Use parental controls to reduce your child's exposure to inappropriate sites. Computers and virus software usually come with them built in.

18. Don't open spam mail and don't click on any links which supposedly delete you from its mailing list except for sites you trust. Doing so confirms that your email address is real, and you may actually download viruses or spyware.

19. Don't open attachments from anyone unless you know what they contain and are expecting them. Even then, they could contain malicious software.

20. Consider a virtual account number when using a credit card online. These are created by your credit card company, and it disguises your real account number. Your regular account will be charged and if anyone steals the retailer's data, the information will be useless. A virtual number has a very limited life span.

21. Don't enter contests operated by unfamiliar companies.

22. Don't assume that an absence of complaints is always a good sign. Fraudulent companies often change addresses and names.

23. Make sure you understand the details of any offer.

24. Be aware of computer "phishing" which is similar to phone phishing in which you are asked for personal information. The email may look official, but businesses don't ask for such information that way.

25. Be alert for "pharming." A virus is planted in your computer and when you type in the address of the legitimate site, you are routed to a fraudster's look-a-like account. Any information such as credit card numbers or passwords can then be stolen.

26. Report phishing to the company involved whether you are a victim or not. Consider a report to law enforcement and fraud.org.

27. Always pay with a credit card so you can dispute charges if you don't receive what you paid for.

28. Don't fall for the "technical support scam." Basically, someone claiming to be from a computer manufacturer or software company calls and offers free software to eliminate a virus that your computer supposedly has. Unless you initiated the call, hang up or the download will likely steal your passwords and anything else on your computer. If you do on line banking, they may drain your bank account.

29. If an email advises that your password has been reset and you need to open an attachment to find the new login, don't open it.

30. Be careful with webcams. Trend Micro advises that the camera be shut off and a lens cap placed on it when not in use. Keep it in an open area so kids don't use it inappropriately and away from viewing private information.

31. Be wary of love scams. One of the most important sources of scams is online dating. The old sayings like "Love is blind," "A fool and his money are soon parted," and "There is no fool like an old fool" really apply. The typical victim is an older woman who is plied with gifts and then asked to send money for airline tickets, divorce costs, travel visa fees, investments, etc.

32. Your computer could become part of a botnet, a large group of hijacked computers that sends out spam or commits other crimes. To reduce the odds of this happening, don't let kids download illegal games or music or visit porn sites. Be vigilant for strange programs, files, or unusual behavior from your computer (redtape.msnbc.com).

33. The internet ads haven't received as much government scrutiny as print ads so there is more outrageous claims there.

Improving the Safety of Children

You can subscribe to wireless services which allow you to track your children though they don't work as well in places where cell phone reception is bad and they don't offer pinpoint accuracy. You can also buy software or services which lets you view your children's text messages and intercept calls.

Taking Vacations and Protecting Your House

There are a number of things you can do to reduce your chances of being a victim. Many are implemented before you leave.

1. Tell few people that you are going. People like to gossip and the information can go far beyond your small group of friends. Do your fellow workers, hair stylist, bartender, your social club, and others really need to know? Tell them when you come home about your great trip. If you are tempted to say anything, considering telling them that you will have a live-in house sitter while gone or that you just installed a burglar alarm system.

2. Never enter information about your trip on a social networking site until you are home. Make sure your kids don't do it either and don't put language in like "We do this every year at Christmas or the 4ᵗʰ of July."

3. Place timer lights in 3-4 different places in the house. The best types are the ones that involve multiple settings. If you set two different on-off periods for each timer, the lights will go on or off 12-16 times. Though you don't want to close all of your blinds, you may want to close some where the lights are on so that a thief can't see in all of the windows. Using fluorescent bulbs saves a lot of energy.

4. Place a loud stereo on a timer. That is better than the power robbing

TVs. However, don't make it too loud that it bothers your pets or neighbors. Place it near the entry door or other places that seem likely to be breached so it is more easily heard.

5. Have a friend or neighbor pick up your mail or newspaper. This approach is better than stopping these services as there will be fewer people who know you are gone. You can stop your mail delivery by going on line to U.S. Postal Service at usps.com/receive mail & packages/ delivery services/hold mail service.

6. Don't let flyers accumulate on your porch or driveway. Your neighbor can take care of those too.

7. Have your lawn watered and mowed as usual.

8. For extra security, consider a house sitter. For longer periods, they can be quite cheap as the person may like a free place to stay.

9. Get an "in house" dog that likes to bark.

10. Put large water bowls in several locations near the house. Paint some ferocious sounding name like "Brutus" on them. Also put some supersized pieces of rawhide near them.

11. Hang "beware of dogs" signs in prominent locations. A sign that lists a known watchdog breed like a Rottweiler, Pit Bull, or a German Shepherd would be a very effective deterrent. You may only want to put up the signs when you leave if you are worried about scaring off friends or delivery persons.

12. Install a security system. If you live close to neighbors, you could install a loud alarm instead of paying monthly for a monitoring system. You only need a stream lined version that secures the doors and a few motion detectors. If you have animals and put in a motion detector, make sure you buy the special ones that pets don't set off. Alternatively, you could put the motion sensor in a room to which the animals have no access. Burglars are likely to enter every room of your house and set it off. You may wish to buy a cellular back-up which will send a distress signal even if your phone lines are cut.

To be safe from criminals at the alarm companies, only select a company that is a member of the National Burglar and Fire Alarm Association. I would also check the internet, and with my friends, neighbors, and the Better Business Bureau for complaints. Monitoring does cost money, but insurance companies may give a small discount for security monitoring. Check several security companies. Some may give good deals to get your monitoring business. You can buy security systems that also come with carbon monoxide and smoke detectors.

13. Get some stickers that mention a security firm and phone number on them and plaster them at every entrance. You could have some printed.

14. Install video cameras. If you can't afford that, buy some fake ones.

15. Alert trusted neighbors when you are gone to look out for suspicious activity. Give them the license number and description of any vehicle that you expect to come regularly. Tell them to call police immediately if they see anyone loading goods on to a truck parked in your driveway, or who appears to be "casing" your property. Ask them to record the license number of suspicious vehicles.

16. Buy a safe. The best approach is to anchor it to the floor (especially a concrete one) with bolts and the bigger the safe the better. Actually a water proof and fire proof container that is hidden in some obscure location (like under some attic insulation) or below ground may be as secure as a safe (which can be hauled off). Of course, you would need to let someone know the location in case something happened to you.

17. Rent a safe deposit box. Contents aren't insured by the bank though it likely would have some liability for loss unless the cause was something like a natural disaster or a war. However, your homeowner's policy likely would offer some protection. Typically, 10% of your building contents coverage is allowed for off site locations. In most cases, you won't reach that value unless you have precious metals, rare stamps or coins, and jewelry. For those, you need a special "rider" or "floater" anyway. Documentation in the form of appraisals and pictures is desirable.

Obviously, it is safer to store here than at home and a box inside a vault is better than those not located there. You need to make sure that the box's rent is paid or the state will eventually seize the property as unclaimed. If you are old or concerned about disability, you may wish to allow a trusted person, who doesn't use illegal drugs, access to the box.

Though fire and theft are occasional issues, the biggest problem is likely flooding which can occur from storms or fire sprinklers going off. Seal your perishables in water tight plastic bags.

18. Never keep your wallet in your back pocket except with a small amount of "decoy" cash. Leave your wallet in the hotel or cruise ship safe and put cash, credit cards, and ID in your front pockets. This is safer than the waist pouches whose straps can be cut unless they have metal embedded in the strap. You can also use those "under clothes" cloth containers and combined with decoy cash will be your safest option.

19. Avoid clothes and jewelry that say "rich foreign tourist, I am easy pickings."

20. Buy fake diamonds like zirconium and leave the good stuff at home. I was once on a cruise in which two guys wore what was reputed to be $10,000,000 worth of jewelry. They brought their own safe along. Their accessories certainly attracted a lot of attention which was their purpose.

21. Consider renting some space in your house to a trusted individual. When you are gone, that person can provide some security.

22. Install a panic button linked to an alarm system.

23. Build a safe room that can't easily be broken into. Have a cell phone in there with "911" being set on the "#1" speed dial. You may wish to buy a prepaid phone and leave it in the safe room. If you keep a gun in there, make sure that you know how to use it and have some practice at a gun range. The odds are high that if you can access your safe room in an emergency and call police immediately, you won't have to use the gun anyway.

24. Never carry your social security card anywhere. Memorize it. If you can't and you must have your number with you, encode it, but leave the card at home. Put the numbers in reverse order and leave off the last four digits which you would put somewhere else in your wallet. Alternatively, you could take the last four digits and put them in front and add a couple of fake letters.

25. Limit the number of cards you carry at any one time to two or three unless you know you are going to a particular store.

26. Use reinforced door jambs and strike plates installed with three inch screws. A secure door jamb may be enough to convince a thief to move on.

27. Buy Grade 1 ANSI-designation locks and deadbolts.

28. Most break-ins occur when you are not at home so put phones and answering machines on low volume.

29. Have someone put the garbage cans out and back as usual when you are on vacation.

30. Use call forwarding so some calls are answered. Thieves may call your house to see if you are home. A better alternative is to obtain an unlisted number.

31. Avoid leaving windows open when you are gone for the day.

32. Don't brag about your possessions. A comment like "I have a huge collection of expensive artwork, old coins or stamps, gold bullion, Chinese ceramics, etc." is sure to get the criminal element interested in your place. If you are so inclined to brag, make sure you have great insurance.

33. Think twice about putting your expensively furnished house on a tour of homes (even for a good cause).

34. Don't leave ladders around that could be used to enter an upper story unlocked or open window.

35. Don't plant bushes that obscure windows. This makes it too easy for a burglar to hide.

36. Avoid booking hotel rooms on the ground floor (burglars can gain easier access) and above the 7th floor (so fireman's ladders can reach you).

37. Hang a "do not disturb" sign on the motel door and leave the TV or radio on to discourage thieves.

Lost Purse or Wallet

To reduce your grief before you lose your belongings, go through your wallet and take out any cards and documents that are not regularly needed so you don't have to account for them. Make a photocopy of the remaining important documents, both front and back, such as medical cards, passport, military ID, etc. Place the photocopy in a secure locked place.

In case of a lost or stolen purse or wallet, do the following:

1. Contact your financial institutions, stores, and credit card companies immediately to stop the unauthorized use of your cards and issue new ones. If you are on vacation, you should have these photocopy records along with you in a separate location from the actual cards and documents. Reporting this loss as soon as you discover it will limit your loss to $50 per card and allow the credit card companies to issue new cards. In most cases, if reported promptly, even the $50 will be waived.

2. Report any theft to the police. Insurance companies won't reimburse for losses unless you report the theft. This act reduces the chances that the loss is not a scam, establishes your claim if anything of value is recovered, and helps protect you from the losses caused by identity thieves. One of your best defenses against fraudulent charges or accounts is the police report.

3. Get your free credit report by calling 1-877-322-8228 or going online to annualcreditreport.com. Under federal law, this is the only authorized source for your free annual credit report. You are entitled to have one from each credit bureau (Experian, Equifax, and TransUnion) each year. If you stagger the requests, you can get one every four months. Don't confuse the above site with freecreditreport.com or consumerinfo. com which are "for profit" sites which provide a free credit report if you sign up for their monthly credit monitoring service. You must cancel the service in 7-30 days to avoid the monthly charges of $11.95 to $14.95.

4. Place a fraud alert on your account with all three credit bureaus. See a later section on this.

5. Contact your motor vehicle agency to obtain new official ID that will be needed for airline travel, driving, and using credit, etc. Have them put a fraud alert on your license. You may need to take other forms of ID to prove who you are.

6. Contact others as needed such as employers, insurance companies, AAA, calling cards, medical plans, and Medicare/Medicaid. It is generally recommended that you request a new account or policy number so fraudulent repairs and medical claims aren't made.

7. If you lose your PDA or computer, then you will have additional security issues depending upon what was on the devices. Always have the information backed up and the devices password protected.

Other Actions to Prevent Scams

1. Buy a cross cut shredder. This device double cuts the paper making it extremely unlikely that your documents can be used. Cut up bank statements, convenience checks, stock brokerage or mutual fund statements, credit applications, and especially anything with your social security or driver's license numbers on them (as long as you don't need them for tax audits).

2. Opt out of receiving offers for credit or insurance. This right is provided by the Fair Credit Reporting Act. You can do this by going to OptOutPrescreen.com or call toll-free at 1-888-5OPTOUT (1-888-567-8688). This is the official site of the Consumer Credit Reporting Industry and is sponsored by the three major credit reporting companies. The opt-out can be done electronically for five years or permanently by mail.

3. If you use debit cards, guard your pin carefully as you will be stuck with any charges that are made or any money withdrawn using it.

4. Be wary of free trial offers. These often involve products or services like insurance, CDs, or magazine subscriptions. If you don't cancel in writing within 30-60 days, you are assumed to be committing to a monthly payment for some minimum period like one year. Sometimes this commitment is done without your knowledge.

If you find yourself a victim, threaten to contact your state's attorney general (go to your state's website or naag.org and click "the attorneys general"), the Better Business Bureau, and the FTC (ftc.gov or 1-877-382-4357). If the charges aren't immediately reversed, then do it and then write a review for the web.

5. Subscribe to a credit monitoring service. I use the lower priced Silver option of Equifax that costs about $50 a year but doesn't seem to be available to new customers. The advisories are less timely but are sufficient for my needs. My main concern is the opening of new accounts in my name. The credit monitoring helps to identify requests for address changes, increases in credit limits, new credit accounts, and negative information like past due bills.

Credit monitoring has serious limitations in its usefulness. The Consumer Federation of America says that many types of identity theft don't show up in credit files such as those involving employment, utility accounts, medical services, government benefits, and account takeovers.

6. Determine your risk of identity theft. There is a free service run by ID Analytics (idanalytics.com) of San Diego California which calculates a score that ranges between 1 and 999 and you don't need to provide your social security number. The process is easy. The higher your score, the more you are at risk of identity theft.

7. Ask employers, schools, and others such as medical providers not to use your social security number as the ID number on any cards or documents or to publicly display it. Most states have laws regarding use of the SSN and the mailing of notices with it. If providers use it, make a photocopy of your ID and cut off four of the numbers.

8. When filling out questionnaires or applications, ask if sensitive information is needed. Leave it blank if not required. Be wary if the questions seem out-of-line for the requester's needs. Unfortunately, your SSN is the standard method for assessing credit and collecting bad debts. Any business can ask for your SSN and some government agencies can require it including tax collectors, unemployment offices, welfare agencies, and the department of motor vehicles and licensing. I personally never rented to anyone who didn't provide his driver's license number (except non-drivers) and SSN (unless they didn't have one).

9. Open bank statements and credit card bills right away to check for fraudulent charges or withdrawals. Investigate and then report suspicious activity immediately. One frequent problem is that you don't recognize a charge because of an unfamiliar name on the statement. Businesses often have legal or corporate names that are different from trade names. There is often a number on the credit card statement to call to clear up the mystery. Another option is to keep all receipts chronologically for each credit card in a separate envelope. Then pull them out when needed. If a charge matches up by the date of the transaction and amount, then it is likely okay.

10. If your employer or any business tosses out old forms with sensitive information on them, ask them to stop and shred them. If you have a lot of material to shred, hire a professional. The cost is relatively low.

11. Reduce the volume of pre-approved credit card offers (that might be stolen) by calling 1-888-567-8688. This takes your name off of marketing lists. You will still be on old lists, including current credit card companies.

12. Buy a locking mailbox for receiving mail.

13. Deposit all outgoing mail at the post office or post office drop box. An easy scam is for a forger to steal your mail with an enclosed signed check, place cellophane tape over the front and back of your signature, and soak the check in acetone (*AARP*). Everything is lifted except the signature and the bank's printer's ink, leaving a signed blank check. The solutions are to pay on line, deposit all envelopes containing checks at the post office or drop box, or use a gel pen which can't be erased.

14. Opt out of allowing businesses to share your financial information.

15. If you are notified that security at one of your credit or debit card companies was breached, immediately begin to monitor your credit files.

16. Close any accounts not being used unless it would greatly impact your credit score, especially those with annual fees.

17. To prevent someone from claiming any sort of benefits, notify the Social Security Administration of a person's death. Call 1-800-772-1213 (TTY 1-800-325-0778) or visit the SSA online at ssa.gov for more information. Social security benefits must be returned for the month in which the person dies and later, but a small death benefit of $255 can be paid to a surviving spouse or eligible child.

If you suspect someone is using your SSN to work, check your Social Security Personal Earnings and Benefit Statement by calling the above number. If you think anyone is claiming benefits with your number, call the Social Security Administration Fraud Hotline at 1-800-269-0271.

18. A further prevention is to notify the three credit bureaus of the person's death. Mail your proof of executorship or marriage and a death certificate to:

TransUnion
1561 E. Orangethorpe Ave.
Fullerton, CA 92831

Equifax
P.O. Box 105518
Atlanta, Georgia 30348-5518

Experian National Consumer Assistance Center
P.O. Box 9701
Allen, Texas 75013

Scammers are known to draw benefits from the deceased. Also don't share a deceased person's social security number with anyone without a need to know it.

19. If you are aware of anyone illegally getting government benefits, call the authorities. You may be able to claim a reward and will keep everyone's taxes lower.

20. Don't change your social security number even if you are a victim of identity theft. The Social Security Administration is probably not going to allow it, and you risk losing too much of your credit and employment history, benefits, and the ability to get credit, open accounts, lease apartments, etc.

21. If your credit card statement is late, call your issuer and be vigilant for the next month. It could have been stolen or simply lost.

22. Check your accounts online regularly though that poses some small risks of its own.

23. Be cautious about buying services that supposedly protect your identity. In a 2009 study entitled "To Catch a Thief: Are Identity Theft Services Worth the Cost?," the CFA studied 16 such services which generally cost $120-180 per year and often found their information "confusing, unclear, and ambiguous…. filled with hyperbole, or missing." They were most impressed with ID Watchdog and ID Theft Alert though none of the companies meet their complete list of criteria.

24. The CFA considers identity theft insurance to be of little value.

25. The ITRC has a fact sheet (130A) on correcting misinformation and errors in medical records (including identity theft).

26. Do something that always reminds you to pick up your credit card. For example, I put my wallet on the counter or restaurant table and hold it with my left hand. When the card comes back, I never forget to retrieve it.

27. Be alert and aware of everyone who has access to your credit records. This potentially could be friends, relatives (especially those with a history of dishonesty), employees, and roommates.

28. Besides the Better Business Bureau, check business ratings for larger companies at Bizrate.com.

29. People can easily reproduce cards so don't let them lie around where others can see or take pictures of them.

30. Void all mistakes by tearing up the paperwork in small pieces. I was in Istanbul and was negotiating to buy a carpet and I thought the price was $800, but the clerk thought we had agreed on $8,000. I quickly grabbed the credit card paperwork and tore it into small pieces. Make sure you know the exchange rate.

31. Because of the growing threat of theft by strangers of children's social security numbers, parents should request a credit report for them once a year.

Necessary Actions if you are a Victim of Identity Theft and Other Information

1. Go to the non-profit Identity Theft Resource Center (ITRC) at idtheftcenter.org and find out what to do if your identity is stolen. They have a Fact Sheet 100 called "Financial Identity Theft- The Beginning Steps" and Fact Sheet 100A for more complex cases. In FS 100, the important steps are discussed including your rights under the law, organizing your case, finding the right people, important terms, assessing the damage, actions to take, collection agencies (see Fact Sheet 116 for more specific help), and additional resources.

2. Then go to a second website sponsored by the California Office of Information Security & Privacy Protection found at oispp. ca.gov/consumer privacy/identity theft. It has an "Identity Theft Victim Checklist." Among other things, they recommend filling out forms to request information on fraudulent charges or accounts and a fraud affidavit. The first form is available on their website (*Consumer Information Sheet 3A: Requesting Information on Fraudulent Accounts*) and the latter at the Federal Trade Commission web site at ftc.gov/bcp/edu/ resources/forms/affidavit.pdf.

While this site has some specifics for residents of California, it also has information applicable to all states. It includes sample letters a person can send to the credit bureaus and creditors of new and existing accounts as well as a summary of the Federal Fair Credit Reporting Act.

3. The FTC (ftc.gov/idtheft or 1-877-ID-Theft (1-877-438-4338)) gives advice for victims including forms to fill out.

4. Trained volunteers at Call For Action will assist victims to resolve problems (callforaction.org or 1-866-ID-Hotline (1-866-434-6854)). You can also find help at the Theft Assistance Center (identitytheftassistance.org).

5. If you suspect your minor child of being an identity theft victim, the California site is a good one to check. In addition, the ITRC has an information sheet entitled "Fact Sheet 120: Identity Theft and Children."

Unfortunately, parents are often the perpetrators by falsely taking out credit in their children's names. In many cases, they are creating large liabilities that take years to cure, can result in a low credit rating, and cause the child to later pay higher than normal interest rates. Such actions cause great stress and ruin family relationships, and the pain is felt by spouses and even the grandchildren.

According to the FTC, relatives including parents are responsible for 6% of the child victims. This crime was almost unheard of a decade ago, and it may go undetected because the parents intercept the mail. Furthermore, a grown child may not report it to avoid a parental criminal record and jail time. Obviously, this decision is a very personal one with great consequences for the family.

Another option for the child includes filing for bankruptcy which clears the obligations but will substantially drop his credit score and will be on the record for 10 years. A second option is to ignore the bills since it will be hard to collect from a minor. This path may be favored for someone who is pre-teen since the record would clear in seven years before he sought long term employment. If the child went to college and graduated at 22, he might have a clear record if the identity theft stopped at 14 (allows for one year to clear).

Another and sometimes better option for a young person with no substantial work history and reluctance to have the perpetrator charged is to file for a new social security number. You can't receive a new number to escape the consequences of bankruptcy, to avoid the law or your legal responsibility (shouldn't apply here), or if there is no evidence that someone is using your number (see *socialsecurity.gov*).

If the person still has the same exact name and address, a new number may be of limited help and the IRS, some state agencies, and private businesses will have some records under the old number. However, once a person moves and applies for a different middle name, it likely will improve the old identity problem. If a person decides to apply for a new number, he will need to prove U.S. citizenship or lawful immigration status, identity, age, and that he is still being hurt by the identity theft. Once the new number is received, the old number can never be used again.

A final option is some arbitration between the family perpetrators and the creditors, usually with a third party attorney who acts as a mediator. The county court clerk or the local bar association can provide names. This process is not cheap. Attorneys will charge $200 an hour and up. This is likely to cost a minimum of $3,000 and could easily reach $10,000 depending upon attorney rates and the number of creditors and their attitudes.

Parents should not ignore a child's pre-approved credit card offers (despite the current law barring it without a co-signer) or the receipt of credit cards, bills, tax notices, or calls from a creditor or collection agency. In such cases, get on the phone and find out what has happened.

6. Find out about your state's laws by going on line and typing "identity theft, ____(your state)." You likely will find some useful information about your protections and requirements for businesses.

7. If you think your mail has been stolen or someone has filled out a change of address for you, notify the United States Postal Service (USPS) immediately. The USPS is listed in the phone directory under the United States Government or online at usps.gov.

8. You can place a free fraud alert in your credit file which can be of three types. An "initial alert" is often used in a data breach situation, but the victim is unsure whether he will be affected. It alerts creditors to use "reasonable policies and procedures." The next is an "extended alert" which requires an official identity theft report and lasts for seven years unless removed by the victim. In the latter case, creditors must contact you by phone or other specified means prior to opening new accounts or increasing limits on existing accounts. The last case is "active duty alert" for military personnel who are stationed away from their normal duty locations. This alert is treated like the initial alert.

You can place a fraud alert by calling Equifax at 1-800-525-6285, Experian at 1-888-397-3742, and TransUnion at 1-800-680-7289. Fraud alerts are supposed to be passed on by each credit bureau to the others, but that doesn't always happen so you should contact all three. The alerts can easily be done by phone. Parents of minor children and personal representatives of others can also place alerts. In some cases, instructions are given at these numbers for doing it on line.

9. You may wish to place a security freeze at the three credit bureaus. This usually stops anyone from opening accounts under your name. If someone merely made a false charge to your credit card, then don't freeze your file. On the other hand, if your social security number, address, and date of birth are in the hands of a criminal, then freeze it. You should assume the worst if someone is opening new accounts in your name.

You can freeze it by mail with a certified letter and certain pieces of information. Go to the websites of the three credit bureaus for more information. If you are a victim of identity fraud and provide the police report, the charges to freeze and unfreeze an account are usually waived. In other cases, the costs vary by state and range from $0-20 each time you want to freeze or unfreeze your account. Credit bureaus make their money from selling monitoring services and credit files so they would rather not freeze accounts.

Each credit bureau will provide a Personal Identification Number (PIN) to unfreeze your account and instructions on how to do it. To open new accounts, you will need to unfreeze your file which can be done for a specific creditor or for a specified period. This freezing and unfreezing should be completed in three business days so you need to plan ahead if applying for credit.

For more information on the process, go to oispp.ca.gov and see "CIS 10: How to Freeze Your Credit Files." Even with a freeze, existing creditors, collection agencies, and some government agencies will still have access to your files. You are still entitled to your free credit report if your file is frozen. Fraud alerts are often ignored by lenders so if you are concerned about continuing ID theft, then a freeze, which can't be ignored, is better.

10. Don't throw away collection letters or statements that you think are not yours. It could be your first warning of identity theft. Call the sender immediately.

11. If someone fraudulently charges something or incurs utilities under your name, you aren't responsible. Sometimes collection agencies ignore the facts. Threaten to contact the Better Business Bureau and your state's attorney general if you are being pressured to pay a fraudulent bill. Then, get a letter from the collection agency which states that you don't owe it and keep that letter forever.

12. If someone steals your checks or forges your information to make a withdrawal from a financial institution, you aren't responsible. You may be asked to provide some documentation, but financial institutions are generally easy with which to work.

13. When someone has used your identity in criminal or civil court cases, the Consumer Federation of America (CFA) advises that you should consider hiring an attorney. Some states like California have an identity theft registry for police to check. Others have an "identity theft passport" program that allows people to carry a card showing that their ID theft has been documented.

14. If you are a victim of cyber crime, file an online complaint with the Internet Crime Complaint Center (CCC) at *ic3.gov*. The CCC sends every complaint to one or more law enforcement or regulatory agencies with jurisdiction over the problem.

15. Other resources for help include: stock broker problems (Financial Industry Regulatory Authority at finra.org/investors); mortgage scams, predatory lending and phony foreclosure rescue scams (freddiemac.com/avoidfraud and NeighborWorks America at nw.org), and identity theft (Consumers Union at financialprivacynow.org).

Results of the ITRC Identity Theft Study and the FTC Report

The following results of a 2008 ITRC study of victims clearly indicate the costs of identity theft.

- Only 34% discovered the identity theft due to an adverse situation. Proactive measures like credit monitoring reduced this problem.

- Other significant types of theft included charges on stolen credit and debit cards without a PIN, check fraud, all types of loans taken out in the victim's name, and fraudulent medical charges.

- Regarding medical theft, many victims reported that someone else's medical information was in their files, and some victims were denied health and life insurance due to unexplained reasons.

- The average out-of-pocket cost to individuals was $739 for an existing account and $951 for a new account.

- Victims reported spending an average of 58 hours to repair the damage to one of their existing accounts and 165 hours for a new one created in the fraud.

- Those businesses reporting losses to the ITRC reported their average loss to be $90,107.

- Many victims reported difficulty in clearing their names caused by an inability to get a police report, bad accounts being reposted on credit reports, fraud alerts being ignored, the inability to prove innocence even with a police report, or simply giving up because of time or family related issues.

- There was considerable negative emotional impact to the victims caused by the identity theft.

According to a 2007 FTC identity theft report, 59% of the crimes involved existing credit cards, 19% were for accounts such as bank accounts and utilities, and 22% involved new accounts and other crimes (such as giving the victim's name to the police when arrested). The latter are the most difficult to resolve because the theft may go on for some time before the victim finds out.

The conclusions that one would draw from the aforementioned are that identity theft is a constant threat to almost everyone; you need to always be on guard; prevention is the best approach; and you need to take quick decisive action when it strikes. However, most people can and do survive identity theft.

My Personal Experience

My family has been the victim on three occasions; once involving a single small overseas charge that appeared to be a test of whether we were watching the account. Another seemed to be an inside job after a telephone sale through a catalog. The third involved stolen and reduplicated checks. In all three cases, we closed the accounts.

Requests for Multiple Credit Reports

In some states such as California, the law allows identity theft victims with a police report to request free copies of their credit report from each credit bureau as often as once a month. Each of the three credit bureaus has different procedures and addresses for requesting your extra reports so go to oispp.ca.gov to find the information.

Business Fraud

A survey (*BusinessWeek*) found that 59% of laid off workers took something of value when they left. Thus, you might want to inventory a person's office before he leaves and limit their access to important information or valuable inventory. This theft issue might even be discussed with the employee who is given a lay-off announcement. Though it is a touchy subject given the circumstances, employees who know that they are being watched are less likely to steal. Among those still employed, the loss is estimated at an average of seven percent of revenues (which seems high).

Digital Abuse and Cyber Bullying

It is dangerous because of the ease of it, the vast number of people who can be involved, and the relative anonymity. It can range from harassing emails to cell phone text messages to more serious stuff posted at online bulletin boards or social network sites. According to the Pew Internet & American Life Project, American high school girls typically send and receive 3,000 text messages per month and often leave their phones on while they sleep. Suggestions for parents to talk with their kids about and to do include:

- Kids shouldn't forward damaging and hurtful comments.
- Kids shouldn't assume that the target will think a comment is funny.
- Kids shouldn't establish a false profile of themselves.
- Kids shouldn't leave their cell phones on while sleeping. Uninterrupted sleep is more important to their health than learning about the latest gossip.
- Parents should be extremely diligent at understanding their problems, become very involved in their child's life, and look for signs of trouble. The child may be reluctant to discuss the harassment for fear that you will make it worse so you need to be persistent.
- Parents should pay the child's cell phone bill. Only 3% of the teens who paid none or a fraction of their bill engaged in sending nude or nearly nude photos (sexting) compared to 17% of those paying their own.
- Parents should set a limit on the number of text messages sent. Kids with no limits were 3 ½ times more likely to do "sexting."
- Parents should develop a cell phone and computer contract with their child. One is available at cyberbullying.us. The provisions might include not visiting inappropriate websites, not downloading or installing any programs without the parent's knowledge, not communicating with people unknown in the real world, not sending explicit sexual information or pictures, and allowing the parent to access the child's files at any time.
- Parents should save the evidence of anything that looks suspicious.
- Parents should encourage kids to support their bullied friends and to report it to the parents, school counselors, and possibly internet providers or law enforcement.

CHAPTER 6

How to Select Credit Cards and Understand and Improve Credit Scores

Selection of Credit Cards

When deciding on which credit cards to have, the most important criteria should be how and why you use it, whether you pay off it in full each month, and how much you spend. Here are some common reasons why people obtain credit cards:

1. As a source of semi permanent credit. In this case, the balance is rarely paid off in full. This is probably the worst reason for using credit cards, especially if they are personal ones which don't allow the deduction of interest. You will want the lowest possible interest rate, probably combined with no annual fee or rewards.

2. Principally for convenience and to get the reward points and you pay in full every month. Then you want those cards that pay the most rewards per $1 in purchases, regardless of the interest rate. However, if you don't spend more than $800-$1,000 per month, then it may not make sense to get one with an annual fee. Many cards pay a flat one point per dollar in purchases while others pay extra points, especially for certain purchases such as those at grocery stores, travel, or those with good credit. Some such as the Capital One No Hassle Miles Ultra card pays two miles per dollar spent (at least when this was written). Be aware that generous card benefits may only be temporary advertising gimmicks.

3. Same as #2 but you carry a balance. If you carry almost any balance, then you should forget the reward points and use the same card as #1.

4. Same as #2 but you hate to redeem points. Then you may wish to carry a "cash rebate" card. These cards vary considerably in their rebates. Some are a flat 1% (one point per $1) or more while others start at less than 1% but pay higher percentages as you spend more. If your spending is limited or you have many cards, then you probably should use the flat percentage cards. If you spend a lot, you may want to concentrate your spending on that one card with progressive cash back rates. Please note that some reward cards accruing points will pay cash, if requested, usually at about 1%.

5. To establish credit. This is one of the best reasons to have a credit card, but you still want to use the one that most meets your needs. Some people may need to begin with a pre-paid card if they have poor or no history of credit.

6. To get elite status so you qualify for bonus rewards or business class lounge use. In this instance, it makes the most sense to focus on the card as the Mamas and Papas say, "Gets you where you want to be."

7. To get the best foreign exchange rate. If you do a lot of foreign travel, this may appeal to you. In that case, you want the one that gives the best combined exchange rate and transaction fee. Some cards have recently increased their fees.

Features of the Credit Cards

The best way to compare credit cards is to line up their disclosure statements next to each other. You should look at the following variables and decide which are most important to you (mostly the interest rates, cash advance transaction fees, rewards, and the annual fee):

- Annual Percentage Rate for Purchases (APR)

- APR for cash advances

- APR for convenience checks

- APR for balance transfers

- Penalty rate (for skipped or late payment)

- Variable rate information- How rates are calculated

- Grace period- time between the statement date and the last day to pay before late fees and penalties are applied- usually 21-25 days

- Method of computing the balance. Usually the average on each day

- Annual membership fee- zero and up

- Minimum finance charge- usually 50 cents or so

- Transaction fee for purchases- usually zero as the merchant pays it

- Transaction fee for cash advances- often 3-5% with a minimum and possibly a maximum

- Transaction fee for convenience checks- often the same as cash advances

- Transaction fee for balance transfers

- Late payment fee- usually varies between $19-39

- Over-the-credit limit fee- usually varies between $19-39. Some have no fee. Mostly higher when over $250

- Universal default- allows issuer to raise your rate for late payments or certain other adverse events

The rewards have been getting less generous and harder to use while the fees and interest rates have risen. Furthermore, the old saying, "There is no such thing as a free lunch" applies here. If you want rewards or no annual fee, the interest rates will generally be higher and/or the rewards lower. IndexCreditCards.com showed the following rate comparisons on May 15th, 2010.

Average consumer credit card rate, overall market	16.74%
Average, non-reward consumer card rate	15.36%
Average consumer reward card rate	17.33%
Average student card rate	16.27%
Average business non-reward card rate	13.75%
Average business reward card rate	15.74%

The average rate has risen dramatically from about 13.75% in March 2009 to 16.74% in May 2010 or nearly three percentage points. The rate increases were due to the anticipated new federal rules. Reward cards charge about two percentage points more than non-reward cards. If you want to check current card rates, go to the above site and click "more on credit card interest rates." It also has a calculator to determine the number of months required to pay off a credit card with different payment amounts and another shows the savings from shifting a balance to a lower interest rate.

You will find a good selection of cards in 7-12 different categories at

CardRatings.com, CreditCards.com, and IndexCreditCards.com. The sites give their top picks from groups in which the cards are separated by high rewards, low interest rates, airline, student, business, issuer, credit quality, and others. The most important consideration is to compare the features that most affect you among your new and current cards.

Credit Card Company Ratings

In 2009, J. D. Power conducted a consumer satisfaction survey of 9,000 credit card users based upon a 1,000 point scale. The results (high is better) are as follows:

American Express	762	Bank of America	687
Discover Card	751	Fifth Third Bank	685
National City	740	HSBC	682
Wells Fargo	724	Capital One	671
Barclay Card	717	Target Visa	665
U. S. Bank	715	WaMu	663
Chase	708	GE Money	661
Industry average	703	Credit One Bank	618
Citi Card	699	First Premier Bank	616
First National Bank of Omaha	689		

The credit card industry has the lowest average rating among the four financial sectors which J. D. Power researches. The others are insurance, banking, and investment services. The credit card industry average rating dropped from 724 in 2008 to 703 in 2009. The three highest ranked firms were identical in both years and a few banks like National City, HSBC, and Wells Fargo actually increased their ratings.

From my personal experience with HSBC, I can understand its below average rating. Despite my very high FICO and a long history with two predecessor credit card companies from which they acquired my account, it cancelled my account and more than 90,000 reward points without warning in 2008 due to inactivity. After reading the fine print, I concluded that it was legal, but in my opinion, unethical. They refused to reinstate my points until I wrote a series of complaints to all my members of Congress, my state's attorney general, *Money Magazine*, AAA, AARP, and the Comptroller of the Currency. When I called to redeem my points, HSBC had established a redeemable limit amount of 20,000 points for an airline ticket which by now required five tickets to use all of my points.

For many months after reinstatement, my credit card statements showed no expiration on the remaining points. Then despite many new charges and using 80,000 points, an expiration of 12/31/2009 showed up for most of the remaining points in August 2009. Their March 2010 policy was to cancel a credit card if not used for four months. I finally decided HSBC really didn't want my business, used the remaining points, and let it lapse.

Your Credit Report and FICO Score

Your credit report (Equifax.com) includes personal information such as your name, Social Security number, current and recent addresses and employers, and date of birth. It also includes details of credit accounts in your name or those on which you are an authorized user and account details like credit limits, payment terms, balances, and payment history. Closed or inactive accounts stay on your file for 7-11 years depending upon the date of their last activity.

It also shows inquiries made by lenders, service providers, insurance companies, and landlords for up to two years. Other items such as bankruptcies, overdue child support, and liens may appear on your record.

There are many items not included such as your medical history, bankruptcies more than 10 years old, gender, ethnicity, religion, your checking or savings accounts, charged-off or debts placed for collection more than seven years old, and criminal records.

The FICO score as developed by the Fair Isaac Corporation basically indicates the risk of default by a borrower on a loan. It is the most important piece of information used to determine your interest rate, credit card features, fees, waiving of fees, credit limits, reward points, and whether you even get a loan. However, lenders use other factors in evaluating you such as income, home ownership, employment history, and time at your current address. They also may use a bankruptcy score such as Equifax's Bankruptcy Navigator Index which ranges from one to 300, with high scores meaning less bankruptcy risk. Banks also have their own internal formulas to gauge your riskiness and how much revenue your business will generate. The only score which you have a federal right to see is your FICO score.

You should find out your FICO credit score by asking lenders who pull your credit file for it or paying one of the credit bureaus. You can also estimate a range by going to **creditcards.com** and running their "Credit Card Calculator." I have an "excellent" rating with a 20+ years of credit history so I ran its "Credit Card Calculator" to determine how various actions would affect my credit score. I found the following:

- Missing one loan or credit card payment (time didn't matter) -65 points
- Raising my ave. card balance from 10-19% to 90-99% of limit -55 points
- Raising my ave. card balance from 10-19% to 70-89% -50 points
- Raising my ave. card balance from 10-19% to 40-49% -25 points
- Applying for 3-5 cards or loans in the past 12 months -15 points
- Applying for 2 loans or credit cards in the past 12 months no change
- Reducing # of loans/cards with a balance from 5-6 to 0-4 no change
- Raising total non-mortgage balances from 10K to 50K   no change
- Raising # of credit cards from 2-4 to 5-8 no change

It is obvious that my two biggest "no-no's" are paying late and "maxing" out my credit cards. Of course, really adverse events like bankruptcy or property foreclosures are even worse. Bankruptcy is worse than foreclosure because it affects most of your assets while the other only affects one. Most of the other factors had no or minor effects. I simulated a person with similar answers to me but with only a 3-5 year credit history. The rating range was about 65 points lower with similar drops for adverse events.

I also checked my estimated credit score at moneycentral.msn.com and got almost the same range. On its home page, click "credit reports" and take the "What's Your Credit Score Range?" test. According to FICO, the following factors affect your credit score:

Payment history	35% (paying on time is good)
Amounts owed	30% (as a % of your credit limit, low is better)
Length of credit history	15% (long is better)
New credit	10% (lots is bad)
Types of credit used	10%
Total	100%

Having many credit sources is fine, just don't carry a high percentage of total debt.

Fair Isaac introduced the FICO Expansion for the 50 million American adults with little or no credit history. The scores are based upon alternative criteria like bounced checks, payday lenders, and rent-to-own. Some financial institutions allow alternative criteria like rent and utility payments in order to qualify for loans. The alternatives are clearly not as attractive as the regular FICO score and might be used to deny you credit.

Strategies for Raising or Maintaining Your FICO Credit Score

1. One strategy that this information suggests is to have a few high credit limit, no annual fee cards that you use only every four months or so and pay in full. This keeps the card from being terminated for lack of use. Cards typically must be used every 4-12 months to avoid this problem. Then concentrate your spending on one or two other cards that are most useful to you. This approach does two things. First, you are less likely to miss a payment with fewer regularly used cards. Secondly, having extra high limit cards reduces your average balance on all cards. In the short run, the net effect of new cards might be small since you will be penalized for both shortening your credit history and possibly getting the new credit cards (depends upon a number of factors). However, lowering your percentage of debt raises your FICO score than the other factors subtract and after 12-18 months, the new cards will help greatly.

2. Another and better strategy is to persuade your existing credit card companies to raise your limit so your length of credit history stays the same.

3. To avoid late or lost payments, consider direct payments. These include automatic deductions from your checking account, on line debits, or direct payment at the actual financial institution. If you are travelling when the card is due, pay in advance unless you have an automatic deduction from your checking account.

4. Space out your new loan or credit card requests.

5. Really manage your credit 12 months before you apply for a mortgage.

6. Borrow from sources not shown on credit reports like relatives, commercial loans, or unsecured lines of credit. Then use the funds to pay down credit that shows up on your credit report.

7. Avoid late payments or disputes on utility, doctor bills, merchant bills, library fines, parking tickets, etc. that are likely to be sent to collection.

8. Get a credit report from <u>each</u> of the three credit bureaus so that you can correct any mistakes that lower your score. If you are thinking about a mortgage, get your free report from one and then pay for the other two. You want to correct any mistakes quickly and long before you apply for a mortgage, if possible. If you find mistakes, ask the credit bureau in writing to fix them and re-evaluate your score. According to the Public Interest Research Group, more than ¾ of credit reports have errors and 29% are serious enough to result in credit denial. Always send copies of documents to verify your claim such as divorce papers which prove you are not liable for someone else's debts.

There is no cost for disputing errors, and the credit bureau is required to respond within 30 days unless it considers the request to be frivolous. It must give you the results in writing and a free copy of your credit report if a change results. If requested, the corrected report must be sent to anyone getting your report in the past six months. If not corrected, you may still place a comment in your file.

Negative information can be reported for seven years and bankruptcies for 10 years, but there is no time limit on information about criminal convictions or that reported for applications for jobs that pay more than $75,000 or credit or life insurance for more than $150,000. If the criminal activity is minor, ask the courts to expunge the records. Many people are doing just that.

9. Canceling credit cards may lower your score. If you are carrying balances, your percentage of total card balance to your total limit on all cards will rise and it also may reduce your credit history life. Your credit life is based upon the age of your oldest account and the average age of your accounts. If you do cancel, hopefully the dropped one has the highest interest rates and the shortest ownership time.

10. Talk with your lender about an unfavorable item. Usually, bad items stay there, but it is worth the effort to try to have a lender remove it if you have just one, especially if your record is clean and fairly long.

Another point worth mentioning is that financial institutions, insurance companies, and employers use more than FICO scores. They will look at total debt, income, and percentage of income used to pay debt and they likely have their own internal formulas. Insurance companies will have insurance scores which include FICO scores but other things like your accident record, zip code, traffic tickets, etc.

11. Avoid hiring a "credit repair" company. Everything you need is right here in this book. Some of these companies are scams charging up front fees of $1,500 or more. Some may advise you to commit fraud or apply for a new identity using a business Employer identification Number (EIN) in place of your social security number. You can be charged with a crime for providing untrue information or obtaining an EIN under false pretenses. These companies often claim inside connections and knowledge of legal loopholes. They can have some charges put into a "pending" mode, but they simply reappear later. For more information, see "FTC- Credit Repair: Self Help May Be Best" by going to bbb.org and type "article 4697" in the search box in the top right corner.

12. Consider contacting a credit counseling organization. Many are non-profit, but still may charge a fee. There are scammers in this field so check them out carefully. Non profit programs are offered by a variety of organizations including many community colleges, housing authorities, military bases, and the U.S. Cooperative Extension Service (look under the U.S. Government in the blue pages of your phone book or online at csrees.usda.gov.). Check them out at bbb.org. Except for government agencies and colleges, I wouldn't use a service that was not accredited by the National Foundation for Credit Counseling (NFCC). To find NFCC members, go to nfcc.org or call 800-388-2227.

The Consumer Federation of America advises against using any counselors that work on commission, charge more than a $50 set-up fee, and more than $25 per month. The American Association of Retired Persons (AARP) advises that any agency that takes less than 30 minutes to review your case or has a one-size-fits-all plan should not be used.

13. Pay down your balances. As credit card companies cancel credit cards or lower limits (both of which lower your FICO score), this approach becomes especially important.

14. Avoid credit cards which don't set a credit limit or don't report your limit to the credit bureaus. This is important for raising your credit score.

15. If you have no credit history, start one now. Obtain a secured credit card by depositing funds in a bank. Don't obtain one unless the lender is willing to give you an unsecured credit card within 1-2 years if you pay on time. Apply for a couple of gas and/or store cards, but only if you can use them responsibly. At this stage, you are likely to find install-ment loans with only high interest rates or with overpriced merchandise. However, if you make a substantial down payment, you may be able to receive a decent interest rate. Eventually, following the advice in this section, you will obtain a good rating.

16. Resist any lowering of your credit limit since it will lower your credit score.

17. Move credit card balances to a home equity loan. This makes sense because the interest then becomes tax deductible (though subject to the AMT discussed later), the rate is usually lower, and it likely will improve your credit score. The downsides are that you may simply borrow more on your credit cards, you may lose your house if you fall behind, and in bankruptcy, the debt is now secured and may not be wiped out.

18. The following will not affect your credit score: requesting your own credit report, employer requests, inquiries from companies offering pre-approved cards, and consulting a credit counseling service.

Quality Ratings and Credit Scores

CreditCards.com has included the range of credit scores for various quality ratings as shown below:

Score Rating	Score Range
Excellent	750-850
Good	660-749
Fair	620-659
Poor	350-619

Fair Isaac lists the following distribution of scores:

Range	% of all scored persons
800 or more	13
750-799	27
700-749	18
650-699	15
600-649	12
550-599	8
Less than 550	7

You will find that those cards with the highest rewards and lowest interest rates and fees are generally reserved for those with high FICO credit scores. For example, an excellent score might qualify you for 1.5-2 reward points per dollar spent while a fair score might only be worth only one point per dollar. Some cards for low rated individuals have four separate fees for set-up, program (similar to the set-up), annual, and monthly. Avoid these cards.

High Cost of Low FICO Scores

Low FICO scores will raise the rate charged for most interest bearing products and many insurance policies. For example, when interest rates on 30 year mortgages were about 4.638% in December, 2009 for those with excellent credit, Myfico.com showed the average interest rates by credit score for a $300,000 mortgage. I have remade the information to show the additional interest rate and the extra interest for the life of the loan.

FICO score	Added interest rate for lower FICO scores	Added interest-life of the loan
760-850	0	0
700-759	.222%	$14,400
680-699	.399%	$25,920
660-679	.613%	$40,320
640-650	1.043%	$69,480
620-639	1.589%	$107,280

Since most people don't hold their mortgage for the life of the loan, the extra annual interest is highest in the early years of a loan. As you can see, the people who are the most financially challenged (low scores) pay appreciably more for their loans than good credit risks. The median score (half above and half below), according to FICO, is 725.

The Credit Card Act of 2009

Most of the provisions of this bill went into effect on Feb. 22, 2010. The bill is fairer to consumers regarding certain card abuses, but the credit card companies responded by changing terms, adding annual or inactivity fees, and raising rates. The important provisions include (*credit-cards.com*):

- Limits universal default. This provision allowed interest rate increases on existing balances if a customer was late on payments to other creditors. This is not allowed on current balances, but is on future ones.

- Limits credit to young adults under 21. Unless a young person has an adult co-signer or demonstrated income, they can't receive a credit card. Be cautious here so an irresponsible teen doesn't ruin your credit. You may want to start with a debit card.

- Establishes fairer due dates and times. Issuers can't have deadlines prior to 5 pm and on week-ends.

- Must apply payments above the minimum to the highest interest rate debt.

- Limits interest rate hikes on existing balances. It would be allowed only in such cases as when a cardholder misses a payment, the index changes for a variable rate, or a promotional rate ends. A 45 day notice is required for any changes and interest rate increases on new transactions can only occur after the first year.

- Gives the right to opt out. Consumers can reject certain significant changes, close the account, and pay it off in five years under the old terms.

- Must allow at least 21 days for payment from when the statement is mailed or delivered.

- Limits over-limit fees. Card holders can opt-out so that a transaction is rejected and an "over limit" fee is avoided.

- Cards must disclose how long it takes to pay off balances if minimum payments made.

- No more double cycle billing. Had allowed issuers to charge interest for a previous month in any month when the card was not paid in full even though the previous month had been paid in full.

- Account opening fees for people with bad credit would be limited to 25% of the credit limit in the first year.

Not everything is covered by the law including business accounts, and credit card companies can still close accounts and lower limits. It also doesn't prohibit new fees like inactivity or annual charges.

Payment Protection Plan

Some banks offer credit card payment protection for up to two years if you are disabled, hospitalized, called to military service, or laid off. Basically, all interest charges, payments, and fees are suspended. One expensive plan is 89 cents per $100 each month which equates to a rate of about 10.68% per year, an extremely high rate to pay for insurance. If your chances of qualifying are 5% in any given year, then that 10.68% is more like an annual rate of 200%.

The Advantages of Credit Cards

1. Using them and paying your bills on time raises your credit score. This is true only if you don't use a high percentage of your credit cards' limits.

2. If you pay in full each month, you receive an interest free loan.

3. You get rewards for a variety of things. Select cards (Schwab, Fidelity, and American Express) allow you to put reward money (2%) into an investment plan while others pay down your mortgage balance. Don't forget to use the points before they expire and they aren't taxable.

4. You can dispute a charge if the product or service is defective or not as advertised. The credit card companies will investigate and try to help settle the dispute. I have won every wrongful charge claimed.

5. Some cards provide extra insurance on auto rentals for "Loss of use." Loss of use is the charge levied by the rental company for the time that a car is being repaired due to some problem you caused.

6. Cards may provide life insurance for travel tickets purchased on the card.

7. Extra warranty protection is sometimes a feature. It may double the warranty up to a year. Check your card's features. You may want to favor a certain card that offers it.

8. Theft and damage protection to replace or repair an item may be offered for up to 90 days of purchase.

9. Credit cards offer easier recovery in the case of theft than debit accounts or checking accounts.

10. Many bills can be paid automatically to avoid missing deadlines including your credit card. However, that automatic payment can be a hassle if you are forced to close the account, and you may need to up-date the expiration date. For payments like mortgages that don't allow this service for credit cards, you can automatically deduct them from your checking account.

11. A high limit card may allow you to consolidate bills.

12. Credit cards give you better exchange rates than buying and us-ing foreign currency. In addition, you are spared the hassle and cost of converting unused currency back to dollars again.

13. I carry 2-3 credit cards in case I have a problem with one. Once a charge was refused because the credit card company had placed a 14 day hold on my payment check. In another case, I was in Chile and hadn't notified an issuer of my foreign travel and the same thing happened.

14. Credit cards offer easier book-keeping, especially if you have one that sends an annual itemization of charges.

15. With multiple cards, there is a benefit from being able to stagger monthly due dates. In my case, I like having them all due at the end of the month. However, if you are paid twice a month, different cycles may be preferable. Many cards allow you to change due dates.

16. By having multiple cards, you can designate one for all business expenses.

17. Multiple cards allow you to negotiate or show favoritism. You might call your card company and tell them that you have a better rate on XYZ bank card. Can they match it or beat it? Or what deal can you give me on a balance transfer? Alternatively, you could favor the card that provides the most benefits or lowest interest rate.

18. Multiple cards give you a back-up if you are the victim of identity theft and you need to close the account.

19. Hotel cards generally have the best rewards (up to 9%) and except for 1% reward cards, are the easiest to redeem.

The Problems and Disadvantages of Credit Cards

1. One big problem is that many people spend more than normal compared to spending only cash. Those less "flush" folks who charge and can't regularly pay their monthly bills in full should stop using their credit cards. I don't advocate cutting them up as it will lower your credit score.

2. Another important difficulty is that the interest rates are often much higher than most other sources of credit and the interest is not tax deductible except on business cards. Only about 40% of cardholders pay in full each month.

3. Credit cards can be cancelled without prior notification for non-use, late payments, and some action that causes you to appear more risky like a drop in your credit score. Your cancelled credit card then lowers your FICO score even more.

4. Fees are too high. Cards frequently have over limit and late payment fees of $39. Suppose you are $200 over your limit, are charged $39, and pay it 20 days after you go over the limit. If one views the $200 as a short term loan from the bank, that $39 fee is an annual interest rate of 351%.

5. Universal default creates a "double whammy." This feature is common, but try to avoid cards with it.

6. You may lose your rewards for any month you pay late.

7. Many cards have expiration dates on rewards.

8. Grace periods may disappear if you are delinquent.

9. If you don't pay in full each month, then you really don't have an interest free grace period. You are charged interest on your average daily balance.

10. The lowest rates quoted on a disclosure schedule are for the best customers and your rate may be higher.

11. Rates may change with overall interest rates or other factors.

12. If you are over your credit card limit and you don't realize it until your statement comes, you will likely be charged for two months of over limit fees.

13. Many people (about 40%) fail to use their reward points and are clueless about what rewards are offered.

14. The deals change constantly. The best rewards may only be teasers that last for a year or two. Then if you cancel and open a new account, it hurts your FICO score.

15. Avoid using convenience checks as they simply encourage you to spend money and incur more high interest debt.

16. Avoid credit card protection insurance as it offers little value.

Other Things to Consider

1. You should add the annual fee on to your interest rate. For example, if your annual charges are $7500, and your annual fee is $75, then you should add $75/7500 (X100%) or 1% to your annual interest rate. This gives you the most complete analysis of what you are paying if you carry a balance when comparing it to a card with no fee.

2. If your credit card company offers a 6 month interest free loan or a balance transfer and they charge you 4%, then the annualized rate of that loan is (12 months/6 months) X 4%= 8%. What the company is hoping is that you will borrow more than you should and won't pay it off in six months.

3. Some credit cards such as American Express allow you to request advance reward points in order to reach the number needed for an award. However, the number allowed is limited and you must charge enough on your card to achieve those points within one year. If you fall short, you must pay for them. This feature has the advantage of allowing card holder more flexibility in points redemption. It is also good for American Express because it forces you to pay a premium for the points (compared to the redemption value) if you fall short and to favor its card when making purchases. It also reduces the possibility that you will cancel the card.

4. You can buy reward points. This makes sense in only two cases. You are close to the number needed for some award like an airline ticket. The second case is where you are going to cancel the card and want to avoid the annual fee by purchasing enough to qualify for an award before the fee is charged. If the annual fee is $50 and the cost per mile is 2.5 cents, you could buy 2,000 reward points for that amount.

5. If you are charged a late, over limit, or phone payment fee, call and protest. If this is your first such charge in 6-12 months, it will likely be waived, especially if you have a high FICO score. If you aren't successful, call back and talk with another agent.

6. Credit card interest rates are high for three main reasons; a high default rate, fairly high bank overhead, and large profits in normal times.

7. A low minimum monthly payment is designed to encourage you to borrow more and spend beyond your means.

8. Don't open an account that raises your interest rate on the first missed payment. You might have missed a payment because you were on vacation, the statement didn't arrive, or your check was delayed in the mail. You should mail your check at least one week before the payment is due.

9. Mail your check in the enclosed bank provided return envelope if you get a mail statement. It is encoded and is more likely to arrive on time.

10. Use your reward points before terminating a credit card. You may lose them or have a very short window to redeem them when you cancel it. Also check your points total. You may want to keep the card if you are close to having enough to qualify for some desired reward.

11. If you are delinquent on a card or don't use it for some period

like 4 months, the issuer may have the right to terminate your card and your miles.

12. Some cards offer bonuses for new card holders and for going paperless.

13. Keep track of which credit cards pay bonus points. If you have multiple cards and they pay bonus points for certain types of spending at restaurants, service stations, transportation, and grocery stores, note that on a piece of paper and keep it in your wallet so you remember which cards pay bonus points.

14. Make sure you do the math on a balance transfer and think about the impact on your credit score (if you cancel a card). Whether a balance transfer is a good deal depends upon whether you will pay it off quickly, the transaction fee, whether it affects your credit score, and the new and old interest rates. Rather than show a complicated formula that would cover most balance transfers, I am simply going to show five cases that reflect the majority of situations.

Case 1- 0% rate for 6 months on money transferred, you pay-off in full in six months. If the transfer fee is 4%, then double it to 8% for the annualized rate. I probably would do the transfer only if it saved at least a $100 per year.

Case 2- Same except 0% is good for the whole year. Annual rate is 4% so do the transfer because the old rate is almost certainly much higher than 4%.

Case 3- Same facts as #1 or #2 except that the new card balance won't be paid off and the interest rate on the new card is the same or lower than the old card. Same decision as #1 and #2.

Case 4- Same as #1 or #2 except that the new card has a higher rate than the old card. In most cases, I would not do the transfer unless it was just slightly higher (1/2% or so), and I was sure that it could be paid off in a few years.

Case 5- The new card has a much higher rate than the old card. You might go for the 0% deal to preserve funds even though the deal raises your interest costs after the 0% period is concluded. However, be careful that you aren't the victim of wishful thinking and end up paying a lot more over the long run.

15. Proprietary cards, used only with one company, are not necessarily a good deal. It mainly depends upon how much you shop at a given store and if you get regular special discounts, other than the one for opening an account. It does become one more bill to pay.

16. Bonus reward points for new cards are appealing, often 15,000 bonus miles or more. Some issuers like Marriott, United, or British Airways allow you to sign up repeatedly and receive the bonus miles. You would receive new credit cards with new numbers so that would shorten your credit history. You can sometimes cancel old ones and get bonus miles to reinstate them as I did with United.

17. Most cards have real credit limits despite the "no preset limit" advertising hype. This ploy is meant to appeal to our ego. In reality, such cards have largely the same criteria as limit cards.

18. Don't ignore a court summons for any debt, regardless of its age. Otherwise, you will end up with a default judgment because you didn't show up or respond. Then you will have to pay it, ignore it at your peril, or appeal it to a higher court. If you are poor, you may be able to obtain free legal services. Collection agencies sometimes resell their accounts two or three times and may be hoping that you won't protest that your bill is past the statute of limitations for collection or that you can't find your receipts.

19. Ideally, you should not pay taxes or pay off other loans with your credit card. In the latter case, it would make sense if the after tax credit card rate is lower, a rare event. If you are really strapped and that is the only option, then try to make it short lived, tighten your spending in most areas, look for other **temporary** low cost options like relatives or a loan from your retirement fund, and put the amount on a card with a low interest rate.

20. Always save your invoices and receipts at least until the statement comes (and longer for taxes) and look carefully at the amount on the credit card slip before you sign it. I bought some t-shirts in Florida a few years ago and didn't bother to use my reading glasses, and the $30 t-shirts cost me $300, but the overage was refunded.

21. Cutting up your credit cards and sending them back in the

bank's envelope will not get you off of the bank's mailing list. You must "opt out" by calling 1-888-567-8688 or contacting the opt-out service online at OptOutPrescreen.com.

22. Go to BillShrink.com to match your spending habits to a reward program.

23. Check out smaller banks and credit unions for better credit card deals.

CHAPTER 7

A College Student's Guide to Saving Big Bucks

In college, I became an educational entrepreneur by seeing how fast I could graduate with my Bachelor of Science (B.S.), Masters of Business Administration (M.B.A.), and Doctor of Philosophy (Ph.D.) degrees. I finished all degree requirements in 5 ½ years and entered the job market about 4 ½-5 years quicker than the average person obtaining the same degrees at the same time and place as me.

In my story, you will see some of the traits or ideas that I advocated in the first two chapters such as risk taking, prioritizing, setting goals, developing strategies, boldness, not panicking, negotiating, persistence, exceeding the minimum, determining your strengths and weaknesses, objectivity, optimism, self discipline, luck, and creativity.

Though I was an educator for 28 ½ years, my prospective on education is different than my university colleagues, who view it as a fine wine to be aged slowly in order to obtain the right balance of wisdom, facts, and mental challenges. However, I think the principal value of education is to efficiently achieve many people's main objective, i.e., learn enough to graduate with a decent grade point in the shortest possible time and get a job. In that context, education is just another business decision.

In business, each investment has opportunities and trade-offs such as how much it costs, the risks, and the timing and size of the income stream. In higher education, we have similar types of choices on the expense and location of a school, the type of accommodations, our major, how to finance school, whether to work, etc. My college experience should be useful in looking at the cost savings of accelerated education.

My College Story

After my 1963 high school graduation, I worked full time all summer at a diner in New Brunswick, New Jersey and had a second job at a fast food drive-in. Despite saving most of my money by living with my brother, I still needed to take out student loans. At the time, it seemed like a good idea to work before starting college. Economically, it was a poor decision.

My parents were supportive of higher education, but they did not pressure me to attend college since none of my known relatives had ever attended. I applied only to our church affiliated Findlay College in Findlay, Ohio and received two partial tuition scholarships but had to rely on student loans and working for the remainder of my support. Because of the scholarships, the cost of attending here was comparable to a state school. However, during breaks, I was working about 700 miles away in New Jersey and lived in central Pennsylvania, about 500 miles away. To be closer to both, I decided to transfer to The Pennsylvania State University in 1964.

After taking the first summer off after high school to work, I had difficulty getting back into an intensive and efficient studying mode. The effect was like an athlete doing no physical activity for three months. **I realized that my most effective and profitable strategy would be to attend school all year around.**

In my case, I changed universities and had three different undergraduate majors; physics, math, and production management. However, I still managed to graduate with the minimum 120 equivalent semester hours. The reason for switching to a business major is that my career interests were more closely aligned to my educational goals. The choice of production management was purely driven by having 100% of my previous credits count toward the major and the degree. I was actually more interested in finance, but that major would have required taking extra classes and delayed graduation.

My undergraduate academic acceleration involved more than just finishing in three years. I also applied for the Honors Program in Business in my senior year. This was a two academic year program that required two semesters of coursework and then the student spent a year doing a thesis. I completed the coursework and the thesis simultaneously in eight months. The reason for entering the Honors Program was to fatten my resume and the quick program completion avoided a delay in graduation.

Accelerating one's academic schedule is not for everyone. If you are in a lockstep program, want a leisurely pace, want to fully enjoy the social aspects of college, have family or substantial work responsibilities, need internships, etc., finishing in less than normal time may not be ideal. For some though, acceleration may simply mean graduating in four or 4 ½ years instead of a stretched out five or six.

In my case, I chose both acceleration and working extra hours in my jobs. While at Penn State, I worked 20-40 hours per week during classes and 60-90 during breaks. However, I still managed to attend the 1964 New York World's Fair, take family trips to New Jersey, a camping vacation to Canada, a spring break in Florida, do some hunting, and see my parents 3-4 times a year. Surprisingly, my undergraduate years were among the most fun of my life.

My situation and what some may feel is a grueling schedule shows my interpretation of Parkinson's law, i.e.,

> **"Your productivity or output per hour can increase as you add work due to forced efficiency and creativity."**

My grades actually improved as I added to my workload.

If faced with the same circumstances again, I would forego working, concentrate on my studies by taking two more classes per quarter/semester, and borrow more money. During the breaks, I would have done advance course work for the next school session. Can you imagine the reaction of a professor who is contacted by a student wishing to start early for the next semester? Among my 15,000 undergraduate and master's students taught during 27 years, it never happened even once. I would have hit the rafters with joy and put five stars next to her name.

When I was in high school, there was no option of taking college credits or advanced placement. Had they been available, I could have cut a semester or more from my college program. College credits taken in high school are among the cheapest credits available since the student lives at home, and there are savings in housing, utilities, entertainment, eating out, and car expenses.

Enormous Savings from Early Graduation

Intensive early graduation has a number of advantages:

- Saves on tuition and housing- In many cases, you can take an overload of courses and pay the same or slightly more tuition.

- Avoids loss of momentum by shifting from jobs to school and back.

- Provides greater earnings and employee benefits as you enter the job market more quickly.

- Raises your odds of landing employment in your field. You will stand out.

- Increases starting pay and likelihood of being chosen for the fast track by your employer.

- Multiplies confidence in yourself.

- Enhances admiration (and maybe some jealousy) by your peers and bosses.

- Augments your odds of being admitted to graduate programs.

How to Graduate Quickly

Ideally, you should encourage your child to take advanced placement tests and college courses while in high school. This experience should help answer some of the following questions about whether your child is a candidate for finishing college quickly. The more "yes" answers to the following questions, the more success the child will have.

- Can the student handle extra mental activities? Some children prefer diversions that involve less mental activity.

- Is your child a fairly high achiever and good at meeting deadlines?

- Are the social aspects less important than other things like money and less debt?

- Will he be in a program which has flexibility?

- Are there enough courses offered that getting them is not a problem? Bigger institutions generally offer more courses and sections so that it is more feasible there.

- Is your child bold enough to seek or push for waivers, exceptions, and special consideration?

One concern is whether one should worry about employment opportunities if one graduates early. As discussed later, 2010 and possibly some years beyond will likely not be good times to graduate. Though most economic downturns are relatively short lived, employment difficulties can linger for a period after that. I personally would ignore this variable. Regardless of when an early finisher graduates, his record will impress employers. Timing college graduation is like timing the stock market, a futile effort.

Some strategies for finishing quickly are:

1. **Reduce conflicts in exam times.** The student needs to be willing to ask the professor for a change in exam times or see the department chair if necessary. Most institutions have procedures for students who have too many exams on the same day or exam conflicts.

2. **Plan ahead.** Some courses may be offered only in certain semesters. To increase flexibility, she may actually want to take some elective or postponable freshman or sophomore courses with multiple sections later.

3. **Sign up for an independent study course.** Ask a professor if she needs help in a special research area, especially after you have taken her class. Typically, independent study grades are higher than average. This arrangement allows the ultimate in flexibility. You do the work during breaks and then sign up the follow semester. Additionally, if the work is good, a student will likely receive a great recommendation and possibly have the inside track on a scholarship.

4. **Avoid professors who give multiple quizzes (especially pop quizzes) and too many exams.** Go online and check a professor's requirements or ask the departmental secretary.

5. **Mix those courses with finals during the final exam week and those which have no finals.** Professors often have the option of giving their last exam during the week before "dead week" (which is actually two weeks before finals week).

6. **Avoid time burning case courses.** In business classes, for example, the history of a company (often including financial statements) is portrayed. The student must then write a solution to the company's problems.

7. **If you are indifferent between two instructors, choose the easier grader.** Employers never ask if Genghis Khan was your professor. You can ask other students who are currently taking a course

for this information or go to ratemyprofessors.com, which claims to have information for 6,000 schools, one million professors, and 10,000,000 opinions. You want to look at their "ease" of grading, but I would give little weight to their "overall quality" ratings unless it is considerably below average. After years of personal experimentation in my classes, hiring many faculty in my finance department at Washington State University, attending teaching method classes, serving on the College of Business's Tenure and Promotion Committee, and visiting the classes of high evaluation teachers, my conclusion is that "personal likability" is probably the #1 factor in student ratings.

8. **If you have trouble filling your schedule, ask the department chair if he will approve a substitution.** If unsuccessful there, contact the associate or assistant dean who may persuade the departmental chair to allow it. Unadvertised exceptions are often made, especially for good students, those who are struggling financially, those trying to graduate, and persistent students.

9. **To fill your schedule, take an online course at a neighboring institution.** Online courses usually don't require day time attendance so it offers more flexibility. Make sure that the course fulfills a requirement in your program.

10. **Can you sign up for credits and pass with just an exam?**

11. **Are there some courses that can be taken "pass-fail?"** I wouldn't do more than one or two because they are viewed unfavorably and shouldn't be done in your major area. For example, a finance major should avoid taking business classes "pass-fail."

12. **Consider starting your job early and completing the last few credits while working.** From the standpoint of the "wow" factor, that strategy isn't as good as completing your credits ASAP, but you get into the job market quicker.

13. **Petition to waive some courses that may have been covered in high school or a lower level course if an advanced one is passed.**

14. **Some people might suggest that this information is anti-learning or anti-intellectual.** The reader should know that in some

countries, there are no exams given in the classes, and you only take a comprehensive exam to graduate from college. Second, the vast majority of information in any class is quickly forgotten, and much of education is simply about getting a rounded prospective. Finally, most new hires are retrained for jobs so only a narrow amount of specific information is actually needed. This may sound like "gaming" the system, but isn't that what free enterprise is about- doing whatever you can to be faster, smarter, and find a competitive edge. That said, I probably wouldn't want my physician to finish his medical degree too quickly.

Figuring the Savings from Early Graduation

After your child has acceptance and aid offers in hand, here is how to calculate the savings from early graduation. Of course, there will be unknowns such as future scholarships, change of majors and schools, medical problems, etc. However, doing the exercise will convince your child of the value of early graduation.

The general rule is:

"The faster a student graduates, the greater will be the financial benefits."

To calculate your own savings, you will need to make assumptions which fit you or your child's circumstances. These include:

- Number of credits to be taken (the more one takes, the earlier she graduates)

- Summer school attendance (same as above)

- Working during the academic year and summer (the less, the better if courses are substituted)

- College credits taken in high school (the more the better)

- Early decision on a major (reduces the potential for lost credits from switching majors)

- Can any courses be waived, challenged, done online, completed as work or independent study (the more the better)?

- What percentage of the needed funds will be supplied by gifts, borrowing, working, scholarships, etc?

- Did your child sign a year's apartment lease, but plans to live elsewhere in the summer, possibly requiring two rental payments?

I will show calculations of college savings based upon some reasonable assumptions. My numbers will reflect the following student:

- A full-time undergraduate

- Paying in-state tuition at a public institution

- Living on campus

- Using student loans. The numbers can be adjusted to reflect different borrowing amounts, including "no borrowing." A total of 66% of students borrow funds with the 2010-11 figures being about $8,000 per year for public school undergraduates (using 2007-08 figures from the National Center for Education Statistics inflated at 5% per year).

- With five cases of graduating in the following number of years: 2.25, 2.7, 3, 4, and 5; only 53% of students finish in five years or less.

My assumptions are:

1. Under the four and five year plans, the student works 10 hours per week during 30 weeks of classes at $8 net of taxes per hour, 30 hours per week during a 12 week summer, and doesn't attend summer school.

2. Graduates find a job paying $35,000 (including benefits of 15%) net of taxes per year after graduation.

3. I assume that the net cost per year of the college for 2010-11 is $14,687 for all expenses after subtracting grants and tax benefits. This includes the 2009-10 figure of $13,988 (*Annual Survey of Colleges*) plus 5%. The rest must come from borrowing, working, or parental or other contributions. Assume costs rise by 5% per year.

4. I assume $8,000 is borrowed each year at 6% interest, but my numbers include interest for five full years for all five cases. For

simplicity, the annual amount borrowed is not increased. For students graduating in three years or less, $10,000 per year is assumed to be borrowed. The interest rate can vary widely, depending upon the loan amounts, when borrowed, type of loans, and income of the parents and/or recipient (see next chapter).

5. The costs for a student attending summer school increase only by the amount of the tuition since her living costs are assumed to be the same regardless of where she lives.

6. I assume a four year program with 120 credits required. Summer session tuition costs $2,500 and involves 10 credits. No extra cost for regular semester tuition for 18 hours. Tuition of 20 hours is $500 extra per semester.

7. All students take 15 credit hours during the academic year except case #1 (who takes less than 15, but is assumed to pay the same tuition as 15 credit hour students) and cases #4-5.

The following cases will compare the financial situation of a person graduating in five years to a number of cases of earlier graduation. Every student will have individual circumstances involving work, time to graduate, net costs, and amount borrowed. The idea is to show an average student.

To figure:

Case #1 (5 years to graduate, works per #1 assumption)

5 year total cost	$81,155
Plus interest on student loans	$6,000
Less student wages	-$26,400
Net cost	$60,755
Cumulative Debt	$40,000

Case #2 (4 years to graduate, works per #1 assumption)

4 year total cost	$63,303
Plus interest on loans (all 5 years)	$5,760
Student wages	-$21,120
Net cost	$47,943
Cumulative Debt	$32,000

Case #3 (3 years, attend 3 summer schools, work 10 hours per week for 42 weeks)

Net cost	$50,021
Cumulative Debt	$30,000

Case #4 (2.7 years, 18 credits, 2 summer schools, no work)

Net cost	$52,922
Cumulative Debt	$27,000

Case #5 (2.33 years, 20 credits, 2 summer schools, no work)

Net costs	$48,588
Cumulative Debt	$23,333

Case #1 has the living costs included for the full five years while the others have it only for the years in college. To have a fair comparison, I will add living costs after graduation to cases #2-5 and subtract the wages earned after graduation for each case. For simplicity, I will assume college living costs of $12,000 per year (approximate value from *Annual Survey of Colleges*). The resulting **"net cash outflow"** in the last column will compare the graduates of cases #1-5 at the end of five years.

Case #	Net cost	+ extra living costs	-wages (after graduation)	= Net cash outflow
1	$60,755	0	0	$60,755
2	$47,943	$12,000	-$35,000	$24,943
3	$50,021	$24,000	-$70,000	$4,021
4	$52,922	$27,600	-$80,500	$22
5	$48,588	$32,040	-$93,450	-$12,822

There is a clear advantage to graduating as early as possible. However, case #5, involving the earliest graduation, is the best alternative. He has the least amount of debt and has recovered all of his college expenses by the end of the 5th year as shown by the -$12,822 (negative net cash **outflow).** Obviously, the person who graduates early may have a higher standard of living and spend more than $12,000 per year for living expenses. This analysis assumes that the graduate gets a job. If the same analysis is completed for a master's or doctoral degree, the net cash outflow advantage would skyrocket for the early graduate.

Another technique for graduating quickly is to attend a somewhat less rigorous school where the workload and competition are less intense. At a place like Harvard or Yale where most of the kids are super bright, graduating in less than three years, might be difficult. As you will note in the next chapter, good students graduating from second tier schools make as much money as the same caliber of student from the top institutions. In addition, if you plan on obtaining an advanced degree, the undergraduate institution is much less important than the graduate school.

The Other Most Important Reason for Finishing Quickly

Finishing quickly sends a resounding message to employers that you are organized, focused, efficient, hard working, determined, and understand what it takes to be successful.

Every employer interviewed after I received my M.B.A. was much more impressed about my having finished my B.S. and M.B.A. in less than four years while working long hours than my grades or courses. I remember one series of interviews at a Fortune 500 company in which they described me as the "Greatest thing since sliced bread." Obviously their selection of bread was limited.

Any student that finishes early will have a leg up in recruiting and later advancement. When comparing two otherwise equal candidates for a promotion, the person finishing most quickly will likely get the new job. This accomplishment becomes part of your legacy and will follow you for a long time. In a competitive job environment with lots of applicants, recruiters are always looking for reasons to keep a resume in a job pool or alternatively toss it out. Finishing your undergraduate degree early is like hitting a couple of home runs in your first baseball game.

CHAPTER 8

How to Choose the Right College and Fund Your Education

Planning Your Finances

Ideally, decisions about financing your child's college education should come early, even before birth since educating them is expensive. They also should be addressed when major events affect your life such as divorce, career changes, retirement, and job losses. Your economic experiences will obviously dictate the answers to some of these questions. The goal here is to think ahead and not wait until your child is in high school to address financing issues.

Financing a college education ranks in the top four lifetime expenditures along with buying a home, funding your retirement, and raising children. I have listed below nine common and important questions about funding a college education.

1. How much can the family expect to save before their children go to college, excluding retirement?

2. Will or should I have more than one child in college at a time?

3. How do private schools differ from public ones?

4. Are private schools better than public schools?

5. Do private schools offer greater advancement and lifetime earnings than public schools?

6. Do I want to shoulder much of the financial burden or let my kids pay for most of it?

7. Should I prefer retirement savings over setting aside funds for my children's college fund?

8. Will I or my children make more money by obtaining a bachelor's degree than by not attending college?

9. What resources can we reasonably expect beyond our own immediate family?

Question #1 will be determined by your family income and size, savings rate, when you start to save, and investment choices. Generally when you start saving early, you should emphasize at least some equity investments. I say that despite the performance of the 2008-09 stock market.

On question #2, the issue is mixed. Having multiple children in college at once allows you to qualify for considerably more than double the financial aid as one child. However, the family budget will likely be stretched more. The other questions are addressed in the following sections.

Public Versus Private Institutions

Though I spent most of my time in public schools, I did attend a private college for a year and had a grant to study private schools from the General Mills Foundation. The private school educational experience will likely differ in that they have smaller class sizes, more limited curriculum, and the students' families tend to be wealthier. In the more elite private schools, the selectivity is very high. Because of more frequent contacts in smaller schools, the average student may experience more bonding.

This issue of whether private schools are better than public ones is tricky. If you were to compare the credentials of the students at the top 20 private schools against the same group of public schools, you would find that the private schools have an edge in student quality as measured by standard criteria. If you have more gifted students, then the courses can be more rigorous. By that measure, the elite private schools would have an edge.

In addition, because of high tuition and big endowments, these top private schools can offer higher salaries and lower teaching loads to their faculty, thus attracting prolific writers and those able to win grants. At the undergraduate level, this might be a disadvantage since these well regarded faculty know that their reputation, salary, and mobility are determined by their grants and articles and not teaching. Indeed, in a 2005 book entitled "How College Affects Students," Professors Ernest Pascarella and Mary Peterson, who studied three decades of research, concluded that the selectivity and prestige of a university had little overall impact upon student learning and teaching quality.

Once you move beyond the top private schools and the better students, then the argument for better education must rest on the different environment, educational emphasis, and smaller class sizes. These arguments need to be weighed against the greater variety of faculty, courses, speakers, facilities, and activities available at the bigger public schools. In my own case, the latter advantages motivated me to transfer to The Pennsylvania State University. I recognize that many people will have small school experiences different from me and prefer them.

Advancement and Lifetime Earnings of Graduates

Aside from these considerations, a key question is whether one gets greater advancement and lifetime earnings by going to a private institution so as to justify the extra expense. My 1970 study for the General Mills Foundation probably casts some light on this issue. I was hired by the foundation to determine why so many of their best executives came from the elite private institutions and not the public ones. I visited some of the most choosey schools like Harvard University, Antioch College, Oberlin College, Dennison College, and a number of the major foundations like the Carnegie and Ford Foundations.

What I found surprised me. My study was conducted during the Vietnam War and the college scene had changed quite a bit from the prior decades. The top executives in 1970 had been educated in the 1930s and 1940s when relatively few people could afford to attend a university. The wealthy would send their children to elite colleges, and these graduates were then hired by other elite school executives so those attending some private colleges in an earlier era probably did have higher lifetime earnings. However, with the passage of the GI bill after World War II and the expansion of the student loan programs, more and more motivated and gifted students started going to public institutions than ever before, and now you see graduates from public institutions in top positions everywhere.

This finding was demonstrated in a 2004 study done at the University of Pennsylvania. The researchers determined that the percentage of top executives from Ivy League institutions at the Fortune 100 companies had fallen from 14% to 10% and the public university graduates had substantially increased their ranks from 32% to 50%. In the past, executives from elite universities were likely to favor graduates from these same selective schools but the swift rise of public school graduates, who may have their own preferences, has likely dramatically diminished this favoritism.

After adjustment for student differences, greater student and parental graduation debt, and higher costs at private colleges, I suspect that it would be very difficult to prove that **net average** lifetime earnings would be higher (and may be lower) for private school graduates with the same career path. A 1999 study done by researchers at Princeton University and the Andrew W. Mellon Foundation compared the salaries of graduates earning degrees from elite schools with another group who were accepted by those schools but elected to attend less prestigious institutions. The two groups ended up with similar incomes. That would suggest that the advantage would go to the cheaper public schools, except for private school students getting large scholarships and grants (not loans).

One can indeed see very large salary differences among the graduates of institutions. For example, at schools like Harvard University, University of Pennsylvania, Dartmouth College, and Stanford University, you will find much higher salaries for graduates of their M.B.A. program than less selective schools (*Business Week*). However, the results must be carefully interpreted because these programs usually require high admission test scores, interviews, and/or significant work experience.

In another study, *BusinessWeek* analyzed the top five executives at the ultra large S & P 100 group. They found that fewer than one out of three executives has an M.B.A. degree, and only half of the that group went to the top ten *BusinessWeek* ranked institutions (though still impressive). The most heavily represented university by far was Harvard with 5.2% or 26 of the 500 executives coming from there. *BusinessWeek*'s top rated school, Northwestern University, only had three representatives. Furthermore, only one out of every 4,000 business school alumni of these top schools ended up in this elite group. It is also interesting to note that only 19% of the students in these elite MBA programs have undergraduate business degrees.

How and Who Should Finance your Child's College Education?

The next questions addressed here are #6 and #7. Some parents figure that they have raised their kids and that the children will reap the benefits of a college education so they should pay for it. Of course, your philosophy about this will depend partly upon your financial circumstances. Parents should not feel guilty if they can only contribute limited funds to their children's education. Furthermore, the funding of the parents' own retirement IRAs or 401(k)s should be given priority over funding a child's college fund. Ideally, they should be funded together. Most parents have 10-20 years of saving left before retirement while their college age offspring have 40-45 years to pay off loans and save for retirement.

One financial strategy is to maximize contributions to retirement, annuities, home equity, and insurance policies which aren't counted against you for student aid and save very little for college. That way the student qualifies for the maximum in student aid. Another advantage of this approach is that if a child should die or choose not to go to college, you are spared the penalty caused by withdrawing funds from one of the educational accounts. The disadvantage of this approach is that when the child is ready to attend college, the parents may be making too much money to qualify for student aid or the overall financial strain on the system may reduce student aid.

An alternative financial strategy is for the parents to focus their assistance on the period after college graduation when the student's financial situation is clearer. The parents could give her a down payment for a house or give annual gifts to help cover the financial aid payments.

The Value of a College Education

The answer to whether you make more money by attending college is still a resounding "yes," but if costs keep rising, then the answer may be less clear. First, you should realize that the higher your family's income, the greater is the chance that a given child, whether a college graduate or not, will have higher income (*Brookings Institute*). Successful families have higher aspirations, better study habits, organization, connections, education, knowledge, fewer divorces, and more drive and that will give an advantage to any child. The following table shows the higher odds of being in the top 20% of wage earners that happens as a result of coming from a higher income family and also of getting a degree.

Family Income	Increased Odds- no B.A.	Increased Odds- with a B.A.
Less than $33,800	Base	280% (from own group)
48,800-65,100	160% (above base)	208%
More than $82,100	360% (above base)	135%

From analyzing the second column, you can see the very distinct advantage that graduates coming from the highest income family (more than $82,100) have compared to the base group. Even without a B.A., that group has a 360% higher chance of being in the top 20% of wage earners than the lowest or base group (less than $33,800). However, the graduates from the lowest income group benefit the most from getting a B.A. As shown in the last column, their odds of being in the top 20% of wage earners goes up by 280% while the graduates from the high income families only increase their odds by 135%.

Another indicator of a bachelor degree's value comes from National Center for Education Statistics, a branch of the U.S. Department of Education. They found that the median **inflation adjusted** (often called "real") earnings of full time workers, aged 25-34 with only a high school diploma, had declined 27.5% for men and 10.8% for women from 1980 to 2006 as shown in the following table:

Median Annual Earnings (adjusted to 2006 dollars)

Year	High School Diploma or GED	Bachelor's Degree or higher
Male		
1980	$41,400	$48,900
1990	33,900	49,000
2000	33,900	53,900
2006	30,000	50,000
Female		
1980	26,900	36,300
1990	24,700	40,100
2000	24,600	41,600
2006	24,000	41,000

While there was a 2.2% improvement in inflation adjusted wages for men getting a college degree, the biggest increase was for women whose wages increased 12.9%. The college wage advantage increased from $7,500 for men and $9,400 for women in 1980 to $20,000 and $17,000 respectively, in 2006.

College graduates are also more likely to get benefits such as health and life insurance, higher employer contributed social security payments, disability pay, retirement contributions, sick leave, flexible hours, and tuition reimbursement. Furthermore, they have a much lower unemployment rate (about 50% lower). Another advantage for college educated men is that similarly educated women, who now outnumber male college graduates, prefer them. This trend shows up, in part, for men aged 40-44, whose "never married" status has increased from 6%, only 25 years ago, to 18% today.

If we took the above figures and assumed a person graduated at 23 and worked until 66, ignored work leaves and unemployment, and used an average of the wage spread between men and women ($20,000 + $17,000)/2 or $18,500, the real (inflation adjusted) extra earnings of college graduates for various assumptions would be:

Assumption	Extra Inflation Adjusted Earnings
A. No increase in annual wage spread	$795,500
B. Same except add 15% for extra benefits	$914,825
C. Same as A except use 3.06% annual increase in spread	$1,605,089
D. Same as B except use 3.06% annual increase in spread	$1,845,852

As you can see, the value of a college education to current graduates is likely to be close to $1 million or more which is a figure recently cited in *BusinessWeek*. A discussion of some of my assumptions seems warranted.

I didn't show a **decrease in** the wage spread because that seems unlikely to happen. Furthermore, if unemployment rates are factored in, that variable would add to the advantage for college graduates. My last two figures do include an annual increase in the wage spread of 3.06%, which was the rate from 1980 to 2006. One could argue both ways on that issue. There are always going to be low skilled jobs and as more people go to college, the unskilled pool might shrink, causing relatively greater demand for them and thus a narrowing of the gap. The counter to that is high legal and illegal immigration will keep the unskilled job pool high and that higher skilled jobs will grow faster than unskilled jobs due to greater use of technology and growth of the service sector. My bet is that the college advantage will continue to grow, probably more slowly.

I assumed that people on average will work to age 66 which is higher than the current norm. This future pattern is discussed in Chapter 20.

The main exception to a longer working age would be childless couples who invest a large part of their savings from not having children and grandchildren (who also absorb money). Obviously, the college educated person who retires early would have less benefit.

The College Board recently came out with a study showing the net benefit of a college degree was about $300,000 over a 40 year working life. They considered inflation and subtracted the cost of an in-state degree. Given the prior information, this figure seems very conservative. It must average in the drop in wages for part-time working or stay at home parents, among other things and of course, subtracts the cost of the degree.

The educational payoff is also high for those with two year associate degrees or those from professional and technical schools such as lawyers, doctors, physician's assistants, and dental hygienists, and those with graduate degrees in business and science. Remember that the financial advantage of certain fields like business, engineering, computers, and science will be higher than others such as liberal arts and the social sciences.

The Perils of Graduating During a Deep Recession (such as 2007-09)

Unfortunately, graduating during a deep recession like the ones in 1981-82 and 2007-09 can cause a substantial short and long term loss in wages. Lisa Kahn, a Yale University economist, used the government's National Longitudinal Survey of Youth to analyze the wages of white men graduating during and after the 1981-82 recession. Those graduating during the high unemployment period earned 7-8% less for each increased unemployment percentage point in the first year than those finishing in better times. The effect persisted for years, slowly dropping to 4-5% per percentage point by the 12th year and 2% less per point in the 18th year. Thus, if the unemployment rate was 7% and it increased three percentage points to 10%, then the decreased wage would be about 21-24% (3% X 7-8%) in the first year, 12-15% in the 12th year, and 6% less in the 18th year. Cumulatively that represents a lot of lost earnings. This finding and the rise in joblessness should give policy makers more incentive to avoid the mistakes leading to the past recession.

Future College Costs

College costs have been increasing at about twice the rate of inflation. I don't believe this trend can persist for a long time as it will make higher education unaffordable to large numbers and will cause the demise of many private colleges. Of course, one could hold down costs by increasing class sizes and/or teaching loads of the faculty, hiring more adjuncts and graduate students, using more technology (such as computerized courses), and employing more distance learning. The most important factor allowing colleges to raise tuition is the fact that the economic value of an education is still quite high. Huge price increases will spur the development of cheaper competitive "for profit on-line learning" and necessitate cost efficiencies in higher education.

To get a feel for the cost of a college in the future, go to FinAid.org and use the "College Cost Projector." This program allows you to enter assumptions about inflation rates which may or may not be accurate, especially for young children who may be 15 years or more away from attending college. What is important is the **"Net Costs"** after grants and tax benefits. According to the College Board's "Annual Survey of Colleges," the total **annual** "Full Cost" and "Net Cost" of attending college during 2009-10 are as follows:

	Full Cost	Grant/Tax Benefits	Net Cost
Public 2 Yr, Commuter	$14,285	$3,000 =	$11,285
Public 4 Yr, In-State, On-Campus	$19,388	$5,400 =	$13,988
Public 4 Yr, Out-of-State, On-Campus	$30,916	$5,400 =	$25,516
Private, Non-Profit, 4 Yr, On-Campus	$39,028	$14,400 =	$24,628

The cheapest option obviously is attending the two year school or junior college and the most expensive are the private and out-of-state options.. Though not shown, the cost of attending college has risen 15% faster than inflation at private non-profits from 2004-05 to 2009-10 and 20% at four year public schools. However, because of large grants and tax benefits, the "Net Cost" has increased slightly less than inflation. Given the national and state budget problems, that trend seems unlikely to continue, and students will likely find the cost of attending college rising at least as fast as inflation.

As an experiment for showing future college costs, I plugged in the 2009-10 average first year net cost of $13,988 for attending a four year public college (in-state tuition) and $24,628 for a private college. I assumed that the child would start college in 15 years and assumed three different inflation factors of 3%, 5%, and 7%. Here are the results for the total cost of attending college for four years:

	Total Cost 4 yrs at 3% inflation	Total Cost 4 yrs at 5% inflation	Total Cost 4 yrs at 7% inflation
Public institution	$91,173	$125,339	$171,352
Private institution	$160,524	$220,677	$301,692

One can see from these results that the future costs are going to be high and that traditional savings accounts with returns of 2-4% aren't going to grow the funds fast enough. The college inflation rate also plays a key role in the funds needed. Increasing the inflation rate from 3% to 7% raises the four year net cost by $80,179 for public institutions and $141,168 for private ones.

Before selecting a school, it is important for the parents and the children to discuss the cost of paying back student loans. One should estimate the likely amount to be borrowed and then calculate monthly and annual payments. People sometimes view the borrowing of money for college as no big deal, but one needs to put that burden into perspective. These loans will compete with funds for raising children, saving for retirement, buying a house and car, and the many other things in life. You want to avoid exceeding the recommended ceiling of debt payments of 36% of gross pay. The cost of paying off student loans is one factor that will reduce the number of children in most households.

Choosing the Best College for the Money

The key question is:

> **"Where can I get the best education in my chosen field for the lowest net cost and time after factoring in grants, scholarships, and total costs?"**

I am not including loans in this analysis as that is money you need to pay back. In many cases, you won't know the answer until you apply because of the delay in awarding grants and scholarships. However, many parents confuse quality with the amount of tuition charged. Some private schools have dramatically raised tuition and seen an increase in applicants.

One method for picking a college is to develop your own scoring system based upon which criteria are important. I would prioritize them and give each one a maximum number of points. In my example below, I picked 12 characteristics with a maximum of 3-15 points. The last step is to evaluate each potential college on your own criteria with 0 to the maximum points based upon your perception of it. Then you add the points and you have a quantitative value for each institution. A sample is as follows:

Characteristic	Maximum points	College A	College B
Net cost after grants/scholarships	15	12	13
Program choices	12	12	9
4 year graduation rate	10	6	9
Academic standing of the college	10	6	9
Crime rate	10	4	6
Friends going there	10	5	6
Technology emphasis	8	6	7
Location	8	3	4
Extra curricular activities	6	5	3
Availability of part-time jobs	4	1	3
Internship programs	4	2	3
Good athletic teams	3	1	2
Total Score	100	63	74

In this example, the maximum score is 100, an easy figure to interpret. College A scored 63 points and College B scored 74 points. Of course, you may simply be interested in only one college such as a parent's alma mater, a local college, one with specific programs, the lowest cost, or where the student's friends are going.

A good internet site for help in selecting a college is Kiplinger.com/links/college. It lists their top 100 of both public and private schools. They factor in selectivity, total cost, aid, graduation rate, and students per faculty.

One should also consider post graduation lifestyle and likely earnings from an intended career. **Payscale.com** lists the starting and mid-career pay for 50 college majors with a bachelor's degree and the information is free. For a fee, you can also assess potential future income by going to HumanCapitalScore.com. It uses GPA, standardized test scores, college attended, and major. Their calculation algorithms were developed by labor economists.

Another good site is **aarpmagazine.org/money**. Type in "jobs" and they provide a lot of information on employment prospects, a free job site with listed jobs, and tactics on resume writing and interviewing.

Perhaps, the best site is found at **bls.gov/oco,** the official site of the Bureau of Labor Statistics (BLS). This link puts you directly into the "Occupational Outlook Handbook" website. Under #3 of "Ways to Use the Occupational Outlook Handbook Site," click on the first letter for the occupation of interest. Then the site lists the jobs under that beginning letter. Suppose you choose "r" for registered nurse. That brings up links for the following information:

- Nature of the work, training, other qualifications, and advancement

- Employment

- Job outlook

- Projections

- Earnings

- Wages

- Related occupations

- Working conditions

- Sources of additional information

When I clicked on "job outlook," the site showed these employment positions are expected to grow 22% from 2008 to 2018 or 2.2% per year. That rate of growth is considerably faster than many other jobs and more than double the estimated rate of growth in the U.S. population from 1990 to 2010. This is the demand side of the picture. One must also look at the supply side (the number of new nurses), but nursing looks like a promising career area. Of course, there may be deviations from BLS's predictions such as that caused by the severe 2007-2009 recession.

The main BLS website also provides data on unemployment rates in selected cities, the economy, and federal and state jobs. This site is a must for anyone prior to entering college to assist in choosing a major. Students should think carefully about careers in fields where there are few jobs and low pay. The best time to make changes in a major is on or before the sophomore year in college. Going beyond that often results in taking lots of extra courses, depending upon your new major.

Sources of Financing

One wants to thoroughly scour the most likely sources for scholarships and grants including employers, fraternal organizations, pageants (like Junior Miss), trade and agricultural groups, community organizations, governments, military branches, and universities. It is truly surprising how many scholarships are offered in some fields like business, engineering, and science to college juniors, seniors, and graduate students. Most are based upon need and/or merit. If you can demonstrate both, you have a leg up on the competition. **However, the most important concept here is that if you don't apply, you will never get any scholarships or grants and you won't know about them without some effort.** Unfortunately, these outside funds will reduce your college's aid but ask the financial aid office to reduce its loans and not the grants for which you might be eligible.

Scholarships set you apart from the others when you apply for a job. I received a Senatorial Scholarship (from Pennsylvania) which I listed on my resume. The fact that it was a state Senatorial Scholarship (not Congressional) and not very big was not volunteered.

Although the amount has probably dropped because of the economy, service clubs, companies, and charities recently awarded about $2 billion in private scholarships (*U.S. News and World Report*) to more than one million recipients. That translates into an average award of $2,000 for one out of every 13 students.

Some elite colleges have large endowments so apply to a number of schools (if you qualify) and even some you can't afford because the most expensive private schools may be cheaper with aid than the "less expensive" ones. If an acceptance comes, ask for a reconsideration of the aid for cases involving the loss of a job, a divorce, an application or evaluation mistake, a competing offer from another institution (bring in the acceptance letter), or simply being short of money. One of the mistakes that people make in life is failing to ask for what they want.

You should be concerned about all four years, not just the first one or two so try to get merit aid adjusted for inflation or you may find that subsequent years have more unmet needs. In addition, consider asking for an extension or a flexible payment plan. Another approach might be bartering. Do you have a printing business, catering service, or some skill that the college might need?

You may want to hire an expert for application assistance. Check with the high school and college guidance/financial aid advisors and consult other parents about finding this expert. I personally wouldn't hire someone to fill out 10 applications, but you might use her for the most challenging one and then employ the techniques and information for the other applications. These experts will suggest themes for applications, extra-curricular activities, summer camps, high school courses, videotaped practice interviews, lectures, and any activity that makes a person stand out.

One area to approach cautiously is agreeing to attend a university if you receive an early admittance decision. Basically, you likely will be granted less aid because of your diminished leverage. Another caveat, as suggested earlier, is to look at the employment picture for your possible career and the demand for graduates from a particular educational institution. This information can be obtained from employers, employees, current and former students, government and private websites, internet searches, and guidance counselors. This is called "doing due diligence" so you don't end up with huge amounts of educational debt and no job.

The granting of financial aid is not simply about need. Because of limited dollars, colleges employ mathematical models for granting it. Basically, institutions want to get the best students for the least money. Your aid will vary depending upon need, your intended major, sex, schools, empty classroom space, your home's location, merit, where your parents went to college, and a number of other secret factors (such as the desire for geographic diversity) that colleges jealously guard.

The number of applications submitted is a matter of choice because of time and money. First, try narrowing down the number of schools based upon my earlier scale. Then consider applying to one or two safe state schools, several private schools in which you would place in the upper 20-25%, and finally a couple of schools that compete with each other in the same geographic area. Surprisingly, competition affects higher education just like corporate America. Be sure to list all preferred institutions on your Free Application for Federal Student Aid so that all institutions can see the competition. Some institutions and states offer free or low cost tuition to need based students or those meeting certain academic standards.

Of course, the best financial aid is often living at home and attending a nearby college, the least expensive usually being a junior college. Junior colleges are known to be easier than most other colleges, but when you transfer, employers will give the heaviest weight to the courses at the four year school.

I don't discourage students from attending a less selective school than the best one for which they qualify. Being a "big fish" in a small pond is often quite desirable. The student is likely to feel less stressed and to get better grades, and with good test scores, has a good chance of getting into a more prestigious graduate school.

Men now represent only 43 percent of college students so they may qualify as the new minority. Thus, one other financial aid strategy would be to apply to schools where your sex is in the definite minority. For example, men at California State University, Long Beach compromise only 40% of the student body while at California Institute of Technology, they represent 69%. To attract the minority sex, more aid might be offered.

In an analysis of 300 award letters, *U.S. News and World Report* found the top 25% of students had 81% of their financial needs met while those with SAT scores 200 points below the top 25%, had just 64% of their needs met. It appears that if financial aid is your primary concern, then some students may need to consider schools below their desired level. In any case, make sure you read a loan's fine print regarding the effect on rates with loan consolidation, the timing of interest rate increases, the loan fee, and any interest rate decreases for automatic deductions and on-time payments, the repayment period, when payments begin and when they are late, the effects of late payments on credit scores and interest rates, when interest begins, etc.

Besides admission test scores, other important admission criteria include high school grades, activities (including volunteer work, school activities, sports, and after school work). That being said, don't let your child be so overloaded that they are stressed out.

I would highly endorse courses and workbooks to improve SAT scores. You might offer your student a reward for formal efforts to improve test scores. The Center for Research on Education Outcomes at Stanford University found that charter school students in a rewards program increased their state reading test scores by 4 percentage points for each year they spent in the program.

Building relationships is often important in getting scholarships. When I was an undergraduate at Penn State, I asked the Associate Dean of the College of Business to be my undergraduate thesis advisor for a special honors program. He was well regarded in the banking field, and I credit his recommendation for my getting the Boeing Graduate Fellowship to the University of Washington. I got an incredible $6,000 which in 1966 covered all expenses for one year. Frankly, though I had a decent academic record, it didn't seem good enough to receive the best scholarship offered.

Scholarships are the number one most preferred source of financing since they are tax free and they make your resume look good. The next most desired are gifts of tax free money (up to the gift exclusion annual limit or unlimited if paid directly to the educational institution for approved educational expenses) and federal Pell Grants and Supplemental Education Opportunity Grants which are based solely upon need.

Parents or their children should explore the possibility of getting funds from relatives and friends. They may be willing to give funds outright, co-sign a loan, or make a loan at below market rates. The latter two are the most likely to cause problems if not repaid. Also you might suggest to "well off" relatives that they consider starting a college fund for your children. The earlier you start the better. Fortunately, your retirement funds and your home equity are excluded from the calculation of your Expected Family Contributions (EFC) which can be estimated at collegeboard.com.

Some schools offer low interest loans but barring those, the ideal for loans is to get a federally backed Perkins loan with mostly lower rates

(5%) and better cancellation privileges than the Stafford or PLUS loans. The Perkins' loan rates are relatively low at 6.8% or 3.4-6% (depending upon the year) for the subsidized undergraduate loans. For both types, the payments are deferred until graduation and there is a grace period of 6-9 months after that.

In the subsidized varieties, the interest is picked up by the government until then. Both the Stafford and Perkins loan are limited in size annually and cumulatively so you may need to supplement that with PLUS loans or private loans. The current rates on PLUS loans are 8.5% in the FFEL third party lender program and 7.9% in the Direct Loan program. You can also get variable rate loans, but these should be consolidated if rates appear to be rising. In order to get a government loan, you must fill out the Free Application for Federal Student Aid (FAFSA), but make sure you shop around as the preferred lender list provided by the institution may not be the cheapest.

In 2010, the student loan program was overhauled by eliminating fees paid to private banks acting as intermediaries, expanding Pell grants, allowing students to cap payments at 10% of income above a basic living allowance (previously 15%), and forgiving loan balances for good payers after 20 years (instead of 25 years) or 10 years for those in public service fields like the military and teaching.

One area worth investigating is the loan forgiveness program. Information on these programs can be gotten from aft.org (sponsored by the American Federation of Teachers), finaid.org/loans/forgiveness, or by calling the U.S. Department of Education at 1-800-4-FED-AID.

Basically, you can qualify for loan forgiveness of Stafford and Perkins loans by teaching in low income areas or after 10 years of full-time public service employment and 120 payments on your loans. The loan forgiveness ranges from $5,000 to $17,500 and is best for people in high demand areas like math and science.

In order to maximize their loans by showing less income, parents or students may wish to:

- Defer income until next year.

- Increase deductible expenses this year.

- Put their child's assets in their name where feasible (after considering income taxes).

- Deplete their liquid assets by giving money to charity, relatives (who then can pay tuition), and your retirement plans.

Private loans are the second least desirable because the interest rates are almost always going to be higher than those obtained from government organizations, are harder for which to qualify, have high loan fees (up to 10% versus 2-4% for the federal loans), require credit scores of about 680, and usually have variable rates. Since private loan rates are based upon loan scores, getting a cosigner with good credit may lower the rate. It is always advisable to get several interest rate quotes, but be aware that more than three quotes may lower your credit score. One option is to split the applications between different parents or ask the lender to use a scored credit report from you for quotes.

Despite the higher rates, 4% of parents prefer private loans since the student is responsible for the repayment. The least desirable loan is a credit card because of higher rates and the inability to deduct interest on your taxes unless it is the only charge on it.

You can get more information from the website FinAid.org, which publishes information about debt levels for advanced and professional degrees, a list of lenders, and tips on choosing a lender. Other good sites include collegeanswer.com by Sallie Mae (a lending concern in Reston, VA), bankrate.com, estudentloans.com, finaid.org, simpletuition.com, and collegeboard.com. Please be aware that some lenders pay a referral fee to some sites, interest rates vary, and a lender may actually own a site. There are also a number of useful books on paying for college by Sallie Mae, the Princeton Review, the College Board, and Kiplinger Magazine.

If you experience trouble making your loan payment, make immediate contact with the organization servicing your loan. You want to take action before fees are charged and it affects your credit score. The U.S. Department of Education advises the following:

- For Federal Family Education Loans, contact the agency or lender that holds your loan.

- For Federal Perkins Loans, contact your loan servicer or the school that made the loan.

- For Direct Loans, contact the Direct Loan Servicing Center online or call 1-800-848-0979 or 1-315-738-6634; TTY users should call 1-800-848-0983.

You can obtain more information by going to studentaid.ed.gov. The worst thing is to be in default because the IRS can seize your tax refund, your wages can be garnished, and the debt isn't discharged in bankruptcy. Most federal loans qualify for forbearance in which payments are put on hold, but interest accrues. You may also be able to increase the borrowing period which lowers the monthly payment and have interest only payments.

Parents should talk with their children about losing their eligibility to qualify for state and federal loans and grants if they are convicted of certain drug offenses while enrolled in college. In such cases, one may want to get a trial delayed and/or your record expunged.

You should explore whether loan consolidation can cut your rate or lengthen your payment time. However, one usually doesn't want to consolidate a private loan with a federal loan as it may increase one's interest rate, reduce the flexibility of repayment terms, or cause the loss of loan forgiveness provisions.

Tax Deduction

Depending your income level, you can receive a tax deduction for higher education costs up to $4,000 for married taxpayers filing jointly. However, you are not allowed to take this deduction and the Hope Tax Credit (worth $1,500 per year for the first two years of college only) or Lifetime Learning Credit (worth $1,000 per year) in the same year. You will need to check with your tax adviser to determine which tax breaks reduce your taxes the most.

Prepaid Tuition Plans

Some states have prepaid college tuition plans so that you can pay now and have the tuition frozen for future students. This represents an excellent way to get a decent tax free return. However, you should carefully research the withdrawal costs if the intended recipient is unable to attend college or decides on an out-of-state school. The prepaid tuition can be paid over and above the annual tax free gift allowance. These funds are considered parental assets so only 5.64% is expected to be used for college bills. In the recent recession, some plans are short of funding because of the poor performance of their investment funds so the rules could change.

Cloverdell Education Savings Accounts (CESA)

The CESA (sometimes called Education IRAs) allows parents and students to put $2,000 aside per year for any beneficiary under the age of 18 or a special needs beneficiary. The contributions are not tax deductible but grow tax free and can be used for qualified educational expenses at most elementary, secondary, and college institutions by an enrolled student. There are contribution limits based upon the contributor's Modified Adjusted Gross Income, and these funds must be contributed by the due date of the contributor's tax return without extensions. The $2,000 limit for 2010 is phased out between $190,000 and $220,000 for married couples.

The tax free distribution can be taken in the same year as the Hope and lifetime learning credits as long as they do not pay for the same expenses. If the CESA distribution exceeds the educational expenses, then a portion of the excess is taxable to the beneficiary and a 10% additional tax is included. A qualified scholarship is not counted against the recipient, and the 10% additional tax is waived if the beneficiary dies or is disabled. To avoid taxes, the unused funds must be distributed within 30 days of the beneficiary's 30th birthday or the full balance must be rolled over to another CESA of a family member. For more information, go to irs.gov.

529 College Savings Accounts

The 529 college savings plan refers to a section of the federal tax code enacted in 1996 which governs them. Basically, anyone can accumulate earnings tax free in a 529 account and use the funds tax free for college. Making this good deal even better is that 33 states and the District of Columbia allow you to deduct all or part of your contributions from your state or D.C. taxes. Some states allow unlimited deductions up to the amount of your taxable income. Subject to certain limitations, 529 contributions are generally excluded from federal estate taxes provided you are not also the beneficiary on the account.

Readers can view the performance of 529 plans at savingforcollege. com and can compare the plans of different states at collegesavings.org, a site sponsored by an organization of state treasurers. You can also call the fund company which administers the plans. Morningstar, the independent research firm that rates mutual funds, evaluates the plans in a "Best/Worst" list in the spring.

Many of the 529 plans have age-based portfolios which are supposed to become more conservative as the time for a student to attend college approaches. This meant that they were to shift out of equities and many did. However, some in 2008 had up to 70% in equities for high school juniors and seniors. Morningstar tracked 3,506 options for 529 plans and 1,098 or 31% lost at least 40% of their value in 2008 (*The Wall Street Journal*). A similar problem was faced by individuals who had "target date retirement" plans which were supposed to become more conservative.

You shouldn't buy a 529 tax plan from a broker since there are many options out there that have little or no buying fee and a low annual expense fee. You should pick one that fits your needs, but remember that past performance is not necessarily a good predictor of future returns.

It is best to find a fund that has an annual expense ratio in the .3%-.5% such as those offered by Utah, Louisiana, Virginia, Oregon, Wisconsin, Ohio, Rhode Island, Alaska, Arizona, California, Delaware, Massachusetts, Nevada, New Hampshire, and Vanguard. The worst states would be those with high annual expense ratios and no deduction for taxes.

To highlight the problem, let's take the following example. Your state allows a tax deduction of $1,000 at a 6% income tax rate for a $60 tax savings. However, they have a high annual expense ratio of 1.5%. If you have accumulated $20,000 in the fund, your annual fee would be $300 (1.5% X $20,000). The annual fee would be five times your one-time tax savings. You would be better off foregoing the tax deduction and investing in a fund with lower expenses.

When you first start investing in the fund with high expenses, the tax deduction might look attractive but as the fund gets larger, the large annual expenses really reduce your net return. It is better to start with the best plan than be mesmerized by the tax deduction. Probably the only time to invest in a 529 plan in a state with a high expense rate and which allows a tax deduction is if the child will be attending school in a short time and you are just starting a 529 plan. In that case, you would be withdrawing the money shortly anyway.

It is usually best to put the 529 account in a parent's name since these assets only count up to a maximum of 5.64% against financial eligibility whereas an account in a child's name will count up to 35%. Many of the 529 plan websites have a savings calculator to evaluate a college savings strategy. You plug in a variety of variables about investments, predicted rates of return, and tuition inflation rates. Obliviously, the results are merely suggestive and you will need to adjust the inputs as circumstances warrant.

At the website collegesavings.org, the following 529 Plan advantages are mentioned (My comments are mentioned in parentheses):

- All money grows federal and state tax free.

- Withdrawals used for qualified higher education expenses are exempt from federal and many state income taxes.

- The account holder retains control of the assets regardless of the beneficiary's age.

- Most plans have low minimum monthly contribution limits, thus being attractive to families.

- The beneficiary can be changed to another member of the beneficiary's family at any time.

- The funds can be used at virtually any accredited college in the country and for tuition, fees, room, board, books, supplies, and required equipment.

- Contributions can be made through automatic payroll deductions or bank transfers.

- Many states offer maximum contribution limits of $300,000 or more.

- 529 plan assets are protected from bankruptcy (This is an important feature in a bad economy).

- Most state plans can be opened directly. (To find your state plan on the web, search by state. For example, if you live in California, type in "California 529 plan," or "California 529 college savings.")

- 529 plans are offered through professional financial advisers who can help choose a 529 plan and an investment strategy to meet your needs. To avoid 529 funds with high annual fees and commissions, hire them only on a flat fee basis as part of financial planning.

- Account owners can make a lump sum contribution of up to $65,000 per beneficiary or $130,000 if married filing jointly. To avoid incurring a taxable gift on this amount, elect to use five years of the annual gift tax exclusion all in one year. After utilizing this provision, the annual gift tax exclusion cannot be used again for the same person until the five year period has passed. Should a donor die within those five years, a pro-rata amount of the gift will revert back to the estate and be treated as a taxable gift.

You should be aware that money withdrawn from your 529 plan that is not used for college expenses will incur ordinary income taxes plus a 10% penalty. Thus, you should consider carefully whether the funds can be spared and whether your kid is really going to college. Furthermore, just like a retirement fund, you should understand the risks of the investment. Additional information can be obtained from Morningstar.com or savingforcollege.com.

If you have young children, your emphasis should be on stocks. Within 3-5 years of the start of college, it is best to become more conservative with greater investment in short or intermediate bonds. You could structure their maturities to coincide with each year of college. The 2007-09 stock performance may be unnerving but as you saw, stocks came roaring back starting in March 2009. If your investment gains are wiped out, you might wait until your child has been in college for a few years and then tap your 529 fund. You could also switch the beneficiary to a younger child, giving the funds more time to recover, and qualifying the older child for more financial aid. This switch also allows an immediate investment allocation change, which is restricted to one per year.

Whenever I "googled" the state 529 plans, I came across Upromise which was featured in an article by *Smart Money*. Upromise is a rewards/loyalty program featuring Citibank credit cards and small rebates of up to 10% with top named companies like General Electric and McDonald's. In 2008, there were 8.5 million households and 650 partners participating.

To obtain all of their rebates which are funneled into a 529 college savings plan, you need to use their credit card, to register your supermarket and drugstore credit cards with a central database, and to download a web browser toolbar that monitors your on-line activity. There are at least two other similar programs including Future Trust and Baby Mint. In this era of junk mail, viruses, data theft, cyber snooping, and the selling of databases, you should consider the risks versus the rewards since rebates and discounts are available from less intrusive programs. The main advantages are that it is a direct saving plan for college and tax free.

Cheap Textbooks

In most cases, except for professional students like doctors and lawyers, my suggestion is to not save most textbooks for future reference. I sold all of my texts, except some Ph.D. texts, but rarely ever looked at those.

To get the best textbook deal, buy used books unless old marks bother you. Check with the campus bookstore or departmental secretary to determine the textbook being used. Then compare prices at Craigslist, AbeBooks.com, half.com, BookPrice.com, campusbooks.com, bookbyte.com, Phatcampus.com, cheapesttextbooks.com, studentmetro. com, valorebooks.com, etc. Your campus bookstore probably will be higher in price, but the books can be quickly purchased and returned. Remember not to mark in new books, or you will only be paid 25-50% of your original cost upon returning them, and some bookstores may not even take them back. Always save your receipt.

You can also rent textbooks at Chegg.com, BarnesandNoble.com, BookRenter.com, CengageBrain.com, and CampusBookRentals.com.

Searching for Schools

You can find plenty of information by searching a school's individual website. Other sites let you select schools based upon a variety of criteria such as urban/rural, selectivity, size, public versus private, etc. These include Petersons.com, the College Matchmaker at CollegeBoard.com, Unigo.com, and the Counselor-O-Matic at PrincetonReview.com (*Money*). Many sites will try to obtain your personal information to make you part of a sales database. *U.S. News & World Report* has an excellent site called usnews.com/payingforcollege which supplies information on schools that are the best values (based on percentage of aid given), schools providing high merit aid, those meeting full need, and a host of other information.

A good option to avoid commercialization is the U.S. Government's site called the National Center for Education Statistics at nces.ed.gov/collegenavigator. The site has a ton of statistics on student profiles, expenses, location, SATs, acceptance/graduation rates, financial aid, and majors.

It is fascinating to analyze the different graduation rates for various schools over four, five, and six year spans of student attendance, the composite SAT scores (average of all SATs shown for the 25th and 75th percentile), and the percentage of applicants offered admission. I picked some schools of varying selectivity as measured by SAT scores and percentage of offers made including some where I taught or attended. This is not a random scientific selection so the conclusions that can be drawn are limited. However, the schools were not "cherry-picked" to make my point. The colleges are ranked by the four year graduation rate with the private schools separated from the public ones. Only the main campus statistics are shown.

Private Institutions	Graduation Rates			Composite SAT	Admission Offer Rate
	4 year	5 year	6 year		
Harvard University	88%	96%	97%	748	9%
Yale University	87	95	96	742	9
Bucknell University	86	89	89	653	30
Denison University	75	79	79	630	39
Washington & Jefferson	66	70	70	578	34
Ohio Wesleyan	61	67	68	593	66
University of Denver	60	72	74	588	74
Duquesne University	58	70	72	558	74
Pacific Lutheran	50	64	66	550	76
University of Findlay	43	53	56	527	68
Public Institutions					
University of Virginia	84	92	93	653	35
New York University	78	83	84	667	37
University of CA/Berkeley	61	84	88	658	24
Penn State University	58	81	84	590	58
University of Florida	53	77	81	625	42

University of Washington	48	71	75	600	65
Florida State University	48	66	69	590	55
University of Texas	47	73	78	598	51
University of Colorado	41	63	67	585	82
Ohio State University	40	66	71	615	59
Washington State Univ.	33	57	63	542	76
University of Northern CO	30	45	48	523	91
Central Washington Univ.	28	49	55	485	80
Montana State Univ.	17	40	48	555	66
CA State Univ.- Fresno	14	36	48	465	68

The reason for including this information is that the four year graduation rates vary considerably and are likely driven by two main factors,
namely, the cost of attending college and the selectivity of the institution. The most selective schools are those with high SAT scores and
a low percentage of student applicants offered admission. Presumably,
students at the more selective schools have more motivation, capability,
and drive.

This information has implications for parents and students in saving
money. If a child attends an institution with a high four year graduation rate, then he will see many kids graduating quickly, and they will
serve as good role models. In addition, the results suggest that parents
and others may not be applying enough pressure on their public school
attending kids. If you average the SAT scores and acceptance rates for
the seven private schools from Denison to Findlay, you get 574 and
56% respectively. The same numbers for the eight public schools from
Penn State to Washington State University are 593 and 61%, suggesting
about the same selectivity for both groups. Yet the seven private schools
have an average four year graduation rate of 59% compared to 46%
for the eight public institutions. There may be some explanations for
the discrepancy such as differences in mentoring (which favors private
schools) and availability of coursework (which favors larger public colleges), but the big driver is likely cost differences.

In looking at the six year graduation rate, the public schools in this
subgroup surpass the private schools, 74% to 69%. Because of lower
cost, the public school students can take longer to finish. The public
schools in this group have added 28 percentage points in the extra two
years while the private schools have only added 10. The higher four

year graduation rate of private schools (at least in the sample) is one factor which helps close the cost gap with public schools. In addition, the private school students on average, enter the job market earlier, another positive factor.

Admittedly, this observation only looks at moderately to highly selective schools, but is interesting nonetheless. Economists would not be surprised at such a finding across all selectivity spectrums. When you raise the cost of attending private schools compared to public schools, you have greater motivation to finish more quickly.

CHAPTER 9

Blasting Through Graduate School in Record Time

The following information is included to show how to save lots of money by being creative and aggressive. I attended the University of Washington's Graduate School of Business in Seattle Washington for my M.B.A. degree. In 1966, the program normally required two academic years of study and included a comprehensive written examination and a six credit (two course equivalent) research paper. Students, who struggled with the latter two requirements, may have taken more than two academic years to finish because the test failure rate was significant and students usually developed their own research paper ideas.

How I Finished my Two Year M.B.A. in One Year

Four primary factors led to my swift completion. The first was the lessons learned at Penn State about how efficiency increased with a greater workload and that the classroom lectures contained 90% of the information needed for most tests. Therefore, I never purchased even one textbook but swiftly wrote lecture notes while always attending every class. During each class, I was always a key participant to clarify notes, but more importantly, to have the professors separate me from the pack. Most of the tests were essay, graded by the professor, and not done anonymously.

When you create a favorable impression and show interest, it influences the professor's attitude about your work. Not having to read textbooks also reduced studying for exams down to a few hours. This strategy was sufficient to get As and Bs in nearly every class.

This experience of seeing how favorable classroom participation generally had a positive effect on test grades caused me to grade all of my student papers and tests by numbers. This kept the cute girls and the articulate students from getting extra credit on tests just because of their class "performance."

In addition, I challenged a number of courses. In the human behavioral area, a two course sequence was required. I petitioned the graduate director to substitute one of my undergraduate courses for the first level graduate core course. He rejected my appeal so I skipped the first course and took the second one. When he was advised of my successful completion of the advanced course, he still refused to waive the basic course. When I began the basic course, the instructor quickly determined that my advanced knowledge would be a problem for his effectiveness. After class, he asked the graduate director to waive the course (which he did).

Finally, for my graduate paper, I conducted a study similar to that done for my undergraduate honors thesis. Using the same methodology greatly shortened the time needed. I made the mistake of telling my research professor that I was replicating the study in the Penn State Honors Program. This information likely contributed to his decision to award a "B." This was a valuable lesson learned about not revealing everything you know. The old adage of "It sometimes shows a fine command of a language to say nothing" applies.

According to the University of Washington, their median 2009 M.B.A. salary plus bonus for their graduates was $88,200. The current non-resident tuition there is $35,763. Today's value of my fast M.B.A. finish (which includes nine months of additional wages, 15% in benefits, and 2/3 of a year's tuition) is $99,927. If we add the additional year of wages from finishing my undergraduate degree in three years instead of four, the total value in today's dollars is $188,127.

It may not be possible to accelerate at some schools so it pays to look around. However, bigger schools with Executive M.B.A. programs or those schools emphasizing maximum flexibility may allow it.

How I Finished my Ph.D. in 19 Months

Like my masters program, I wanted to finish as quickly as possible. The requirements for a Ph.D. at the University of Colorado (Boulder campus) were that you take a selection of courses, pass comprehensive written and oral exams, and write a long dissertation (somewhat like a book) incorporating original research. Besides having a major field in finance, I also needed core courses and a secondary field of study. I chose international economics for the latter because of the speed with which the field could be completed with relatively few extra courses.

During my first semester, I received an assistantship from a real estate professor who was in the last phases before retirement and only interested in doing the bare minimum. I wanted to be seen by the faculty and to have a nicer office than the windowless Ph.D. dungeon in the basement so I offered him a deal. If he would let me use his office, I would do research for him, answer his phone, and teach some of his classes at the Denver Campus. The courses included basic real estate and real estate law.

Most Ph.D. students took their courses and passed their comprehensive exams and then started to work on their dissertations for 1-3 years. In November, after 10 months and while still taking courses, I began my research and completed it by August, in nine months. The selection of one's dissertation committee is critical because some members keep adding endlessly to their expectations. I carefully selected my committee to reduce graduation delays.

Because the faculty saw me every day, they assumed that I had been there for three years. The actual time was 19 months. Most Ph.D.s who finished required three or four years, and a substantial percentage never finish.

CHAPTER 10

Forty ways to Get Discounts and Other Money Saving Methods

This chapter represents a broad array of techniques to save money. It helps to be bold, but even if you are not, asking for discounts gets easier with practice. In addition, many of these approaches work by phone so you can start off anonymously. Remember, the worst they can say is "no." I should add that one's request should be based on a reasonable and fair approach. Many times, I have not sought discounts where the price was fair or the circumstances did not warrant a discount.

In businesses like antique stores where prices are often negotiable, I will suggest 25% or more off the price depending upon my perception of their mark-up. The higher the mark-up, the more likely you are to receive a discount. The best places for negotiation are independent stores (not a chain), antique stores, jewelry stores, auto/off road/implement dealers, furniture stores, craft fairs, second hand stores, collectible dealers (stamps, coins, etc.), flea markets, garage sales, and foreign countries.

I always avoid praising an item because that signals a person's willingness to pay more. Words like, "That is the most beautiful wingding I've ever seen" or "I've craved one of those all my life" will get you full price.

Quantity Discounts on Merchandise

Buying in quantity leads to discounts more than any other technique. I always ask for quantity discounts though my success rate was not as good in chain stores until the 2007-09 recession.

Even if my plan is to buy more than one item, I don't always offer this information right away. Your very best strategy is to get a discount price on one and then say, "How much more will I save if I buy two or how about three?" If you tell them right away that you want multiple items, you may only get one discount. The exception to this is where you are expecting to buy a large quantity of items, and then the information is volunteered up front. I have received large discounts in bulk buying when remodeling or building apartments or motels, even from the big box stores except Walmart.

Free Delivery Discount

An alternative to a price discount is to ask about free delivery.

I Have my Own Truck Discount

If you have your own truck, ask for an extra discount for picking the items up yourself.

Manager or Owner Discount

The best discounts are usually obtained from the owner or manager and you will receive the best price by asking to have her contacted. Once at Sears, I bought a washer and dryer, some sports equipment, and two TVs (including a big screen) and received an extra discount from the manager. At Loews, I bought a quantity of fans and was told there was no contractor discount but got one anyway. The same successful result also occurred at Home Depot. The managerial discounts work best at small independent stores, but the request has worked virtually every-where in all types of stores and most foreign countries.

Beat the Competitor's Price Discount

If a competitor is running a special, ask your store to beat it or at least match it.

Male Discount

On average, research suggests that males seem to get bigger discounts than females, especially in buying cars. I am not sure if this is be-cause females are less bold or whether it is a cultural bias. Anyway, you might want to test this by having the female negotiate a discount and walking away and then have a male do it later in the day. However, just the process of being willing to walk away may generate a higher discount for her.

The Unadvertised Discount of the Day

You will never obtain unadvertised discounts unless you ask. It is best to inquire about one before browsing to avoid having the clerks believe you have already found a desirable item. Once I decided to purchase an "expensive" watch costing over $100 but not over $200. There was only one store in my community that had what I wanted. Upon entering the store, I informed the clerk of my price range and that I would only buy something on sale. Mysteriously two cases of watches were offered for unadvertised specials of 20% off.

Damaged Goods Discount

I have regularly spotted items with small flaws and gotten up to 75% off. This past year, I noticed a pair of reading glasses that had a small scratch off to one side which did not affect the viewing area. A 33% discount and a free new Harley Davidson glasses case were negotiated. If you see flaws, missing buttons and minor stains on clothes, ask for the discount.

Not Quite What I Want Discount

One frequently effective discount method is to inform the person that the product is not quite what you want. For example, if you see a small old crock at a store or flea market and you really wanted the large size, mentioning this might get you a substantial discount.

Work Efficiency Discounts

Sometimes I ask for a work efficiency discount. For example, I had the timing belt on my car replaced so I inquired as to the sequence of work. Replacing the timing belt required that the antifreeze be drained and the water pump removed. I was able to have the water pump and the antifreeze replaced only for the cost of the materials. In other words, the three jobs were combined into one. I could also have had the fan belts replaced for just the cost of the belts. Sometimes mechanics will separately add the standard book cost of labor for each item even though some of the items are interconnected.

In another instance, a sporting goods store was having a closing season special on ski equipment and at the same time was offering 10% off on anything in the store if you showed your ski pass. I was buying some discounted ski merchandise and asked about getting the 10% off on the stuff already offered at 40% off. The clerk was not willing to grant my wish but on appeal to the manager, it was approved even though I did not even have my ski pass with me.

At another ski shop in late spring, they had only a few ski items discounted at 10% off. When asked, the attendant indicated that their biggest sale (40-50% off) occurred over the Memorial Day weekend, but would offer 30% off now. Since I was planning to be gone then, I asked for an extra 10% off and she accepted.

Special Return Discount

Last year, I spent about $400 on a new fly rod and reel. About two weeks later, the store advertised a 20% off special on any two items. I asked the clerk if I could get a retroactive discount and she said, "No." So I said, "Well I'm bring them back and get a refund and then immediately buy them again." I received my $80 off.

The Walk Away Discount

Before the discount discussions with store employees, I form my idea of how much to offer and will walk away if the price is too high. This technique works well in foreign countries where they know you are a tourist and will likely not return. In some cases, I have given a store employee my cell phone number to call me with a later discount offer. In some cases, I will go back to the clerk before leaving a store and give them a last chance. They may be on the fence about giving you the discount but may decide to give it as you leave the store.

The Hard Nosed or Desperate Seller's Discount

Sometimes when I really don't care about an item or have reached my budget limit, I will offer a ridiculously low price. These discounts are usually 80% or more. On occasion, I have purchased the entire contents of the unsold items at yard sales for $10-50.

Company Discounts

What discounts does your company or corporate partners offer on a wide variety of merchandise, services, and vacations?

The Old Split the Difference Trick Discount

Many times after hard bargaining, the price still is not satisfactory. So I offer to split the difference between my last offer and their last offer. This technique frequently works. I bought a 1961 Corvair in 1967 with 49,000 miles on it for $262.50. The car was in perfect shape but was the victim of Ralph Nader's book "Unsafe at Any Speed." This book highlighted some mechanical faults which never affected my driving.

After hard negotiations, the owner offered to sell it for $275 as a counter to my $250 offer. Then I asked if she would split the difference. Interestingly, I drove the car for 11 more years and sold it for $125.

Opportunistic Discounts

One of the advantages to reading a lot and having multiple interests is that you can take advantage of bargains when they appear. I have had an interest in old letters and envelopes. Once, at an antique show in Spokane, Washington, a vendor had about 30 old stampless letters sent from Ohio and Pennsylvania during the 1830s. I bought them for $2.50 a piece and resold them for $35 each. Another time at an estate sale, I paid $4 for 20 pieces of Washington state correspondence that were sent in the 1880s before Washington achieved statehood. These were resold for $40 each. I have also resold old rods, reels, and old tools purchased cheaply.

My best opportunistic discount occurred in 1983 at an antique auction in Ipswich, Massachusetts. My wife, four kids and I were on a 6 ½ week tour of the east coast. About half of our luggage was on the roof rack. This auction was poorly attended because of a very large two day auction nearby and a nasty thunderstorm. The auction had a huge amount of middle grade material that had been planned for a two day sale. The prices were incredibly low so we bought tables full of stuff and old trunks.

After making some individual sales to people at the end of the auction and selling some items to an antique dealer the next day, we paid about $10 for several thousand dollars worth of antiques which I latter resold. I stacked the trunks high on the roof. There have been scores of these kinds of deals over the years. The above is just a sampling.

Throw in This Added Item to Make the Deal Discount

On some bigger items, when I thought I had extracted the best price, sometimes I will ask that some small item be thrown in to make the deal. I asked for a variation of this at a pre-wedding golf course activity. I was paying for about a dozen rounds of golf and asked the manager if he would throw in three free buckets of driving balls to honor the groom and he agreed.

Bought a Big Item from You before Discount

Several years ago we had moved out of Pullman and I hired a general contractor to build our new house. Anyway, the general contractor had paid a paving company $17,000 to pave our long driveway. I later needed some gravel so I asked the price for a truckload. **After he quoted the price**, I explained that his company had been paid $17,000 for paving our driveway a couple of years ago and would he give a good customer a discount. He immediately gave me a 25% discount. I went back to the same company several times and received free buckets of gravel and asphalt patch.

Cash Discounts

Many businesses will give a discount for paying in cash if you ask. I never accept anything less than 10%, but I usually try to wrangle some other discount first. Before I joined AAA, I would ask for a business or government discount on motel rooms. Now the best price is almost always the AAA rate. However, I still ask if they can beat the AAA price. Surprisingly, I have only been asked once for my AAA card at check-in.

Double Purchase Discount

I was at a fun center with my grandson and noticed that you got a free game of bowling if you purchased $5 worth of tokens. So I asked if you received two free games with the purchase of $10 in tokens, the amount I had planned to spend. She said, "No" so I handed my grandson $5 and said we would both like $5 in tokens and each received a free game of bowling.

Substandard Rooms, Service or Food Discount

If I complain about a service or ask for a discount, I give consideration to the circumstances and who is with me since some people get embarrassed. Whether you ask for a discount or not, my philosophy is that you are doing a service to the owners and managers to advise them of problems. You also should not have to pay the same price if the product or service is not as expected.

I remember having my family at a cottage on Orcas Island, Washington in Puget Sound. The toilet actually stopped flushing so we had to go in the woods. Sadly, I was only able to get a 50% discount. Because it was the peak season in August and I had paid in advance, I wasn't able to charge it and then dispute the charges.

On another occasion, I had asked for a wake-up call to catch a 5:30 A.M. flight and we also set the motel's clock radio. Because we were flying to a cruise and it was leaving that day, we also set a portable alarm. The call never came and the hotel's clock radio mal-functioned. I was surprised that two of their wake-up systems did not work so I got a full refund at Hampton Inn. That one little gesture has gotten them more business from me.

At the Sheraton Hotel in Fort Lauderdale, Florida, I was using their gym when a weight machine malfunctioned. Actually the hotel was very lucky. I was pressing about 400 pounds with my legs when the seat pin slipped out and the seat snapped back with great force against my spine. I was not injured but did get a modest room discount. At the same hotel on another occasion, I also got a discount when the air conditioning was not working properly, the electric door lock malfunctioned, and there was a problem with the sink drain. To get the best discount, **you** should propose the discount amount such as 50% off or a couple of free days' stay instead of simply letting them suggest the amount. They are likely to lowball you.

Slow Restaurant Service Bonus

If the service is particularly slow, I may ask for a free dessert.

Happy Hour Discount

If a restaurant has a bar and you are there during happy hour, go to the bar and order your drinks before sitting at the tables. Alternatively, ask your table waiter for the happy hour price and tell him that you wanted him to get the tip on the drinks. If he refuses, go over to the bar for your drink order.

I am Taking my Business Elsewhere Discount

If you ask, you may be able to get interest rates or fees on credit cards, phone bills, cable, internet, etc. lowered or waived. The most success comes when you have a competing offer in hand and can cite the actual offer or your contract is near expiration. It is best to insist on speaking with a supervisor.

Ignorance Discount

I had a situation where there were very substantial roaming fees on a cell phone. I hadn't read the fine print and claimed ignorance and the charges were cut in half. Ignorance usually only works once.

Upgrade Discount

I have had some fees and charges reduced or waived by agreeing to an upgrade.

Really Awful Movies Discount

On a cable bill, I watched several "pay per view" movies for a few minutes and did not find them appealing and was able to have the fees waived.

End of Season Discounts

Most stores will have some end of season discounts. Late in August, I was at nursery to buy some scrubs. I asked about an end of season discount for some scrubs. I received 40% off on regular priced item for which I would have paid full price.

Customer Appreciation Day Discount

Some stores have customer appreciation days every year. Ask to be put on their mailing and email lists.

Senior Citizen Discount

There are a surprising number of businesses which offer discounts to persons 55 years or older. I was in Whole Foods Market (which specializes in natural and organic foods) and asked about a senior discount. Much to my surprise, they give a 10% discount on Wednesdays and it was Wednesday. Shopko offers 10% off on the first Wednesday of the month.

My Best Friend in Line Discount

I have used a variant of the quantity discount with customers standing in line with me. This only works for places where discounts are likely. Basically you make friends with someone in line and offer to combine their merchandise with yours in order to negotiate a bigger discount. The savings are split in proportion to the price of each party's goods. It is best to negotiate a percentage amount off so that the calculations are simpler. Recently, I went to a sporting goods store offering big mark-downs on shoes and then a "two for one" special on all of the marked down shoes. I successfully asked a customer in the shoe area to combine my pair of shoes with his to get the special discount.

Phone Call Discount

Discounts are sometimes more easily negotiated on the phone. Car purchases are one of the best commodities but this technique can work with almost any typically discounted purchase. I simply call the business and say that I am willing to spend X dollars and would like a 20% discount (or whatever). The more I expect to spend, the greater the discount requested. Always make sure you ask for the name of the person agreeing to the discount. In the case of the car, I might offer $300 over invoice. It is helpful if there are multiple stores offering the same goods so that you might say, "There are eight stores selling these items (can include other cities you visit) and if you aren't interested, I will call the others."

Persistence Discount

I recently bought a blue ray DVD player that failed within 4 months. It was difficult to identity anyone who actually could do the warranty work. After my persistence, the manager finally authorized a new one at no cost. On another occasion, a commercial washer failed several times within the 90 day warranty period and then again after the warranty, so we got a free replacement. It was tempting to write off the dealer, but obviously, he wanted my business.

Not Quite Finished Discount

In some cases, you may not want someone to finish a job and need some rationale to figure the discount. I once was having a two part shower enclosure put on a tub. The first part was a fixed panel and the second part was the door. They were having a difficult time installing the door and were thinking about chipping some tile. Since the tile could not be matched if a mistake was made, we decided to terminate the job. The owner contended that he had already bought the door and had ordered two different ones, both of which were the wrong size. Finally, he agreed to charge ½ of the price based upon the fact that he installed ½ of the two panels.

You Forgot My Discount

On a number of occasions, I have had store employees forget my discount. It is always recommended to look at the invoice for each item to see if the proper discounts were given. If there is no paper tape, then you can estimate in your head or carry a small calculator.

Passed Over the First Time Discount

Sometimes a business that has refused your first request for a discount will be more flexible on a second request. Recently, I was flying with a special cruise and air package from the U.S. to Germany. Due to bad weather, I was rerouted from Chicago to San Francisco and had to fly economy class instead of business class. I applied for a partial refund due to the class change. My request was denied because the original ticket was based upon a special cruise package.

On the way back from Germany, the audio/video system malfunctioned. So I faxed the letter that refused my first refund to the same individual and asked for some credit for the loss in service. In the letter, I also asked that my new request be shown to his supervisor. I was awarded $100 per ticket. Incidentally, I could have refiled the original request for the partial refund with a higher level supervisor, but decided to accept their rationale. In my opinion, this should have been some compensation since the business class fare was times the economy class.

Creative Discount

Sometimes you can get creative and get a discount. I was able to get a discount when I took my young grandsons to a store selling Pokemon cards. I asked the owner for a "first time Grandpa brought the kids to buy Pokemon cards discount."

Last Week of the Season Discount

Some seasonal businesses like skiing or shops in tourist areas that close often offer or will accept substantial discounts during the last week of the season. When I was touring the Greek Isles during the last week of October, a number of shops were closing until April and were offering great bargains.

Special Day Discount

I have often asked for a special discount on my birthday or anniversary, sometimes as a kind of a joke, and it has often worked.

Off Brand Discount

The driveshaft broke on my Ford "pull behind" mower. The cheapest part available from a Ford dealer was $700 so I got the part number and called another dealer selling off brand parts. This one cost only $152.

Actual Going Out of Business Discounts

This is one of the best times to buy especially if you have rental properties. I have purchased thousands of dollars of merchandise from such sales. My favorites are plumbing and hardware stores. I have stocked up on water heaters, toilets, light fixtures, paint and painting supplies, roofing materials, lawn and garden instruments, etc. that lasted for years. Of course, you only want to buy what you are sure to use. The discounts increase toward the end of the sale, and I typically wait for at least 30% off. I have often negotiated additional volume discounts during the sale.

One caveat on "going out of business sales" is that prices are often marked up and then discounted. Stores often show a suggested retail price and then their own regular "discounted" price. The liquidator then re-prices the merchandise up to the suggested retail price. If a 10% discount is being offered, it may actually be the same as the store's last regular price. You can often tell this by peeling the sale tag back to reveal the true price. Be aware that some businesses offer these sales when they are actually moving or aren't even going out of business.

I Just Thought I would Ask for a Discount

There are situations in which you might think you couldn't get a better price. Ask to see the store manager, owner, or landlord.

Drugs

The expiration dates for prescription and non-prescription drugs are roughly a year, but most are perfectly fine for a longer period if stored away from high heat and humidity. I asked my doctor about the shelf life of drugs, and he indicated that the expiration date is short because the products are usually not tested for a longer period. It is in the interest of the pharmaceutical companies to have you throw them away and buy new ones. Personally, I use most drugs for several years after the expiration date. My anti-histamines did lose effectiveness after two years. Check with your pharmacist or doctor before following this advice.

Merchandise Exchange Strategy

Sometimes you will be told that refunds aren't available without a receipt or can't be returned after 30 days. Don't believe it without asking. If the manager finds out that you shop often, he may grant your wish.

I once unsuccessfully tried to return a defective arrow that cost about $1 and another time an $8 elk bugle in its original never opened package. In both cases, it was obvious that the item had been purchased there and the reluctant owners lost a long term customer. In the later case, he implied that I might be lying about it. The lack of customer service cost him over $30,000 in sales over the next 25 years. On my way out, I handed the elk bugle to him with the explanation that he might need to resell it to recoup his future lost profits from my business. Here is an example of being "penny wise and pound foolish."

I do recognize that stores try to protect themselves from shoplifting by strict return policies. However, in my case, I was dealing directly with the owners whom I had known for years. In any case, most established businesses will at least give you credit for the merchandise.

I once bought a Timex sports watch at 60% off. Unfortunately, the band had broken after three months. When I went back to the store without a receipt, they did not have the exact model in stock. However, they had a more expensive model (not on sale) that I liked even better. I asked the clerk to check on its cost to see if an even exchange would be possible. In the meantime, I explained that I would be shopping for other things. The idea was to create the notion of my being a volume shopper. When I came back with new purchases, the more expensive watch was traded even up for the damaged one. I had considered offering to pay the difference in price but the situation seemed like an interesting segment for this book.

Dumpster Diving

Having been a landlord in the university town of Pullman, WA for 31 years, I was amazed at the usable stuff thrown away by college students at the end of the school year or left in their apartments or on the premises. At affluent private schools, it is likely even worse. The finds include mountain bikes (I quit collecting after 10), nearly new clothing, towels, bedding, furniture, CDs, DVDs, computers, good food, dishes, watches, stamps, money, sports equipment, software, storage containers, and unmentionables. I could have had a lifetime supply of student notebooks. Some had only their courses name written on the front. No wonder they flunked or dropped the course. In fact, I am using one recycled notebook to record information for this book.

A person could sell unneeded items to second hand stores or use the stuff himself. Your best bet on selling to second hand store sales is to find one not located next to the university as it will be inundated with merchandise at that time. If ever in dire straits, I would head for the college student dumpsters. Despite recycling bins, a big portion of the reusable items are thrown in the trash, including aluminum cans which pile up after big sporting games, Mom and Dad's weekend, homecoming, etc.

For college dumpsters, the treasure trove is best just before or during final exams, especially at the end of spring term. Go to the university's website and check the final exam schedule or its calendar. Then call the local disposal service and find out when pick-up is scheduled for that location or ask a tenant. Do your scavenging on the day before pick-up, Sunday is a sure bet since there usually is no Saturday or Sunday pick-up. I used to set aside items for charity, and then people started stealing the stuff so I packed smaller items to my warehouse.

There is also quite a lot of usable merchandise thrown out by furniture stores, office supply stores, big box stores, supermarkets, and lots of other businesses. I would be careful about eating perishable products during warmer months.

Food Wasting

It is always a challenge to remember to eat leftovers, but this is an important part of savings and wealth accumulation. To reduce leftover waste, try placing a piece of masking tape on the container and marking the date on it. Most foods seem to last 4-5 days if cooked and refrigerated properly. Another good idea is to have one or two leftover nights per week. Depending on the leftovers, I may make a mini stir fry and add some leftovers. If there is no time to eat cooked leftovers, most can be frozen.

Of course, it is just as important to avoid having non-leftovers spoil. On leftover night, you might look in the vegetable and other bins to see what was still in there. Letting food spoil not only costs you money but will result in more trips to the store and wasted time and vehicle expense. Remember to look at the expiration dates on food containers of dry and canned goods. Most properly stored food will outlast the dates, but it is best to use the food as soon as possible.

Sometimes, I buy food that is nutritious to experiment and find it is not too tasty. Once I tried buckwheat and quinoa which are kind of like oatmeal but neither was to my liking. So eventually I combined a small amount of each with the better tasting oatmeal and none was wasted.

Eating Out

I don't expect most of my readers to be as radical in saving money as I was as a teenager. During my high school years, my dad (a pastor) and his family were often invited to dine at parishioners' homes. Because we were so poor, I would contribute by eating only that one meal for the day and would stuff myself "to the gun holes."

Contrary to some claims, eating out is always more expensive for the same quality and quantity of food than eating at home. To cover overhead and profit, a restaurant except those serving fast food, is going to charge you three or more times the cost of the actual food. For example, a shopper's cost of two non organic eggs, two slices of toast, hash browns, and coffee is less than $1.50. The restaurant is likely to charge $8 or more (including tip). It would not take more time to cook (not including gourmet dinners), shop (assuming you are buying lots of other groceries), and clean-up (if you have a dishwasher) than to drive to a restaurant, wait and eat and drive home. You must also factor in the expense of getting there which the IRS currently estimates at more than 50 cents per mile.

You might find it an interesting exercise to compare the cost of the food used to the price of your next restaurant meal. Of course, I am mindful of the fact that some people do not like to cook or the less acceptable excuse of not being able to cook.

Don't forget to bring home the leftovers or consider splitting or sharing your meal. It is truly surprising how much food is wasted. To avoid food poisoning, you should ask the waitperson for a bag of ice to put with the food or try to refrigerate within 45 minutes or less *of being served*.

Be aware that ordering ala carte is usually more expensive than ordering set menu meals. Sometimes the wait staff makes strange choices. I once had a 50% off coupon and wanted to order ala carte. The waitress said that you could only apply the discount to one item or a whole package breakfast. So I ordered a package breakfast and shared the extra food with my companions.

You should always carefully check any bill as my experience is that the error rate is at least 10%. The errors include charging you for the wrong items and items not ordered or calculating the amounts incorrectly.

Tips

The American average now is apparently between 18-19%, up from two percentage points five years ago. I suspect in the current economy that it will drift lower. Remember that in some restaurants, the tip is included for large groups. If the service is bad, you should consider reducing it, but don't punish the waiter unless it is clearly his fault. Also, waiters often divide the tips with busboys and hosts so you would be punishing them as well.

It does seem that tips are expected almost everywhere from shuttle drivers (if they help with the bags, but only a couple of dollars), room service (check the menu and/or the bill to see if it is automatically applied), bartenders, chamber maids ($2-5 per day), bellhops ($1-2 per bag), tour guides ($2-5), and babysitters, barber/hair stylists and taxi drivers (10-15%) and mail and delivery drivers (only at Christmas). Of course, any tip is better than none at all. *The Wall Street Journal* offered a number of websites to help with tips including fodors.com (sightseeing guide and tipping abroad), ivchamber.com (hotels), emilypost.com, and iparenting.com.

Food Shopping

If you have the storage space and don't let the food spoil, buying in bulk or large sizes is usually cheaper. You should always check the price per ounce or per piece. I also buy quantities of food with long lives so as to cut down on trips to the store which saves time and money. Large sizes are also good for the environment as they often have relatively less packaging.

I do use coupons but am careful to only use them for items that are really wanted. It is easy to purchase undesired or overpriced goods just to get a discount.

Cut down on waste and pollution by buying reusable cloth bags for any kind of shopping. They hold more weight without breaking, are easier to carry than plastic bags, and fit more easily into your cargo area. It is important to keep them in your car as one inevitably forgets to bring them. If you do have plastic or paper bags, try to reuse them at the grocery store or for other uses like trash.

Regular Store Sales

One way to remember discounts is to note them on your calendar, especially big ticket or large quantity items. Most stores have recurring sales on Memorial Day, Mother's Day, Fourth of July, Christmas season, etc. Frequently they will have the same type of goods on sale every year. For example, when I had 15-20 construction workers on site at one time during the summer, I would buy about 40 twelve pack cases of soft drinks on July 4th for $1.99 each. They would last to the end of summer.

Be friendly with the sales clerk and they will tell when the sales are likely to occur and what type of merchandise is on sale. A call to the store may produce just as good a result, particularly if you identify yourself as a loyal customer. **Remember to write these sale dates on your calendar and transfer them each year to the next year's calendar, just like you do (or should do) for anniversaries, birthdays, etc.**

Reuse and Recycling

As we move into the period of energy scarcity and environmental concerns, the first question to ask is "Do I really need this item?" Once you make the decision to buy, try to reuse or recycle the packaging or shipping container. However, it is a good idea to keep some boxes around for charitable donations, trash disposal, storing or mailing items. Boxes also make great toys for children. I built a rocket ship for my grandsons out of tall boxes, duct tape, and a magic marker. Remember that when you throw a reusable item away, the trash disposal company must truck it and the land fill must store and process it. Wherever possible try to buy items with the least packaging.

One method of recycling is something I have never seen anyone else do.

I reuse most mailing envelopes that I get except a few like the United States Post Office Priority mail envelopes. I simply cross off my name and any mailing bar code in the lower right corner, readdress, apply my return address, and affix new postage. If you prefer, you can buy white labels and put over the old address.

Used large envelopes are great for storing tax returns and receipts. I especially like those flexible Fedex envelopes. For my income taxes, I mark each envelope in black magic marker and sort receipts by category. Every year, I empty the contents of tax returns no longer needed and reuse the marked envelopes (see tax chapter for how long to keep receipts).

You should re-use those pre-addressed stamped (not metered) envelopes from charities by simply crossing out the address and any bar code. Stamped envelopes that are mistakenly addressed can be similarly recycled. For many years, I used over a thousand envelopes purchased for $2 at an estate auction. I never buy notepads because I make them by cutting up old mail, faxes, and drafts of this book which have an unused side.

Hobbies

The cost of hobbies varies greatly depending upon what gear and vehicles are used, your accommodations, and how far you travel. I am not suggesting that a person abandon a great love or activities with friends to save a few dollars. However, you may wish to analyze your interests from the standpoint of how much they cost per day or hour of recreation.

All costs should be considered. For example, suppose you like golfing and also camping in an RV. If the RV is used only for recreation, then you need to consider depreciation, license, insurance, interest costs, the alternative investment return on the RV's equity, fuel, storage, and repairs as well as the daily space rental costs. You might find the RV is costing you $500-1000 per day of actual use. One special problem with RVs is that tires, batteries, hoses, fan belts, windshield wipers, and oil often need replaced with relatively few operating hours because of age. In fact, you may be better of renting an RV. Golfing, of course, would have its own set of costs, but you don't necessarily need to include all of your vehicle depreciation since it would likely be used for other purposes. Though some depreciation is related to the number of miles driven, more is related to aging.

In any case, one should at least look at the comparative costs of different hobbies of interest. One of the least expensive can be stamp collecting. You can buy collections and pick out what you want. Then donate the rest to charity with possibly a nice tax deduction if you itemize.

CHAPTER 11

120 Consumer Tips for Saving Money

The following tips will save you a modest amount to a bundle of money depending upon your spending habits.

1. Pay and bank online to save trees (paper), fuel (mail delivery), money (checks, stamps and envelopes), and time. You can view the continuous rebalancing of your checkbook, automatic withdrawals and deposits, and problems and unauthorized withdrawals more quickly. People worry about on-line theft which must be weighed against mail theft and late payments. However, banks generally protect customers against on-line theft.

Even with on-line banking, you can still choose to pay some bills by mail. In addition, you should consider depositing your paycheck automatically (in case of bad weather, illness, and vacations), synchronizing your automatic payments with your monthly deposits (to avoid being overdrawn, leave at least a few days leeway because of holidays and weekends), and use a cash cushion for errors and unexpected expenses.

2. Buy at yard sales. Buying at yard sales saves lots of money. To be efficient, go to yard sales when there are many of them, usually on Saturday and during the warmer (not hot) and dryer months. Plot your strategy to hit as many as possible by choosing those closest together. Go early before the stuff is badly picked over or go late when the best bargains are available. "Yardsaleholics" usually start arriving 30 minutes before the official opening time though I don't recommend it. Check your local newspaper and Craigslist. The prices are often as little as 5-10% of original cost.

A great option for planning your yard sale strategy is found at YardSale-TreasureMap.com. Plug in the town, day, and radius in miles and hit "search." A Google map pops up giving you the location of many yard sales. Click on the red balloon and the street address, sale time, and items for sale come up.

3. Sell at yard sales. After conducting many yard sales, I will never have another one because it takes a lot of time; the majority of stuff never sells; you have to worry about the weather; and then one must pack up the unsold stuff. I now donate my unwanted items and take a tax deduction (see Chapter 17 about tax deductions). Yard sales are warranted in the following cases:

a. You need quick cash.

b. You do not file Schedule A, thereby missing a charitable tax deduction.

c. Your marginal tax rate is very low, 20% or less (see Chapter 1) so that your tax saving from charitable donations is small.

d. Your income is too high and you lose much or all of the benefit of charitable tax deductions. In that case, you may not need the money. Maybe then, you should let your or a neighbor's kids handle the yard sale to benefit from the experience.

e. You like the social aspects of a yard sale.

f. You are bored and it is something to do.

g. You like income that the government doesn't tax.

One should be aware that the 2008 consumer product safety law makes it illegal to sell recalled products even at yard sales. Though the law is unlikely to be enforced at yard sales, one should be aware of the recalled items as both a buyer and seller. Recall information is found at recalls.gov for all government agencies.

The two main concerns are toys that pose a choking hazard and lead based paint. You can test for lead based paint with lead testers costing $13 and up (plus shipping) at leadinspector.com, Ebay.com, and professionalequipment.com. Additional information on regulations, recalls, and laws can be obtained from the U.S. Government's Consumer Product Safety Commission (cpsc.gov/businfo/regsbyproduct).

4. Buy at a second hand store such as Goodwill Industries. This is a good second choice to yard sales. The trade-off is that you will find tons more stuff at the store with less junk, thus saving time and travel, but usually at a price of 2-3 times that of a yard sale. In Spokane, Washington, they used to have a collectibles day where the better merchandise was offered. Books were the biggest bargain as I would buy first additions for 50 cents to a dollar and resell at prices of 20-50 times the purchase price. In addition, thrift stores often have "everything in the store half price" or "fill a bag for $4" sales. Check with the employees to find out when such sales occur.

5. Buy antique decorations and furniture. Most new furniture and decorations decline in value as much as 50% when it leaves the store. Medium to high quality antiques often cost the same or less than new furniture, hold their value much better, and are often easier to resell. Don't buy the cheapest and look for antiques that have eye appeal. Antiques make great Christmas, house warming, and birthday presents too.

6. Send Christmas, birthday, and other holiday greetings by email. One can make individual cards with your computer. I certainly wouldn't woo a significant other or recognize your spouse's anniversary this way, but there may be occasions when it would be okay, especially as the world goes "green" and money is tight. Creating your own rhyme or "heartfelt" message can have special meaning. The younger generations are probably the most receptive to this approach.

7. Send donated cards. Every year, I receive six or more batches of Christmas or other cards asking for donations. Because of my support for many charities, I don't always send in money. However, it is wasteful to throw them in the trash so a few are used and the rest donated to charity. The envelopes could also be used to mail bills and the blank portion of cards cut up for notes.

8. Attend one of the thousands of government auctions by the General Services Administration, U.S. Customs Service, the Small Business Administration, the Federal Deposit Insurance Corporation, the U.S Marshall's Service, the Internal Revenue Service, every state, and many cities and counties. These entities auction excess property, confiscated assets of criminals, goods of those with overdue taxes, property of failed businesses and banks, abandoned goods, etc. The items include almost every conceivable asset imaginable. Check newspapers, contact the agencies directly, or go on line.

Many goods can be located at usa.gov. Type in "us auctions" or specific branches like "ustreasury.gov" or "gsaauctions.gov" (General Services Administration or GSA). The GSA is the general clearinghouse for U.S. Government auctions. Unfortunately, you or someone else usually needs to pick up the merchandise, and many auctioned goods have no photos. A secured check or a valid credit card is essential.

Links to non-internet auctions can be found at "surplussales.gsa.gov." You will find a buyer's delight in great prices often caused by having multiple identical items, used goods, and antiques that are less likely to be noticed, properly identified, or enough of them to attract antique dealers or retail customers.

In any auction, the best bargains occur toward the end of the auction when most people have left, the auctioneer is tired, and people are running out of money.

9. Avoid buying bottled water. Bottled water is one of the biggest environmental disasters ever conceived, with as much as three gallons of water required per gallon of bottled water (*Green Builder*). According to the Pacific Institute, a research outfit in Oakland, CA, making the plastic bottles, filling and shipping them produced 8.4 million tons of carbon dioxide in the U.S. in 2006. It is now an $11 billion business (*Business-Week*) in the U.S. which translates into about $35 per capita, and 90% of the bottles end up in landfills. In 2004, the average U.S. consumption of bottled water, according to the Earth Policy Institute, was 22 gallons per capita.

The bottles most commonly used for bottled water have a 1, PET, or PETE stamped on the bottom. There is some concern with the leaching of the chemical antimony used in making the bottles (*Reader's Digest*).

The American Association for Cancer Research reports that hard plastic bottles with a #7 in a triangle may allow Bisphenol A, a cancer-linked chemical to leach into the contents. My main concern would be from filled bottles left in warm conditions, especially over longer periods. To avoid this problem, use bottles quickly, rinse or wash after every use, fill your own with cheaper tap water, or buy bottles made from aluminum or stainless steel which have no Bisphenol A. It has been reported that some water cooler jugs may also have this chemical.

A 1999 report on bottled water came from the Natural Resources Defense Council (*Reader's Digest*) which studied 1,000 bottles from 103 brands. About 1/3 of the bottled water brands had at least one sample that contained chemical or bacterial contamination that exceeded state or industry safety guidelines.

Bottled water is held to less stringent standards than tap water and can cost several thousand times as much per gallon if purchased individually. About 25% of bottled water brands are simply tap water. When buying bottled water, look for brands with NSF certification or that belong to IBWA (International Bottled Water Association). If the certification is not on the bottle, go to bottledwater.org or check out brands at nsf.org.

If your water tastes bad, buy a filter like Britta or PUR which is much cheaper than bottled water. They will remove the lead from water in old pipes, but some filters are reported to remove fluoride, which, according to the Fluoride Action Network, is good. According to that group, 97% of western Europe does not put fluoride in drinking water.

10. Avoid extended warranty contracts. Extended warranties typically have much higher mark-ups than the product being sold. Most failures occur in the first year when the problem is covered by the manufacturer's warranty or after the extended warranty period is over. *Consumer Reports*, the nonprofit magazine that tests products, has suggested four products that might warrant extended warranties. They include hot running plasma TVs, laptop PCs, elliptical trainers, and treadmills.

One serious problem is forgetting about the warranty. Another is having conditions that are expensive to meet. I had a relative who paid for an extended warranty on a rebuilt transmission. When later reading the fine print, she found out that the transmission had to be serviced every 12 months and repairs only made at an authorized dealer located in that state. This servicing requirement is not standard practice and almost guaranteed that most consumers would never collect on the warranty. If you have already bought a warranty, many states give you 30 days to change your mind and receive a full refund.

11. Watch out for hidden fees. Businesses and banks are charging consumers a host of fees. A recent study by the Ponemon Institute, an independent business research firm and published in a new book, *Gotcha Capitalism*, found the average adult paid $942 in fees per year. These were associated with cell phones, hotels, air travel, insurance, banks, ATMs, credit cards, cable/satellite TV, internet access, etc. Some of the fees are not disclosed and others are buried in the fine print. It pays to read the entire contract and then ask the clerk, "What are the fees and are they all disclosed?" Consider asking if some can be eliminated or reduced. Even if this strategy fails, you will be aware of the charges, and you might decide to make changes to reduce them.

The following percentage of consumers studied successfully resolved their complaints about the fees:

Category	% successful
Pay TV	20.2
Cell Phones	26.8
Insurance	28.9
Hotels	37.0
Internet	51.5
Credit cards	64.6

There are two messages here. The success rate is high enough that one should consider complaining if the sum is large or for the principle of it. Secondly, there are some categories like the internet and credit cards where it is really worth complaining because of the high success rate.

12. React quickly when damaged goods are received. Take pictures of the damaged items and immediately inform the shipper and the vendor. I had some unique artistic pottery shipped from South America. Two of the pieces were damaged and since I had paid with a credit card, I could have refused payment. I emailed pictures of the broken pottery to the seller. Even though both pieces could be fixed with glue, the vendor allowed us to keep them and to pick two new pieces.

13. Avoid pre-paid funerals. Both AARP and the Funeral Consumers Alliance advise against them. The funeral home may close its doors, be bought out, or misappropriate funds. AARP advises that you open an interest bearing account at a local bank that pays your named beneficiary, who, upon your death, pays the funeral home. Be sure to name a friend or relative in good health and not the funeral home.

If you do decide to purchase a pre-need plan, read the fine print, ask questions about refunds, the ability to transfer to another funeral home in case you move, the flexibility to increase or decrease your funeral spending plans, and where the funeral home is investing your money. Considering the size of the investment, one might consult an attorney about the contract.

14. Carefully give gift cards. They are more prone to be lost or forgotten than cash and 25% are never redeemed. One also has to be concerned about a store changing hands or going out of business. Furthermore, a study in the *Journal of Experimental Psychology: Applied* concluded that people who receive gift cards spend more than when given the same amount of cash. Gift card givers should emphasize those cards which are likely to be redeemed and not forgotten. The giver may even want to ask if it has been redeemed.

Gift cards now must not expire in less than five years and no dormancy fees are allowed unless cards have been inactive for at least one year. Some cards, such as prepaid phone cards or cards redeemable at more than one vendor, can still have expiration dates, and cards with this feature should be totally avoided.

15. Trade gift cards. Unwanted gift cards can be traded at MonsterGift-Card.com, PlasticJungle.com, or GiftCardRescue.com. Be prepared to lose 20-40% depending upon the popularity of the card. Typically, you receive cash via Paypal or select a new gift card. You must go to the site, register, and then send in your card. Another option would be simply to use it for something or buy gifts for others. Some stores will actually let you receive cash for any or all of the card's value. Check this option before losing your money and your time.

16. Take and develop pictures cheaply. Buy a digital camera if you are one of the relatively few people without one. You can buy chips that hold hundreds of pictures, view and edit the results, and print only the best ones. I download my pictures on to my computer with a cord from my camera to a USB port. Then I send them to Snapfish.com for processing at 9-12 cents apiece plus a small delivery charge. It is easy and saves money, time, and gas. The quality is excellent. SnapFish will often give you a better price at the end of your order to double your prints. If you need extra copies, then order them after your initial order but before you finalize the order.

17. Buy forever stamps at the post office. To maximize your return, use all of your old stamps before the rates go up and then buy a year's supply of the "forever stamps" at the old price. The rates go up in increments of 1-2 cents. If you use 50 stamps a year, don't bother.

However, if you use 50 stamps a month and stamps rise by 2 cents, then my strategy saves $12 per year and some trips to the post office. In this case, the purchases are like an investment with a 9% annual rate of return that is tax and risk free. If extra trips to the post office to buy stamps are included, the rate of return is much higher than 9%.

18. Watch the register as items are being tallied. Often, the price hasn't been reduced for specials.

19. Buy only printers that use a large "toner" cartridge. The printers with small "inkjet" cartridges do not last long and the cost of ink per page is high. My rough estimate is that the small cartridges cost about 3-4 times as much per page as a refill by a firm such as Cartridge World. If you need color copies, then you are stuck with the small "inkjet" cartridges unless you can justify one of the large printers.

20. Change your printer's typeface to save ink and change cartridges less often. Printer.com tested different types and found the best in order were: Century Gothic, Times New Roman, Calibri, Verdana, Arial, Sans Serif, Trebuchet, Tahoma, and Franklin Gothic Medium. The differences were startling. Century Gothic used 30% less ink than Arial. You can also prolong your printer cartridge by reducing the font size.

21. Printing online material seems to create considerable waste. Always check to make sure you aren't printing unwanted items like comments, reviews, copyrights, footnotes, and disclaimers. When printing or copying, consider printing both sides of the paper.

22. Plan early to enjoy cheaper shipping methods. People use a variety of services to expedite shipping such as express and Priority Mail. By planning ahead, one can avoid some of these extra costs.

23. Pack your garbage down. When I had many apartments, I saved $12,000 per year by getting into the dumpsters and jumping up and down. This practice allowed smaller dumpsters and fewer overflows (which are usually charged a large premium). I always wore rugged boots to avoid getting cut with glass or stuck with a hypodermic needle. One should stay toward the middle of the dumpster or hold on to the sides. Once when jumping upon some cardboard, I sprang all of the way out of the dumpster and landed on my butt on solid concrete from five feet up. I was not seriously injured, but the shock to my system was so great that I could not speak for at least three minutes.

Homeowners can essentially do the same thing by getting smaller cans and packing them down. A large coffee can filled with concrete with a hook for a rope or a 4" x 4" post makes good compacting tools. Just be careful that the can isn't packed so tightly that the contents can't be dumped.

Hauling excess garbage to the dump yourself is much cheaper than using the disposal service. In addition, the trash companies might charge $3-4 for a single extra can but $10 for three small trash bags so have an extra can available. You will also save money by keeping your recyclables out of the trash. Most communities have special recycling containers for which a customer is charged whether they are used or not. If overflow trash is caused by not using the recycling bins, you are paying extra unnecessarily.

Also, if you travel frequently or have a second home with infrequent pickups, you might ask for special pick-ups instead of paying for regular service.

24. Inquire about intermittent insurance and phone/cable/other utility service. Many utilities allow services to be temporarily disconnected with either no or a substantially reduced charge during the suspension. There are often shut-off restrictions on the minimum number of days or the frequency of shutoffs. Be sure to check for restart penalties. Also be careful that you are not shutting off some essential function like a burglar alarm or your furnace in winter. Intermittent insurance works great for cars left at vacation homes because it looks like someone is there, and many companies let you turn off all but the comprehensive with a 30 day minimum.

25. Don't shop when you are depressed. Research indicates that unhappy people spend more in total and pay more per item.

26. Be careful of less desirable substitutes. Some services or products simply aren't as good as the original. I really like many store brands, but their ant-acids are horrid.

27. Buy the biggest container of a product that you can buy if it is cheaper per ounce or per piece. My wife buys shampoo by the half gallon and refills smaller bottles. This works well with almost any product as long as it is used during its useful life. That includes paper, plastic, canned foods, office and school supplies, and many frozen and dry foods. You might wish to carry a small calculator for those stores not listing the price by the piece or ounce.

Of course, you will need to consider your storage space and your likelihood of moving. One key is to remember to rotate and use the oldest first.

28. Join the Free Cycle Network (FN) at freecycle.org. FN is a six million member international organization of nearly 4,700 groups in 85 countries. The participants give away good and excellent quality goods with no strings attached. However, some rules prohibit asking for expensive items, trading animals, making a request more than every two weeks, or asking for money and food.

Two alternatives are FreeSharing.org, which has 900 groups composing 400,000 worldwide members, and ReUseItNetwork.org with groups in most states. These two organizations are similar to FN, but encourage the reuse of even non-working goods like appliances. A smaller free site is throwplace.com.

29. Use Layaway plans. One alternative to credit card purchases is buying stuff on a layaway plan. For a fee of $5 to $10, your merchandise is held until it is paid in full. No interest is received, but there are no exorbitant credit card interest charges. Because of rapid technological changes, this option is not suitable for most electronics.

30. Sell your unwanted gold jewelry. When gold prices are high, consider selling some. However, if it has artistic or antique value, this may be a mistake. Take it to a jewelry store for a free appraisal. Don't ask for an "insurance type" appraisal which can cost up to $100. Then take it to several jewelers and pawn shops for purchases prices. Because of hundreds of complaints to the Better Business Bureau of theft and low-ball appraisals and a class action lawsuit, don't send it to a mail order buyer.

31. Avoid rent to own. Customers sign a contract agreeing to pay so much per month for new furniture. At the end of a fixed period, they own it but at a great mark-up. If they fall behind in payments, there could be additional charges or repossession, and all payments would be for naught.

They would be better off buying the merchandise somewhere else with interest free or low interest financing or using a credit card with a modest interest rate. Then pay the charge in full during the same time as if they rented it. Better still would be to buy good used products at yard sales, newspaper ads, second hand stores (like Goodwill), E-bay, and Craigslist and save 70-90%.

32. Use coupons and sales alerts. Subscribe to a Sunday newspaper. The coupon savings can easily be several times its cost. You may wish to buy several copies regularly or selectively when great deals show up. Also, look on-line for coupons. Your coupon savings will be limited if you tend to emphasize the cheaper store brands, but these brands are commonly a better deal than the name brands even with coupon savings.

You can find some coupons and weekly store sales in your area by going to mygrocerydeals.com. I would emphasize that it is never a good idea to buy something simply because of a coupon. In addition, ask a competitor if he will honor another store's coupon. Some stores will offer a discount on all merchandise if a certain amount like $50 to $100 is purchased. These are often the best deal when offered by grocers since you can combine this discount with specific product discounts.

A site which has links to many other coupon sites is mommysnacks.net. Its links include Coupons, SmartSource, RedPlum, Organic and Natural Sites, Coupon Surfer, MommySavesBig, Coupons Inc, Hot Coupon World, Shortcuts, P&G Esaver, UpromiseCoupons, and Cellfire. The latter four sites allow you to load coupons on to your shopping card. Then there are manufacturer and store specific sites such as BoxTops4Education (General Mills), Eat Better America (General Mills), Pillsbury, Betty Crocker, Albertsons SS, Eversave SS, Safeway SS, Meijer Mealbox, Walgreens SS, and A Full Cup (Target).

Another useful site is HotCouponWorld whose users compile hard copy printable manufacturers' and groceries' internet printable coupons/coupon links from the Sunday newspapers. However, one problem is that the site isn't always updated and some links are dead.

Another good one is moneysavingmethods.com. This site goes far beyond rebates and coupons. It has sections on how to earn money blogging, online offers, high interest checking accounts, being paid for surveys and research, bank offers, trial offers, and transferring prescriptions. An interesting feature of this site is that there are step by step instructions for each of the suggested approaches.

Other sites include RetailMeNot.com (offering 150,000 coupon codes), FatWallet.com (2,400 stores), CouponMom.com, CouponCode.com, CNet.com, DealDivine.com, SavingPiggy.com, ShopLocal.com, Wise-Bread.com, SlickDeals.net, and Groupon.com. Some sites earn a commission when a customer makes a purchase. Some non coupon discount sites include Bluefly.com (offering designer goods) and two fashion invitation only sites called Gilt.com and Ideeli.com.

If you seriously wanted to probe the web coupons and rebates, you should definitely set up another email address so you could pick and choose responses and not mix them in with your regular and personal ones. One could easily be overwhelmed by junk mail. Keep your coupon stack next to your grocery list. You could organize them by expiration date, food category, or importance.

33. Apply for rebates. The most important advice about rebates is to follow the instructions, meet all deadlines, and keep a copy of everything sent (including the bar code). Mark the date mailed on the documents with a reminder on your calendar about the expected date for the rebate. When you get the check, write "received" on the calendar in case you forget its receipt. If the company claims to have sent an undelivered check, ask them to reissue the check and put a stop payment on the first check or to send a copy of both sides of the cancelled check.

Let me relate my potentially bad experience with an appliance maker in getting a $50 rebate. I had sent the paperwork in and had omitted the serial number since the appliance had not yet been delivered to my second home. My wife had planned to be there in a couple of weeks, and I wanted to make sure that the rebate forms were timely. I received a legitimate rejection form so the paperwork was resent with the serial number. They again denied it as not being timely even though the deadline was almost one month away. This time I resent all of the paperwork with a letter that included a "cc" to my appliance store and I got the rebate. Be cautious as rebates may be mailed in junk mail type envelopes, and people sometimes forget to cash them.

If the amount is $50 or more, consider sending the rebate request by "certified mail, return receipt requested." That gives you proof that the company received it. If the rebate is later than promised, immediately call the company. Not sending a rebate is a violation of Federal Trade Commission (FTC) rules. You might also use my strategy of putting "cc" to the store manager on the "complaint" correspondence to the manufacturer. In my case, I didn't actually send a copy to the store, but the manufacturer didn't know that. If the situation is still not resolved, file a complaint with the FTC at ftccomplaintassistant.gov.

34. Don't go early to liquidation or "going out of business" sales. In such sales, some prices are actually raised by the liquidation company and then lowered. I never go before the discounts are 30%, and most of my purchases are for 40-80% off. However, I really stock up. In recent liquidations of two stores, I bought $1,000 in items with an average discount of over 50%. These purchases provided a five year supply of tennis and hiking shoes, fishing gear, trousers, gloves, socks, shirts, underwear, and sunglasses.

Don't forget to look for damage, instructions, warranty information, missing parts, and accessories. Always charge the merchandise on your credit card, and even though all sales are final, I would still contest them to your credit card company if you find the merchandise is damaged.

35. Look for special deals through your memberships in groups such as AARP, AAA, your employer, professional association, etc. AARP and AAA offer a wide range of discounts.

36. Favor breakfast or lunch out over dinner. It is definitely cheaper and you are probably less likely to overeat. Check out places where kids eat free. Look for two for one offers. Skip the drinks, dessert, appetizers, and the special for the day (typically more expensive). Have your drink at home before you go. Go out on your birthday and call ahead to see if anything special is done (like a free dessert) or check the website of the restaurant. You can often find nutritional information there too. Ask for the senior discount. No one has ever requested proof of my senior status so I must not look like a "spring chicken." However, I was carded by a bar in the Anchorage airport in 2008. God bless 'em.

You can go to the website of restaurants.com and pay $10 for a $25 coupon which is good at a few restaurants in a geographic area. Other sites include Wow-coupons.com which will show you coupons and rebates, but offers at some websites have expired, and many sites require you to register for a club or newsletter.

37. Regularly check competitor's prices for everything. Include cell phones, cable/satellite, burglar alarms, health clubs, credit cards, interest rates/fees, lawn care service, telephones services, etc. It usually pays to bundle services such as your land line, cell, internet, and cable/satellite. The best time to negotiate is just before a contract expires, but the ploy may work even in the middle of a contract. One place to compare prices for almost anything and anywhere is the website, thefind.com.

38. Set aside a buying and negotiating day. People often are annoyed by having to negotiate on everything, everyday (not for me). An alternative is to devote a whole day once every six months for obtaining better deals on revolving purchases. Mentally, it makes things easier. I called my satellite provider and said, I have been a good customer for many years, can you give me a discount? She didn't offer one so I asked to talk with the supervisor. She offered $10 per month off for 5 months. I said "How about $20 per month?" She agreed.

39. Live a lifestyle which you can afford. This lifestyle should be dictated by your income, expenses, family size, age, and savings and adhering to this book's philosophy.

40. It's the thought that counts. Based upon recent studies at Stanford University (*Journal of Experimental Psychology*) and the University of Virginia (*Social Cognition*), it appears that expensive gifts are not valued any higher than much cheaper ones. This finding also included engagement rings. For male recipients, the thoughtfulness of the gifts (picking something unique) was very important, but any gift was appreciated by the ladies. Most people probably have a value band of acceptance, in part based upon the giver's and perhaps receiver's net worth and/or income. I would take this information as suggestive. If you are making $100,000 per year, a fiancée would likely not view a $500 engagement ring favorably unless she simply wanted a band.

41. Use skilled personal trainers only to learn proper techniques. That is a good idea to help avoid injuries. Enlist a friend or significant other to split the cost. Then after your one month of sessions, find a no-frills gym for about $50 a month or less. My gym has a special rate for people who come before 4 PM and on week-ends. Before you make a long-term commitment to a gym, pay on a monthly or per visit basis to see if you will go regularly. Avoid signing a long term commitment unless there is significant savings and before reaching an agreement, try to negotiate for the same rate without the term commitment (or for a shorter one). In addition, cross out any clause that allows them to close the facility and have you work out at a less convenient one. Many places offer group fitness classes which can be more fun than individual lessons.

42. Work out at home. Purchase cheap used equipment, the basic essentials being weight and cardio machines. Supplement that with exercise, movement, and stretching videos. Using videos and having exercise partners are helpful in aiding you to stick with a routine.

43. Look for cheap or free recreation. These include classes, recreation, and leagues at public pools and gyms, churches, bowling alleys, city leagues, and community centers. Bowling alleys have surprisingly cheap leagues for those who want to engage weekly.

44. Walk regularly. You can determine your own distance covered with a cheap pedometer. Put on your walking shoes and take a few normal strides and then stop as you complete a stride. Measure your stride in inches from toe to toe. Then use the following to calculate your distance walked: (Stride/12 inches) X (pedometer steps/5280 feet). To illustrate, consider the following example:
    Stride (toe to toe) = 22 inches
    Pedometer steps = 10,000
    Distance traveled = (22 inches/12 inches) X
    (10,000 steps/5280 feet= 3.47 miles

45. Favor the off season when possible. That is for anything that is normally more expensive during certain seasons including vacations, hotel, car rentals, tree trimming, marriage, holiday shopping, lawn equipment servicing, carpentry, painting, tax accounting work, etc. For example, you could file for a tax return extension and then ask your accountant for a break in fees to do it after April 15th.

46. For repairs, choose the business that meets your needs. A local muffler replacement shop, for example, might offer a better rate than the national chain Midas. If price is your number one criterion, then use the local store. However, if you expect to own the vehicle for a long time, Midas would be superior for exercising a lifetime guarantee though most people never benefit from it because they lose their paperwork or don't keep the car long enough.

47. Earn a "Time Dollar." At timesbank.org, a social change movement, you can earn a "time dollar" by voluntarily working an hour for others. In return, you earn the right to have work done for you. I am guessing that incidental activities like this are not pursued by the Internal Revenue Service, but technically, any barter received should be reported as income.

48. Try to have your rent lowered or not at least raised. This is more likely to work toward the end of a lease if you have been a good tenant and are signing something other than a month to month lease. You need to have as much information as possible when you call. The answers to the following questions will help determine whether the landlord will likely view your rent request favorably.

Do you live by yourself, use fewer landlord supplied utilities, and have less wear and tear than a couple? Do you have a pet (not likely to be viewed favorably)? Have you been a long time tenant? Is the landlord offering specials to new tenants (check the newspaper, Craislist, etc.)? You can press *67 on your landline phone to disguise your call. Are vacancies up in your building and the surrounding area? Have you paid your rent on time? If you were late, did you call the office to let them know? Have you bounced any checks? Have you whined about this and that? Is your apartment kept clean? Have you partied and disturbed the other tenants? Are you on good terms with and know the names of the office and maintenance staff (they may go to bat for you)? Do you have a good credit record? Are you still employed? Do you leave junk all over your yard?

Landlords want good tenants and may make concessions if you ask them. If the office staff turns you down, ask them to contact the owner. Better yet, ask to see or talk with the owner. Be sure to mention all of the positive things just mentioned. If you are pressed for money and local rental conditions warrant it, you might ask that your deposit be reduced and applied to the rent.

49. See if you are eligible for food stamps. Many people eligible for food stamps don't get them including about one third of people aged 60 and over (*AARP Bulletin*).

50. Use a comparison shopping site like Shopzilla.com. Print off the lowest price and go to your favorite store and ask them to beat it by 10%. You should increase the price by the shipping costs and reduce it by any sales tax savings.

51. Research a product before you buy. Amazon.com and Epinions. com are good places to do that, or you can buy a subscription to *Consumer Reports*.

52. Forego cable or satellite TV. Use rabbit ears or a house top antenna. With the new digital programming, these devices allow much clearer signals than in the past. You can also view TV shows on your computer or stream them from your computer to your TV. The major networks (Fox, CBS, ABC, and NBC) allow you to download shows (with ads) from their websites. You can also go to Hulu.com and can see 1,700 past and present TV shows such as Family Guy, Glee, Chuck, Saturday Night Live, House, Modern Family, The Office, and The Simpsons as well as hundreds of movies.

You can also view shows at MSN TV, Veoh, TidalTV, Joost, AOL, and Miro. Some people use illegal file sharing at sites like "The Pirate Bay" using software such as Tomato Torrent (*MSN Money*). However, given some large judgments in court cases and legal fees in defending yourself, this would be a risky venture.

53. Plan your food menu by sales. Instead of planning your food menu and then buying, reverse this process and don't plan until you see the sales. I also think it is a mistake to ask the kids what they want. Present them with a variety of nutritious foods and then give them choices. Otherwise, you will be serving a lot of soda, pizza, hamburgers, hot dogs, and dessert. All of these choices have a limited place in a balanced and healthy diet.

54. Consider alternatives to standard phones. You might want to drop your landline and use "Magic Jack" which plugs into your computer. For international calls, one can route calls over the web (Voice over Internet Protocol) to your cell phone or computer for a fraction of the old cell phone rates, and the VIP rates are comparable or cheaper than standard phones. Companies offering VoIP include Sunrocket, Vonage, VoIP.com, Skype, and ITP. Companies such as Gizmo, Rebtel, and Truphone offer software to install on your internet accessible cell phone. The call quality and coverage is sometimes a problem in less developed areas of Asia and Africa. Of course, when your computer is involved, a power outage (unless you have battery back-up), or a problem with your server could disrupt your phone service.

55. Use prepaid or minimum charge cell phones. Some people use cell phones only for emergencies or to check on their kids. In that case, you will save money by foregoing a more expensive plan.

56. Get free videos, books, movies, and games. Go to SwapTree.com. You list your tradable items by their IBSN. The site, with over 100,000 items, then lists the merchandise in your desired category available for trade. You just pay shipping to the other exchanger who is rated by the users.

57. Become a multi-generational family. According to a recent AARP study, 6.6 million households had at least three generations living together, a 30% increase since the 2000 census.

58. Buy reconditioned tools. If the product packing has been opened, the product can't be sold as new. It is often send back to the manufacturer, and it may be new or just slightly used. The manufacturer then inspects, tests, repairs, and repackages the product along with a full warranty. Companies such as ToolKing.com (1-800-696-8665) then sell the reconditioned items for discounts up to 75% off of the new retail price.

59. For smaller repair jobs, try to get a time (hourly rate) and materials bid. You will usually do better than a fixed price bid though there are drawbacks. A contractor may send his worst guy and, for simple jobs, it doesn't matter. If the job is more complicated, you want an experienced worker.

60. Don't pay for work until you are satisfied. For work at your place, that isn't a problem, but an unpaid mechanic may refuse to release your car. However, you can dispute a credit card charge or stop payment on a check. The former is preferred since there is no fee and you have 60 days from the billing statement date to protest the charge.

61. Consider phone cards. They make sense if you don't make many long distance calls, regularly frequent areas where you don't have cell phone reception, or are concerned about abuse of your long distance service (by friends or relatives). Don't buy ones in which the minutes expire. Some discounters and warehouse clubs sell minutes for as little as 3-4 cents. I would stick with cards sold by major stores as one of the problems appears to be that some cards don't deliver the number of minutes promised, and there are often undisclosed connection fees. Read the card's fine print.

62. Beware of auction fever. Over the years, I have spent many thousands of dollars at auctions. You can find great bargains there, especially non-antiques. However, some people succumb to auction fever and overbid. The best approach is to set a limit on any item and not go over it.

63. Rent a spare bedroom. If you are elderly, you might be glad for the extra company and security. Always run criminal and credit checks.

64. Rent your own stuff or rent from others. You can either rent from professionals or other consumers or rent your own goods at Zilok.com. The site has a wide range from vacation rentals to electronics to power tools.

65. Consider tutoring. Do you have a special skill like scientific training, language, tax preparation, music, etc.? Then place an ad, contact K-12 schools, senior citizen groups, community groups, and other interested parties. Consider listing your services on LivePerson.com where professionals offer their skills to people willing to pay for them. The services range from financial advice to psychics.

66. Get discount or free food. On the internet, type in "share," "foodshare," or "foodshareAmerica," to find many options for getting free or discounted food. Many of the groups are affiliated with SHARE (Self-Help and Resource Exchange). Also try typing in those words plus your city and state.

67. Forego expensive wines unless you are an expert with wine tasting training. In a sample of 6,000 blind tastings, six researchers including two from Harvard and Yale Universities concluded that non-expert wine tasters slightly preferred cheaper wines when they didn't know the price. I ran this same experiment twice using light colored beer and had the same result. In fact, the most preferred beers were Keystone, Buckhorn, and one labeled "Beer."

68. Forego expensive running shoes. Researchers from the University of Dundee in Scotland tested nine pairs of running shoes, three models from three major shoe manufacturers. The prices ranged from $80 to $150. All identifying marks were covered and 43 men rated the shoes for comfort and were asked to estimate the price of the shoes. The runners could not estimate the shoes' prices, and there was no difference in comfort ratings by price or brand.

69. Consider off-the-shelf orthotics (arch supports). Over the years, I have had much difficulty with my plantar tendons even in ordinary walking and paid $300 for some custom made orthotics about 20 years ago. Then I found a much cheaper and surprisingly better substitute.

First, I only buy shoes which have a very stiff core. This is determined by grabbing the heel and the toe at the same time and placing my thumbs on the bottom center of the shoe's sole (arch). If it bends more than slightly, I don't buy it. Then I buy the arch support called "Superfeet." The green color is best for me, followed by the blue one, and my least favorite is the more expensive orange color. Of course, the original arch is removed first.

70. Favor clothes that can be washed rather than dry-cleaned.

71. Try home dry cleaning products instead of a professional.

72. Processed food generally costs more than the fresh or frozen varieties. The price differential is even greater for whole dinners.

73. Don't use those machines which charge 8% or so to dispose of your loose change. Instead, use your change when buying, give it as a tip (except pennies), donate it to charities (often found at check-out counters), or give it away at Halloween or to your neighborhood kids (that you know).

Actually collecting change is a great way of accumulating funds for investing and everything else. Many banks have coin counters which will take all U.S. coins and process them at no cost for customers.

74. Instead of spending your rebate, tax refund, bonus, or inheritance, invest them in interest bearing accounts, bonds, equities, or some tangible investment.

75. Automatically deposit your paycheck in your checking account. Then have your bank automatically deposit money in a savings or brokerage account.

76. Buy discounted tickets. Many sites offer tickets such as StubHub. com, PremiumTicketsCheap.com, VividSeats.com, DiscountSportsTickets.com, TicketLiquidator.com, BroadwayBox.com, and TheaterMania. com. Some tickets are discounted, some are not. For theatre or sports tickets, the best deals are often half priced tickets on the day of the show or game. To find a source, type "half price theater tickets" or "discount sports tickets" followed by the name of the city in your browser.

77. Buy a house full of furniture for heavily discounted prices. The area around Jamestown, High Point, Hickory, and Thomasville North Carolina is one of the world's foremost locations for furniture showrooms with goods from 3,000 manufacturers. Go to highpointfurniture. com for contacts and locations. With discounts you can find on the web or with information using web pricing, you may not need to schedule a trip there, but if you want to visit the southeast, you can see an immense selection of goods there.

78. Buy used luxury goods. Portero.com offers 500 luxury brands of jewelry, watches, and goods at large discounts.

79. Take on odd jobs. Can you walk dogs, pick up poop, house sit, mow lawns, paint, or do minor repairs? For some jobs, you may need a city license.

80. Do work online. One very legitimate site is Mechanical Turk run by Amazon.com. People are paid small amounts to evaluate a product description, take a survey, write phrases, look at videos, etc. I looked at 150 random entries and about 85% pay 10 cents or less, but take 10-30 seconds to complete. Some are rather bizarre such as one "business" which paid nude females $1 to pose with a sign reading "Hi! Tasty Prawns." Associated Content also pays for online work and it claims almost two million articles. However, this site must not pay much as it mentions having paid out $1 million.

81. Eliminate fees for extra cable or satellite TV boxes. Boxes are often $5 per TV. Eliminate unused ones. They can be turned on or off quickly (usually at no charge) by calling your provider.

82. Buy a membership at a discount warehouse like Costco, Sam's Club, or a bulk distributor.

83. Try a dollar store.

84. Use only the amount of detergent recommended. The low water washers take less soap, but people often use too much.

85. Pay small bills in advance. For recurring bills under $20, pay them in advance for 4-6 months to save time and/or postage.

86. Find unclaimed money. There are tens of billions of dollars in unclaimed dividends (including stock dividends), payroll checks, checking and savings accounts, class action lawsuits, utility deposits, and insurance proceeds. Companies, by law, must turn these funds over to the state government for holding. With my propensity to watch everything, I thought there is no chance of me having unclaimed money. At "claimed.org" I clicked on the states in which I had lived, and found money from Abercrombie & Fitch. That site, representing the National Association of Unclaimed Property Administrators, has links to "Other Sources for Unclaimed Property" such as VA and railroad benefits, tax refunds, U.S. savings bonds, holocaust benefits, and international links. My find would have paid for several copies of this book.

87. Reduce your catalogs and junk mail. To reduce your junk advertising mail, sign up with DMAchoice.org, sponsored by the Direct Marketing Association (DMA). The DMA is a trade association of businesses who agree to not market products to you or sell your name to others. The cost is $1, but not all marketers are members.

Another option is catalogchoice.org, endorsed by the National Wildlife Federation and the Natural Resources Defense Council. I signed up for this free service after getting at least 2,000 catalogs per year. My volume has decreased some but not enough.

Another option is 41pounds.org which costs $41 per year and 41 pounds is the average amount of junk received by American households each year. They will contact direct mail companies and supply you with a quantity of stamped, pre-addressed postcards to send to the offending companies that continue to send magazines. One third of the fee is given to your choice of community or environmental organizations and that portion may be tax deductible. In all of these options, you will need to send postcards or go on line and manually delete names from an approved mailing list.

88. To opt out of credit card offers, go to optoutprescreen.com or call 1-888-567-8688, the official credit reporting industry website and phone number.

To reduce other unwanted mail from mail list brokers (Experian and Polk Company) and national mailers sending coupons and circulars (Mailbox Values, ShopWi$e, and Val-Pak), go to reduce.org. That site also has suggestions for businesses to remove unwanted mail.

89. Shop at salvage supermarkets for substantial discounts on over-stocked items. The products are usually inspected and are damaged, over manufactured, mislabeled, or about to expire. For a list of stores, go to andersonscountrymarket.net/directory.

90. Compare prices in different supermarket aisles or cases. You may find that the prices vary for the same or different sizes (per ounce) of the product.

91. Compare prices by using smart phones to scan bar code labels. You will need to download apps such as ShopSavvy.

92. Get free firewood by contacting tree cutters or builders (don't burn treated wood like plywood, some beams, particle board, and glue-lams).

93. Share tools like weed whackers, leaf blowers, and lawn mowers by cooperatively buying with friends. Of course, all must share equally in maintenance or maybe one person could contribute no money in exchange for overseeing the maintenance.

94. If you have multiple lawns to mow, maybe you can negotiate a bulk discount with a provider or pay one of your neighbors less than the cost of a service.

95. Save on funerals. Donate your body to science. Contact major university medical schools which normally will have small or no charges.

96. Housework is a good work-out. Consider foregoing the gym cost, the lawn care service, and the maid (we should all be so lucky) and do the work yourself. These tax free savings are particularly valuable.

97. When you cook, do large batches and freeze some. Every year

I cook a large batch of game birds in a pressure cooker for tenderness. Then I make about 15-20 servings of wild bird vegetable soup using produce from the farmer's market.

98. Flooded basement. For occasional water in the basement, there are several actions to solve the problem. First, make sure your gutters and downspouts are clear and that the downspouts are either connected to a **working** drain or that they shed water away from the house (preferably five feet away and downhill). Additionally, the dirt from the uphill side of a foundation can be removed and water proofing applied to the concrete foundation wall.

Water problems can occur for a house sitting at the bottom of a hill. To solve this problem, dig an 18" deep (or deeper) trench at the base of the hill, put plastic on the bottom (and up to the top on the side facing the house and two inches on the other side), and fill it with drain rock, sloping it away from the house. More serious problems may require a sump pump or an excavation along the uphill side of the foundation footings. In the latter case, you may need to put perforated plastic drain pipe along the base of the foundation and cover it with drain rock to channel the water along the base of the foundation and away from the house.

Once, I solved a water problem caused by not having a roof overhang in which water was blown against the house during heavy downpours. I created a downward slope away from the house and covered multiple layers of plastic with decorative rock.

99. Non food products are often cheaper in the discount stores than in grocery stores.

100. Consumer Reports found that some female oriented products are up to 50% more expensive than men's. Two examples are blade razors and over-the-counter menstrual pain relievers (which have the same ingredients as male oriented pain drugs).

101. Be crafty when returning products. I returned some "burned out" seven year guaranteed fluorescent floodlights purchased at a big box store three years ago. When I returned them, the clerk insisted that the original package was needed. So I picked up some new bulbs, cut open the packages, and handed them to her.

102. Buy goods through GoodShop.com which connects to over 1,000 retailers and donates an average of 3% of the purchase price to your favorite charity.

103. Start your own babysitting co-op, preferably with neighbors, work colleagues, and friends. It can be formal with rules and a board or simply small and informal. The most important issues are having a safe environment, fair and balanced scheduling, and sickness and behavior rules.

104. Be cautious about joining large class action lawsuits. I have joined a number only to receive token gifts, small vouchers for airfare requiring me to go to an airline office to buy tickets, and other stuff that was useless or required me to buy more products to receive a discount. Many class action lawsuits seem designed to line the pockets of lawyers who agree to an effectively low settlement for the defendant company in exchange for large attorney fees.

105. Buy used DVDs, CDs, and VHS tapes or rent them. The latter are particularly cheap because most people have switched to DVDs. I purchased 100 VHS tapes and 15 DVDs on Craigslist for $50 and another 129 DVDs for $120. These movies were mostly blockbuster, "chick-flick," and action movies with 2 ½ stars or better rating.

Renting DVDs on-line is extremely easy. Netflix, for example, has 100,000 movie titles that can be delivered postage free each way in one business day for 95% of people. It has deals ranging from their "two a month" deals for $4.99 to $16.99 per month for to their "three at a time" specials. Their higher priced deals include free access to 12,000 movies and TV shows via a Netflix device or your computer. Of course, you can rent them at rental stores, McDonald's (for $1 movies), some food stores, or your local library (possibly get them free).

If you subscribe to a movie channel package, you may wish to note how many movies in a month are watched and calculate the cost per movie. You may find it is cheaper to use "pay per view" for each movie which usually costs $1.99- 4.99 or rent them.

106. Most people like caller ID. See if you can turn off "call waiting" and save money. It is often bundled so that may or may not work.

107. Get good professionally supervised and less expensive work at local university veterinary clinics and schools for hair styling, physical therapy, dental professionals, massage therapy, etc.

108. Bring your own drugs to avoid the overpriced hospital prescriptions and non-prescriptions.

109. Avoid battery powered toys or use rechargeable batteries.

110. Consider having Christmas or Thanksgiving early or late to avoid the travel crush and save money on gifts.

111. Many older farsighted people can avoid buying custom glasses and simply use over-the-counter reading glasses. It doesn't work for some conditions or if the eyes' corrections are too dissimilar. For the latter case, of course, you could buy two different glasses and change out the lenses. Buy online at DebSpecs.com, which has glasses up to +12 diopters.

112. Some on-line courses are free. Check at education-portal.com.

113. Save old Christmas wrapping for re-use or save the colored Sunday comics section.

114. Make your own mulch by composting and reduce yard and garbage waste.

115. Look for grand opening specials and prizes. I loaded up on fishing flies when a local Orvis store opened.

116. Get some owner's manuals free at sites like manualsonline.com or usersmanualguide.com.

117. Look for "kid's eat free" restaurants.

118. Reuse large oversized (good condition) shoe laces for holding keys or whistles.

119. Eat produce in season. Out of season produce costs more, due to less supply and greater transportation costs.

120. To avoid moving company problems, do the following:

- Stick with the major companies for interstate moves so that you have a real person on the other end to address concerns.

- Check out the business by going online to bbb.org (the Better Business Bureau) and check the number of complaints within the last 36 months.

- Use only licensed movers and ask to see their license.

- The police may be reluctant to become involved without widespread evidence of fraud. In 2005, Congress passed a law called the Safe, Accountable, Flexible, Efficient Transportation Equity Act which gives authorities and consumers more authority to go after crooked movers.

- Your best chance of recovery for damaged merchandise occurs if you check the contract's option for "full value protection." The higher the BBB rating the less likely you are to have problems. There is considerable mark-up in this insurance.

- Show all goods to the mover when he is making an estimate.

- Find out whether the estimate is binding or whether the truck needs to be weighed. If the latter, you should watch the truck being weighed before loading and check for a full fuel gauge. Then after loading, accompany them to see it getting weighed again. If the fuel tank was not full, check it again.

- If you pack, make sure to be finished when the movers arrive.

- Measure the distance that the movers will have to carry stuff to your new front door. List that on the contract and specify any extra charges for distance. Same goes if there are no elevators and the stuff must be carried up the steps.

- Make sure that the moving truck can navigate to your new house. When I moved, my new driveway was too twisty so a second truck was rented and loaded and unloaded several times. I paid the truck's driver directly for the time and the extra truck. Then the moving company owner billed me another $1,000, but I refused to pay it.

- Verify that the company you hired is going to do the move. Sometimes, a company will subcontract the work, creating another headache.

- Ask if the moving company will be using inexperienced day laborers who are more likely to damage goods. Pass on the ones that do.

- Never sign the moving agreement without reading it and clarifying your questions and don't accept a telephone estimate.

- After delivery, only sign when everything has been accounted for and any missing or damaged items noted on the moving company's paperwork. Make sure to get a copy for making a claim. If goods are missing, find out how soon a claim must be filed.

- The American Moving and Storage Association estimates that one in five moves involves a claim. That figure likely goes down as a mover's BBB rating goes up.

- The Federal Motor Carrier Safety Administration, the Department of Transportation, and the state transportation departments are responsible for ensuring the safety of the trucking industry. However, they are often understaffed and bad movers simply shut their doors and move to another location with another name. No BBB history or a being a new company is a red flag.

- Some moving companies will hold your goods "hostage" if not paid. The best defenses against this are to carefully select your mover and pay with a credit card so you can dispute charges.

- The mover's liability coverage is limited to about 60 cents per pound which is very low for almost anything. See if your homeowner's policy covers moving. If you have a high deductible, maybe you should lower it for the move.

- Another option is to rent a truck and move it yourself. In most cases, you can safely rent on-line and sometimes obtain a substantial discount. For example, Penske offers 22 percent off for AAA members booking on line.

- The biggest problem is underestimating the physical strain and the packing and loading time. One option is to hire strong kids or even moving company workers to load and/or unload your truck while you just do the driving. One nice thing about this option is that you know when your goods will arrive.

- Buy the fattest case hardened lock that will fit on the truck's latch. When traveling, always park in well lit areas, against a tree or building, or so that the truck can be seen from the hotel's front desk or an all night restaurant. Minimize the number of nights parked with a loaded truck.

- You can also use a service that delivers a container for self packing (such as Upack.com). They allow three days to pack and the same to unload.

- It is often better to sell or give your goods to charity and take a tax deduction than to ship them. Energy tax credits are available for new appliances.

- To save money, consider packing your own non-breakables. That way you can label the stuff at your leisure.

- Here are the "red flags" indicating a possible scam (some from moverscomplaints.com):

1. One estimate is particularly low.

2. Their advertising does not contain a legally required license number.

3. Their website doesn't have a local address or insurance or license information.

4. The mover has been open for only a few years (could be a new business).

5. It has changed addresses and/or names recently.

6. At the company's office, there are no trucks with its logo and license numbers painted on the doors.

7. The moving company demands a cash deposit. Most don't but it shouldn't be over 10% of the moving cost.

8. Offices and warehouses are in poor or dirty condition or non-existent.

9. The mover claims your goods are fully covered by its insurance. Actually, you must select valuation coverage and pay for it.

10. It doesn't agree to an on-site inspection and offers you an estimate over the phone or internet without seeing your goods.

11. You aren't offered a free publication called "Your Rights and Responsibilities When You Move." Unscrupulous movers don't want you to see this.

CHAPTER 12

Extreme Measures for the Ultimate Penny Pincher

This chapter is devoted to my deceased parents, the most loving and caring people on the planet. They were teenagers at the start of the depression and never forgot the lessons of conservative and frugal living. Most of the items in here would be endorsed by them.

This chapter focuses on the more extreme measures of penny-pinching which become more fashionable in hard times. However, if you are a Prada wearing, BMW driving, metro-sexual, you might want to skip this chapter which is for the truly frugal, extremely poor, or the ultra "green" environmentalists.

1. **Save the extra plastic utensils and napkins from fast food places and airlines.**

2. **If covering a bowl or anything with plastic wrap, hold it over the item being wrapped to measure it.**

3. **Don't over boil an egg as it will be reasonably hard in 6 minutes of boiling time and turn the heat down when it starts to boil.** In fact, you can turn the heat off a few minutes before completion and it will continue cooking. This is not desirable for precisely cooking soft boiled eggs.

4. **Ignore the recipe to cook pasta uncovered and cover to save heat.** Once boiling starts, turn the heat on low to avoid boiling over and stir occasionally.

5. **Use only ½ the water specified for pasta.**

6. **Don't leave water on when brushing your teeth.** Use a cup for rinsing and don't fill it up.

7. **Ignore the Crest packaging logo which shows a toothbrush with two inches of toothpaste.** Using that much is messy and requires more water. My rule is that you only need enough toothpaste to cover the width of your toothbrush, not the length of it.

8. **To squeeze all of the toothpaste out of the tube, place the tube on the counter and press with your fingers or buy one of those toothpaste rollers.**

9. **Some people use their tea bag twice in one day.**

10. **Some people are opposed to cremation, especially for religious reasons.** However, it costs far less than a casket, gravestone, and plot. It takes less time to visit an urn, and you don't use scarce earth for burial or have annual maintenance fees.

11. **Poo do, pee nee.** About 30 years ago, during a California drought, this phase became fashionable. It obviously is suggesting that you flush only after a bowel movement-BM (that term is even grosser than the suggestion).

12. **I was really, really reluctant to write about this next one, but it will save you lots and lots of headaches and money.** People often plug up the low flush toilet when taking a bowel movement (BM, also called #2). This blockage is caused by two things, namely, way too much toilet paper (TP) and/or balls of TP being too large. You can double flush and waste water and TP or do the following: Take about four squares of TP and double it into two squares. If the TP is thin, use eight sheets and fold twice. Using the end where the TP is fully attached (not the loose ends), fold about ¼ of the TP again. Take your index (pointer) finger and place in the middle of the folded up portion. Wipe and then fold another 1/4. Repeat again getting 4-5 wipes from the four sheets. This process can be repeated 2-3 more times without clogging your toilet. I have only clogged my toilet once in 15,000 BM flushes with low water toilets. Now your teenagers will have extra TP to "TP" someone's house.

13. **To unclog a toilet, use a large plunger (with about 7" of rubber). Fill the bowl to just below the rim (to create extra pressure), then plunge like crazy.**

14. **To conserve heat in the bathroom during cold weather and to make your shower warmer, plug up the shower drain with your foot or a rag.** The only down side is the additional soap residue on the shower floor.

15. **To reduce the size of the towel needed, "squeegee" your body after your shower by cupping your hands and running them down your legs, arms and the rest of your body that you can reach.** Smaller towels cost less and take less water and soap to launder.

16. **Let the most cold tolerant person take the first shower so the shower is warmer.**

17. **If your house is cold in the morning, consider taking your shower in the evening.**

18. **Use a conditioning shampoo, instead of shampooing and then conditioning your hair.** This saves water and time.

19. **Avoid conditioner/shampoo bottles with a narrow neck or ones made from hard plastic.** It takes more time getting the product out of the bottle.

20. **Here is a use for motel lotion bottles.** If your hair is dry, apply a dab to your "hard to manage" parts. This works like conditioner and is similar to Brylcreem, a popular hair product in the 1950s and 1960s.

21. **Before turning on your shower, take the lids off of your shampoo and conditioner and have everything else nearby.**

22. **When entering the garage, forgo opening the main electric door when possible and just use the manual side door.** You save electricity and garage door repairs.

23. **Change into your older, less fashionable clothes when you come home from the office.**

24. **Cut off your long pants when the knees are worn out and make shorts out of them.** Out of date clothes now look less dated.

25. **Many soup cans are of the "don't add water" type.** You can still rinse these with a little water and add to the soup.

26. **If you have multiple battery powered watches and one stops running, consider not replacing the battery until the last one stops working.**

27. **Make your dental floss last longer by leaving it connected to the container.** After pulling out about eight inches, put the container next to your mouth, If you need more, you don't have to cut another long piece, saving money and an annoyance.

28. **Buy the narrowest scotch tape available.** Using ¾ – 1 inch wide tape is usually wasteful. Your best value comes from buying a tape dispenser and then buying the large rolls.

29. **Scrap food into the garbage instead of washing plates before putting them into the dishwasher.** Alternatively wipe them with a used napkin.

30. **Men can stretch their time between haircuts.** When hair is short, blow dry and comb straight back for a fuller look. When longer, air dry and comb to the side and it will be flatter and look shorter.

31. **Have someone cut your hair.** The two biggest dangers are having your ears nicked (as my dad did to me) and a bad haircut. The latter is often the result of cutting too much off. You can also trim your own hair. Cutting around the ears is easy but cutting a half inch along the sides and back is not difficult. Comb horizontal sections down and snip off a little at the end. The little razor combs by Conair are too imprecise. Self cutting is especially easy for curly hair, just nip off the ends of the curls.

    A relative of mine uses a self cutting vacuum system by Flowbee (Flowbee.com, with vacuum, $99.90) He is so well groomed that I was shocked by his revelation. Another similar system is offered by Robocut (Robocut.com, $94.44 with vacuum). These two sites have a spirited debate on which product is the best, but my source says they are both excellent. These systems seem to work best for short hair.

32. **Dishwashers are a great modern convenience and use less water than washing and rinsing the dishes as long as they are full.** For the truly "green" person, there is an even better option. Wash and rinse your dishes in 2 separate pans with none going down the sink. Then use the gray water in toilets by dumping the water directly into the bowl flush or use it on the garden. My family recycled our dish and laundry water because our shallow wells often went dry.

33. **Don't buy multi-watt lamps unless truly needed.** They cost more and the bulbs are much more expensive. You can use single watt bulbs in multi-watt lamps.

34. **Be sure to get your free floss, toothbrush, and dental tool (with rubber tip) from your dental hygienist and ask for several.** Most hygienists want you to request their services so they are often generous with giveaways.

35. **Use both sides of your note pads.** Cross off the used side so you don't get confused.

36. **Bring home the leftover portions of your shampoo, lotion, conditioner, and hand soap from the motel.**

37. **Buy a 10-12" long spatula with a 1" wide blade to remove the "hard to reach" contents from mayonnaise, peanut butter, and jelly jars.** The spatulas with wide blades don't do the trick.

38. **Avoid dirtying another container by placing a piece of foil over leftovers in a can before refrigerating.** For that matter, you can eat directly from the original container unless it is metal and the food needs to be heated. Plastic lids that fit on cans are also available.

39. **Reuse plastic bags.** If they had unwashed vegetables or fruit in them, turn them inside out to reduce exposure to any substance on the former contents. For other bags, reuse them if they had dry contents like crackers, chips, and pretzels in them. Throw away bags that contained refrigerated products unless the contents had their own separate bag.

40. **Reuse empty dog food bags for trash and cat food and cat litter bags to pick up the used kitty litter.**

41. **Plastic bags that cover the newspaper or bread can be used for lunch or sandwiches.**

42. **Emily Post or Miss Manners would love this one.** Eat out of the microwave safe container if not too large.

43. **Make your own cheap microwave meal by filling microwave safe containers with your leftovers (sounds yummy, huh?).** Place

the container in a freezer rated plastic bag or cover with aluminum foil and freeze. When microwaving, remove any non-microwavable cover.

44. **Don't wash pots used to boil eggs.** The pot is already sanitized.

45. **Save leftover over pasta sauce from becoming moldy by freezing it with the jar placed on its side.** There is a risk of cracking from the sauce expansion, but half filled jars are usually okay. The left-over sauce can normally be reused or added to soups.

46. **When baking fish in a pan, line with a double layer of foil so the juices don't find their way to the pan.** The use of foil avoids having to wash the pan and the outer layer of foil can be reused if the juices don't leak through.

47. **Don't throw away bread crusts which are good for toast or soup dipping.** When young, my brothers and I fought over the crust from my mother's delicious homemade bread.

48. **If your bread is stale, toast it.** To freshen bread, put a few drops of water in the bread bag and microwave for 10 seconds.

49. **Eat bruised fruit first as it becomes moldy the quickest.** It is often the most vine or tree ripened and frequently tastes better.

50. **Ask the wait staff at the restaurant about the portion size.** If large, you may want to order less, take it home, or offer it to guests by saying, "I hate to see all of this delicious food go to waste, would someone like some or want to take it home." Don't be shy as either a giver or receiver.

51. **The U.S. seems to be a throw-away society that has gotten worse with affluence.** During the Great Depression, there was a saying, "Make it over, wear it out, make it do, or do without." (*The Bulletin*)

52. **Save your old shoelaces and buttons.** When I was young, we had this giant collection of buttons to use. The bottommost button and those on the sleeve are least noticeable so you don't need to exactly match them.

53. **Save those thread kits from cruises and motels.** They really save time if each color comes with its own needle. Be careful in disposing of the needles. Stick them in something solid like a melon skin.

54. **Wear similar mismatched socks in boots and higher sided shoes.** Be sure you aren't going to the doctor or the airport security area.

55. **Avoid white or very light colored shoes.** They scuff and show the dirt more quickly.

56. **When buying shoes that need polish, make sure that matching polish is available.**

57. **When empty, remove the plastic liner from the cereal box to find extra cereal.**

58. **Avoid unwanted holiday gifts by providing a list to givers.**

59. **I have tried applying powder and liquid pre-shave before using my electric shaver. However, I obtained the same results by swabbing my whiskers with water before shaving and it is gentler on my skin.**

CHAPTER 13

What you Need to Know to Buy and Maintain Vehicles

Buying New Cars

Since 1973, my wife and I have purchased 10 new vehicles. For eight of them, I paid anywhere from $3,000 below the dealer's invoice (not the window sticker) to a high of $300 over. I always told the dealer that my business was contingent upon him showing me the car's dealer invoice. Now, of course, the reader can check Kelley Blue Book (kbb.com), vehix.com, Edmunds.com, or autotrader.com to obtain this information.

Buying the car was sometimes an ordeal where the salesman would haggle for hours. Finally, I wised up and would go into a showroom knowing exactly what I wanted. My offer was given to the salesman and I gave him 15 minutes to convince the sales manager before leaving. Occasionally, it meant buying a car in a neighboring town, but mostly the method was successful.

Except for the "hottest" models, a discount can usually be negotiated, often by alerting the salesman that there were **specific** competing models and that price was the last main hurdle. Sometimes, a dealer will pretend that he only has one or two cars that fit your needs and can't possibly sell them at your price. In such cases, I patiently wait until a desired car becomes available at my price. On one luxury car, I was told that it might take a month or more to locate my preferred car. I said, "Fine" and the car suddenly appeared within a few days when another "buyer" backed out. The dealer probably traded cars with another dealer. Actual buyer prices are available from TrueCar.com.

On many new car sales, dealers receive a "hold back" from the manufacturer so that their gross profit is more than the amount of any markup for the car's dealer invoice. They may also receive special dealer incentives. Except for luxury brands and "hot" models, new cars can normally be purchased at a few hundred dollars over dealer invoice or even less with incentives and when new models are coming out. Before negotiating, scan the lot for last year's models. Higher numbers means lower prices. Remember the worst a dealer can say is, "No." Your best strategy in getting a great price is your willingness to walk away. The salesman knows that if you leave the lot, he has likely lost the sale. Give him your cell phone number and tell him you are going to make offers on other cars. If he is the only dealer for a particular brand in your area, pick out another similar competitor's brand and tell him the same thing.

In evaluating cars, one should look at any incentives such as customer rebates and low cost financing offered by the car dealer. If the low cost financing is of little interest, ask to apply the savings to the purchase price. The value of a four year zero interest rate financing deal can be estimated as follows

Length of loan = 4 years

Amount borrowed = $20,000

Monthly payment = $479 per month with normal financing

Total paid = $479 X 48 months = $22,992

Interest saved =
Total payments - loan amount = $22,992 - $20,000 = $2,992

A zero interest dealer loan would therefore save $2,992 in interest charges. For a higher rate like 2%, the savings would be less, but would be calculated by substituting the total payments for the $20,000. Of course, if the vehicle is used for business purposes and the interest charges deducted as an expense, the actual after tax savings are less. Any bank, credit union, or even a car dealer can calculate your payment under different interest rates, or you can Google "amortization calculators" on the internet.

Before accepting a dealer car loan, check with other sources to determine their rates. Credit unions often have the best rates, and some have very minimal membership qualifications. If a special dealer interest rate is offered, ask if the deal can instead include a further reduction in price. Then compare the monthly payment and interest rates from other lenders using that reduced price. No matter how good the new car deal is, your total costs of owning will be lower with a good used car. Your best option often is to keep your current vehicle.

If you expect to lose your job, don't buy a new car. If one is desperately needed, consider a good used one but rush before losing your job. Once unemployed, you won't qualify for a loan.

It is important to consider depreciation and overall costs for a given brand and model which is available from Consumer Reports' *New Car Buying Guide* or free from Edmunds.com using their "True Cost to Own" formula. The biggest cost is first year depreciation of **new** vehicles which ranges from 10% to over 33% with lots of cars in the 20-26% range. It seems to be lowest in the cheaper models (though some like Porsche and Lexus do well), those with good quality reputations, and the most popular vehicles. At Edmunds, this information is presented by model for the last five years. The financing costs shown do not include principal payments as it is assumed that the car can be sold for the purchase price minus depreciation. Edmunds also has vehicle ratings, new car comparisons, best used cars, consumer reviews, and manufacturer history.

Two other useful sites are cartalk.com and cars.com. The sites have many interesting features including expert and consumer reviews, the top cars to buy (based upon three criteria, namely, frontal and side impact crashes, reliability, and fuel economy ratings within their class), safety recalls, rebates, tax credits, currently recommended cars, vehicle donations, researching a car, Kelley Blue Book values, fuel efficiency for used cars, and buying and selling a car.

Cars.com provides a really important feature by showing the 10 best cars (and some trucks) by resale value, mileage, popularity, safety, initial quality, customer service, cash back, color, American content, and 14 best by class. They also display the 10 worst in resale value and mileage. The following table shows the 10 best and worst by resale value as determined from the *Automotive Lease Guide* and are based upon three years of depreciation.

Best Rank	Make/Model Style	Resale Value	Worst Rank	Make/model Style	Resale Value
1	Mini Cooper Hatchback	66%	1	Cadillac DTS 1SA	30%
2	Mini Cooper S Hatchback	65%	2	Ford E-150 XL	30%
3	BMW 1 series Coupe 128i	64%	3	Chrysler Sebring LX convert	30%
4	Mazdaspeed3 Base	62%	4	Mitsubishi Endeavor LS	30%
5	Honda Fit Sport	61%	5	Dodge Dakota 2WD Ext Cab ST	31%
6	Mini Cooper Clubman	61%	6	Lincoln Town Car Signature Ltd.	31%
7	Ford Mustang GT Coupe	60%	7	Nissan Titan (2wd) King Cab XE	31%
8	Madza3 s Sport sedan	60%	8	Mercury Grd Marquis LS	32%
9	Toyota Prius Hatchback II	60%	9	Jeep Commander (2WD) Sport	32%
10	Honda Insight LX	60%	10	Ford F-250 (2WD) XL	32%

The 2010 ten best are mostly small foreign models and the 10 worst are mostly large domestic ones. These figures change every year and American cars should be higher in future ratings. I checked some of these values against Edmunds.com and found them to be close to these figures for dealer trade-in. Private party sales and dealer prices would be higher.

One obvious conclusion from the above is that there are great bargains to be had from the "worst rank." If you wanted a three year old truck or an SUV, you can buy them for about 30% of their new sticker price, assuming these figures are accurate. The ability to hold car value is affected by past quality problems (many American cars and Kia) or current ones for a top brand like Toyota. Often times, the market overreacts to the problems or doesn't correct quickly for improvements in quality. Be on the look-out for great values when this occurs. Furthermore, if you plan to lease a vehicle, the highest lease rates will be for those vehicles suffering the largest decline in resale value.

Consumer Reports also has quality ratings on used cars as does JD Power at JDPower.com. *Consumer Reports* gives information by model but JD Power also reports by brand. Interestingly, three American brands; Buick, Lincoln, and Mercury, were among five that received five star ratings for 2010 in "overall dependability." That highly suggests that American cars will move up in resale value, and their more recent models are undervalued.

If you want to help American car companies, check the American content at cars.com. However, I would ignore their "American Made Index" because it factors in the sales of the vehicle. Thus, popular vehicles with less American content will score higher than those with less sales and more U.S. content. They do provide the National Highway Transportation Safety Administration's (NHTSA) ranking of cars based upon domestic content and where assembled. Those cars being cancelled are excluded. The top 10 NHTSA rank is:

Vehicle	Domestic-parts Content	Assembly Location
Ford Taurus	90%	Chicago, IL
Lincoln MKS	85%	Chicago, IL
Toyota Sienna	85%	Princeton, IN
GMC Savana 1500	82%	Wentzville, MO

Chevrolet Exp. 1500	82%	Wentzville, MO
Buick Lucerne	81%	Detroit. MI
Chevrolet Malibu	80%	Kansas City, KS
Honda Odyssey	80%	Lincoln, AL
Toyota Avalon	80 %	Georgetown, KY
Toyota Tundra	80%	San Antonio, TX
Toyota Venza	80%	Georgetown, KY

The most heavily represented American companies are Ford and General Motors while Toyota takes the top spot for foreign car makers. Just because a model is sold by an American company doesn't mean it has much American content. The Chevy Aveo is built in Korea with just 1% of American content.

Buyers interested in a "green vehicle," defined as one with the lowest carbon footprint in manufacturing and driving, should look at each new car's green rating at auto.yahoo.com by clicking on the "green center." This information was launched by Yahoo in consultation with Environmental Defense, a nationally recognized environmental organization. Each car is scored with a maximum of 100; the highest rating for 2010 is 82. The greenest cars are natural gas and electric hybrids, followed by some gasoline and diesel powered vehicles. There are 100 rated cars with the best being small ones.

One way to get a starting price for a new car is to go to Carsdirect.com where you specify make, model, and options and get a local dealer's price. Use this information to negotiate with other area dealers. When I typed in "Ford, new car dealer, Denver, CO," I was linked to lotpro.com with 18 Ford dealers listed. Each one could give an internet price, but you may wish to call some to avoid a flood of emails. Though, for those lacking the ability to hang up on persistent salesmen, deleting emails may be less time consuming and mentally draining than phone haggling. You should show all dealers at least your first offer. AAA and other outfits will negotiate for you as they have prearranged discounted prices. Personally, I prefer to haggle. Of course, always test drive your intended vehicle and maybe more than once.

One option is to buy your foreign car in the U.S., take delivery at the factory, and combine that with a vacation. Six European car manufacturers (Volvo, Audi, BMW, Porsche, Saab, and Mercedes) have had recent programs that allow that. The savings can be substantial, and the car companies may give additional funds for air travel, lodging, and meals. After your vacation, the car is shipped to you without charge, except transportation charges from the port to your home.

Most states have "lemon laws" which require the manufacturer to refund your money for some new cars that can't be fixed. Go to your state's website (such as Florida.gov) and type "lemon law." Remember to follow the required procedures such as writing to the manufacturer and giving them a chance to fix the problems. I certainly had two General Motors lemons.

One question often asked is whether to buy a discontinued brand like General Motors' Pontiac and Ford's Mercury lines or from a bankrupt vehicle manufacturer. If the firm is liquidated, you will be just another claimant in line. If the firm reorganizes, it won't be able to stay in business without honoring warranties, even on discontinued lines. There will be spare parts and people to repair them with or without a warranty for a long time. Those persons keeping their vehicles for many years are the only ones who should buy such cars, which will experience a substantial loss in value from being less in demand and harder to resell.

Car Dealer Tricks

The following are more car buying tips and car dealer tricks from caranddriver.com, editorial.autos.msn.com, and carbuyingtips.com.

- The salesman will have a worksheet with four elements: purchase price, down payment, monthly payments, and trade-in value. Focus on one item at a time and take it slow. If you show too much interest in your trade-in value, for example, he likely will raise it but then offer you a higher purchase price.

- Negotiate without regard to any rebates which come from the manufacturer and usually apply regardless of the price. Get a great price and then have the rebate deducted instead of having a check mailed to you. Be cautious if you are told the rebate is only offered to those buying certain extras.

- Don't tell the salesperson what size of monthly payment you can afford. Negotiate first on purchase price and then discuss payments **AND** interest rates.

- Delivery charges, titling fees, and some other closing costs are inevitable extras. Most other fees like undercoating, fabric and paint protection, insurance, special finance charges, and warranties are unnecessary or over-priced.

- The dealer may get an interest rate quote and then bump it up and pocket the difference. The financing contract is simply another product for sale.

- Never sign a bill of sale with blanks or terms that are "subject to bank approval."

- Never drive the vehicle off the lot until all paperwork is complete. The dealer may pretend you have a loan, let you drive it for awhile, and then advise that the deal fell through. You will be asked for more funds and charged a higher rate. This scam is used for people with bad credit.

- Ask to see the title. If the dealer owns the vehicle, he should have it. If she says that she can get it, be cautious. She may have not paid for the car yet.

- If you have a co-signer, make sure he signs on the same page as you and not on a separate sheet of paper.

- Pay off the loan on your vehicle before trading it in. This makes sure the dealer doesn't "forget" to do it. If you don't, then make sure that it says on the contract that the dealer will do it. However, if the dealer goes out of business, the loan will still be your responsibility.

- Know your credit score before buying your vehicle. Some dealers will low ball your score to convince you to accept higher interest rates.

- Dealers may say that your online bank or credit union check is no good and then offer you their own higher rate financing.

- The deal is about to close and the salesman advises you that the bank requires an extended warranty costing $1-2,000 or an extra fee to close the deal.

- "Dealer prep" or "destination charge" may be on the invoice, but the factory already pays for this service which requires about two hours. Refuse to pay it or go to another dealer.

- Never buy a dealer's car with an "As Is, No Warranty." Get at least a 30 day warranty and a guarantee in writing that it wasn't in an accident. It could have been previously wrecked, and the dealer lied about it, he didn't bother to check the database, or it may not have been registered in the records.

- If you currently have a long term car lease, don't fall for advertising that tells you the dealer will pay it off. The penalties must still be paid, and they will be rolled into a new and higher loan.

- Car salesmen sometimes hound people until they give up and buy the car. To avoid that, give them a wrong phone number.

- Ask about third parties covering warranties. If they go out of business, you will be stuck.

- Never fill out a dealer credit application if you have your own financing.

- The dealer may offer to throw in some cheap extras like floor mats with low value to divert you from the price negotiations.

- If you are told that the price is only good until the end of the day, don't believe it.

- Never write a check until the paperwork is complete and filled out.

- The following are rare but do happen. The salesman asks for a check to show your seriousness before the agreement is signed. Never fall for that. Second, the salesman goes to the manager's office and leaves his intercom on to eavesdrop. If concerned, move to a lobby area to discuss the deal. Finally, the salesman misplaces the keys to your trade-in to keep you there. You could bring two sets of keys. This trick used to be abbreviated "GTK" for Get Their Keys.

Lease Versus Purchase

The advantages of leasing are:

- You can drive a newer car that is generally under warranty.

- The down payment is usually small compared to the vehicle's value.

- For the same monthly payment, the leased vehicle will be higher valued than one financed.

Leasing a vehicle is rarely a good financial option because:

- It is much harder to evaluate than buying.

- You may drive considerably above or below the allowable amount in your contract which can be costly because of unused miles or add-on premiums for extra miles.

- Early termination may cost thousands of dollars in fees.

- You have no equity in the car at the end of the lease period.

- Payments never stop until the end of a lease.

- You can't alter the vehicle in a permanent way.

- You will be charged for excess wear and tear and every noticeable scratch which is likely to be greater than the car's drop in value.

- The advantage of buying increases after the loan is paid off.

Business users benefit the most from leasing because the lease costs are deductible. Depreciation (the decline in the car's value) is the costliest expense for a newer car, but its deduction, even for business use, is severely limited by the IRS code. However, it is fully charged by the leasing company in its rates. The IRS allowed depreciation is inadequate except for low priced cars that hold their value exceptionally well. Remember that lease terms are negotiable just like the purchase price of a vehicle.

Safety Issues

A lot of safety information is shown at iihs.org, a site assembled by the Insurance Institute for Highway Safety. Click on "Consumer Brochures" to find insurance losses by make and model. By clicking "vehicle ratings," you can enter the same vehicle information and find their crash test results, the evaluation of seat/head restraints for neck injuries in rear impacts, and the listed safety features. It also lists the top safety picks for the past four to five years.

Another excellent site is safercar.gov which is sponsored by the U.S. Government's National Highway Transportation Safety Administration (NHTSA). It includes government crash safety ratings, defect investigations, early warning reports, safety recalls (involving motor vehicles, child seats, tires, motor vehicle equipment), rollover prevention, air bags, safety latches and tethers, and tire ratings. Safety data are also available at the fee based site "consumerreports.org."

According to safercar.gov, people are 75% less likely to be killed in a rollover when wearing a seatbelt; 33% of all fatalities annually are caused by rollovers; and taller and narrower vehicles are most likely to roll over.

To locate the top 10 most stolen cars (as compiled by the National Insurance Crime Bureau), go to statefarm.com. An alternative is found at CBS5.com which features the top 25 from CCC Information Services Inc. Its data were supplied by 350 property and casualty insurers in North America.

A recent study by the Virginia Tech Transportation Institute has shown the riskiness of texting while driving. Long haul trucks were fitted with video cameras over an 18 month period. Their collision risk was 23 times greater while texting than when not. In the period just before a crash or near crash, the average driver spent about five seconds looking at their devices. At 60 miles per hour, they would have covered 440 feet or 140 feet longer than the space between the goal lines of a football field. According to a study by the National Safety Council, 28% of all accidents are caused by cell phone use (including texting).

Wearing seat belts is extremely important. The U.S. Department of Transportation estimated that 1,652 lives could be saved and 22,372 injuries prevented if U.S. seatbelt use rose from 83% (2008 figure) to 90%. Every passenger in your vehicle should be required to wear them before the car is started, and you should insist that your kids have the same policy for their passengers.

According to NHTSA, 68% of the drivers and passengers aged 16-20 who are killed at night did not buckle their seatbelts with 57% in the daytime. The nighttime fatality rate stays above 60% through age 44 and declines to 52% for ages 55-64, and 41% for those older than that. Since 83% of drivers wear seat belts, the unbuckled 17% have more than tripled their death rate. To drive the safety aspect home to teens, try getting an injured paraplegic, who did not wear a seatbelt, visit high schools.

A University of Buffalo study of U.S. automobile crashes from 2000-03 concluded that riding in the back seat is 59-86% safer than riding in the front seat, and the middle back seat is the safest (25% safer than riding next to the rear windows). For teen drivers, this would be a trade-off because the back seat rider is safer in an accident, but the driver is more likely to have an accident with back seat passengers.

Another important and touchy issue is the age of drivers and their accident rates. According to a 2007 report from the Government Accountability Office (GAO), the number of fatal crashes per 100 million miles driven based upon age is:

Age	Crashes per 100,000,000 miles
16-24	7.0
25-34	2.5
35-44	2.2
45-54	2.0
55-64	2.0
65-74	3.0
75 & up	7.7

The most accident prone drivers are the youngest and oldest drivers. However, those 65 and older, despite having high accident rates, actually have the fewest fatal crashes per driver because of less driving and the avoidance of tough driving conditions. To reduce the accident rates of older drivers, some people advocate requiring drivers (at least older ones) to renew their licenses in person. According to a 2004 study in the

Journal of the American Medical Association, this approach reduces accident rates because badly impaired drivers tend not to show up.

Pet Friendly Vehicles and Businesses

To find the most pet friendly vehicles (and information for safely transporting pets), go to barkbuckleup.com. The criteria for the top 10 selection included ease of pet and human access, ventilation, pet friendly surfaces, and accommodating kennels of various sizes. Four of the top 10 vehicles were made by Ford with another two by Chrysler. The site also rated the top airline (Southwest), the top hotel (Sheraton), and the top retailer (BassPro Shops).

Buying and Selling Used Cars

When buying a new vehicle, I never trade in my old one. To find out the true value of a potential trade-in, tell a new car dealer that you don't have any trade-in. After negotiating your best price, then ask for a trade-in price. That is the only way to gauge its true worth to the dealer. You should advise him that his price must be good or you will sell it yourself.

The two most used pricing guides are Kelley Blue Book and the National Automobile Dealers Association (NADA) guide. Dealers like to buy using the lower NADA prices and sell at the higher Kelley price. NADA now has 3 wholesale categories; "rough," "average," and "clean." At kbb.com (Kelley Blue Book), there are 3 vehicle prices. The first is the dealer asking price based upon original selling price, age, features, condition, and mileage. The second is a lower price for sales between private parties. The third is the dealer cash price or real trade in value of your car. Kbb.com also has the latest rebates and incentives, most researched cars (shows buyer interest), and a research car finder that matches your interest (price, category, mpg, and features).

Some other interesting things about this site are the ability to research title problems, ownership history, and accidents for a used car. They offer a records search through carfax.com for $29.99 for one car search, $34.99 for ten searches within 30 days, and an unlimited number for $39.99. If you are shopping for a used car, it might be worth buying this service. Sometimes cars that are flooded or wrecked are bought as salvage and resold as undamaged cars. This is illegal, but it does happen. Apparently, there are good cars with bad reports and bad cars with good reports. If in doubt, have the car investigated by a trusted mechanic.

A cheaper alternative to this search is the site **nmvtis.gov** which stands for National Motor Vehicle Title Information System. The site was created by the U.S. Department of Justice, and it links to the two providers of information, Auto Data Direct, Inc. and the CARCO Group Inc. A total of 73% of the U.S. vehicle population is represented in the site with 37 states and some salvage yards and insurance companies having some degree of participation. You can find out if a car has been stolen or has been in a flood or major accident.

Another useful site is autotrader.com which provides pricing for new and used vehicles, the top ten most popular cars, a car comparison feature, an opportunity to sell your car on-line, and a variety of other features. Also look at Autobytel.com and MSN Autos.

I have only traded one car into a dealer and it was a piece of junk. To illustrate the trade-in dilemma, a couple of years ago, I bought a new car and had a 2000 Acura 3.5 RL to sell or trade. Its original window sticker was over $44,000 and I paid about $41,000. Based upon Kelly Blue Book at kbb.com, the starting dealer asking price was $19,300, the private party sale price was $15,600 and the dealer purchase price was $13,300.

After the purchase of our new car, I questioned our new car salesman, and he thought that he could sell the Acura for at least $17,000. On the internet, similar cars were advertised as high as $24,999. I offered the car at $19,995 but did not get many calls until the price was lowered to $16,995 and then I received 12 calls in three days. The sale price was more than $3,000 above the dealer's likely offer and about $1,000 above the KBB private party price.

A used car will typically sell for 15-20% more than a dealer trade-in offer, assuming you first determine his rock bottom new car price. Dealers will often give you a high trade-in after marking the new car up considerably. They may make more money selling better used cars than the more expensive new ones. Some people still like the trade-in option to avoid having to deal with unknown people, bad checks, and complaints about the car plus the time and inconvenience.

In any case, never accept anything but cash or a cashier's check in a private party sale. If the amount is substantial, meet the buyer at the bank and watch the teller make out the cashier's check. About 15 years ago, I accepted an $1,100 personal check for a car and it promptly bounced. This local person was given three days to make it good before my call to the police. With this threat, the money was quickly replaced.

Here are some more tips for buying a used car:

1. **Look for signs that the speedometer has been rolled back or spun forward past 100,000 (for those that only go to 99,999).** Look at the condition of the seat, seat belts, and pedals. They should reflect the amount of wear on them. If the pedals are new, seats are quite worn, and the speedometer says 60,000, it may actually be 160,000.

2. **Engines should start rapidly.** Before starting it, lift the hood and feel the engine. If it is warm, the owner may have started it earlier to disguise the hard start.

3. **The idle should be steady.** Some four cylinder cars have a rougher idle than 6 cylinder ones.

4. **Check the oil change sticker.** If it has been a long time since it was changed or reflects an abnormal amount of miles or is missing, it may indicate a problem with overall maintenance. Of course, the owner might change the oil himself, just ask. The oil on the dipstick should not be unduly dirty.

5. **Check the exhaust when you start for bluish smoke and during a test run after it is warm, let off the gas for 20 seconds and then hit the accelerator.** Check the rear view mirror for smoke. Whitish smoke in cold weather is normal. That isn't the kind you worry about. You can also idle the car in park and then hit the accelerator to check the exhaust.

6. **Look at the paint under the hood to see if there are paint color differences near the fender.** It may be signs of an accident and a repaint job.

7. **Turn the lights on and after a few minutes, start the car.** The car should start easily and the lights should quickly brighten indicating that the alternator is working. It is best to point the lights toward a building or wall so the brightness change can easily be seen.

8. **Look for corrosion around the battery terminal.** A little is normal but lots indicate an old battery and a car that has not been serviced for a while. Check the warranty sticker on the battery for its age.

9. **With your foot on the brake, shift the automatic transmission between drive, neutral, and reverse.** If there is much of a hesitation, it indicates considerable wear. When driving, listen and feel the transmission shifting up and down. Watch for long shift times or clunks.

10. **Bring a pad and look at the underside of the vehicle while running.** Do you hear unmuffled exhaust leaks? I once had a 1955 Ford with a leak on the upper side of its exhaust pipe just in front of the back seat. I was driving home from college with all of my belongings when the car filled with smoke. The carpeted floor was burning and the floor was orange hot. Acting quickly, I flooded the floor with water from a creek, both putting out the fire and creating a steam bath all the way home.

11. **To test the clutch, run at high rpm's in second or third and then shift into the next higher gear, especially when going up a slight hill.** If the engine races, but the car doesn't, the clutch is likely worn out. Ideally, the clutch should have about 1-1 ½ inches of free play. When the petal is pressed, it should move easily before you feel resistance.

12. **Turn the steering wheel while parked and with the engine running.** There should be very little free play, i.e., the wheels should turn almost instantly.

13. **Drive the car with the radio off and the windows closed.** Listen for whining, clunking, vibrating, and rattling sounds.

14. **Private parties are more likely to know a vehicle's history than a used car salesman.** Ask specific questions about maintenance and repair records, current problems, how long they have owned it, etc.

15. **Used car dealers won't tell you that many of their vehicles were purchased at auction or from another dealer who didn't want them on his lot.** However, one advantage of dealers is their

ability to reduce your search time and increase your knowledge about car values. It may be worth visiting some car lots just for the education. The best option is to buy a two-four year old, highly rated, one owner car from a private party.

16. **Never pay for a car without obtaining its title or pink slip to make sure the vehicle is not stolen.**

17. **Be leery of a private seller that won't meet you at his home.** You may want to copy his driver's license number and birth date. Also note the license number of the vehicle she is driving.

18. **Your safest choice is to pay a mechanic $100 for an analysis.** Ask to see any certified checklist from the selling dealer and make a copy for the mechanic to review. Certified vehicles will cost an average of about $1000 more than similar non-certified ones (CNW Marketing Research Inc.) because they have undergone detailed inspections and usually come with a warranty. Their warranties are essentially the same (with possibly a few more items) as any other dealer's "built-in" warranty. Frankly, I would use the $1,000 for repairs and skip the warranty..

19. **The best prices are often in December and January because people have spent much of their available funds for Christmas, and in cold climates don't want to shop.**

20. **Some cars are more popular and therefore overpriced in certain areas.** Foreign cars are more in demand in coastal states as compared to the Midwest. When gas prices are higher, gas hogs are in less demand.

Financing Your Vehicle Purchase

One of the key strategies for lowering your interest rate is to improve your credit score which is discussed in Chapter 6. Don't assume that any particular source of financing is cheapest. When calling lenders, know your credit score so that you can get a phone quote. The last place to check is the dealer. You want to walk into his showroom with your quotes in hand. Check out the following financial institutions:

- The banks where you have checking and/or savings accounts
- Credit unions, often the cheapest

- Mutual savings banks

- On line banking such as myautoloan.com, moneycentral.msn.com, Eloan.com, and Capitalone.com.

Most on-line banking sites will give one or more no obligation quotes. However, they require your social security number, and too many credit checks can lower your credit score. One way to use the on-line services is to call their toll free lines, tell them your credit score, and ask for a quote. If they refuse, hang up.

Probably my favorite website for providing detailed information such as a specific lending institution, phone number, and interest rate is moneycentral.msn.com. When checking loans, ask about the rate and monthly payment for specific maturities. The cheapest interest rate is usually for 36 months and often 48 and 60 months are the same with another jump at 72 months. It is not advisable to go beyond 60 months because of the higher rates and to avoid having a vehicle's value become less than the loan balance.

How Long Should You Keep Your Vehicle?

The most economical approach is to keep your car for 10 or more years. I have owned three that long and one for 21 years that was recently traded in during the "Cash for Clunkers" Program. I have only been stranded once in 48 years of driving when a spark plug fell out. There were a couple of close calls when I was either near a repair shop or knew how to fix a problem. Most cars and trucks today will last 250,000 miles if properly maintained.

Keeping a car for a long period lowers your insurance premium because your vehicle value falls. When it is 7-8 years old, consider dropping the collision insurance which pays for vehicle replacement. You also are likely to have paid off your car loan by then. Your main costs for a newer car will depend somewhat on how many miles you drive, but include depreciation, fuel, insurance, and financing. As your car ages, all of these costs will drop except fuel costs and repairs which will go up. Nevertheless, your savings will dwarf these increased costs. The fuel economy of a properly maintained vehicle shouldn't drop very much. After 21 years, my 1989 Trooper got the same gas mileage and had the same compression ratio as when it was new.

The main drawbacks to keeping an older vehicle are that the safety equipment on newer vehicles has been improved, emissions reduced, dependability increased, and fuel economy enhanced. When selling a used car, the first interval worth considering is the 36,000 mile mark at which higher maintenance costs usually first appear, but these are much smaller than the drop in other costs.

At 60,000-90,000 miles, depending on driving habits, your risk tolerance for a breakdown, and your vehicle, you may want to change your water pump and timing belt (at the same time), perhaps some fan belts and hoses, and replace the battery and fluids (rear-end and transmission). In my 1989 Isuzu Trooper, no fan belts or hoses were ever changed though they were checked regularly. A mileage of 100,000 seems to be a psychological barrier that makes a car harder to sell.

Finding Good and Honest Mechanics

Bad reputations tend to get around. When I find a mechanic who tells me that some work isn't necessary or that it can be done later, then chances are that this person is honest. Of course, you need more than honesty, you need a good repairman.

After moving a few years ago, I needed to find a mechanic. The easiest thing to do is go to the yellow pages, but that is not the ideal route. The best advice is to ask locals, especially a parts dealer. I went to a Schuck's store and asked to speak privately with the manager. He may have multiple loyalties because he sells parts to various automobile repair shops. I basically asked him if he owned my make and year of car, where would he take it to obtain good and honest work at a fair price. The recommended mechanic was the best one that I have ever found.

Later on when some auto body work was needed, I asked the good mechanic for his advice. I got bids from his suggested source and two others. His recommended shop yielded the lowest price, the work was excellent, and he told me which businesses to avoid. The AAA website (aaa.com) also has mechanic recommendations.

You have three problems in selecting a mechanic, namely, knowing whether a mechanic is knowledgeable, honest, and fairly priced. The solution is to get referrals and estimates if you still feel uncomfortable. Various studies have shown that a substantial percentage of repairs were unnecessary, not done, or completed improperly.

Consumer Reports provides some insight into whether independent repair shops or dealerships are best. It surveyed 349,000 vehicle owners and found that 84% were "very satisfied" with the service from the independents and 77% from the dealerships, a gap of 7 percentage points. The difference was even greater when an actual repair was done with the independents getting the highest rating 75% of the time but dealerships only 57%, a spread of 18 percentage points. The dealers are also on average 34% more expensive than independents according to a study done in six large U.S. cities by the Automotive Aftermarket Industry Association. The dealers were especially high priced for front brake pads and rotors, radiators, starters, and water pumps. A certification like AAA or Automotive Service Excellence (ASE) is a good indication that a mechanic has proper training and tools.

The good news for domestic dealership brands is that five of them landed in the top 10 (Buick, Saturn, Mercury, Cadillac, and Lincoln) for service and repairs. Lexus was #1. At the bottom of the list were mostly foreign makes including Mazda, Nissan, Jeep, Suzuki, and Volkswagen (last place).

If you have a written estimate, go to repairpal.com for repair prices gathered from thousands of shops around the U.S. They will also email repair quotes for your specific vehicle, have user ratings for repair shops, latest service bulletins, answers to common questions, user reliability ratings, and an online account can be set up to show your repair records and to offer maintenance reminders. I was pleased to find that my repair shop had the highest rating in my city.

My Repair Horror Stories

Let me mention some of my bad experiences. As a college student, I took my cute Corvair with a floor shift in for an oil change. The next day the mechanic called and said he could not get it into gear. The most likely reason was that he had disconnected some linkage, but it is possible that one of the workers had been driving it. I paid $125 to have it fixed, but should have stopped payment on the check and alerted the Better Business Bureau, the Chamber of Commerce, the State Attorney General's office, and the parent company as it was one of the major oil company stations. Make sure the mileage is written down on the repair order to determine if anyone has been driving it (other than occasional necessary road tests).

On another occasion, I purchased a new 1978 Chevrolet that had two serious problems. First, the car would surge forward while driving. I took the car to a dealer (not the one from whom it was purchased), and he returned it without fixing the problem. I took it back and suggested he call the regional office to determine how to fix it. This time the surge problem was corrected, but the car used 25% more fuel and smelled like rotten eggs.

When contacted, the dealer suggested patience. Eventually, I tore the carburetor apart and determined that he had drilled out its jets. On older cars, the fuel was feed into the engine through small holes at the base of the carburetor. By enlarging the jets, he had seriously violated rules from the Environmental Protection Agency. He admitted the illegal tampering, paid me $350, and changed the oil and spark plugs. I should have forced him to buy the car.

The second problem with the same car is that five new clutches wore out in 40,000 miles, averaging 8,000 miles per clutch. I should have tried to apply some lemon law statutes to the defect and hired an attorney. When I wrote to General Motors' corporate headquarters, I was advised that my driving style was at fault. In my 46 years of driving mostly stick shifts, I had never replaced a clutch. My theory is that the rear end gear ratio was wrong.

This experience and the next one help explain why General Motors lost more than half of its U.S. market share in the past few decades and went bankrupt. Despite this bad experience, I actually bought another new Chevrolet in 1982. It was a station wagon with a six cylinder engine which began stalling at stop lights in the first three minutes of driving. There was a five year guarantee on the emission system and the problems started about three months before it expired. However, I ignored the problem and went to have it fixed after the warranty ran out.

I tried several auto shops with no success. The problem was that the carburetor was running too lean until the engine warmed up. Finally with great reservation, I took the car to the same dishonest Chevrolet dealer mentioned above and personally spoke with him. I had hoped that he would treat me differently and would have amended his errand ways. Boy was I wrong.

I called the dealer after a couple of days and asked if the car was fixed.

He said no and that there was a strong gasoline smell in the car. About a quart of gas was in the crankcase with the oil. The gas certainly was not in there when it was delivered. I later asked several auto shops about this event, and the only logical explanation is that the gas was deliberately added. It appeared to be an attempt to damage the engine by diluting the oil. In fact the engine was damaged. The car had never used any oil but now a quart had to be added every 1,000 miles.

I immediately pulled my car out of there and changed the oil. I then took the car to a Chevrolet dealer in another town, explained the stalling problem, and told him to keep the car as long as needed. He kept it for five weeks. I paid him and as I was driving down the road, it stalled at 20 miles per hour, causing a loss of power steering and brakes. Needless to say, my money was refunded in full.

Frustrated, I went home, got a paper clip and a piece of elastic, hooked it to the carburetor valve, and the problem was solved. Despite one apparently dishonest dealer and about three months of attempted repair, I fixed the problem in 20 minutes for 15 cents. Unfortunately, my wife was so unhappy with the vehicle that she refused to ever drive it again. Despite having owned six General Motors cars, the last episode ended my relationship with them. My message here is that if you have misgivings about any car or dealers, look elsewhere.

My last sad tale involves car dealers who push unneeded products on to unsuspecting consumers. As part of most oil changes, the hoses and fan belts are examined for bulging and aging signs. During my 45 years of driving, I have never had a hose or fan belt break. However, a new dealer convinced one woman to change every hose and fan belt even though the car was only three years old with about 25,000 miles on it.

Taylor Vehicle Purchases to Your Needs

Sometimes we invest (yes, invest) in vehicles that are rarely used. I have been through that with a jet boat and an RV. Before you buy that "toy," consider the whole range of costs as found on Edmunds.com "True Cost to Own." Do you really need that extra vehicle or several large ones? Also, who is going to drive it? Do you want your teenager with a high potential accident rate driving a vehicle that rolls over more easily (many SUVs), has lower crash ratings, a higher repair incidence and theft rate, poor traction, and no airbags. You can get the information for these factors at the websites mentioned in this chapter.

Speeding and Tickets

I can't encourage you to speed though most Americans do it. In times of economic distress when town budgets are under great pressure, and some police forces are in danger of budget cuts, some jurisdictions will issue more citations.

It is especially important to watch your speed and driving in small towns. About 14 years ago, I was towing a new boat purchased in Lewiston, Idaho through Colton, Washington, a small town in southeastern Washington. The boat was being towed to Pullman, Washington, about 35 miles away. I was given a ticket for not having a transit permit and another for not having adequate mirrors on the towing vehicle. The fines totaled about $200. After researching the law, it was clear that the mirror requirements were vague so I went to traffic court and the fines were reduced to the cost of a transit permit or $12.

One option regarding tickets is simply to say that "I did the crime, so I'll do the time." However, we are so dependent upon our autos for travel that this approach may be very costly. You should consider fighting most traffic tickets if there is a reasonable case for a reduction. Some states, like California, mandate insurance rate increases for certain types of tickets or others like New York charge more with multiple offenses. In addition, some ticket points can result in canceled insurance; placing a person into a high rate insurance program, restrictions on who can drive your vehicles (like your children), major insurance rate increases, or a license suspension, causing extra expense and inconvenience and possibly the loss of your job. Thus, you could pay for the ticket in multiple ways.

Here are some ways to avoid tickets or get them reduced (consult your attorney).

1. **Don't drink or do drugs and drive.** In some states, a DUII can be issued even if you pass a "breathalyzer" test if the officer feels you are impaired.

2. **Avoid driving when in a state of unusual emotional shock, have a really high fever, and/or have any other substantial impairment.** Such people are inattentive to their driving.

3. **Regularly check the lights on your vehicle.** Having burned out lights encourages cops to stop you.

4. **Obey the law.**

5. **Don't carry a loaded gun in your vehicle unless you have a concealed weapons permit and unless you do, keep any guns in the cargo area and unloaded.**

6. **Use cruise control to limit your speed.** Many people get caught speeding because of inattentive driving, especially in more powerful vehicles and going down a hill. In many states, you aren't exempted from tickets even while passing another vehicle. Whenever I encounter a speed trap when walking or see a policeman in a store, parking lot, or on a ski lift, I often ask about what speed over the limit triggers a ticket. Invariably, you need to be at least 12 mph over the limit, but less during inclement weather and in some small towns. However, some officers have a ticketing threshold of 15-20 mph over the limit.

   One of my friends received a ticket for going five mph over the limit on an interstate highway. He had his foot amputated and was driving with a prosthetic foot. The judge found his exaggerated sympathy letter compelling and the ticket was dismissed. There was a funny side to this story. The traffic on the interstate was travelling about eight miles per hour over the speed limit and we were not quite keeping up with the flow. Since we were splitting the driving, I had offered (about 10 minutes earlier) to split the cost of any speeding ticket. He declined the offer.

7. **When an officer has stopped you, place both hands in a visible location on the steering wheel.** Always carry your insurance card and produce it and your driver's license as soon as requested.

8. **An officer is more likely to issue a ticket to uncooperative or disrespectful drivers.** I think saying "Yes, sir" or "Yes, officer" is a good start. As a professor, I remember how good it felt when the military or ROTC students came into my office and were so courteous.

9. **Apologize for your actions and try to be sincere.**

10. **Most jurisdictions have guidelines about handling traffic stops and whether tickets are discretionary.** In fact, most officers have made the decision about issuing a ticket before approaching your vehicle. If you have a legitimate excuse for speeding or being distracted, then it may help to say you just got laid off, have diarrhea, are a single unemployed mother, your house is in foreclosure, are going through a divorce or your long-term relationship just ended, just lost a loved one, have massive medical costs, just got an organ transplant, had a yellow jacket in my car, were on the way to the emergency room, your house just burned down or was robbed, are having a bout of salmonella poisoning, can't support your family if you lose your license, are living on unemployment, etc. At 20 mph over the speed limit, any appeal is likely to be ignored unless you were going to the emergency room. Additionally, the officers have likely heard every conceivable story, and the chances are poor that an appeal will succeed.

11. **Barring a good excuse, your best approach is probably to indicate you were going with the flow of traffic.** This situation is in fact what happens to many people. Then apologize, apologize, and apologize. Unfortunately for men, being an attractive female driver apparently helps with some male officers. About 20 years ago, I had three very sexy co-ed tenants who told me they had never gotten a ticket, despite having been stopped a number of times. Apparently, the officer's radar was not focused on their car.

12. **If all else fails, plead for a warning citation or a ticket below your actual speed.** If he is unsympathetic and he starts to write up for a ticket for the full speed, ask to see the locked speed on his radar gun and when he last had it calibrated. Once you make these last requests, you will likely get the ticket unless he has failed to take these actions. I think it is a legitimate question to challenge a ticket if the officer can't show you the locked speed.

13. **One helpful thing is that points for tickets are usually not transferred from one state to another.** Check to see if your home state is notified about out-of-state tickets and from which states.

There are some defenses that work in traffic court. First, you may have been cited under the wrong code. I once had a fine thrown out because of being cited for making a u-turn on a green arrow at a traffic light.

There was no green arrow.

On another case, I requested a hearing and both the policeman and I delayed the trial. When it stretched beyond 90 days, the judge dismissed the ticket because the delay exceeded the statutory requirement for a timely hearing. If the policeman doesn't show up for the hearing either because he is too busy, it's his day off, he forgot, or he is on vacation, the judge often will dismiss the case though some jurisdictions allow the officer to leave a written statement.

Once, when speeding, I used a legitimate defense by telling the officer that the car was brand new, much quieter, and more powerful than my old clunker. Though true, this didn't work even though several officers have told me that they sometimes let people go with this explanation.

In another case, I was cited for parking over one hour in a "one hour" zone near Washington State University in Pullman. The ticket was deserved, but the police allowed a fraternity to park its fire truck there in two spaces for days at a time. I called the officer and pointed out this "uneven justice." He stated that they had no other place to park it, and he wouldn't rescind the ticket. Thereupon, I asked him how he and the city would respond to a front page article and picture about the fire truck in the local newspapers, and complaints to the mayor, the city supervisor, and the city council. His tone abruptly changed and the ticket "disappeared." The fire truck was moved onto the fraternity's property.

In another case, my wife was given a ticket for going 40 mph in a 25 mph zone during rush hour. It was unlikely that she was going that fast at the point where the ticket stated the infraction occurred. I hired a student to ride in my car while driving past the site about 10 times at the time listed on the ticket. Because of traffic congestion, I was never able to achieve 40 mph. The student provided a notarized statement about his observations. It is possible that the officer had pointed his radar a quarter of a mile up the road where the traffic speeds were faster, and his radar clocked another vehicle going in the other direction.

Most speedometers are off a little bit simply based upon tire wear and a ticket may be suspended or reduced for that reason. You would need some proof either by hiring someone to check your speedometer or doing your own test between road signs and possibly tying it to brand new tires or oversized tires. You also may have success with the following arguments or strategies if you have a sympathetic judge:

- Speed trap was at the bottom of a long hill. I knew one judge who dismissed every such case until the police stopped putting their radar traps there.

- Town makes its living off of speed traps.

- As previously mentioned, just got a new car and it is quieter and faster than my old one.

- Judges want to be fair and impartial, but he might have sympathy for adverse events just mentioned in #10. Some proof would be helpful, if available. The judge has heard thousands of excuses and some people are liars. However, other judges might say, "Been there, case dismissed or more likely, fine reduced."

- Going to traffic school.

- If you can determine the judge who will hear your case, attend his trials a few days early and see what appeals work or what information is needed.

- Calibration on the radar gun wasn't up to date.

- You asked to see the radar gun's locked speed, and the officer wouldn't show it to you or it wasn't there. Some of the newer radar automatically lock in the speed.

- The radar caught me when passing. Though this may not be a legitimate defense, a judge may still reduce the ticket.

Speed and Red Light Cameras

These can be permanently mounted or mobile. To find the former ones, go to speedtrap.org where users identity locations of them. Some radar/laser detectors can sound an alarm for GPS locations of fixed cameras. A few defensive court tactics include asking for the camera's service and calibration records and indicating that the picture of a license plate doesn't indicate who was driving. However, a judge is likely to ask who was driving and whether you will testify to that.

The Worst Traffic Ticketing States

Various studies (Wagner/Garrett and Makowsky/Strattman) do suggest that giving tickets not only generates revenue but also reduces traffic accidents. Rankings for the traffic ticketing by states from worst to best was developed by the National Motorists Association based upon 17 criteria including speed traps per capita, freeway speed limits, helmet laws, and restricted cell phone use (which I favor). The rankings of the states from worst to best are:

Rank	State	Rank	State	Rank	State	Rank	State
1	New Jersey	14	California	27	Missouri	40	Wisconsin
2	Ohio	15	Michigan	28	Texas	41	Utah
3	Maryland	16	Vermont	29	Oklahoma	42	So. Dakota
4	Louisiana	17	Maine	30	Nevada	43	Indiana
5	New York	18	Florida	31	Georgia	44	Minnesota
6	Illinois	19	Pennsylvania	32	Connecticut	45	No. Dakota
7	Delaware	20	North Carolina	33	South Carolina	46	Kentucky
8	Virginia	21	Alabama	34	Iowa	47	Nebraska
9	Washington	22	Rhode Island	35	Hawaii	48	Montana
10	Massachusetts	23	West Virginia	36	Arkansas	49	Idaho
11	Colorado	24	New Hampshire	37	Alaska	50	Wyoming
12	Oregon	25	Arizona	38	Kansas		
13	Tennessee	26	New Mexico	39	Mississippi		

Eight of the top ten worst states are densely populated states in the east, and the best states tend to be lower population states in the west or mid-west.

Aggressive Driving

According to the NHTSA, one third of all accidents and 67 percent of fatalities are linked to aggressive driving. Everyone should report the license number, make, model, and color of vehicles driven by aggressive and DUII type drivers. Parents should also advise their kids not to "give the finger," shout obscenities, or react to these drivers, but simply to report them. Aggressive driving is thought related to low self-control personality traits of sensation-seeking, anger, and impulsivity. Allstate Insurance Company found that teenage female drivers are considerably more likely to drive more than 10 mph over the speed limit, drive aggressively, and talk on the cell phone than teenage males.

Money, Safety, and Environmental Saving Travel Tips

I will now include a list of activities that will save time and/or money and reduce carbon emissions (some of the last tips are from gassavers.org).

1. Make several stops during the same trip.

2. Pick the lowest carbon method of travel. *Greentips* of the Union of Concerned Scientists indicates that 75% of your carbon emissions are saved by taking the bus, one of the least expensive forms of transportation.

3. If you have multiple cars, drive, if possible, the most fuel efficient one.

4. Avoid rapid acceleration and stomping down hard when passing. A properly planned pass may sometimes avoid using the passing gears. If you accelerate rapidly, your automatic transmission may go down two gears. Look ahead for slowing traffic or changing traffic signals and adjust your speed far in advance. Gradual slowing down will reduce transmission, clutch, and break wear and will increase fuel efficiency.

With a manual transmission, shift to higher gears as quickly as possible and no later than recommended by your owner's manual. Shifting less quickly wastes fuel and wears the engine somewhat more due to the higher rpm's of the motor. I usually shift up about 5-10 mph faster than the owner's manual suggests as long as the car isn't lugging or on a hill. Tachometers can indicate how much fuel is being wasted. At 3,000 rpm's in third gear, the car is using about 20% more fuel than a car at 2,400 rpm's in fourth gear. In my 1989 Isuzu Trooper, I shifted into 5th gear at 35 mph. Make sure you always use your overdrive gear unless pulling a heavy trailer or in mountainous terrain.

5. Idling produces carbon so if more than 30 seconds of idling is expected, shut off the engine because you get 0 mpg. Vehicles with larger engines waste more gas. Whenever picking up the newspaper or mail, talking with friends, stopping for road construction or at any drive-up window, etc., I turn off the engine. Restarting the engine does put a little more wear on the starter motor, starter solenoid, ignition switch, and battery (in conventional cars). If none of these has to be replaced during your ownership, then you have earned 100% of the fuel saved and helped the environment.

6. Keep your air cleaner reasonably clean between interval changes.
Using a vacuum cleaner or tamping the air cleaner on the ground works
fairly well. Using a high pressure air hose may enlarge the filter's holes.
Never wash a paper filter.

I never change my air filter in my cars out of warranty. However,
I won't recommend this because it would be contrary to your owner's
manual and the advice of most mechanics. The logic behind changing
air filters is that there are tiny particles that are trapped by your air
filter (that can't be blown or sucked out) so they must be changed at
least every 12,000 miles to allow air to flow freely. If that were true,
my fuel mileage would have dropped; the cars would be hard to start;
and they would run rough. None of this has ever happened. Put me
down as a skeptic of the "tiny particle" theory. I don't change air filters on my tractor (16 years now) or lawn mower either, but you must
clean them. If an oil/gas mix is used and the oil gets into the filter, I
change them.

**7. Make your car last longer by following the manufacturer's recom-
mendation for oil and filter changes.** I looked at the owner's manual
for four cars. The 1989 Isuzu Trooper recommended 12 month intervals
or 7,500 miles. A 2007 Lexus said 5,000 miles or 6 months, and a 2007
Honda Element had a gauge which gave you the amount of the useful
life left. It appears to be based on 7,500 mile intervals. I typically go
about 5,000 miles even if it takes six months. For some of my vehicles
used less than 4,000 miles per year, the interval is 12 months.

If you live in damp climates where more moisture comes into the carburetor during use, have mostly short trips, tow heavy loads, and/or
drive on dusty roads, 12 months is probably too long. The danger of
longer intervals is contaminants (including water) that degrade the oil.
However, these are mostly a function of the amount and type of use.
It is probably true that you will get a little more lifetime mileage out
of your engine if you change the oil every 3,000 miles, but is it worth
the time and money? You could save about $400 and 10-20 hours of
waiting in 100,000 miles by changing oil every 5,000 miles instead of
3,000. The short trips are worse because a cold engine uses more gas,
and usually it involves lower speeds and gears which cause the engine
to run at more revolutions per minute for each mile driven compared
to highway driving.

I have a back-up generator for my house which runs about 17 hours per year on a 20 minute weekly test run. I change the oil about every two years.

8. Make sure your tires are inflated to the car manufacturer's specifications. These are usually found on the door or door frame on the driver's side and are more specific than the tire manufacturer who usually lists the maximum allowed. Check the pressure on a regular basis to maximize safety, fuel economy and tire wear. Both over-inflation and under-inflation are bad. Over-inflation causes uneven tire wear and a rougher ride though you are likely to get better mileage, and it may blow out if too inflated. I did that on a bicycle tire and got a rude toss to the pavement.

Under-inflation causes your tires to run much hotter than normal, cuts your fuel economy, may damage your tire by undue flexing, reduces your vehicle control, shortens tire life, lengthens braking distance, and might cause the tire to separate from the rim, possibly causing an accident. I had a near accident from this very occurrence. I was passing a large semi-truck on the San Diego Freeway with my windows open while a helicopter passed overhead. By the time I realized that some of the loud noise was from a tire that had deflated, my tire had shredded and separated from the rim. Obviously I lived to tell about it.

The National Traffic Safety Administration figures that under-inflated tires account for 500,000 traffic accidents every year and a 2001 Department of Transportation study found that as many as 80% of the cars on the road have tires under inflated by 10% or more and half by 20% or more. Some new cars have automatic tire deflation warnings on the dashboard, but you can also buy special color coded valve caps from Brookstone (1-866-576-7337) that warn you. It is hard to determine if radial tires are low on air so the best procedure is to check all tires with a gauge.

9. Avoid Tire Failure and Pick the Right Tire. Based upon a 2003 study by the U. S. Department of Transportation and the NHTSA in Phoenix, it is clear that tire failures are more common in older tires with more mileage, carrying higher loads, being driven in hot climates, and at higher speeds. Exposure to sunlight and coastal climate also ages tires. Some tires had much less decline than others, especially those with higher speed ratings. Experts recommend replacing at risk tires.

However, it would seem prudent to travel slower, especially in the hottest weather and when carrying heavier loads with degraded tires.

To determine a tire's age, check the tire's four digit date code that shows the week and year of manufacture. On newer tires, the code is on the outside sidewall, but on older tires, it is on the inside. There is no magic age at which a tire should be replaced as it depends on usage and tire design. However, if you see cracks in the sidewall or the tread is down to 2/32 inch, it is time to replace them and obviously the older the tire, the more likely you are to have a problem. To determine inadequate trend depth, insert a George Washington quarter into the center of your tread with his head in first. If you can see every part of him, buy new tires.

If you live outside of the snow-belt, consider buying the same tire brand as currently on your vehicle. The manufacturer is likely to choose the most fuel efficient tires possible. Aggressive off road, snow, and water shedding tread patterns usually burn more fuel.

Install your snow tires no earlier than necessary and remove them as soon as they are not needed. Studs reduce your fuel economy, are noisy, and wreck the roads, but are good on ice, though with little advantage in snow. All season tires are the best all around value and also save the time and cost of mounting winter tires and remounting your summer tires. In addition, with two sets of tires, you may need to replace both sets prematurely due to age. In some snowy states, mud and snow rated tires are required when driving in mountainous areas.

Understanding tire inscription is useful. If a tire is rated as P195/65R15 88H, the "P" stands for passenger (tire), "195" is the width in millimeters, "65" is the ratio of height to width (aspect ratio), "R" is radial, "15" is the diameter in inches, and "88H" is the load index and speed symbol.

At safercar.gov, tires are rated by traction from AA to C, by temperature rating from A to C, and for wear rating from 0 to 800. This information is also on your sidewall. The tread wear base rating is 100 so a tire rated 400 will last four times as long as the 100 rated tire. The traction rating shows the ability of the tire to stop on wet roads, but this rating doesn't appear to translate into gripping in snow. Those with a less aggressive tread pattern have more rubber contact with the road and probably stop better on wet roads and not so well on icy roads. The following is a distribution of the tires manufactured for each rating.

Traction Rating	% of tires	Temperature	% of tires	Tread wear	% of tires
AA	3%	A	27%	500 & above	8%
A	75	B	59	401-500	20
B	22	C	11	301-400	32
C	>than 1%			201-300	25
				Below 201	15

I checked the tires on two 2007 cars. The Honda had Wrangler HP's with a tread wear rating of 340, a traction rating of A, and a temperature rating of B. The Lexus's Michelin tires had respective ratings of 440, A, and A. Since the Lexus costs about twice as much as the Honda, one is not surprised by the better tires.

Obviously, the higher rated tires will cost more, but which is the better choice? One would expect that the tires with a higher rated tread wear would also have higher temperature and possibly traction ratings. It doesn't appear to be the case. For example, Michelin Hydroedge has a tread wear rating of 800 but only a B temperature rating and an A traction rating. By contrast, the Michelin Pilot Cup with a tread wear rating of 80 has an AA temperature rating and an A traction rating. I looked at eight tire lines and couldn't find any discernible pattern nor any evidence of which tires fail the most.

Personally, here is what makes some sense. First, I would insist on a radial tire rated A for traction and never accept a temperature rating of C. If I lived in the desert southwest or another place with lots of heat and sunshine, did a lot of high speed driving in the summer, or pulled heavy loads, I would only choose a tire with a temperature rating of A.

Low mileage drivers might want to pay less and buy a lower rated and cheaper tread wear tire so that they are replaced before being too old. If you drive 4,000 miles per year, it doesn't make much sense to buy an 80,000 mile tire that lasts 20 years. The only caveat is that the better rated tire may be safer, but all should be replaced after 5-7 years according to the tire dealers I contacted. However, tires will last longer if the vehicle is parked in a garage or at least out of the sun.

Since the tread wear rating is linear (a 200 rated tire lasts twice as long as a 100 tire), a value rating for tire purchases could be developed by dividing the tread wear rating by the price. For example if tire A has a rating of 250 and costs $50, the value rating would be 250/50 or five. If tire B rates 270 and costs $70, the ratio is 3.85 so tire A is better because it offers more wear for the money.

10. Know the accuracy of your speedometer and odometer. Your speedometer reading is based upon the rotation speed of your tires. It is helpful to check this speed using marked test sections on the freeway or the white and green mile markers along most roads. When using the latter method, do this for 10 miles and keep your speed at exactly 60 miles per hour. The mile markers are not exact and I have found variations of up 1% in adjacent states using the same vehicle. I don't know if this variation was human or equipment error or some scam of road building companies.

At a constant speed of 60mph, the 10 miles should be covered in exactly 10 minutes or 600 seconds. Also check your odometer for accuracy. If it takes 10 minutes and 20 seconds (620 seconds) to cover the course, then your actual speed is 600/620 X 60 mph= 58. If your odometer reads 10.2 miles over the 10 mile course, then your odometer reads too high by about 2% (10/10.2 X 100%). To compensate for this error, fuel economy calculations would need to be lowered by 2%.

Badly worn tires will cause your speedometer to record a higher speed and your odometer to register more miles than new tires, and thus over-estimate your mpg. This happens because the old tires will turn more often than new ones. A 27 inch diameter tire with only 2/32 of tread will show a speedometer and a fuel economy reading that is about 2% higher than a new tire with 11/32 of tread. At a speed of 60 mph, that is 1.2 mph more and for 25 mpg, that is an additional ½ mpg.

Wide tires provide more traction and stopping ability and cost more but will lower your fuel economy because of extra weight and wind resistance.

11. AAA says that at speeds over 40 miles per hour, fuel economy is best when the windows are closed and the air conditioner used if needed. Open windows create drag on the car and the wind and noise tire a driver. Having just one window open would not reduce your fuel economy as much as using the AC. One option especially for those with-out air conditioning is to carry a wet wash cloth and sponge your face and hair periodically. Especially in dry climate, the evaporation really cools you off. In addition, except for contact wearers who suffer from direct air, channeling all vents to your face makes you feel cooler.

To quickly vent hot air, open all windows for a few minutes on sunny days before starting the car. Also, if you partially open windows, always open one on both sides. It greatly increases air flow. As an experiment, open the driver's window about 1-2 inches and notice the air flow. Then open the passenger's side by the same amount and you will notice increased air flow on the driver's side.

12. Driving in windy and cold conditions consumes more fuel so consider taking longer trips in good weather.

13. Don't fill up your fuel tank unless it is at least down to ¼ tank. I let mine go down to 1/8. It is a challenge in newer models because the "low fuel" light may come on when the tank has 3-5 gallons left or about ¼ of a tank. It is best to leave at least two gallons in the tank as there may be moisture or sediment in the bottom which would be sucked into the fuel filter and carburetor. If an 18 gallon tank is filled when only half full, the car is lugging around an average of 108 pounds of gas. At ¼ full (the real ¼, not the gauge reading), the average is 90 pounds or 18 pounds less. Of course, you need to regularly look at your fuel gauge or notice when the "low fuel" light is on. The exception to letting your tank carry less fuel is for rear wheel drive cars in snowy areas where you want extra weight.

14. Look on the map and take the most fuel efficient route. Freeways and major thoroughfares may offer better fuel economy with less stop and go driving (depending upon the location and time of day), and flatter terrains are also better. When possible, plan your trip so that you make right turns instead of left ones across traffic which are not as safe and often require waiting. UPS, the giant package delivery company, reduced its deliveries by 30,000,000 miles and saved 3,000,000 gallons of fuel in 2007 by doing this.

15. Save your fan motor and get better mileage by having the vent on "open" when running the heater. Most cars are actually warmer (compared to not running the fan) when the outside vent is open. However, some cars may not permit defrosting the windshield with an open vent. Conversely, you may wish to close the vent when running the A/C as the outside air makes the A/C work harder. It should be noted that some car manufacturers recommend always keeping the vent open with exceptions for blowing dust, smoke from burning fields, or exhaust fumes. Presumably, this is a safety issue to keep the oxygen level up in the car, particularly when there are smokers or lots of passengers.

16. Consider activities when there is less stop and go traffic. Maybe that means going out to dinner after rush hour or golfing early in the morning. It may mean scheduling vacations during the week or on less popular weekends.

17. Invite a friend to go with you for a day of fun. You might join a club to find others who want to share a ride.

18. If possible, vacation, do leisure activities, and work closer to your home.

19. Don't carry extra weight like tools, chains, or sand bags unless needed. I removed the two back seats of my Honda Element for better fuel economy and more space. The smaller vehicles are usually more affected by the same amount of weight because of less reserve horsepower.

Also non-permanent roof racks and carriers should be removed when not needed for long periods. Using a car top roof carrier can cut your mileage by up to 15%. Bigger vehicles with powerful engines would be affected somewhat less.

20. Consider riding coach instead of first or business class. The carbon emissions in coach class must be close to half that for business or first class.

21. Using cruise control will normally save fuel because a vehicle's speed is more constant. The exception to that is when you are driving in hilly country. Cruise controls tend to accelerate and down shift more rapidly when going uphill as compared to using moderate manual acceleration. This problem can be reduced by accelerating gently above the cruise speed. Some cruise controls will downshift several times, i.e. going from fifth gear to third.

22. Many roads have grooves worn from studded tires and large trucks. These grooved areas are usually rougher, have more potholes, and retain water. You will have slightly less tire wear, more stopping power and control, and better gas mileage by avoiding these grooved areas. On a two lane road, I typically drive on the right side of these grooves so as to be further from the adjacent lane. You should only drive within the stripped area and be alert for parked cars and pedestrians. In a four lane divided highway, I usually drive on the left side of the grooves when in the passing lane.

23. In most situations where a driver loses control, he was driving at an unsafe speed. The vehicle was being asked for more traction between the road surface and the tires than was feasible. It is important to anticipate the need for changes in speed and direction and do them gradually rather than suddenly.

24. Even though modern cars are not supposed to need a "break in" period, I still would not drive the car over 60 miles an hour or accelerate rapidly for the first 1,000 miles. Also don't drive at constant speeds during the break-in periods.

25. If a vehicle is regularly used for heavy towing (not a light fishing boat), make sure to gear down properly and change the oil more often. When towing, the vehicle consumes more fuel, thus putting more contaminates in the oil. It may also run hotter in warm weather.

26. Buy an electric car, which ignoring the purchase cost, is by far the cheapest to operate, though we don't have good numbers on repair or battery replacement costs.

27. Park where you can pull forward so you don't use gas or have to shift the transmission to back up. In a double spaced parking area where the space in front of your stall is free, this means pulling into the front space.

28. Avoid short trips, especially in cold weather, because your oil is stiffer, requiring more fuel to drive the pistons, and the engine runs richer, necessitating more gas.

29. Don't warm up your car in winter, but accelerate slowly in really cold weather. If your windshield gets covered in frost, place a cheap cover over it. Scrape all windows before starting the vehicle.

30. Use window shades to block the heat build-up in summer when parked to reduce A/C use.

31. Don't use premium gas unless the owner's manual specifies it. Otherwise, you are just throwing your money away. If you use premium gas, some stations carry it without ethanol at a greatly inflated price.

One hundred percent ethanol gets only about 2/3 the mileage of straight gasoline. According to the National Highway Traffic Safety Administration, 100% ethanol has 34% fewer BTUs than gasoline. The ethanol requirement is one of the most costly, environmentally damaging, and consumer and taxpayer wasting laws ever enacted. Even at 10% ethanol and 25mpg, you lose about 1 mpg in each gallon of gas. Ethanol costs more to produce and has tax subsidies so you pay at both ends of the pump. Ethanol might be more feasible and desirable if produced from byproducts like tree harvesting waste though supply problems might exist.

32. Avoid extended warranties because on average you will be dollars ahead to put the payments in a bank account and purchase the repair directly. This includes new cars and any aftermarket service being offered. The reason is that profit margins on the warranties are high, and there may be fine details like requiring lots of maintenance that is time consuming and expensive. Don't respond to telemarketers trying to sell extended warranties. The federal government is suing Voice Touch Inc. and Transcontinental Warranty Inc. who are responsible for a wave of one billion "robo-calls" trying to get consumers to extend expiring vehicle warranties.

33. Don't overfill your crankcase with oil. It can damage the seals, gaskets, and your air cleaner. Check the owner's manual for the correct amount. The wrong dipstick or one that is not fully inserted may give an incorrect reading. Use the motor oil specified in your owner's manual. Most oil change places won't look in your owner's manual so know that ahead of time. If the oil grade is too heavy, the car will use more fuel. If too light, it causes more engine wear. Always check your dipstick after commercial oil changes to insure that your vehicle wasn't under or overfilled. My mechanic says not to use synthetic oil unless you do from the start. I tried putting a quart in my Acura at 60,000 miles and it started using oil. Also, diesel engines often require different oil than gasoline engines.

34. Be careful when using a high pressure hose to clean your engine. It can force water into places that cause corrosion or electrical problems or damage fragile housing covers.

35. Unless there is lots of competition at a freeway exit, those locations are likely to have higher gas prices, especially those far from metropolitan areas.

36. Some people recommend buying fuel at night or early in the morning when it is cold and the fuel is denser. I highly doubt whether there is any effect since the fuel is in underground tanks in large quantities and daily temperature movements in the tank would be slight. If there is any effect, it would be after a week or so of prolonged cold.

37. Avoid filling up on the week-ends or holidays when there are long lines which cause you to idle your vehicle and waste your time.

38. Check the gas prices in any area by going to gasbuddy.com. Gas prices can vary considerably by location and state. For example, the best fuel prices in Las Vegas, Nevada are about 20 cents cheaper per gallon than in Los Angeles, California. Similarly, Newark, New Jersey's gas prices are about 35-40 cents a gallon lower than in Manhattan, a part of New York City. Fuel prices are worth considering when travel planning. In general, the southern and midwestern states seem to be the cheapest. Locations for alternative fuels like compressed natural gas or biodiesel can be found at altfuelprices.com.

An alternative and fun site is AAA's fuelcostcalculator.com, which figures the cost of fuel for a trip based upon your make and model.

39. Instead of waiting in a fast food drive through, park and go inside. This usually saves time and fuel. In fact, be courteous and turn off your engine at the "drive thru" windows so the attendant doesn't breathe fumes containing carbon dioxide, nitrogen oxide, and volatile organic compounds.

Also, don't idle your car when waiting for children at school. They breathe 50% more air per pound than adults and their developing lungs are more susceptible to damage from pollutants. Pollution worsens asthma and that is the most chronic problem in school children.

40. Share a ride. Join a car pool. You can join a carpool and offer or get a ride at eRideShare.com. Back in the 1960s, I picked up almost every hitchhiker in sight including women traveling alone because I hitchhiked hundreds of times myself. In addition, Penn State had a bulletin board to post your name for sharing a ride. I once had four people sign up to ride with me when my front left wheel suddenly developed a terrible shimmy causing me to drive only 35 miles per hour. The trip was 300 miles long and it took three extra hours, but they all elected to go. Now, most people including me, never stop for hitchhikers due to the danger.

ERideShare offers a number of safety tips which makes ride sharing safer such as copying picture ID's, meeting in a public place, calling him back at the phone number given, and asking for references. I would also email the make, model, color, and license number of the vehicle to a friend and advise the driver of your actions.

Other sites worth checking out include ridester.com, goloco.org, zim-ride.com, NuRide.com, and craigslist.com (click "community" and then "rideshare"). The first two charge a fee of about 10% based upon the driver's price. There may be an insurance issue if passengers are charged so check with your agent.

41. Fix dents to make your car more aerodynamic and keep its value.

42. When gas prices get high, inquire about free gas offered by hotels and motels. Just search the web by entering "motels, free gas promotion." You might also inquire at destination places as well or the Chamber of Commerce in that location.

43. Take the train or bus, ride a bike.

44. The U.S. Government has a website called fueleconomy.gov. It includes tax incentives on new vehicles, the lowest gas prices in each major city, a discussion of alternative fuel vehicles, a method to calculate your car's energy impact, and an interesting section with the current and past high mileage vehicles. The world record for a high mileage vehicle was set in France in 2005 and is a hydrogen powered vehicle called PAC-Car II that achieved 12,666 miles per gallon.

45. Make sure that your gas cap is on tight. On newer models, you will hear it click. A loose cap will cause gas to evaporate which wastes money and is bad for the environment.

46. Take advantage of the frequent oil/filter change and car wash specials. Call servicers with prominent yellow page or newspaper ads and ask to be put on their email lists. I can usually get an oil and filter change for less than $25 and often less than $20. Doing your own oil change might save $10-15, but then you must dispose of it. Hopefully, you would never dump it in the ground or down the drain. According to the Environmental Protection Agency (EPA), 200 million gallons of used motor oil in the U.S. are improperly disposed of each year. Five gallons is enough to contaminate one million gallons of drinking water. The Union of Concerned Scientists recommends the following for do-it-yourselfers:

- After draining the oil, but before removing the drip pan from under the car, close and secure the drain plug and check for leaks.

- If changing the filter, drain it for a minimum of 12 hours and combine this oil with that drained.

- Reuse your drip pan. Do not rinse the residual oil in it down the drain or into your yard. Tilt the drain pan and let the oil collect, then pour it into your used oil container. Wipe the pan out if necessary with a disposable paper towel.

- Place absorbent material like cat litter or sawdust into spilled oil and then dispose of it in the trash.

- Take used oil to a recycling center or oil change facility (the latter may not take it unless you regularly do business there). Mark "used oil" on the side with a magic marker.

47. Most accidents occur on sunny dry days (*Traffic* by Tom Vanderbilt) so it is important to drive defensively even in good weather.

48. If you live in a location that uses lots of road treatment, consider washing the underside of your car to remove harmful residue. However, driving in a couple of wind driven heavy rainstorms will probably clean your car fairly well. Favor facilities that recycle their water.

49. Periodically change your engine coolant so that your radiator works properly. I have to admit to never having changed it in my old Isuzu. My trusted mechanic said it was fine. Always use pet friendly coolant to save them from severe illness or a painful death. The coolant in your radiator should be rated for the lowest winter temperature likely to be encountered. If you live in southern California and drive to a ski area, protection is needed for far lower temperatures. Having a cracked engine block caused by frozen and inadequate coolant is costly. Coolant is also better for the A/C than all water.

50. For bad weather areas, AAA recommends that you keep an ice scraper, a blanket, a change of clothes, a collapsible shovel, a gallon of water (which may freeze), some energy bars, a small bag of sand or cat litter, and a flashlight in the cargo area. Putting these items in a trunk would be better to discourage a break-in.

51. Small cars cost more to insure than large cars, primarily because of the greater injury and death rates to its occupants. This reduces some of their lower cost advantage.

52. If your engine is not running properly, has a shimmy or whining sound, or backfires, have it checked out by a professional. In the past, I worked on my own cars, but they are now too complicated except for changing spark plug wires (mostly a waste of money unless the car has 150,000 miles on it), spark plugs, fuses, fuel pump, water pump, starter motor, fan belts, and a few other things that haven't changed a lot. Use the same mechanic, who will know your car and have records to show what has been done (to remind us when we forget).

53. I check my mpg at every fill-up and play a game to beat my best record for town and highway driving. One should recognize that wintertime fuel economy is lower because of a longer warm-up period, more dense air (cold molecules are closer together), and stronger winds.

54. My vehicles typically obtain 1-4 mpg better than the EPA estimates. This feat is achieved by taking my own advice. What you should realize is that my conservative driving means the oil requires fewer changes, the engine has run fewer rpm's, the transmission has shifted fewer times, the brakes are less worn, and the operating costs are lower than an average driver. That means the car will last longer.

The EPA mileage ratings have been revised lower to reflect faster acceleration, more aggressive driving, and higher speeds. At fueleconomy. gov, you can see the old and new ratings for all cars from 1985 and later. The EPA mileage estimates are produced in controlled laboratory conditions by the manufacturers using specifications of the federal government. The EPA reviews the results and tests about 10-15 percent of the vehicles in their own National Vehicles and Fuel Emissions Laboratory.

55. Teens should be carefully monitored while driving. Parents should establish written driving rules that teens sign which prohibit cell phone use (except for an emergency), drinking alcohol, eating and drinking, and more than one passenger (who should ride in the front seat). Teens are easily distracted by conversations from the back seat.

Though they might ignore what you say, setting rules and explaining the reasons for them is more likely to produce a safer outcome than no rules. A Western Washington University study shows how distracted people are when using cell phones. Only 25% of users walking across campus noticed a clown riding a unicycle while wearing a bright colored costume, a red nose, and large red shoes.

56. Save your maintenance records. This helps in selling and advertising your vehicle, and you won't forget what and when something was done. Make a copy of any receipts needed for your annual tax deductions, but keep the originals in a separate file for each vehicle.

57. Do a visual inspection of your car on a regular basis. Check the tires for bulges, uneven wear (caused by poor alignment or incorrect inflation), and sidewall cracks. Check the hoses for leaks or bulges, and check the lights and turn signals, including any trailers. I was once in an accident because my trailer lights weren't working. I was turning left and a passing car didn't realize it.

58. Don't ignore dash lights like "check engine." You will ruin the engine with continued driving if the oil pump is not working or the oil drain plug has fallen out.

59. In parking lots, try to park where only one or no cars are adjacent to yours and park on their passenger side. Lots of times the neighboring car has one occupant (the driver), and this will reduce the number of dings on your car. I like to park a few inches from a planting strip so only one car is next to mine, and my car will be positioned far enough away to allow a full door swing.

60. Keep your car under a carport or in a garage as much as possible to reduce the effects of the sun, dirt, bird droppings, and tree sap.

61. Wax it periodically and more if left out in the weather to prevent rust and preserve paint. Don't forget to clean the interior and attack upholstery stains ASAP so they don't become permanent. Vehicles in good condition are more likely to be kept longer and have higher resale value.

62. For older cars, consider using junkyard parts for replacing expensive ones like the rear-end and transmission. Inquire about the mileage on the parts and request a 30 day guarantee in writing. Most salvage yards can buy and sell on the internet or you can deal directly. Negotiate hard and check multiple sources. Getting a used intact transmission is far cheaper in both labor and materials than rebuilding a transmission. If you have a $3,000 car that may last 30,000 more miles, it doesn't make much sense to spend $2,500 rebuilding the transmission that will last another 150,000 miles when you can probably save 50% and lots of shop time.

63. Driving a car or truck is riskier than taking the bus, airplane, or train.

64. Don't buy a four wheel or all wheel drive unless needed. Except on some big engines, it lowers fuel economy by 1-2 mpg.

65. Stick shifts tend to achieve EPA mileage ratings that are 1-2 mpg better than an automatic except for a few cars like a Honda Element.

66. Larger engines have lower rated fuel economy than small ones. Going from a four cylinder to a six cylinder generally costs you about 1-3 mpg unless the six cylinder has a transmission with more gears.

67. To obtain the best fuel economy, buy a two wheel drive, four cylinder, stick shift. However, that prescription may not fit your requirements. Also keep in mind that it is harder to sell stick shift cars, especially to women. In countries with high fuel prices, stick shifts are the norm, even in buses.

68. Avoid buying vehicles that use premium gas. They are usually high performance ones with more powerful engines. You are hit twice because typically the cars also get poorer mileage. Your extra fuel cost for premium seems to vary based upon the price level of gasoline. When the national average for regular gas was $2.17, the extra cost of premium fuel for a vehicle driven for 100,000 miles and getting 18 mpg would be about $1,150, but almost $2,000 when it was costing $3.65. There are lots of nice cars that don't use premium gas.

69. Diesel prices skyrocket when demand is high. When regular was at $2.17, diesel was selling for about 9 cents more per gallon than regular, but at $3.65, the differential was 60 cents. Keep this in mind when considering the purchase of a diesel powered vehicle. One nice feature about them is being able to make fewer stops at the service station.

70. The major oil companies sometimes promote their gasoline by saying that it keeps your engine cleaner with better gas mileage because of additives. I always use discount gas and have never seen a difference in performance or mileage.

71. Use a gas card only if there is actually some savings or reward above a normal credit card including the annual fee.

72. Driving in the far left freeway lanes during "stop and go" traffic will, on average, reduce transmission shifting, clutch and brake wear, and get better fuel economy. The reason is that the right lanes are more impacted by oncoming merging and exiting lanes. Of course, there are always exceptions based upon accidents and freeway design.

73. After shutting off the gas station pump, get some extra gas by squeezing the handle and draining the hose. If the hose sags, you can lift it up and get a few more drops.

74. Special gas saving and horsepower increasing devices mostly don't work. I did see a major network special on TV about an expensive car modification car that purportedly offered such advantages. If it works, the major car companies would pay billions for it. I remain skeptical of all of them until they are proven effective through independent laboratory testing or a major car company begins to utilize them.

75. As a leftover habit from the Great Depression and gas rationing in World War II, my dad would turn the engine off and coast in neutral. There are two issues, namely, coasting in neutral and turning off the ignition. In a modern fuel injected car, fuel delivery is shut off when coasting so no fuel is used. There might be a slight bit of fuel saved because gearing does retard the vehicle some. Nonetheless, I have spoken with several mechanics who have seen transmissions ruined when coasting so that it is not worth the risk. As far as shutting the engine off, you lose the power assist for steering and braking (they still work), and there may be a possibility in some cars of locking the steering wheel.

76. If a car pulls in one direction on a straight road requiring pressure on the steering wheel to stay in your lane, then the front end is out of alignment. This costs you money in two ways, namely, your tires wear out more quickly and it reduces fuel economy. You should correct the problem unless rotating the tires fixes it.

77. Don't ride your brakes. This occurs because some people seem to have a fear of not being able to stop in time, or they follow too closely to the car in front of them. This wastes gas, wears out the brakes, and causes more transmission shifting. One cure is to use the right foot for both the brake and gas pedals.

78. Avoid being pressured to buy, sell, or trade in a vehicle. In most cases, taking your time is the best strategy.

79. Make sure any dealer incentives such as free wash jobs or oil changes are in writing.

80. High profile vehicles and especially those that have been jacked up in the air after purchase get really bad gas mileage because of the extra weight and wind resistance. The EPA fuel mileage estimates don't apply to such cars.

81. Don't top off your tank because spilled gas releases benzene and other toxic pollutants. Topping off is even illegal in some states. In addition, the extra gas will clog your vapor control system, making it inoperable. It will eventually evaporate, but be of no benefit.

82. Good products for removing scratches in your vehicle's paint are rubbing compound and GS-27 Scratch Remover. Both work on any color of paint.

83. Your warranty is not voided (by law) if an independent garage does warranty work on your vehicle. However, you may be denied reimbursement unless authorized dealers are far away.

84. Fueleconomy.gov has much information on driving, tax incentives, car comparisons, and extreme mpg.

85. Time your gas purchases for rising and dropping prices. Though service stations may use some index for pricing gas, often they raise or lower it based upon delivery prices. Find out from your gas station what its delivery days are. When prices are rising, buy the day before a delivery. When falling, buy a few days after delivery. They are likely to be lowered more slowly than raised unless the competition is offering better deals.

86. According to a study by Firestone, radial tires produced 7-10%

more fuel economy than non-radial tires which are mostly sold for trailers. If you pull a trailer frequently, consider radial tires at replacement time.

87. Don't respond to ads warning of the danger of worn shock absorbers. Obviously, they play an important role, but safe driving and carefully maintained tires are of more value.

88. Drive at moderate speeds to realize better fuel economy.

Consumer Reports reported the following mileage for three speeds on two vehicles:

Speed	Toyota Camry	Mercury Mountaineer
55 mph	40 mpg	24 mpg
65	35	21
75	30	18

The mpg for both vehicles rose by 1/3 when slowing from 75 mph to 55mph. The higher speeds put more carbon into the environment, greater wear on your car's engine, and contaminate the oil more quickly because you are dumping additional fuel through the engine for each mile driven. It is truly a tradeoff between travel time versus vehicle savings and the environment. I suspect that the mileage of those cars with six or more speed transmissions don't lose as many mpg's at higher speeds due to lower RPMs.

89. Don't tailgate to avoid rear ending a vehicle that stops quickly or does something unexpected. I have seen recommendations for staying three seconds behind the car in front. At 60 mph, that is 264 feet or almost the length of a football field. That is only practical on lightly traveled roads. Another better rule is one car length for each 10 mph. Most cars are 15-17 feet so at 60mph, that would be about 96 feet, somewhat more feasible.

90. Road hazard warranties are not worth the cost. Few tires fail unless the tread is badly worn, and then you receive only a prorated discount for the new tire based upon unused tread. My only tire failure was in 1968, and it was probably caused by under inflation.

91. If you need to move your car a few feet, put it in neutral and push it (but not on a hill).

92. Personal fuel savings are after taxes so it is worth more than the same money earned.

93. Listen to the traffic reports to avoid congested areas.

94. If your car is used regularly, use a block heater in winter so that the engine is close to optimum temperature when first started.

95. Carry loads on or in the rear of your vehicle instead of on top.

96. Reduce accessory loads such as heated mirrors, defrosters, heated seats, DVD players, and lights when safe for better fuel economy and fewer repairs.

97. Avoid wheel spinning when possible to reduce vehicle and tire wear and improve mileage.

98. Do telecommuting.

99. Use park and ride.

100. Sell unneeded vehicles.

101. Use the heater only after the engine is warm.

102. Time your stop sign approach so that you arrive just as the car ahead of you pulls out.

103. Don't waste money on gas additives that supposedly increase mileage.

104. Many cars have helpful displays which show continuous mpg or the effects of different rates of acceleration on fuel consumption. However, some displays are not accurate. I repeatedly checked a 2009 Suzuki Grand Vitara and found the reading too high by almost 7%.

105. Always leave the overdrive engaged on automatic transmissions unless you are pulling a trailer in hilly country.

106. Carry loads in your vehicle instead of pulling the extra trailer weight. It is definitely safer and more fuel efficient. If you are carrying toxic or flammable cargo, then you should use the trailer.

107. Maintain tire pressure on trailers and prefer trailers with a

profile no higher than the towing vehicle.

108. Let the safest and most efficient person drive. She follows the tips in this chapter.

109. Calming music as opposed to fast tempo or heavy metal is more likely to result in conservative driving.

110. Don't start your car until you can immediately pull into traffic.

111. Avoid parallel parking.

112. In snow, follow the tracks to reduce rolling resistance.

113. Close the sunroof to avoid drag.

114. Except when there is a tailwind, bad weather always reduces mpg.

115. If your accelerator is stuck, shift to neutral or turn the ignition off. I prefer the former because the power steering and brakes require less effort.

116. The color of your car affects your accident risk according to an Australian study. The safest color was white and the worst were black, grey, and then silver. The effect was especially pronounced at dusk and dawn.

117. Never leave any pet or person in an enclosed car to avoid death from heat exposure. An average of 37 children has died annually in the U.S. since 1998 with most being 4 years or less. A body temperature of 107 degrees F is considered lethal and children gain heat faster. There were deaths in 47 states with the highest per capita deaths in the southern latitudes. According to several studies by Professors Jan Null and Anna Gosline, the temperature gain inside a closed car is quite rapid even when the outside temperature is 72 degrees F, and the gain was about the same for all starting temperatures (72-96 degrees). The gain was 45-47 degrees in 60 minutes and 80% or 37 degrees in 30 minutes. The effect is worse on sunny days and in dark cars with dark interiors. Leaving the windows cracked had little effect.

118. If you are interested in hybrid vehicles, go to hybridcenter.org for comparisons and state and federal incentives.

119. If you want to get out of an existing car lease without paying termination fees or want to assume one without the large down payment, go to swapalease.com or leasetrader.com.

120. According to a survey by AAA, two-thirds of dog owners travel while playing with, petting or feeding their dogs. Ideally, the dog should be restrained by a harness attached to a seatbelt. Unfortunately, many dogs, including mine, will chew through all harnesses.

Note: Check with your automotive professional for confirmation and further guidance on these suggestions.

CHAPTER 14

Tons and Tons of Travel Information and Savings

I couldn't resist this Oct. 9th, 1903 quote from the New York Times regarding air travel: "The flying machine which will really fly might be evolved by the combined and continuous efforts of mathematicians and 'mechanicians' in from one million to ten million years."

Voluntary Bumping in Air Travel

Bumping, as you probably know, occurs when you lose your booked space on an airplane because the airline has sold more tickets than there are seats. They do this because people don't show up or miss connections so they make more revenue by overbooking. If you want to reduce your chances of being bumped, always reserve your seat and print out a boarding pass. Of course, do the opposite to increase your chances.

Volunteering to be bumped can be a good deal for you. You may receive cash, a discount toward another ticket, or a voucher for a round trip on that airline. I have done it a number of times. However, you should be cautious. If you are offered vouchers or a discount, ask if there are any restrictions, including expiration and black-out dates, whether they can be used on the cheapest fares, the allowable lead time for making the reservations, and whether the available seats are severely limited in number. The best award would probably be a straight dollar amount with no strings attached. The second best would be an unrestricted, non expiring ticket.

Also pay attention to the announcements. If the airline starts raising the voucher amount, immediately go to the desk and make sure the new offer applies to you. Don't assume your award will be automatically raised.

Be certain that you have a confirmed seat on a later flight and expect more including a free motel room if you are delayed overnight. If the airline doesn't use your seat, ask for your old seat or an equivalent one back.

Involuntary Bumping

Sometimes, the airline can't find enough volunteers so there is involuntary bumping. In these cases, the Department of Transportation requires the following:

- The airline gives you a written statement describing your rights and how the carrier decides who is bumped.

- If the airline arranges other transportation scheduled to arrive at your final destination within one hour of your original flight, you receive no compensation.

- If you arrive between one and two hours late (up to four hours on international flights), the airline must pay you the lesser of your one way fare or $400.

- If the arrival is more than two hours late (four hours on international), the compensation doubles to a maximum of $800.

- You get to keep your original ticket and use it on another flight. If you choose to make your own arrangements (preferable if there is an expiration on the new ticket), then you should request an involuntary refund.

- There are some exceptions and conditions to the above. For more information on some of these and other issues in this chapter, go to airconsumer.ost.dot.gov/travel tips and publications/fly-rights. This is an official site of the Department of Transportation.

For European travel, you may be able to win compensation for bumping, flight cancellations, and long delays. In 2004, the European Union passed the Air Passenger Bill of Rights. To file a claim, simply log on to EU-claim.com and fill out the brief form. There is no cost unless they collect in which case you pay 27% of the proceeds and an administrative fee.

Complaining about Poor Service and Inconvenience

When the Queen Mary left Fort Lauderdale in 2007, the ship hit a sand-bar and damaged the ship. It took three days to repair and the ship had to miss all ports on South America's east coast in order to arrive on time in Santiago Chile. The cruise line offered a 50% refund for that leg which seems generous to me since I prefer sea days. However, the passengers were "steamed" and got a full refund after the company's president flew in to meet the passengers. The point here is that sometimes if the collective complaint is loud enough, the refund will exceed the loss. I was on the second leg of the cruise and did not receive any money. Here are some other tips.

- The compensation should be commensurate with the loss. Be specific about what you want. If you think you deserve a voucher for $200 or a free round trip (hopefully unrestricted ticket), say so. Nevertheless, the airlines haven't made much money in some years so take that into consideration.

- If they lost your luggage, make a claim before you leave the airport if possible. On my two occasions of lost luggage, I wasn't required to make an "on-the-spot" list of missing items. You are entitled, up to their limit, to get full replacement cost.

- Frequent travelers will often receive more attention and compensation than occasional travelers at airlines, cruise lines, and hotels.

- If the gate attendant isn't helpful, you should write a complaint letter, again asking for fair compensation. If you don't, a letter of apology will be your reward.

- Avoid calling them "scumbuckets" and saying that you will never do business with them again. They are more likely to respond if you appear as a truly aggrieved party who will be a repeat customer.

- Reduce your likelihood of a bad experience by taking early morning flights originating at your airport (to avoid delays of planes coming from other airports and it gives additional chances to take a later flight). Have only carry-on bags and avoid connecting flights or at least allow a minimum of one hour between them (and preferably more especially to areas with snow, international flights which may take off from a far out terminal, and during holidays). Allow extra time (at least a day) when connecting for a cruise.

- If the airline's offer doesn't satisfy you, then go to small claims court where the legal rules are relaxed and attorneys are not allowed though you may consult one. However, first go to the website of the airline and look at the "contract of carriage" to see the terms of your contract with the airline. Unlike regular court, you won't be paid for your inconvenience, just your actual losses like having to pay for another flight, lost luggage, hotel, meals, taxis or auto rental, etc. If the amount claimed exceeds the small claims court limit in the state where you purchased the ticket or there is unusual "pain and suffering," then you can go to district court and also collect attorney fees if you win.

- When complaining or making reservation, keep a paper trail of persons contacted along with dates and time, and what transpired, especially if there are special requests like non-smoking, first floor, or handicap accessible rooms.

- In a discreet way, you should mention your affiliations such as AARP, AAA, your company, and trade groups. If you are deemed to be part of a larger group, you are likely to receive more attention. You could say something like "Mistakes are made but I belong to _ _ _ , and I am sure that most members including me expect them to be corrected." If the agent is resistant to provide help after that, I would not be so subtle. I would say something like, "I prefer to settle this now in a way that satisfies both of us. However, if you won't respond to my legitimate complaint, I plan to write to these organizations and request an investigation and will encourage _ _ _ to publish their findings in their magazine. My travel agency and their affiliates, as well as my many friends and family, will also be alerted."

Airline Air and Tiredness

Ever wondered why you feel tired after flying. You have the usual explanations of changing time zones, getting up early, hassles at security, sitting around the airport, and boredom. However, you can add cabin air to that list. According to federal regulations, commercial airplanes are pressurized to approximately 8,000 feet (*National Geographic Traveler*). Since most of us live at altitudes of less than 2,000 feet, we are subjected to much less oxygen than normal. This level of oxygen can cause some difficulties for people with decreased circulation due to lung, heart, and brain disease. The solution is to walk around and get the heart and lungs working, drink water, and avoid alcohol and caffeine.

The good news about airline air is about half of it comes from outside the plane and the airplanes have good HEPA filters. However, the air tends to be dry which may irritate respiratory linings.

One Way Fares

It is still surprising that you find one way fares that are the same price or higher than a round trip. I checked 13 domestic and round trip destinations on a number of travel websites and found trips to Athens and Venice where the round trip fare was cheaper than the one way ticket. If you find more expensive one way fares from the traditional sites, you should have your travel agent contact a wholesale consolidator such as McAbee Tours (1-800-622-2335).

I have tried plugging in "cheap seats", "consolidator", and "one way" fares to find the best prices to Athens and looked at many sites which scanned other sites including Expedia, Priceline, Farecast, Orbitz, Trip Advisor, ATI Flights, Airfare, CheapOAir, Budgettravelinc., Airgorilla, Kayak, BookingBuddy, Tripmania, Travelyahoo, Sidestep, and Cheap Tickets. The prices of the one-way ticket were about the same or higher than the round trip ticket. The variation in prices was quite sizable with one way coach being from $787 (including taxes and fees) to $1232. The business class ranged from about $2300 to $4690. The $2300 fare actually had coach seats for the U.S. leg.

The results of this analysis are obvious. Don't depend upon just one site, make sure the price includes fees and taxes, and check to see if the same class is used for every segment. Also consider flying two different airlines instead of one for a round trip. You may find better connections, fewer stopovers, and better prices that way.

Occasionally, a flight to a more distant city is cheaper than the shorter flight to its hub. For example, American Airlines had several direct flights from Los Angeles to Dallas/Fort Worth which cost $233 for a one-way, non-stop ticket. If you booked the same flight but listed your destination as Omaha, Nebraska, the ticket was only $141. In this case, you buy a ticket to Omaha and deplane in Dallas. Of course, you could only have carry-on or your bags would go to Omaha. If you were going round trip, you probably should buy two separate one way tickets since if you didn't show up for the Dallas to Omaha segment, your return flight might be cancelled.

The Best Deals

The best deals are going to occur on those flights with lots of unsold seats. On most travel sites, you can go through the booking process but not actually buy the ticket and see how many seats are still available. The lower prices are likely to start showing up about three to four months before departure on those empty planes. They may again occur 45-60 days in advance. If you book directly with the airline, you may be able to get a refund or a credit for the difference if ticket prices drop.

The worst prices often occur about 0-4 weeks before departure (and sometimes earlier) during certain days of the week. The best chance of snaring a last minute fare is in competitive routes. Before playing the waiting game, always check the available seats and book at least 30 days in advance unless you really don't have to fly. If the airline will match any fare drop, you can obviously book earlier. Some sites such as Orbitz will automatically refund the difference up to $250 per airline ticket or $500 per hotel reservation if one of their customers gets a better deal through them. Farecompare.com offers a number of tips for saving on airfare including (some comments added by me):

- The cheapest time to travel is the first flight in the morning, followed by the lunch hour and at the dinner hour and just after.

- The cheapest days are Wednesday, followed by Tuesday and Saturday.

- Don't forget the discount airlines including AirTran, Southwest, Jet Blue, and Virgin Airlines. Note: You need to go to the Southwest Airlines site directly as its pricing doesn't show up when searching other websites. (For Europe, discounters include Virgin Express, Air Berlin, EasyJet, and Ryanair; for Asia, check out SpiceJet, Air Asia, Tiger Airways, and Jetstar).

- Fly the cheap foreign airlines but beware of hidden fees.

- Fly the big hubs like New York, Chicago, Los Angeles, Atlanta, etc. as the increased competition keeps fares lower. However, the big hubs may mean bigger delays so check the flight and airport "on time" information sites shown later in this chapter.

You can sometimes obtain cheaper fares by booking with a regional carrier in a foreign country. Go to azworldairports.com and look at the arrivals and departures to see what airlines serve your destination city. You can find airlines that serve a region at Kls2.com, but the first website focuses on which airlines serve your preferred airport. Then go to those carriers' website. You can also check out specialized travel websites like Zuji.com for Asia and Opodo.com for Europe.

Because of computer operator errors, some airlines have unintentionally offered amazing deals. Some honor them; some don't. One option is to file a small claims court action against a defaulting airline. The results in court are mixed, but likely will favor the airlines because most state laws protect businesses when such mistakes are made (*The Wall Street Journal*).

Poor Deals

The quality of business and first service varies considerably from airline to airline. I remember a KLM flight from Amsterdam to Athens in which business class was charged. However, the seat size and spacing was identical to economy class. The meal was slightly better and they only filled two of the three seats. To avoid this kind of problem, check the type of the airplane and seating arrangements by calling the airline or in many cases, looking on its website. Also, I would recommend complaining as this sets a very bad example for others offering "business class."

Price Drops

Some websites such as Farecast.com, Airfarewatchdog.com, Travelzoo. com, ShermansTravel.com, Hotwire.com, and Yapta.com will send an alert if prices drop on your preferred airline itinerary. Unfortunately, these alerts don't always feature the best prices, and sometimes you are alerted to the same price as you were originally quoted. It appears to be partly an advertising ploy to keep that website's name in front of you.

Each of these sites has some unique characteristics. Airfarewatchdog. com, for example, features the 50 top fares of the day, allows you to pick the frequency of fare alerts, and will show numerous best prices from any chosen departure city to a host of other cities and the duration of these deals. You can also pick an arrival city to get the best prices from a variety of cities to there. This site would be very useful to someone whose travel plans are flexible and will choose the destination based upon the airline price.

Some sites like Yapta and Orbitz will either directly give you a refund if the price drops or will assist you in getting one. The airlines vary in their price reduction programs. Alaska/Horizon will give you a credit toward a future flight for the difference if contacted within 90 days of the flight's booking. On the other hand, Delta will match the fare if you find a cheaper fare within 24 hours and give you a $100 credit.

Price Increases

If you absolutely must travel by air, you shouldn't wait for the price drops. The waiting game is most dangerous if the number of available seats on an airplane isn't available online or through the airline agent. I have been stuck with higher fares when waiting more often than I have benefitted from lower ones.

Sometimes, airlines don't run sales despite many unsold seats or they may not run a special if only one leg of your flight is near capacity. That happened to me when going to Athens.

I would be especially careful about waiting too long when booking for the high season or to cities served by one or two airlines. Another area of caution is when flying to a city that is an embarkation point for a cruise ship, especially if you are flying business or first class. On the date that the cruise ship expects full payment (usually 90-120 days prior to the cruise), vacant seats often disappear quickly.

The Best Travel Sites

Consumersearch.com listed the best travel sites as follows:

Category	Site	Comment
Overall	Kayak	Searches 140 airline, travel, and other travel websites.
Discount Travel	Hotwire	Shows good clearance fares.
International	Vayama	Covers 190 countries. Lots of good info and links.
Luxury Hotel	Priceline	Best is when you bid, especially on last minute travel.

Some travel experts consider Momondo.com as the best site because it covers almost 700 sites. However, when I checked it, there was no option for business or first class travel, and you needed to return from the same airport at which you arrived. In other words, no "open jaw" itinerary was possible.

One booking site that I won't use again is Easy Click. I booked a U.S. hotel and had to pay a cancellation fee (it was disclosed) of $25. Then when I received my credit card statement, there was a 3% transaction fee. My credit card company told me that the motel was booked from Israel and so an international fee was added. I ended up getting a much better deal later at Expedia and a fantastic last minute special at the hotel. From now on, I won't book with any site that has cancellation fees or books from a foreign country.

Using a Travel Agent

Some people book all trips on line, some exclusively use an agent, and some like me, mix them. It is sometimes more frustrating dealing with a travel site though they often do have 24 hour service. Travel agents are useful to reduce stress, if you fly a lot, have a complicated multi-airline, multiple stop itinerary, or need visas.

Travel Packages

If you are looking for special deals on last minute flights or motels, you might try lastminute.com, lastminutetravel.com, and VacationsToGo.com. However, some of the deals are often the same as standard websites. Furthermore, one produced what appeared to be bait and switch. On its homepage, it listed a 4.5 star hotel in downtown San Francisco for $146. When I clicked it, a four star hotel in Oakland for $156 came up. Likewise, a four star in New York City for $122 produced a three star hotel. No names or addresses were given. They also listed $10 per night deals but after extensive searching, I couldn't find one.

Taxes

You may wish to consider the taxes levied by cities on travelers when figuring your budget. These taxes include general sales taxes and discriminatory taxes for lodging, car rentals, and meals. The five cities with the **highest taxes** and their amounts (*National Business Travel Association*) in 2009 were (based upon some assumed spending):

1. Chicago, IL $40.99/day
2. Seattle, WA $37.95/day
3. Dallas, TX $37.26/day
4. San Antonio, TX $37.20/day
5. Houston, TX $36.83/day

The five **lowest** are:

1. Portland, OR $21.49/day
2. Detroit, MI $22.37/day
3. Honolulu, HI $22.55/day
4. Fort Meyers, FL $22.91/day
5. Fort Lauderdale, FL $23.69/day

The low tax cities are in states with no general sales tax like Oregon and Hawaii or with low travel taxes like Florida. The high tax cities have both. Some cities have lower total taxes than others, but one would expect low taxes in most of the cities of Oregon, Michigan, Hawaii, and Florida and high taxes in most of the larger cities of the high tax states.

Points Exchange

Some airlines allow two people to exchange miles from one carrier to another. The service is called Global Points Exchange and can be found at Points.com. The fee ranges from 4/10 cents to about eight cents per reward point (miles) depending upon the airline and the quantity. Some major carriers including American, AirTran, Alaska, Continental, and Delta participate. Each exchanger must have a frequent flier program in both participating airlines.

When points are exchanged, your total points don't change unless the exchanger agrees to a trade of more than one to one. Before exchanging miles, you should consider using them for goods, magazines, or possibly selling them back to the issuer. Banks often offer to buy them for one cent each. In addition, you might consider buying miles instead of exchanging them so that you actually receive more miles for the money spent.

Loyalty/Frequent Flier Programs and Airline Ratings

You will get the best deals if you are loyal to an airline, hotel, or cruise line. They have an incentive to treat their best customers well. The best situation is to obtain "elite" airline status and qualify for no baggage fees, special check-in (including separate boarding lines and security), priority on stand-by, free upgrades, premium seating, lounge use, and early boarding. Loyalty may qualify you for a better rental car, a cruise discount, or on board ship credits. In hotels, you will get the best up-grade deals if you arrive late in the day for one or two days' stay or during slack periods.

If you can't get a frequent flyer seat on say Delta Airlines, try going to one of its airline partners in which you have award points. For example, Delta, Continental, Northwest, and Alaska are all partners so you may be able to book a flight through one of Delta's partners on that Delta flight. American is also a partner with Alaska but not the others just listed.

For some small airlines, you can accumulate frequent flyer miles in the name of the larger partner. I recently flew COPA Airlines and collected the miles on Continental. The advantages to this approach are that you qualify for more awards and your expiration date for miles is extended.

J. D. Power and Associates does customer satisfaction surveys (using seven criteria) among airline customers. You may wish to consider this information when traveling and choosing frequent flyer programs. The rankings carry a star rating with five stars being "among the best;" four stars is "better than most;" three stars is "about average;" and two stars is "the rest." The 2009 and 2010 rankings for traditional carriers are:

Carrier	Rating (stars) 2009	Ratings2010
Alaska Airlines	5 (2008-10 top award)	5
Continental Airlines	5	4
Delta Airlines	4	3
Northwest Airlines	3	-
American Airlines	3	3
Air Canada	2	3
United Airlines	2	3
US Airways	2	2

For low cost airlines, the ratings are:

Jet Blue	5 (2009-10 top award)	5
Southwest Airlines	4	3
WestJet	4	3
AirTran Airways	2	2
Frontier Airlines	2	2

In researching frequent flyer options, I found large differences in the number of points required for similar itineraries. Sometimes, it is the result of one airline having used up all of its cheap awards. Therefore, before committing to one or several airlines and credit cards, do the following:

1. **Decide where you most frequently travel.**

2. **Then go to Kayak.com or some other travel websites and plug in the destinations and see which airlines serve your preferred routes and offer the best prices.** You should focus on trips that are not last minute where you often pay high prices. Note which airlines have the most flight options.

3. **Now go to the airlines' websites for those serving your destinations.** Look for frequent flyer black-out dates. Most have two or three tiers of miles required, depending upon the peak travel dates and how far in advance the flight is booked. Simulate a number of trips by looking at various lead times from 90-330 days. Some airlines are more generous than others, and some will have more flight options which increase your chances of getting mileage awards.

4. **You may wish to avoid an airline with just a few desired flights serving your airport as it may eliminate or cut back on service.**

5. **Next look at the number of partner airlines.** How many of those fly to destinations you want?

6. **Now consider which credit cards you want?** Of course, you will look at interest rates, annual fee, and other factors. If you use an airline credit card, you are likely to book their cheapest award for about 15-25,000 miles while non-airline cards often require 30,000, may limit the amount paid toward a ticket, or may simply pay 1%. The airline credit cards mostly have an annual fee and the less generous cards often do not.

One strategy for picking up extra miles is to open a new credit card. Banks or the airlines often give at least half the miles needed for a flight (and sometimes all of the miles) and some like Alaska Airlines offer cardholders an annual two for one ticket coupon (second ticket costs $99).

Another approach is to cancel a credit card. Often they will come back with an offer of 10,000 to 20,000 extra miles for reopening your account. United Airlines has done it in the past, but I am not sure who is currently doing it. However, that action could have negative effects on your credit score unless the bank shows you as a continuous card holder.

7. **Next look at their mileage expiration policy.** It is more desirable to have cards where the expiration date is pushed out each time you have an activity in your account, in contrast to a set expiration date.

8. **Other tips.**

- Is there a minimum award per flight (like 500)? This helps for short flights.

- You should regularly use miles so they don't unduly accumulate in case the airline goes bankrupt (they may still honor them if they emerge from bankruptcy), the bank cancels your card and all of the miles (like HSBC did to me), the rules become more restrictive, or they drop partners (hotels, cruise ships, retailers, and other airlines).

- Remember to always use your frequent flyer number when booking a ticket and check your ticket to insure that it is there. Even after booking the ticket, you can call the airline with your frequent flyer number, enter it online, do it at check-in, or enter if after the flight (save your boarding passes).

- You can usually book awards for others but make sure to book it in the traveler's exact name as it appears on their official ID. Also, remember that birthdates are needed to book a ticket.

- If you are not a frequent flyer member when you book a ticket, you can usually join before your trip or at the check in desk. You may also be able to join after a trip and still receive miles.

- Carriers do limit seats on an airplane so remember to book early.

- There are deadlines for using most miles but they are usually extended by any activity that uses or accrues miles. If miles are expiring, buy a magazine subscription for some family member.

- Some airlines like American and Alaska allow one way awards at ½ of the round trip ticket and their one way fares are half price. This allows maximum flexibility because sometimes one can snag a good deal by combining miles in one segment with purchased tickets on another.

- To accumulate awards faster, two people might share a charge card.

Two great advantages of frequent flier miles is that you can buy tickets for others without feeling like you are using real money, and you may avoid arguing with your significant other about ticket purchases.

Some uses are much better deals than others. For example, magazine subscriptions give you much better than 1% which is at the low end of frequent flier award values and the average value of most cash award rebates. First or business class travel, upgrades, and overseas flights are usually better than 1%. Deals that take you from the east coast to Alaska, Hawaii, or Asia, from the west coast to Europe, or in less competitive routes, are usually good values.

Anything paying less than one cent per point (1%) is a terrible deal. You might as well have a cash back card. A $250 airline ticket which can be had for 25,000 points is the equivalent of one cent per point. A good deal is probably an award ticket that pays 1.5-2.5 cents. A great deal is 2.5-3.5 cents and a fantastic deal is over 3.5 cents. Every year I snag at least one fantastic deal. If you don't let points expire and you average about 1.5 cents per point, then you are generally ahead in favoring a mileage card over a cash back card. However, you should factor in the extra work to use the award miles and the annual fee.

On a recent February trip, I flew to Fort Lauderdale, Florida and came back from Orlando. I have miles in a number of different airlines. However, I waited too long after award reservations began to find the best deal (with the fewest miles). So I checked the on-time performance of various flights and the history of the wintertime performance between the various airports (discussed later). Then I booked a one way award ticket with American Airlines (for 12,500 miles) and paid $160 for a return trip through Salt Lake City (#1 rated on-time airport) on Delta. United Airlines (which didn't offer "one way mileage" tickets at half the round trip rate) wanted 25,000 miles for a one way ticket and Alaska Airlines needed 20,000 though it would have accepted 12,500 on a flight two days later. Delta wanted 80,000 miles for the segment.

Checked Baggage

Since the majority of airlines charge for luggage when booking coach, that gives everyone an incentive to pack light and use carry-ons. It also saves time picking up luggage, making claims for lost luggage, problems rerouting your luggage from a delayed flight, shopping for replacement items, itemizing lost items, and a lot of frustration and anger. If you are checking baggage, then always carry-on everything needed for two days.

One alternative is to ship your luggage by ground or air carrier which reduces hassles and lost luggage. The fees are considerably higher than airline charges. You can check them out at luggageforward.com, xsbaggage.com, and luggagefree.com. For domestic travel, I would stick with FedEx ground service which is cheaper than the other services.

Here are some more baggage tips (some from airconsumer.ost.gov):

1. **Check in for your flight by the suggested time.** Even if you are able to make your flight, your baggage may not be loaded on time.

2. **According to the Aviation Consumer Protection Division of Department of Transportation, the risk of losing a bag (or possibly damaged) is:**
   Least   Non-stop flight
                One or more stops but no change of aircraft
                Change of aircraft but not airline
   Most   Change of aircraft and airlines

3. **If you really need to avoid lost bags, try to book a non-stop flight, stay on the same airplane, or have all carry-ons.**

4. **Make sure you receive a claim check stub for every bag checked.** Ask the agent what the three letter code is for the airport to which the bags are being checked and double check that before the bags go down the conveyor belt. When you make an on-line reservation, the code will be shown.

5. **Remove straps and hooks from checked garment bags so they don't get caught in the baggage processing machinery.**

6. **Buy very colorful luggage or put big distinctive ribbons or tags**

on them so that others don't grab yours by mistake.

7. **Don't be late to the baggage claim area.** It reduces the chance that someone will accidentally take or steal your bags. Try to position yourself so that you will be among the first to claim your bags or at least see the bag coming out of the chute.

8. **Some bags seem to invite inspection.** My long duffle type bag is regularly opened, possibly to find weapons. The Transportation Security Administration (TSA) leaves a note indicating that it was inspected.

9. **If an agent feels that your luggage is unlikely to survive the trip, she should advise you.**

Lost or Damaged Luggage

Never leave the airport without making a claim for lost or damaged luggage with your last carrier. Be sure that they fill out a form with the agent's name on it. Get a phone number, not the reservation number for following up. Ask for a cash advance for necessities if away from home. Obtain the reimbursable item list and keep receipts for those purchases. Tell them you expect them to deliver the bags free of charge when found.

Except on cruises, I almost never check luggage. According to SITA which tracks baggage information for airlines and passengers in 220 countries, 30,000,000 bags are lost each year. A total of 98% of lost bags are recovered.

Some "hard core" travelers make a list of their luggage contents and **stash it in a carry-on (in case the checked bags are lost).** Consider keeping a couple of years' worth of clothing and accessory receipts or credit card statements in case verification is needed.

Keep luggage tags until your bags are found and check the contents immediately if your bags appear to be open, damaged, or unlocked. If that does occur, immediately inform the airline by phone. Make a note of the date and time of the call and with whom you spoke. Only those locks which can be opened by TSA are allowed. Use them on all checked baggage.

The airline will usually pay to repair or replace your damaged suitcase and its contents, but may insist on a depreciated value. It may refuse to pay for fragile or poorly packed items, especially if your suitcases show no external damage. The 2010 limit for lost or damaged bags is $3,300 per passenger (airconsumer.ost.gov). You may be able to purchase "excess valuation" when you check in, but the airline may refuse it for certain items.

The reimbursement limit for international flights that originate in the U.S. is based upon the Montreal Convention and is remarkably lower. The limit is 1,000 "Special Drawing Rights" (go to imf.org and type in "Special Drawing Rights") and changes daily. Currently, it is less than $700 per passenger. This limit also applies to domestic segments of international flights. You may be able to purchase "excess valuation" coverage, but your homeowner's insurance and some credit cards may provide additional coverage. The percentage of unreturned bags is so low that I always self insure.

If you are dissatisfied with your offer from the airline, you can file a complaint with the DOT at DOT Aviation Consumer Protection, 400 Seventh St., SW, Suite 4107, Washington, DC 20590. See tsaclaims.org for more details.

Carry-on Baggage

Most airlines have rarely enforced carry-on weight limits. During 2010 for the first time, I saw some passengers challenged on size (luggage that is). There is some variance in bag size allowance among the airlines, especially foreign ones. The worst case seems to be that the bag is taken at the gate and you are not charged. The size and weight limits can be found at farecompare.com.

Airlines often allow oversized carry-ons as long as they can be safely accommodated. These exceptions often include fishing poles, art and advertising portfolios, delicate scientific equipment, and human organs.

Some items may not be counted towards the carry-on allowance of one standard sized bag and one smaller personal item. These include coats, hats, umbrellas, reading material, diaper bags for ticketed children, FAA approved child/infant seats occupied by the child, wheelchairs and other mobility devices, medical supplies and small medical equipment, small musical instruments, food, and ashes in an urn. Check with your carrier's website. You and your kids can pack lighter by personally carrying these items. Those with many carry-ons to be stowed in the overhead bins should be at the head of the boarding line and should have a seat toward the back half of the aircraft. People are carrying on more bags and if the plane is full, those in the back may fill up the front bins.

Transportation Security Administration

The TSA is responsible for screening airline passengers in the U.S. and it provides a lot of information in its website (tsa.gov) about packing, things that set off metal detectors, security tips, pets, head coverings, shoes, body piercings, acceptable identification, and prohibited and allowed items. Many dangerous items are allowed in checked baggage, but most flammable, disabling, compressed, and explosive materials are prohibited. **Make a photocopy of your TSA required ID and keep it in another location away from your actual documents.** If your ID is lost or stolen, you will be still able to board.

Back-up Plans

One of my back-up plans is always to carry the name and phone numbers of my travel agent and all airlines as well as my frequent flier numbers. If the airplane is late and I'm likely to miss my connection, then I call them before leaving the aircraft. The last thing you want is to be 50th in line for rebooking. My first call would be to the airline on which I'm booked to see if the connecting flight has been delayed. Your stewardess may be able to find out. Make sure your traveling companions have a cell phone too in case you want to make multiple calls to different airlines and/or your travel agent.

Airline Fees

There are a variety of fees which airlines charge and many domestic ones can be found at farecompare.com including:

- Reservation by phone (per person)
- First and second checked bag (each way)
- Seat selection priority/leg room
- Beverage/snack packet
- Meal
- Alcohol

- Oversize bag (each way)
- Overweight bag (each way)
- Standby/confirmed seat
- Travel with pets (each way)
- Unaccompanied minor (per flight)
- Curbside check-in
- Non-refundable ticket change
- Priority boarding
- Fuel surcharge
- Checking in at the airport and not on-line
- Travel insurance (may need to opt out)
- Infant charge

Since fees change, you should check for possible changes in your airline's website. For example in 2009, Alaska Airlines allowed one free bag. The second one cost $25 and the third one $100. Then they changed their policy so that the first one was $15, the second, $25, and the third was $50. Generally, the airline will stick to the charges in effect when you purchased your ticket. Baggage fees may be eliminated for "elite status" fliers, first or business class travelers, military personnel, and specific other people. Depending upon the airline, it may be cheaper to check an overweight bag than to pack an extra one.

You may wish to consider indulging in other perks such as day passes to the airlines' VIP lounges, more leg room, and priority screening. My wife and I disagree on one element of travel. She insists on flying first or business class, and I don't think it's worth the money. On long trips from the east coast to Asia or from the west coast to Europe, the upgrade premium can be $3,000 or more. That can pencil out to about $100 per hour of flying time. For $1, I can take a generic sleeping pill in coach and not be much aware of space differences or amenities. Check with your doctor.

Credit Cards and Currency Conversion Rates

I wanted to find out the best way to spend money in a foreign country so I called several banks and AAA. When considering this issue, you need to look at the foreign transaction fees as well as conversion rates from the country's currency to the dollar. I called four credit card companies and AAA and got the following cost for a 100 euro transaction in November 2009, using either cash gotten in advance or charged on a credit card. The first four are credit card transactions.

	Conversion rate	Dollars	Trans. fee	Trans.cost	Total cost of 100 euros
Bank of America	1.487	148.70	1%	1.49	150.19
Chase	1.50	150	1%	1.50	151.50
CitiBank	1.487	148.70	3%	4.46	153.16
HSBC	1.487	148.70	3%	4.46	153.16
AAA (cash)	1.584	158.40	$7.50	7.50	165.90
Bk of Am (cash)	1.569	156.90	$7.50	7.50	164.40

All of the six above sources knew their transaction fees quickly, but getting the currency conversion rates was a little harder for some. Based upon this small sample, you should be aware of the following:

1. The credit card conversion rates shown are close to the official rates published in the *Wall Street Journal on-line*. Except for Chase, the credit card rates all appeared the same. I was quoted 1.48 by two of the banks, but I'm assuming that they simply rounded the official rate.

2. The main difference among the four credit card sources is in the transaction fee. Bank of America offered the lowest total cost on the credit cards checked. You probably will not find lower rates as Visa charges a 1% fee to the banks. The fees are not the same to every cardholder. Bank of America, for example, has cards with a 3% fee. Many banks likely offer the 1% fee to their best customers.

3. If you aren't planning to spend much overseas, then don't worry about which credit card to use. However, in a 3,000 euro transaction (about $4,500 when checked), the Bank of America card would save $90 over the Citibank and HSBC card.

4. I would look for those cards with a 1% fee, but people with lower credit scores probably won't be offered that rate. Furthermore, with banks tightening restrictions, it is likely harder to find.

5. When using cash, your deals are not nearly so good because of high fees and poor conversion rates. In my 100 euro purchase, the extra cash cost was about $15 or 10%. The $7.50 fee is for any amount so your relative transaction fee drops with higher amounts converted.

6. One problem with using cash is having to convert excess amounts back again and getting the same lousy conversion rate and fee.

Therefore, rarely use cash except for foreign businesses like taxis and small vendors.

7. Your best deals in getting foreign currency may come with debit cards using ATMs, especially if you can find an affiliate of your bank. The ATM fees may be waived, and you will likely get a good exchange rate. However, non-affiliated banks will charge fees and may offer a poor exchange rate. Check the website of your bank for foreign affiliates.

8. Cruise ships often will often carry local currency, and their rates for small amounts are reasonable.

9. Many foreign shops will accept dollars. Even with a poor conversion rate, you are often better off to spend dollars because they don't charge a special transaction fee, and you don't have the re-conversion problem. The excess foreign currency often results in another problem, spending it just to get rid of it.

Other Travel Tips

1. **Bring your cell phone charger and charge your cell phone before leaving.**

2. **If you have older folks who are a little forgetful, you may want to help them pack.**

3. **Make a list of what you want to bring and copy it for your next trip.** Start it a week before you go. For recurring trips, my preprinted list saves time and items are not forgotten.

4. **If you are thinking of bringing pets, check out farecompare.com which lists pet policies of the domestic airlines.** Some airlines don't allow pets, others won't carry certain breeds, and still others require all pets to be in the cabin. The charges can be expensive.

5. **Be courteous to other passengers and flight personnel.** It is true that you get more with honey than vinegar.

6. **Never check luggage containing anything with great monetary or personal value or something that is irreplaceable.**

7. **Fly to important events a day or two early especially to areas with inclement weather or for cruises.**

8. **If a loved one dies, ask for the last minute "Bereavement rate"** for air travel. While no great bargain, it offers flexibility, usually a discount from full fare, and the ability to change the flight without penalty. I was asked for proof when seeking one to attend my mother's funeral. The special fares are often restricted to situations involving the death of an immediate family member.

9. **Don't assume that you can't obtain a refund on a cancelled trip.** Check the airline's **contract of carriage.** Be persistent if it is due to a good excuse like the death of a close relative, a natural disaster such as a wildfire or a hurricane, or a personal medical emergency. If you anticipate a change in your flights, you may wish to book something other than the lowest non-refundable discount fares.

10. **Be flexible about dates.** You might get a better deal.

11. **When it comes to frequent flyer programs, your best deals come when you book early before the allotted cheap tickets are gone.** After that, the required miles go up. You can book 330 days in advance. Sometimes, the fares are not in the computer that early.

12. **Always check the airline's and hotel's website before booking at a travel website.** Making a change is easier with direct reservations. Airlines are often unforgiving about charging for passenger initiated schedule changes, but when my brother required heart surgery, the frequent flyer miles were reinstated without penalty. Request changes ASAP since if your hotel reservation has some likelihood of being rebooked, the business may be sympathetic.

13. **Know the cancellation policy before you book.**

14. **Repositioning cruises such as going from Europe to the Caribbean or the western U.S. to Asia offers the best price per day of sailing.** For those like me who prefer sailing days to port days, this is ideal. If traveling during cold months when storms are more likely to occur, I prefer going from west to east to reduce the chances of heading directly into the winds and the storm churned waves.

15. **There is quite a range of cruise prices** based upon cabin size and location, decks, crew to guest ratio, quality of food, size of

ship, number of port stops, tips included or not, and drinks included or not. The lowest rated ships seem to have the most last minute specials.

16. **In most cases, your best cruise fare is usually obtained when the new bookings come out** and typically you are given an extra discount for scheduling during a current cruise.

17. **Always check alternative or nearby airports which may have better weather, less traffic, lower prices, and/or fewer people.** Make sure to note the departure airport. In 1967, my wife and I took a private New Year's Eve gambling flight from Long Beach, California to Hawthorne, Nevada. When we landed on the return flight, the airport looked different at 4am after a night of revelry. We had actually landed in Burbank, a fact the stewardess had failed to mention. Fortunately, the pilot was contacted and stopped the airplane as it taxied down the runway.

18. **The cheapest flight is not always the non-stop (shorter) flight.** Look at the pricing for one more stop than your shortest route. You might save $100 or more. However, in bad weather or when you just can't afford to be late, take the flight with the fewest stops. Also the more stops, the more your checked baggage is handled unless you stay on the same flight.

19. **Fly on a major holiday like New Years, Christmas, and Thanksgiving** to reduce the delays in security lines and check-ins, minimize lost luggage, and better avoid bumping. In many years, reduced prices were offered on the actual holiday.

20. **Advanced purchase tickets from bankrupt airlines are not likely to be honored by surviving airlines.** However, where there has been a code share in which the flight was actually operated by the bankrupt airline but booked through a survivor, the ticket is likely to be honored.

21. **Always purchase your ticket with a credit card.** The credit card companies usually give you 60 days from the billing date to dispute a charge so you should be able to get a refund during that interval.

22. **Donate your "about to expire" frequent flier miles to charity**

and get a tax deduction. Use the purchase cost that the airline charges for buying miles as your deduction value, usually 2-4 cents per point. Don't forget to print off the donation sheet and the buying cost of ticket miles for your tax records.

23. **Discounted group fares for 10 or more are often available.**

24. **Be aware of Deep Vein Thrombosis (DVT),** also called "economy class syndrome" which occurs from sitting too long in a cramped space and can cause blood clots to form. The most susceptible people are those with recent surgery or injury, are overweight, have cancer or varicose veins, or who have joint problems. You should move your legs by walking or stretching, drink extra water, and if your doctor approves, take aspirin.

25. **Look for free or cheap entertainment** such as street musicians and other acts; take walks in historical locations and on beaches; and go to museums, festivals, free TV shows being taped (reserve in advance), free sightseeing (europetours.eu and globalgreeter-network.info); etc. It is worth visiting some town websites covering your itinerary and look for specials at various websites (such as Disney World and travel sites). Some travel books have coupons in them, or you may find them at your motel.

26. **Try some new locations instead of going to the same vacation spot every time.** Personally, I try to visit new cities every year. However, recurring vacation spots have several big advantages, namely, you know what to expect, can receive the best deals, and they are often less stressful than exotic new locations.

27. **Check out the conditions, exceptions, and add-ons before you book any flights, motels, cruises, and excursions.** These extra fees must be disclosed in advance, but often only on a business's website. The staff, if asked, will identify them. Look for charges for parking and valet, taxes, handling and service, add-on gratuities, fuel and energy surcharges, in room safe (even if not used), mini-bar restocking, resort usage, leaving luggage with bell staff, fax and internet, phone calls, cancellation and early check-in, deliveries, and anything the provider can get away with. If you determine them in advance, you can protest them (if applicable) before booking. However, you often have some success in avoiding them

at the front desk. The most outrageous fees that I was ever charged was a $10 local phone call fee from the Intercontinental Hotel in Athens, Greece and the $160 charge for a 30 minute water taxi ride to the Venice airport.

28. **Before booking your airfare through the cruise line, find out their airfare price and compare it against what you find on line or through your agent.** The cruise line may not get the best connections, be shunted to airports with a high percentage of delays, may not obtain the lowest price, get less desirable seats, or have longer flight times or more stops. Don't forget to add on the extra cost of ground transportation to the ship when comparing the two fares. Some cruise deals include the airfare. Ask about the discount if you book your own.

Cruise lines vary in pricing airfare. Some give good deals; some don't. I would always book my own hotels before and after a cruise because the cruise lines' mark-ups are too great. My only concern is the safety and security of ground transportation in third world countries. We solve that by booking at or near the hotel chosen by the cruise line. Then we ask the hotel to recommend the name of a safe taxi company. If you actually book through the hotel, they will likely mark the price up.

29. **Remember that the all-inclusive fare of the cruise line often doesn't include tips, drinks, spas, pictures, shore excursions, merchandise, special restaurants, etc.**

30. **Some of the food, except on the highest rated ships, is pretty ordinary**, but still acceptable for the average diner. On some ships, like the Queen Mary, you can upgrade to "grill class" for better food.

31. **Shore excursions are marked up as much as 100% by the cruise line.** Some can be purchased more cheaply by buying directly from local tour operators or you can hire a taxi to go sightseeing. If four people share a taxi, they can cut the cruise line excursion price per person by 75% or more. Make sure that you are back on board by the departure time. The ship will wait for late arrivals on a cruise sponsored excursion but not an independent one. Check out shore excursions at CruiseCritic.com.

32. **Consult your tour director on board ship or your hotel staff when going on your own in some countries.** I would always recommend going in pairs and ladies are safer with a man. My wife had a terrible experience in Istanbul, Turkey with a taxi driver. I got off at an earlier stop and she continued on alone. He basically threatened her, and she ended up giving him about $70 for a $6 trip. It is best to note the license or cab number of every taxi before getting in.

In India, we also had a bad experience. We rode a three wheeled taxi called a tuk-tuk. We asked to see the sites but were taken to shops in which the driver received a commission for any purchase. The driver bought gas and stored it in a two liter plastic bottle on the floor in this open air tricycle. When you consider the lack of traffic lights and the amount of vehicle and pedestrian congestion, this taxi was a "deathmobile."

In another situation, two of our dinner companions related how they went with a person promising "extra ordinary deals" where the locals shop. They were basically led into a "seedy" area and blackmailed into paying about $100 to be taken to the ship.

In most poor countries, there are pickpockets everywhere. My kids and I were laying on several blankets and beach towels in Acapulco, Mexico. They went down to the water, and I was laying there with a money capsule about two inches from my neck. It was silently swiped.

I have also had a number of European encounters with pickpockets. The most noticeable was in Florence, Italy. In a museum, I noticed a sign in Italian which warned of "Gypsy pickpockets." Not 50 yards from the sign, a woman thrust a baby into my chest and her hand immediately went into my back pocket. She was given a not so gentle elbow. Be careful when anyone approaches and wants you to read something or wants to be very close.

33. **Especially in poorer countries, anyone, anywhere can be robbed.** In Buenos Aires, one of my fellow cruisers was wrestled to the ground while on a daytime ship sponsored tour and his gold watch and expensive camera were stolen right in front of the screaming tour agent. Leave your good stuff at home, but even cheap imitations might encourage criminals.

34. **As part of excursions, the ship may take you to shopping centers where it may receive a cut of your expenditures.** In such cases, you are less likely to obtain the best prices.

35. **Discuss the vacation and its possible downsides with the family.** While you are expecting a lot of fun, many vacations have unexpected and stressful events like flight delays, bad tour guides, and undesirable weather. If prepared, travelers are more likely to take adversity in stride.

36. **Travel during the off season.** Some places like Hawaii, Florida, and the Arizona national parks have fairly decent weather just before or after the peak tourist seasons.

37. **Buy a $10 Senior Pass for free lifetime admission** to national parks and many Forest Service, Fish and Wildlife, Bureau of Land Management, and Bureau of Reclamation sites. The pass holder and three adults aged 16 and over are admitted free as well as anyone under 16. You need to apply in person at one of above agencies.

38. **Some airlines give discounts when luggage fees are paid online.**

39. **Most airlines charge a fee for tickets purchased by phone.**

40. **Alternatives to taking more bags may be to use a laundry service, a Laundromat, or do some hand washing in the sink.** Most cruise ships have free Laundromats though getting one sometimes requires rushing to them when they first open in the morning (or maybe just before) or while the ship is docked.

41. **You can't receive a refund for taxes and fees on an unused domestic ticket.** However, some foreign airlines apparently will refund those on foreign travel.

42. **Check with a travel agent before booking a cruise deal on the internet.** Agents, specializing in cruises, may find the same or better deal and also give some shipboard credit (a credit against which you can charge). Some cruise lines will pay cash for unused credits.

43. **On a cruise, check with the spa people to see when they offer specials.** There is always a panic to book as soon as you are on board, but you may get better deals a few days into the cruise. One option is to book early space for later in the cruise, then ask for a discount or change times if specials are announced. The specials are most common when the ship is in port.

44. **Some spa treatments are really cheap in foreign countries.** I paid $15 for a one hour massage in Bangkok.

45. **Some people like to fly on the more expensive private jets.** If you are so inclined, you might contact boutique charter services like Talon Air or XOJET (*Fortune Magazine*). You can save money if you fly on the week-ends, book an empty leg, fly on Thanksgiving or Christmas day, are flexible about the airports (that have lower landing fees), fly with strangers, or take the return flight from winter flights to Florida (for example).

46. **Check out the weather that historically occurs at your preferred travel times.** One method is to go to a city or country's web site and type in "weather" in the search box. Another method is to go to ncdc.gov, the site of the National Climatic Data Center of the National Oceanic and Atmospheric Administration. Choose "free data" on the left, then choose HCS6-4 (free data file L) for foreign data (shows the averages for 1931-60). This file lists 800 stations around the world with maximum and minimum temperatures for January, April, July and October. It also shows average precipitation for each month. From the latter, you can gauge humidity which is an important component of comfort.

For the U.S., choose file "CLIM 84 Daily Normals" (free data C) and then select the state and then PDF Format or ASCII format. The information on average temperatures and precipitation is given for each day of the year.

For current weather and predictions, go to weather.com or the airline websites. Many states also offer road condition reports and even webcams.

Sometimes you get surprised by the weather. About 15 years ago, I went to Tahiti in February. I had checked the average maximum and minimum temperatures which didn't vary much for any given month. However, the rainfall was at least 11 inches per month from December through February. It was too hot and humid for anything except swimming. A better choice would have been the less rainy months of May to October.

47. **Be careful to look for extra fees when booking overseas discount airlines.** Look for an "opt out" box on travel insurance.

48. **Double check your reservation information.** Check the dates, times, the spelling of names, and the airport. The name on your ticket should be identical to that on your government issued photo ID. Otherwise, you might be delayed enough by airline or security personnel to miss your flight or be charged by the airline for reissuing the ticket with the correct spelling.

49. **Reconfirm your flight by phone or on-line before going to the airport.** I would also print a boarding pass and check luggage by computer. You can also go to a kiosk (TV type screens) at the airport and check in to save time.

50. **Most on-line web sites, travel agents, or airline reservation assistants can tell you the make and model of your aircraft.** Some people avoid the smaller and noisier aircraft. Airlines sometimes charge for business travel when you are really getting coach seats. I flew "business class" from Amsterdam to Athens on KLM Airlines and got the same identical seat and leg room as the coach passengers. Commercial flying, even with the smaller planes, is much safer than driving. The smallest planes, especially those carrying 1-4 people, have dramatically more fatal accidents than larger planes. To view the accident statistics, go to the National Transportation Safety Board site at ntsb.gov. Click "accident and incident reports."

51. **Temporarily held reservations are usually cancelled in 24 hours (unless booked).** Make sure you have actually purchased the ticket by getting a confirmation number. Some on-line printouts look like tickets.

52. **Have your e-ticket or printed ticket in your hand before leaving for the airport.** If you don't have on-line access, then mark a note on your calendar to remind you that a ticket is being mailed.

53. **Jot down the number of your ticket and carry it separately.** If your ticket is lost or stolen, the airline can more quickly process your refund and may be able to immediately issue a replacement ticket.

54. **When changing flights, a ticket agent may wish to credit your account and then issue a new set of tickets with a second charge to your account.** To avoid future hassles, insist that the old ticket values be credited against the new ones with any difference charged or credited to your account.

55. **An airline is required by law to provide a credit to your credit card within seven business days after receiving a refund application.** If you have trouble with the airline, **write** to your credit card company within 60 days.

56. **If you anticipate that a cruise line, hotel, or airline might cease operations, I would consider other providers.** If you wait to within the 60 day period and charge it, you likely can still get your money back. Keep in mind that a bankrupt business may reorganize and then honor your reservation.

57. **Airlines are not required to compensate passengers if their flight is delayed or cancelled, only if they have been bumped due to overbooking.** There are no federal requirements about what airlines should do for delayed passengers at the airport. Each airline has its own unique policies.

58. **International travel doesn't operate on the same rules as domestic travel.** To find them, ask your travel agent or go to a provider's website.

59. **Some cities or sites offer discount tickets to attractions.** Go to citypass.com if you are planning to visit Atlanta, Boston, Chicago, Hollywood, Houston, New York, Philadelphia, San Francisco, Seattle, Southern California, or Toronto. The savings can be 40-50% of the admission price and of course, the full savings are only realized if you go to 5-6 attractions out of the normally 7-9 choices. AAA and many attractions offer discounts at their websites. Also check brochures in your lobby, travel magazines, and local newspapers.

60. **Some amusement parks allow a discount for a particular day or after a certain time of day.**

61. **Look for package deals for motels, admissions, and food.**

62. **People value experiences over the long term more than most possessions.** This was determined in a 2003 study by psychologists Thomas Gilovich and Leaf van Boven. Instead of leaving your friends and relatives a pile of money, take them on a trip. This preference for experiences likely depends upon the amount of money given and the assets of the recipient.

63. **Avoid being ripped off by a taxicab driver who takes the long route to your destination.** Go to TaxiWiz.com or TaxiFareFinder.com to calculate the cost in many cities.

64. **There are many travel related scams especially in poor countries.** Avoid giving out information about your plans or that suggests you are a rich American.

65. **Your best last minute travel deals may come from your frequent flyer programs.** Be sure to provide your email address to receive news and discount codes.

66. **When preparing to travel, lay out all your clothes and all your money. Then take half your clothes and twice the money** (Susan Heller).

67. **Some memberships like AAA and AARP qualify you for discounts on moving van and vehicle rentals, Amtrak air ambulance services, road rescues, tours, and motels.**

Trip Cancellation/Interruption/Travel Insurance

Trip cancellation insurance provides reimbursement for prepaid, non-refundable expenses (like flights and cruises), emergency expenses (such as medical), or transportation back home because of a covered reason which causes the trip to be completely or partially cancelled or delayed. Apparently, travel insurance use has risen dramatically from about 10% of Americans taking cruises, tours, and international trips before the 9/11 bombing to 30% today (*U.S. Travel Insurance Association*).

I travel regularly and have never bought trip insurance and never will. Typically, there are exclusions allowing the insurer to avoid payment. Most policies don't cover concerns about terrorism and when they do, it must occur in one of your itinerary cities close to your departure date. You likely won't collect for concerns about swine flu, sudden business problems, airline strikes or bankruptcy, or the fear of a hurricane unless you purchased one of the more expensive policies.

Coverage ranges from 5-10% of the cost of the trip, but you shouldn't purchase more than you want. Anything over 5-6% is excessive. If you skipped the insurance priced at 6%, and your hotel, cruise, and plane fare for 20 trips averaged $3,000 per trip, you would save $3,600. At 10%, you would save $6,000. Apparently, the reason that trip insurance is so expensive is that a fairly high percentage of people file claims.

Buying trip insurance seems most sensible for an expensive cruise or tour or for elderly people who are more prone to death, disease, and accidents, but have no pre-existing condition likely to be excluded. Remember that airlines are supposed to refund the money for cancelled flights if you can't be rebooked. Frankly, **self** insurance is much more cost effective in the long run than buying travel insurance.

Alaska Airlines lists the following reasons for collecting on travel insurance (my comments in parentheses):

- Serious and unforeseen illness, injury or death to you, a covered family member, or a traveling companion.

- Natural disasters or bad weather which results in a complete cessation of services for at least 24 consecutive hours (airlines and hotels may waive rebooking fees and non-refundable deposits).

- Employer termination if you have been there for at least three continuous years.

- Fire, flood, burglary, vandalism, or a natural disaster making your home uninhabitable.

- Emergency medical, dental, or transportation required during your trip. (Your regular insurance may cover these expenses).

- Travel delay. Offers reimbursement to cover additional accommodations and travel expenses due to a delay of at least six hours. (The airline might provide this also).

- Baggage delay. You can purchase essential items if baggage is delayed by at least 24 hours (the airline likely will provide some funds for this)

- Provides 24-Hour hotline help for medical, legal or travel related emergency.

There is a new travel policy out that is known as "delay" insurance which pays for hotels and meals if your flight is delayed for some specified period. For round trip tickets, it sells for $50 or less on cheaper routes. Again know the terms of your policy, but my advice is to save your $50 and put it in a fund for emergencies. You will accumulate far more than you will ever likely use, and you won't have the hassle of filing claims.

It is generally recommended that you don't purchase insurance through your cruise line or travel agent as they may go bankrupt and/or may not offer the best rates. Instead go to InsureMyTrip.com which offers 100 policies from 18 carriers. You are more likely to find a cheaper price tailored to your needs. Most policies exclude pandemics and epidemics.

Before buying insurance, check to see if your credit cards on which a trip was purchased or your homeowner's policy provides some limited coverage like life insurance or possibly medical evacuation. Another possibility is Elderhostel which includes some coverage at no additional cost. Its coverage is not likely to be very comprehensive, but might be sufficient for some people. Medicare does not cover health care expenses outside the U.S. so older travelers should make alternative arrangements.

Travel Information

The Center for Disease Control and Prevention (cdc.gov) provides a wide variety of information (including links to other sites) on:

- Most country's description

- Travel notices and advisories

- Safety and security information

- Registering with the U.S. Embassies (for long stays or in dangerous countries)

- Health and food safety tips

- Disease inoculations and symptoms

- Travel and visa documents

- Scams and crime, penalties and reporting

- Passports

- What to do after you come home

- Driver's license requirements

- Children's issues

- Country special circumstances

- Traffic and aviation safety

- Road conditions

- Medical facilities

Travelers can also receive some information on diseases and food safety from the 193 country World Health Organization (who.int), but the site is less informative and harder to use than the CDC's.

The U.S. Department of Transportation's website at airconsumer.ost. gov. has considerable relevant information. These include health tips, airline safety, filing complaints, consumer help groups, contact information, and publications of other state, local, and federal groups with concerns about safety. The others include the American Society for the Prevention of Cruelty to Animals, Better Business Bureau, Federal Trade Commission, U.S. Department of Agriculture, U.S. Customs Service, and the Department of State. You can find such varied publications as "Travel Tips for Older Americans," "Kids and Teens in Flight," "Telemarketing Travel Fraud," "Traveling by Air with your Pet," and "Accessible Travel" (for handicapped services).

Travel Scams

There are many travel scams around which offer free or unbelievable deals. Some scams are just that- you get nothing. If you are within 60 days of billing, you should be able to get a refund by notifying your credit card company in writing. Fax and send the notification. If a lot of money is involved, I would send the notice certified with "return receipt requested."

It could easily be a scam if:

- You can't leave for 70 days or so, putting the departure beyond an appeal to your credit card company.

- The deal is far better than anything else you can find from known sources.

- The seller contacts you "out of the blue."

- Caller ID shows an area code outside of the U.S. though many legitimate call centers are there.

- You are pressed to make a quick decision.

- The company has no street address.

- You must attend a seminar, buy the airfare to get the "free" motel, rent the overpriced motel room to get the airfare, and/or pay for expensive extras.

- They aren't willing to tell you the name of the airline.

Avoid the deal if the company offers no firm information on the lodging, departure date, airline, and the full cost and details of the trip. Get telephone numbers, names, and addresses for lodging, airlines, and cruise ships. Call the motel. Is it really on the beach? How many stars is it rated? What are user reviews?

Consumers should contact the Better Business Bureau or a recognized travel group to identify any complaints about the travel company in the U.S. and Canada. Web sites displaying a clickable "BBB On-Line Reliability Seal" show that the business is a member in good standing.

Choosing Airlines and Airports

People can employ many criteria for selecting a flight including the number of stops, time of day, loyalty programs, and cost. However, two other statistics may be useful, namely, the percentage of on-time flights of the airline and the airport as provided by the airlines and compiled by the Bureau of Transportation Statistics. You can, for example, determine the percentage of on-time flights (defined by being no more than 14 minutes late) between any two cities for specific months and the overall record for individual airports and airlines. Some airlines have far more take-offs at key times than they can reasonably hope to accommodate.

I was curious to see if there were substantial differences among warmer climate airports and colder ones. I looked at 17 major airports and found a slight disadvantage to those in the snow-belt. Most averaged on-time ratings of 70-76% during Dec. 2007 to Feb. 2008 and Dec. 2008 to Feb. 2009, but two airports did not. Chicago O'Hare averaged 59% and San Francisco International registered 61%. Fortunately, two neighboring airports had substantially higher ratings, Oakland at 76% and Midway (Chicago) at 74%.

Of the large cities checked for a six year period from 2004-09, **the best were**:

Airport	Arrival Rank	Departure Rank
Salt Lake City	1	1
Chicago Midway	2	
Minneapolis	3	6
Phoenix	9	5
Portland		2
Washington D.C.		4
Los Angeles		7

The worst were:

New York City	29	28
Miami	25	30
San Francisco	28	26
Atlanta	23	24
Dallas	18	27

You may wish to consider this information when allocating time between connecting flights and choosing routes. Please understand that ratings do change. To check on your specific flight, airport (both destination and origin), or airline, go to transtats.bts.gov, then click "data and statistics," then "airline on-time statistics," and then finally the category in which you are interested. If you want to research airports and airlines but not flight numbers or just going from one specific airport to another, it is faster to type in the following: transtats.bts.gov/OT_Delay/OT_DelayCause1.asp?pn=1.

Your reservation agent can provide a less specific on-time performance rating for a given flight. A flight rating of "8," means that the flight was no more than 14 minutes late between 80-89.9% of the time. On-time information may also be shown on travel websites.

You can also use J.D. Power's customer satisfaction surveys to choose airports (jdpower.com/travel/ratings/airport). Its ratings include six factors: overall customer satisfaction, baggage claim, check-in process, airport accessibility, terminal facilities, security check, and food and retail services. The airports are divided among small (fewer than 10,000,000 boardings annually), medium (10,000,000 – 30,000,000), and large (over 30,000,000). The 2010 five star ratings for "overall satisfaction" were as follows:

Large Airports: Charlotte Douglas International
                     Denver International
                     Detroit International (top award)
                     Minneapolis/St. Paul International
                     Phoenix Sky Harbor

Medium Airports: Kansas City International (top award)
                     Portland International
                     Tampa International

Small Airports: Indianapolis International (top award)
                     Southwest Florida International

Unless you have lounge access, you may wish to check out the site "sleepinginairports.net." The lowest rated airports for sleeping are JFK, LA International, and Chicago O'Hare. You may wish to pack an inflatable mattress and an alarm clock.

House Swapping and Free Couches

A fairly popular vacation program is the direct swapping of houses throughout the world. Homeexchange.com (same as houseswap.com) claims to have 28,000 listings while Homexchangevacations claims 32,000. The annual membership for the former is $99.95, but the second year is free if you don't score a house swap in the first year. The latter is about $116. A third, the vacationexchange.com, allows indirect swapping where one of the parties gets credit to stay in a third property.

Another more intimate version is allowing someone to sleep on your couch for free. There have been more than 1 ¼ million successful couch surfers in 61,254 cities in 232 countries. This service (couchsurfing. com) is free.

Rental Cars

1. **One of the most expensive and least needed costs is for daily collision insurance or loss damage waiver which can run $7-$15 per day.** Check with your insurance company, credit card company, and travel club for existing coverage.

2. **Refill the fuel tank to avoid the huge premium charged by rental car companies to fill it.** Sometimes a cut rate deal is offered to fill the tank, but it may be based upon supplying a full tank of gas (which you likely didn't need).

3. **Your best deal, if you are traveling within a state, is a local car rental company, not one of the national chains.**

4. **Renting off of the airport site is often much cheaper than renting on site.** Most off-site rental companies have shuttles to pick you up and your taxes and fees may be lower. To find them, type "rental car companies," followed by the city and state or go to CarRentalExpress.com which serves 300 independents in 1500 locations in 30 states. They claim to save you 15-30%.

5. **For longer trips, check to see whether you have "unlimited mileage" or not.** The extra mileage costs can add up quickly.

6. **Ask for senior discounts based on age or AAA and AARP membership.** Do this only after asking for their best price.

7. **Note any vehicle damage before leaving the parking lot and ask for an inspection upon returning and get a signed copy of it.** Consider snapping a few pre-rental and post rental pictures, preferably with a date stamp on the picture.

8. **Keep a copy of both the rental car agreement and final invoice.** If no one is around at your departure, leave a note requesting an invoice. Then compare the invoice with your credit card billing statement.

9. **If you are later charged for a repair, ask how they determined that you caused the damage.** Request a copy of the repair invoice, the replaced parts, and pictures of the damage. If the repairs or pictures occur in another city than the car return location, you have a strong case to refuse payment. Furthermore, don't let them assess normal wear and tear. If necessary, go to small claims court to make them prove you were responsible.

10. **A car reservation does not guarantee that the car you choose will be on the lot.** Generally, it refers to a class of car. If you are upgraded to a larger car, refuse to pay more. If they downsize you, ask for an adjustment.

11. **Try reserving a compact and then asking for a free upgrade at the counter.** If they have extra larger cars, they may allow it.

12. **If you don't want to hassle with a car rental at the airport, take a taxi to your hotel and have the car delivered there, often for free.** If the car isn't needed right away, you can save on both parking and rental charges.

13. **Vehicles kept for more than 24 hours will be charged extra.** I called four car rental companies and was given the following information (may not apply to "elite" or "gold" status):

Company	Grace time allotted	When full day's rate is charged
Budget	29 minutes	1.5 hours late (after the 24 hrs)
Enterprise	29 minutes	4 hours late
Hertz	30 minutes	2 hours late
National	28 minutes	2 hours late

When booking your airline ticket and renting a car, keep this information in mind. Of the four companies, Enterprise has the best "lateness" deal, but policies may change with economic conditions. This is the only rental car company that received a five star rating from J. D. Power and Associates. Hertz and Alamo were awarded four stars and National and Avis only three.

14. **Check a rental car company's website.** The rates may be cheaper than by phone and may vary at any given time so check several times. Also, you might receive a better price by calling the rental agency in the pick-up location. A local agency knows its inventory better than an 800 operator. Since there is usually no cancellation fee, rebooking a reservation only consumes your time.

15. **Be aware that the rental car company may charge extra for things like a GPS, satellite radio, and a baby seat.** If they try to charge extra for something you don't want on your car, refuse to pay it and give them a choice of providing another car. GPS can be used for tracking your vehicle so privacy issues may be a concern.

16. **When using coupons, find out where they are honored and any black-out dates or other special stipulations like a minimum rental time or a Saturday night requirement.**

17. **Hotwire.com often beats the named car rental companies at similar locations like airports.** They don't give you the name of the company until you book the deal. You might take the Hotwire price and try reducing it by 10-15% and bidding at Priceline.com.

18. **Another alternative is to ask your preferred company to beat the Hotwire price or provide an upgrade.**

19. **Remember to cancel a car reservation or you may be charged for your "no-show."**

20. **Be paid to deliver cars or incur a minimal charge for relocating them (check autodriveaway.com).**

Hotels

1. **If you had a bad experience, ask for fair compensation.**

2. **Settle your hotel bill the night before** when you aren't pressed for time, there is no line, and you can dispute charges.

3. **Hotels are sometimes keeping gratuities themselves instead of giving them to the help.** If they are adding sales taxes to the gratuity, then the hotel is keeping the money for itself (*The Wall Street Journal*). Such a policy should definitely be protested.

4. **It is a good policy to negotiate discounts and other amenities in advance.** After you have gotten a price but **before** making a reservation, ask for free parking, a complimentary breakfast, or an upgrade. When you show up at the hotel with a confirmed reservation, it may be too late for a discount but do try anyway. The best approach is to mention local vacancies and a competitor's best deal. Alternatively, call your motel without mentioning your reservation. Then see what kind of deal you can get before checking in. If they have extra rooms, your last minute request may be favorably received.

5. **Remember to cancel your reservation if your plans change.** Most hotels and motels charge for "no shows," and the policy varies from allowing a free cancellation by 6 PM to the entire cost being "non-refundable."

6. **Motels and hotels should be cautious about accepting partial payment.** In one of my motels, a businessman wrote a bad check for about $2,000. After much harassment by me, my staff, and the police for theft of services, he finally paid $800 of his bill. After the payment, the police informed me that since he showed good faith that it was now a civil matter. I didn't inform him of that, and he eventually paid in full.

CHAPTER 15

Water and Energy Saving Techniques

Every time you save water or energy, you reduce carbon emissions and put money in your pocket. Here are some tips for both.

Exterior Water Use

1. Modify automatic sprinklers. Adjust them for changes in temperature and moisture levels. Consider turning them off after a rainstorm or reduce the running time when the temperature cools. In some less harsh climates, those with high humidity, and those with water holding clay soils, watering might be cut back or eliminated if you don't need a green lawn all summer. You can also install moisture sensors which can automatically adjust watering to soil moisture.

2. Apply water during the coolest parts of the day to reduce evaporation (usually at night or early morning). Unless this causes some problem with your plants, it will help your electrical utility which pumps the city's water because you are consuming during a period of low demand.

3. Mow the lawn less often. A lawn mower emits far more pollution than a car because the exhaust emissions are poorly controlled. A lawn that is 2 ½-3 inches long requires less water than shorter grass because the roots of the grass and soil are shaded.

4. Use plantings that require less water. Check with your local nursery and state extension agents.

5. Recycle newspapers. In gardens, you can cover newspaper with dirt or mulch to hold in moisture and create composting.

6. Sweep the driveway. This gives you good exercise and is better than hosing it off.

7. Don't run pond waterfalls at night or in colder weather. If you have a pond with fresh water coming in and you have a water fall created by pumping water, you can put the waterfall on a waterproof timer so that it doesn't run at night. For ponds without fresh water, however, the lack of full time circulation may cause algae build-up.

8. Install a rain barrel at the bottom of your gutters for watering your yard and garden.

9. Disconnect your gutter from city sewers and connect a disperser that helps water your lawn.

Interior Water Conservation

1. Flush less frequently. When a severe drought occurs, cities often encourage more extreme conservation. In such times, people may resort to flushing under the rule "pee, nee. poo, do."

2. Replace the toilet. If you have an older flush toilet from the period from about 1990 or before, you can save money by replacing the toilet. The current standard flush is 1.6 gallons. Those installed prior to early 1990s have a capacity of about 3.5-5.0 gallons. There is a new brand from Australia by Caroma and one by Kohler with two buttons that allows a different flush for solids versus non solids. The solid flush is the standard 1.6 gallons while the non solid flush is .8 gallons. Reports are that the lower flush works for many solid flushes. I found these regularly in restrooms and higher end motels in Europe.

To determine the savings by replacing your toilet, you need to check your water bill for the cost. If your water company charges by the cubic feet, then multiply the number by 7.5 to get the number of gallons. Make sure you include the sewer charge. There are other variables that may complicate the calculation such as higher summer rates and the use of a flat rate plus usage charge. You can obtain that information from your water billing company or it might be on your bill. Let's assume that the variable portion of the water and sewer cost is 3.5 cents per cubic foot or about 1/2 cent per gallon. The cost per flush with various tank sizes then is:

Tank size	Cost/flush	Flushes/day	Cost/year	Flushes/day	Cost/year
5 gallon	2.5 cents	10	$91	20	$182
3.5 gallon	1.75 cents	10	64	20	128
1.6 gallon	.8 cents	10	29	20	58
Caroma					
(ave-1 gal)	.5 cents	10	18	20	36

You can buy low flush toilets costing from about $80 and up. The savings is quite substantial, particularly when replacing the older high flush toilets. For example, if you have several people using one toilet, resulting in 20 flushes per day, and you have the five gallon capacity, the annual savings of replacing it with a modern 1.6 gallon unit would be ($182-58) or $124. You can quickly estimate your monthly cost per gallon by the following formula if you don't pay a basic or flat fee:

Cost per gallon = (Monthly bill) divided by (cubic feet used X 7.5).

For example, if the bill is $50, 133 cubic feet is used, then the number is gallons is 133 X 7.5= 998 gallons. The cost per gallon is $50 divided by 998= .50

If you have a flat fee plus a volume fee, then the formula is: Cost per gallon = ((Monthly bill- flat fee)/ cubic feet used) and then divide that by 7.5.

You can determine your toilet size by shutting off the water in back and noting the desired water level mark on the inside of the tank or on the overflow valve. Then flush the toilet. Next fill the nearly empty tank with a measured amount of water from a milk carton or other container. With this information and your cost per gallon, you can calculate your annual savings from installing a modern toilet:

The time required to recover your money will depend upon whether you install the toilet yourself, its cost, usage, the capacity of the toilet being replaced and your local water rates but is likely to be within eight months to three years. Furthermore, on a new toilet, you also save by having 3-5 years before some parts need replacing.

3. Take shorter showers. Wet down and then take a sponge bath or simply be faster in the shower. Don't use it as a place for meditation.

4. Take showers which generally require much less water than a tub bath.

5. Install low flow shower nozzles. Low flow nozzles spray two gallons per minute, about 50% of the old variety. To calculate the savings, I used the following assumptions: 4 six minute showers are taken per day, a two gallon per minute new shower head replaces a four gallon one, water costs 1/2 cents per gallon, the water heater is set to 120 degrees with 85% hot water and cost of one cent per gallon to heat the water. I also show the effect of dropping the shower length to four minutes.

	Gallons Saved	Water Savings	Heat Savings	Total Saved
Low water shower head	17,520	$88	$149	$237
+Reduce shower to 4 min.	23,360	$117	$199	$316

A shower head with a low water spray annually saves many times its cost. Some can be purchased for less than $15. The combination of shorter showers and low water shower heads saves tons of money.

6. Fix dripping faucets and running toilets. I have seen **huge** increases in water bills in apartments with running toilets, but even a dripping faucet can use large amounts of water. Place a one gallon container (or any measured size) under a dripping faucet. If it fills up in four hours, you are wasting 2,190 gallons per year. If it is hot water, then it would drain a 50 gallon water heater 44 times a year.

7. Only run the dishwasher when full. If spotting on dishes from hard water is not a problem, turn off the hot dry cycle, especially in the non-heating season. In the heating season, open the dish washer door and let the heat out. Dishwashers can use up to 30-40% less hot water than hand washing.

8. Use the low water setting for less than full loads in your washing machine. Better yet, buy a washer which uses less water. Each washer has a Modified Energy Factor (MEF) which takes into account the amount of water and dryer electricity saved. A typical one saves 6,000 gallons of water per year based upon washing one load per day. Remember that much of that is hot water. Check out *Consumer Reports* or other consumer ratings before buying a low water washing machine. Some problems are caused by not using high efficiency liquid detergent.

9. Employ other small ways to save water. Do you need to run the water while brushing your teeth? How long does it take to wash your hands? I had a college roommate who spent 10 minutes washing his hands. Of course, if you like long hand washes, turn off the water while scrubbing, a good idea even for short washes.

10. Wear items more than one day. Most Americans change their underwear and socks every day, but otherwise most clothes can be worn again before washing. Avoid white and very dark clothes which easily show dirt and need to be washed more often. Brush off dust with your hand and then use a damp cloth to remove any excess.

Frequent washes cause your clothes to fade more quickly and lose their shape. Dark clothes show color fading more than light clothes. The best colors for longevity that survive multiple washings are gray, medium and light brown, and patterns. Clothes with rough patterns like corduroy are also good. Fleece seems to be especially destroyed by washing.

11. Install aerators in your faucets. It reduces the flow by as much as 50% without reducing pressure. If your aerator has more than 2.5 gallons of flow per minute or it shows no rating, replace it with one that rates 1.5 gallons or less. They cost less than $2 each. Some utilities will reimburse commercial users with lots of faucets.

12. Check for water leaks. A monthly check of your toilets and faucets for dripping water is a good idea. If your water usage seems abnormally high, turn off all water uses and check the water meter. It is usually on the house side of the sidewalk, often with an oval shaped concrete lid. Lift off the lid and if the needle is spinning on the meter, you likely have a leak on your side of the meter. Next turn the water off at the meter using a crescent wrench, a hooked nose pliers, or a special tool.

The meter should stop spinning. That means that the leak is definitely on your side of the meter and your responsibility to fix it. Turn the water meter back on and go inside the house. Now turn the water off where the "main" comes into the house from the meter. Now check the meter again. If the meter is still running, then you likely have a broken water main pipe. Immediately, shut the water off at the meter and don't turn it on unless you urgently need it. Call a plumber. If the meter stops, then you have a leak somewhere in your house which is the preferable problem.

Now call your water company to determine if they will adjust your bill since the leaking water didn't go into the sewer system. It may simply have a once in 12 month adjustment for such problems.

If your toilet makes a dripping sound, but you can't see anything obvious, it may be that the flapper has a slow leak. To test, place 10-15 drops of food coloring in the tank. If the color appears in the bowl within 15 minutes, your flapper is bad. If it doesn't appear, then the valve assembly is likely bad. This problem will cause the tank to overfill into the overflow pipe.

13. Avoid frozen pipes and/or damage to your house by:

- Disconnecting hoses before the freezing season starts. The cold can work its way back into the wall from water in the hose at the faucet connection.

- Draining those outside faucets after shutting off the inside shut-off valves. Leave them open in case you have a slight dripping. The water will likely evaporate or at least won't fill the pipe and freeze. Those faucets most at risk have a shut-off that goes straight down rather than back into the wall.

- Placing insulated covers over older outside faucets after closing any inside shut-offs. The modern ones generally don't need it except in very cold climates or where you fear a power failure, especially when traveling.

- Insulating outside walls in crawl spaces with water pipes. This will keep your house warmer too.

- Wrapping water pipes in unheated areas with an electrical heating coil or pipe insulation. These unheated areas include crawl spaces, attics, and basements.

- Opening cupboard doors of sinks in houses with pipes in outside walls. You may wish to do this even in modern houses when on vacation in case the power goes off and your heating system then fails.

- In older houses, letting a faucet run that is furthest from the street in really cold weather. A stream the size of a pen refill is sufficient. Galvanized and the newer plastic pipes resist freezing much better than copper pipes.

- Leaving your furnace on low and not off (depending upon the climate). In most houses, this means at least 50 degrees. In poorly insulated houses with pipes in outside wall, you may need 60 or more degrees. If you have someone checking your house daily, you can leave it on a lower setting.

- By not heating frozen pipes with an open flame. The heat will go back into the wall and possibly catch the house on fire. Use a hair dryer or heat lamp for heating. Plumbers have special equipment that can thaw metal pipes more quickly.

• Caulking around pipes where they enter the house.

14. If you have low income, see if you qualify for discounts on utilities and plumbing repairs (assisted by the utility).

15. Avoid rinsing dishes. Instead scrape them or use an already used napkin. Most dishwashers can handle small bits of food. Some things like grated cheese or oatmeal need to be scrapped really well.

16. Turn off the water to the washing machine when you go on vacation to avoid a disastrous uninsured problem.

17. Use less water in toilet flushes by bending the lever holding the float on old tanks, by adjusting mechanisms in newer tanks, or placing a brick or plastic jug filled with water and gravel.

CHAPTER 16

Maximizing Your Heating/Cooling/Electricity Savings

Energy Loans, Rebates, Tax Incentives, and Tax Credits

If you are contemplating a new or remodeling project or the purchase of new appliances, check with your local utility, state department of energy, local contractors, and the IRS tax code for loans, rebates, and tax credits for energy efficient buildings and equipment. Some states have programs that allow tax credits for some appliances, fuel cells, heating and air conditioning systems, wind and solar systems, water heaters, boilers, insulation, window replacements, and alternative and hybrid fuel vehicles. Here are some things to check and do with your state's energy department and/or your local utility:

- Find out what qualifies. For example, some incentives are not available for oil heated homes in many states.

- Don't give up easily. The websites of some states require digging to find all of the incentives.

- Check all sources **and** call several. You may find incentives from more than one. Your utility, state, city, and the federal government may all have programs with incentives.

- Determine if you can receive a free energy audit. This is probably the best way to receive the most incentives unless you are simply buying an appliance.

- Does your state allow residents or non-residents without a tax liability to transfer the tax savings to someone else? Some do.

- Check the makes and models to be sure they are approved **before you buy or sign a contract.**

- Don't miss compliance dates. Some states and utilities may allow you to apply 30-90 days after the work is done, but don't depend on it.

- Which incentives require an inspection before the work?

- Which inducements require pre-approval?

- Some incentives require an approved and licensed contractor. Sometimes they are more expensive than unapproved ones. I would get a bid from the latter and use it as a negotiating tool. Don't be afraid to ask for a price reduction simply because a contractor is on some list.

- Visit dsireusa.org for a list of federal and state incentives. In most cases, the combination of incentives and lower utility bills makes the high efficiency units a good deal.

- Don't be fooled by terms like "Energy Miser" and "Energy Saver" as they have no standard meaning for efficiency, rebates, or tax credits.

- You can find out the state solar incentives by going to findsolar. com. They have a color coded map (by *Cooler Plant*) which reflects the net cost of a renewable energy system and any special loans and property tax reductions. You can find more detailed information on state rebate and assistance programs by looking at its "Database of State Incentives for Renewables and Efficiency." The top ten states ranked by incentives are:

     1. Louisiana
     2. Oregon
     3. Connecticut
     4. Massachusetts
     5. New York
     6. Hawaii
     7. North Carolina
     8. Wisconsin
     9. Illinois
     10. Minnesota

For solar, you could also check the following websites: ases.org (The American Solar Energy Society established for professionals and advocates in 1954) or seia.org (Solar Energy Industries Association, the leading trade group established in 1974). These sites have a variety of information and lists of contractors.

- Federal tax credits are available for consumers to cover 30% of the cost up to $1,500 in credits for existing homes in 2010. This includes windows and doors, insulation, roofs (metal and asphalt), HVAC, water heaters, and biomass stoves. Through 2016, tax credits are available to cover 30% of the cost with no limit for existing homes and new construction for geothermal heat pumps, solar panels, solar water heaters, small wind energy systems, and fuel cells. For the complete details and the specifications needed to qualify, go to energystar.gov. In most cases, the qualifying products reduce the energy needed for heating and cooling, but do cost somewhat more. The site also covers tax credits for home builders and commercial buildings.

- Some utilities have buyback programs to purchase excess power generated by residents. The cost of solar, wind, and other power generating and heating sources have come down due to government and utility assistance and more competition.

Cooling and Heating Ideas

Check with your heating/cooling professionals about these ideas.

1. Use your furnace fan to draw outside cool air. If you live in a safe community where night time temperatures cool off to at least 65 degrees, you could benefit from the following procedure. It works for a one or multiple story buildings. During the potential air conditioning season, block off the cold air return duct at the furnace with some cardboard so that all air would be drawn from outside the house. If you don't have windows in the furnace room or an adjacent room, it won't work.

Next, isolate the furnace room and the outside window(s) by closing all doors beyond that window and the furnace room. Then remove the bottom cover of the furnace so that the cold air return is drawing cool air from the outside. Turn on the fan in the evening and then off early in the morning before the outside temperature becomes higher than the inside. This works best in low humidity areas like the west where nights are cooler and the humidity is low.

On the hottest days, you could open every upstairs window and at least a few on the ground floor to increase air flow. The hot air rises drawing in the cold air. Depending upon the outside temperature, one might cool the house by as much as 15 degrees, possibly eliminating the need air conditioning.

Before opening ground level windows, you may wish to consult with local police about the likelihood of burglaries at night in an occupied home. Of course, if you have an alert dog, that may be the only deterrent you need.

2. Run your A/C with open windows in dry climates. One of the questions sometimes asked is, **"Should you open the windows with the air conditioner running?"** If you live in a humid climate, then absolutely not. One of the advantages of an air conditioner is that it lowers the humidity of the building and eliminates that "muggy" feeling.

However, in a dry climate where outside humidity levels are 10-30% and temperatures drop rapidly at night, consider opening the windows once the outside temperature is near the inside temperature. Humidity isn't a problem here even at night.

The outside air will help cool the house more quickly than the A/C alone. Furthermore, the house will continue to cool even after the desired "sleeping" temperature is reached and the A/C shuts off.

This strategy works particularly well if you have upstairs windows that can be opened for cross ventilation and even better if you have duel climate zones or two heat pump/air conditioners, one on the ground and one on an upper floor. If you only run the downstairs A/C, it pushes the hot air up where it is cooled by the open windows.

3. Attic fans can help cool a house. A large temperature controlled attic fan, placed at the highest roof or attic point and away from sleeping quarters, will help cool the house. The fan can have fairly dramatic effects if both the attic access and the windows on your lowest floor or basement are opened during cool nights. In most newer homes, the attic access is made with one or two layers of sheetrock for fire protection. Removing that safety barrier is the key danger of this approach. A fire marshal would advise against leaving the access door open. Solar powered roof fans are also an option. Large attics may require two temperature controlled fans.

I will alert you to one word of caution that I have never experienced. Attic and whole house fans may possibly create a back draft for your combustion appliances like a gas furnace or water heater. The concern is that the fans would create such upward force so as to suck the burning gas fumes back into the house instead of exhausting them. I would suspect that such cases are most likely to occur with the windows closed. Most modern appliances are well enough designed that this problem shouldn't occur (especially with the windows open) but **be sure to check with your heating specialist.** You could also look at the flames in your appliances to see if they are being sucked back or burning straight up.

4. Cooling the attic will also lengthen the life of your shingles, reduce your A/C's use of electricity and damaging moisture in your attic, and lessen the deterioration of items left there.

5. Reduce attic heat by using ridge vents at the peak of your roof in conjunction with soffit vents. If your daytime **attic** temperature is more than 20 degrees higher than the outside air, the load on your A/C will be quite high. Generally, the greater the vertical distance between your ridge vent (outlet for heat) and the soffit vents (inlet), the greater will be the air movement and heating reduction.

According to B.R. Stewart (Texas A & M University), natural ventilation is the most economical, and fans can't be justified on a cost/benefit basis (at least in Texas). The quantity of ventilation air depends on vent area, temperature rise, and wind movement. Tests show that you need one net square inch of inlet/outlet area (equally divided) per one square foot of attic area with roof slopes of 3/12 to 5/12. National standards appear to require only about ½ of this. Notice that the term "net" is used because only about 60% of some prefabricated vents is open area. I personally agree with this as I tested one new building with insufficient ventilation and found a 60 degree increase in attic heat.

6. Install ceiling fans and use portable fans to feel a few degrees cooler. Window fans should be placed on the side of the house with the coolest outside temperatures, likely the north side (which has the least sun causing the house and nearby vegetation to absorb the least heat).

In dry climates, fans tend to dry your eyes, especially when sleeping, so you may want to have them blow over a container of water, not run them at night, or add a humidifier. Dry air feels cooler against the skin because your natural moisture evaporates more quickly.

7. Try some cheap A/C. One inexpensive method is to freeze a block of ice in a milk carton and have the fan blow across the ice toward you. The best effect occurs if the ice is removed from the milk carton and set in a pan. If you don't, make sure that the carton hasn't split while freezing.

8. Stay cool by wetting your top bed sheet and for the real polar bears, put it in the freezer.

9. Turn the furnace down to 68-70 degrees in winter and the A/C up to 76-80 in summer.

If you have **fury** animals, you can probably turn the heat further down in winter while on vacation. I asked four veterinary clinics and was advised that 50-55 degrees was fine for cats and dogs in good health. For short haired varieties, however, somewhat warmer temperatures may be more ideal. However, I wouldn't raise the summer temperatures any more unless you have a basement for them.

10. Consider using a heat pump (in conjunction with a furnace in cold climates) to increase energy efficiency. Heat pumps can be used for both heating and cooling, and they do save money but do not heat as rapidly during cold temperatures as regular furnaces. After installation, check the temperature coming out of the register. It should be 20-25 degrees hotter than the room temperature or about 85-90 degrees. I had one new heat pump and furnace incorrectly installed so that they came on together, and the register temperature reached 120 degrees. The problem was caused by a thermostat programming error. The heat pump made a squealing noise after a half hour or so.

11. Professionals recommend that the heat pump be inspected every year and every five years on other systems. When asked, one installer, told me to just hose the heat pump off every year and make sure that nothing is clogging the intakes.

12. Keep your doors and windows closed as much as possible when running the furnace or A/C (except as noted in #2).

13. Keep garage doors closed in the heating and cooling season (unless the garage is unattached to the house).

14. Clean or replace your air conditioner and furnace heater filters

regularly. This increases the efficiency and life of the appliances. Depending upon conditions, it may be necessary to service filters every two months. I have seen recommendations for monthly servicing, but after having experienced 500 housing years (10 rental units owned for 10 years is 100 housing years) with A/C, heat pumps, and furnaces in multiple locations, two months is the soonest that I would service them. Some electronic filters may be washed in the dishwasher (check your owner's manual), but others may not.

15. Put a fan in front of your window A/C to move the cool air further into the house.

16. Shade your heat pump during cooling days with an awning or shade trees but make sure you don't block the air flow. Don't plant trees or scrubs so close that the vegetation grows into the vent, and don't plant vegetation that loses its leaves.

17. Don't put lamps or other heat producing devices like toaster ovens, TVs, and computers near your A/C thermostat as it will cause the A/C to run more.

18. If you live in a dry climate, consider using a "swamp cooler" instead of an A/C. They are cheaper to buy and use about ¼ the energy of a regular A/C.

19. Replace older A/C units since they aren't nearly as efficient. You can check on your A/C's efficiency by holding a thermometer on the register and then at the return air grill. The register should be 14-20 degrees colder than the cold air return. An A/C that is not cooling to that level could be low on refrigerant or have leaks.

20. Remove window air conditioners in winter.

21. Clean the spines on the outside of your A/C regularly. I simply hose off the spines or use a brush. Check your owner's manual for cleaning instructions or call your heating specialist.

22. Don't install larger cooling units than needed unless you require rapid cooling. Be aware that some new heat pumps which have higher energy ratings actually run longer than older less efficient ones. That happened to me when I went from a 10 SEER rated heat pump to a 16 SEER. However, the new pump was quieter than the old one.

23. Install white or light colored window shades and drapes to reflect heat away from your house. Dark ones absorb heat.

24. Adjust your window coverings in the cooling and heating seasons. In the morning, close your window coverings facing the sun during A/C necessitated weather and at night during heating days. Heavy drapes are better than blinds. **Exterior** shades, awnings, or trees, which keep the sun from hitting your windows and building, cool more than inside shades. During the heating season, remove any exterior coverings on the south and west side (where practical).

I conducted an interesting experiment on two successive sunny days in my home's alcove room during one July. My goal was to compare the room's inside temperature with the light colored fabric blinds open to the temperature with them closed. On both days, the 7am outdoor temperature was 60 degrees and the inside temperature was 67 degrees. The outside temperature rose to the low 90s.

The room has five double pane low-E windows facing east, but is not separated by any doors or partitions. The house was built in 2004 and the room receives sun for about five hours.

I compared the temperature in a shady part of the test room all day to that on a thermostat located in the home's center. On the blind closing day, the temperature in the test room started out one degree below the thermostat and never got more than one degree above it. By 11 pm, it fell to one degree below the beginning temperature. On the open blind day, the test room reading rose to three degrees above the thermostat and was still one degree above by 11 pm. It is clear that opening blinds even with low E windows causes a lot of solar heating that seems to penetrate furniture and floor coverings.

25. I ran another experiment in my bedroom. I have two small storage cabinets whose bottom sits about two inches above the floor. Both are positioned over the registers, but there appeared to be plenty of space for the air to circulate. During a very hot summer day and night, I moved one completely off the register and the A/C cooled the room two degrees more. Thus, I wouldn't put anything over a register that doesn't have at least 10 inches of clearance. You should likewise avoid blocking baseboards, wall heaters, and radiators, not just for heating efficiency but also because of fire and melting danger.

26. Plug unused chimneys and insulate attic doors and pull down ladders. Make sure that a large note is placed in any fireplace in case someone forgets about the sealed chimney. For the chimney, you can place an insulation filled bag in the bottom and on top, use rigid foam installed with construction adhesive or buy an insulated cover. Make sure your damper is always closed when the fireplace is not in use.

27. Dress for the seasons. People can add layers of clothing in winter and wear the bare essentials in summer (whatever that is), including no shoes and socks. You will especially notice how cool you feel if you are barefoot on wood or tile floors.

As people age, they are often more likely to notice temperature variations due to poorer circulation. For the heating season, you can buy nice insulated jeans and khakis from Aramark at Aramark-uniform.com (1-800-388-3300). The clothes are very durable and modestly priced (especially during sales), but sorry no designer jeans. For short hot periods, try dampening your face, hair, and even your clothes.

28. Use a timer or manually reduce pool and spa heating during off-peak or non-use periods.

29. If you have a water bed, keep the covers on to retain heat. Turn the heat off or at least down when on vacation. Consider using a timer to adjust heat.

30. Paint the outside of your house a light color. This reduces the heat absorption and lengthens the time between painting due to fading. In some small European cities, you are either required by law or encouraged to paint your house white.

31. Install white or light colored shingles to reflect the sun. A light roof may be among the cheapest cooling methods and doesn't cost much more to install. In the winter, you might recapture some heat with a dark roof, but with cloudy weather and a low sun angle, probably not much. It is estimated that a white roof could save 20% or more in A/C costs. The most savings occur in hot and sunny climates with a long A/C season. A cheaper method than shingle replacement is to paint your roof white with a special paint.

32. Landscape for energy efficiency. In areas that absorb the sun during the cooling season, avoid landscaping that employs unshaded rock, cement, and asphalt. These hard materials absorb tremendous amounts of heat which radiates after the sun goes down. Instead, prefer native plants, ground cover, and drought resistant grasses that use less moisture. In cold climates, fescue is good and for hotter regions, Bermuda grass.

Grow vines on trellis or plant trees that shade the whole house. In cold climates, prefer trees on the south and west sides that lose their leaves in the winter so you can get radiant heat from the sun. During the summer, notice how much cooler parks with lots of trees are than unshaded areas. The plantings will also help block the wind which cools your house in winter and will lessen storm run-off. According to the Department of Energy, trees can reduce the air temperature within their shade cover by 25 degrees F and surrounding air by up to 9 degrees F.

33. Use solar screens. This fabric, costing less than $1 per square foot, blocks up to 90% of the sun and doesn't obscure your view.

34. Buy a programmable thermostat. This device allows multiple settings and will automatically raise and lower your temperature at different times of the day. If your utility has time of day pricing for electricity (requires a special meter), consider accelerating electrical use during off peak hours. For example, if rates are cheap from 5-7 am, you might want to warm or cool your building at 5-6 am instead of waiting until people arrive or get up at 7-8 am.

I would only buy a new thermostat with a humidity reading. In dry climates, the readings might encourage you to add a humidifier to your heating system or buy a portable one. With a humidistat, you will notice how opening windows changes the moisture level, and you may be able to equate dry, itchy eyes and skin and sometimes nosebleeds to low humidity. Of course, allergy season may cause similar reactions. Adding extra moisture in dry climates also reduces static electricity and the possible warping of wood floors or furniture.

In wet climates, the gauge can help you correlate "muggy" feelings with indoor humidity which isn't the same as that outdoors and will vary depending upon your type of heat. You might decide to leave the humidity alone in the winter when it makes you feel warmer and run a dehumidifier in warmer weather with or without the A/C. Personally, my ideal indoor humidity is 34-44%.

35. Shop for home heating oil and propane. In most larger communities, prices are competitive so shop around and ask for any discounts (senior, quantity, repeat customer, etc.). If you plan to own your home for many years, it might pay to install a larger tank to take advantage of volume and time of year discounts. Check to see if you can rent one. In one of my businesses, I pay $5 per year to rent a 500 gallon tank. I also negotiated a special pricing that gives a low flat rate mark-up on the propane.

Water Heaters

1. Turn the water heater down to 120 degrees (recommended ranges are 115-122) since much of your usage is simply to keep the water hot. Use a thermometer in running water to measure it. Test only after the hot water has not been used for at least four hours. Higher temperatures increase the danger of scalding.

For gas water heaters, simply turn the dial to adjust the temperature. For electric water heaters, pop the electric breaker before adjusting. Unscrew the two covers and test to determine if the power is off at the heating element using a cheap $3 tester found at any hardware store. (You don't actually have to turn the power off to adjust. It is simply a safety feature). The tester has two probes with a light that detects power. Retest the temperature again the next day, especially if adjusting downward since well insulated tanks take time to cool.

2. Businesses should consider using a timer. These work for electric or electronic ignition gas water heaters. If hot water use is not too heavy, the heating can be stopped prior to closing since the water heater will stay warm for hours. Then it can be programmed to restart early on the next work day. Some commercial bathrooms appear to have no hot water (often in gas stations). Though having only cold water is a poor business decision, owners should remove the hot water handle or hang a sign so people don't unnecessarily run the water waiting for warm water.

3. Turn the power off to your water heater. When you are gone for a few days, flip the circuit breaker for electric water heaters, and for gas ones, turn the heat to its lowest setting without shutting off the pilot light. However, if the room is unheated and there is a danger of freezing, you may want to leave the temperature up. For longer inactive periods, consider shutting off the pilot light. It can be easily re-lighted with one of those long handled barbecue lighters.

If you have never turned off your pilot light, the re-lighting procedure is simple. Read your instructions or consult your heating/plumbing specialist but for most gas water heaters, the following will work.

- Before shutting the pilot light off, remove the access cover at the bottom of your water heater. When the water heater is not heating, shine a flashlight to find the pilot light. That is the exact point to place the barbecue lighter when relighting.

- Locate the black (usually) knob that has three positions: "off", "on", and "pilot." It is located on the outside and toward the bottom of your water heater.

- Now turn the knob on your water heater control valve to "off" and the pilot light will go off.

- To relight, turn the knob to "pilot" and push down it and hold. It will take a few seconds for the pilot light gas to reach the ignition point.

- Ignite the barbecue lighter and hold at the ignition point at the same time as you push down.

- As soon as the pilot light is back on, withdraw the lighter, but continue holding the knob down for about 45 seconds.

- Release the pressure on the knob and the pilot light should stay on.

- Then turn to "on."

- Leave a note in a conspicuous place like the toilet seat reminding you to relight the water heater because it takes 2-4 hours to reheat. People will often become upset if they discover the problem the next morning when taking a cold shower.

4. Add an insulation blanket if your water heater, especially an older one, is in an unheated space.

5. Consider an electronic ignition for your gas and oil appliances when buying new ones. Pilot lights can cost $7-10 per month and may add unwanted heat to the house. With the electronic ignition, one doesn't need to worry about pilot lights.

6. Size your water heater to your needs. When considering a water heater, you should know your family's "first-hour rating" (FHR), the amount of water your household uses during its busiest hour. You can reduce the FHR by staggering showers, dishwasher use, and clothes washing throughout the day.

Gas water heaters generally heat up more quickly than electric ones and under current pricing (and probably for decades) are cheaper to operate in most places than electric ones.

7. Check the energy factor (EF) for your water heater. The EF determines how efficiently the water heater operates with typical ranges of .75 to .95 for electric water heaters and .5 to .7 for natural gas ones. The higher the numbers, the more efficient they are, and the more likely you will get a rebate or tax credit when buying a new one.

8. Tankless (on-demand) water heaters are becoming popular. They are considerably more expensive, but they take up less space and are much cheaper to operate. They use energy only when they are needed as no standby energy is needed to keep the water hot. I have heard stories about problems with them so ask several dealers about that.

Insulation

Insulation keeps the heat in during the winter, out during the summer, and temperatures more uniform throughout the house. Insulation is measured in R values and the higher the "R," the better it does its job. Windows are rated in "U" values, a similar rating. Insulation comes in rolls, loss fill (that can be blown in), rigid foam (which has higher R values and is sold in 4' X 8' sheets or larger), and liquid foam that can be spayed into cracks. The majority of homes built prior to 1985 or so probably have inadequate insulation in most places.

1. In most climates, raising the attic insulation level to R38 or more is probably the most economical way to save on heating and cooling. The next best and probably more expensive would be insulating cathedral ceilings and then do walls, floors, crawl spaces, and basements. The cathedral ceilings may be difficult, but you should insulate them if you replace the sheeting on your roof.

2. Insulate and seal heating/cooling ducts wherever possible, especially in areas you don't want to heat or cool. You can buy insulated pipe wrap and tape to seal the joints.

3. Use insulation with a high recycling component, especially from non-petroleum sources. Such insulation requires less energy for manufacturing, fewer new resources, and reduces waste. In any case, every type of insulation that raises the R-value will substantially reduce energy use and pollution as compared to that generated by the manufacturing process.

4. Buy an insulated cover for your outdoor pool and spa. If your spa is not well insulated, you can stuff insulation around the framing and use spray insulation in poorly insulated spots. Be aware that fiberglass insulation attracts mice so you may need traps. There are large cage type traps in which I have caught as many as four mice in one evening. I resist using poison that accidentally kills raptors after eating the mice or kills your own or your neighbors' animals.

5. Caulk and weather-strip. Caulk any of the following which is located in an outside wall or ceiling or next to an adjacent unheated space:

- Doors and windows
- Plumbing pipes
- Electrical outlets and switches
- Sill plates (usually on top of a basement wall)
- Recessed lighting and ceiling fans
- Attic accesses
- Chimneys

Check the directions for the sealants. Use caulk for small cracks and expanding foam sealant (much more expensive) and flexible foam material in long coils for bigger gaps. For doors, use a sweep on the bottom and weather stripping around the door. The foam weather stripping is easy to install but generally doesn't last as long.

6. Any time a wall is opened, insulate. If there is a water pipe, make sure you insulate between the outside wall and the pipe. If you put the insulation toward the room side, you will increase the likelihood of a frozen pipe. Consider putting solid insulation with a higher insulating R value in 2" X 4" walls, but make sure it fits snugly.

7. Use climate and health friendly spray to install foam insulation. Foam insulation has traditionally been sprayed on walls using chlorine containing agents. Ask for chlorine-free agents such as hydro fluorocarbons (HFCs), carbon dioxide, or water (*Union of Concerned Scientists*).

8. Use heating tape with a thermostat or timer to protect pipes or gutters from freezing.

9. Apply Low-E coated film to windows to reduce heat loss in winter and heat gain in summer.

Window Replacement

As far as replacing older windows with double pain low E windows, the cost effectiveness depends upon heating and cooling costs, the length of time you expect to own the structure, the types of windows installed, the federal and state and utility tax incentives, the effect on resale value, etc. Help for estimating the merits of such replacement can usually be found by contacting your local utility and/or your state energy office.

Storm windows are a lot less expensive and easier to install than new windows. To install the latter, you usually need to tear up the siding and reframe the window and do repainting. The disadvantage of storm windows is the need to remove them unless you get the preferred sliding ones.

For windows, you should consider the following:

1. **Install windows with a low U-factor.** The range is generally from .2- 1.2. The value shows the heat transfer between the inside and the outside of the house. Lower values reduce A/C and heating costs, but cost more. Aluminum windows typically have higher U values. Generally, only low U-factor windows qualify for tax credits and rebates.

2. **Window glazing (Low-E) and argon gas lower the U-factor and still allow most light through.** Glazing also reduces the damage that sunlight causes to fabrics and other materials. This aspect of heat transfer is unrelated to solar heating.

3. **Install windows with a solar heat gain coefficient (SHGC) appropriate for your area.** SHGC ranges from zero to one and

measures the fraction of solar radiation or heat allowed through a window. High numbers transmit more heat. Thus, you want a high value in cold climates for winter solar heating and a low value in warm climates. Of course, having a sizable roof overhang helps greatly in cold climates so that you get the heat gain in winter but not in summer.

Lighting

1. Replace incandescent bulbs with fluorescent ones. The latter typically use 70% less energy and last many times longer, up to seven years. I don't like fluorescent lighting for reading though if you have opaque light covers, you may not notice much difference. One option with a double socket light is to use one of each or have fluorescent overhead lights but an incandescent reading lamp. Excessive use of fluorescent lights for reading before bedtime has reportedly been linked to insomnia and some people get eyestrain and occasional headaches from reading with them.

The savings are most dramatic if you live in an area where the air conditioning and non-heating season are long. Incandescent bulbs give off a lot of heat, and the air conditioner must work harder to cool so you pay twice for the light. The most savings are realized by replacing the bulbs in the rooms most frequently used.

Fluorescent lighting seems to be fairly well tolerated for exterior use. If you leave lights on for long periods, you will realize great savings. There are specially made flood lights and "roundish" bulbs that look similar to incandescents.

If a 60 watt incandescent bulb used five hours per day is replaced, and your electricity costs 10 cents per kilowatt hour, it would save about $7.67 per year which would exceed the cost of the bulb. During the A/C season, you would also save on cooling costs. The longer lasting fluorescent bulbs would also save time spent shopping for and replacing bulbs. If you have old fluorescent lights, replace them with the newer ones which are much more energy efficient, and some have more pleasing light spectrums.

You should choose those that have a low level of mercury in them. The Environmental Working Group recommends the following:

Brand	Mercury per bulb (mg)	Average life span (hrs)	Where to buy
Earthmate Mini-Size Bulbs	1	10,000	Energy Federation
Litetronics Neolite	1	10,000	1000bulbs.com
Sylvania Micro-Mini	>1.5	12,000	Amazon.com
Sylvania DURA (reflector)	>1.8	15,000	Conservation Mart
Feit Ecobulb	>2.5	8-10,000	Amazon.com
Maxlite	1.2-2.5	10,000	Amazon.com
Philips with Alto	1.2-2.7	8-10,000	Black Energy

2. Clean the light covers and bulbs once or twice a year to increase light output.

3. Use task lighting or natural sources instead of overhead lighting.

4. Install automatic lighting timers that turn lights off and on as you need them. For example, your stairways outside your home may only need to be lit from dusk until 10pm. Businesses may want night lighting that goes off at daybreak.

5. Use low wattage bulbs when possible for closets and hallways.

6. Remove extra bulbs in bar or track lighting or use lower wattage bulbs. However, high wattage incandescent bulbs (like 100) last much longer than low wattage ones.

7. Install dimmers where you are likely to use them. The energy savings are directly proportional to the amount of dimming. They don't work on fluorescent lights.

Appliances and Other Equipment

1. Buy energy saving appliances and those with energy saving features. Focus on those that have Energy Star ratings awarded by the U.S. Department of Energy and the U.S. Environmental Protection Agency. Anything over ten years of age is likely very inefficient and will cost hundreds of extra dollars in utility bills. You can go to the government's website at energystar.gov to see all of the products that qualify and the criteria for getting the Energy Star rating. Look for the yellow energy guide which is stuck to many appliances. You can compare the average annual energy costs (not adjusted for your area) for comparable models (like refrigerators with 18 cubic feet of space).

For A/Cs and heat pumps, one should become familiar with their SEER (Seasonal Energy Efficiency Ratio) ratings. The SEER is the number of BTUs it removes from the surrounding air divided by the number of watts it uses. The higher the SEER, the more efficient the unit and the lower the energy cost.

The greatest improvement in efficiency over the past 15 years has come from low water clothes washers which use about 70% less energy, followed by refrigerators with 40% less, and A/Cs with about 30% less.

2. Replace or eliminate old freezers and refrigerators. Can you use a smaller refrigerator or freezer or a side by side combination? Remember to check for rebates. Some utilities will haul the old ones off for free or many actually pay for them (usually $25-30).

3. Defrost freezers on a regular basis to increase energy efficiency of the coils. Most are not frost free. When there is a ¼" thick coating of ice on the coils, it is time to defrost.

4. Unplug a "party" refrigerator until needed. Make sure it is clean or it will smell. It is usually best to prop the door open, but that presents some danger to small children.

5. Keep your refrigerator out of direct sunlight and away from the warmth of heaters and heating vents, dishwashers, washing machines, and dryers.

6. Keep your refrigerator and freezer full to better retain the cold, as long as you aren't wasting food. The cold escapes more quickly from sparsely filled appliances. Store water filled containers inside to increase mass.

7. Keep your refrigerator at 37-40 F degrees and your freezer at zero to five F degrees. Vacuum or at least check the coils or the rear grill covers once a year. To facilitate this, buy only machines with rollers. Check the door gaskets to insure a tight seal. If your door seal is worn out, your appliance likely should be replaced.

8. Don't block interior air vents or your appliance will need to work harder.

9. Cover all liquids in the refrigerator or freezer so evaporation doesn't cause it to run longer.

10. Operate your clothes washer, dryer, vacuum cleaner, and your dishwasher in the evening or week-end. This is good for two reasons. First in the summer, it doesn't add heat to the house during the hottest part of the day. Secondly, after 8 P.M. or the weekend, utilities have excess capacity.

11. Wash and/or rinse clothes in cold water and only full loads. If you do wash a small amount of clothes, use the low water capacity setting. This cuts down on soap too. Use special detergents for cold water.

12. Whenever possible, dry multiple loads of laundry at once because each load will use the residual heat from the previous load.

13. Dry heavy clothes separately from lighter clothes to reduce drying time.

14. Vacuum lint out of your dryer duct or use a leaf blower from the outside (to keep carbon fumes from entering your house). After cleaning, note the amount of dryer exhaust force so you become more aware of future clogging.

15. Clean the lint filter in the dryer after each load.

16. Use your high speed spin cycle to extract as much water as possible from the clothes.

17. Consider outside drying of some of your clothes during warmer weather. This may not be time efficient but is good for the environment and they smell so good.

18. Use the short cycle on your dishwasher.

19. Open the dishwasher to air dry the dishes or use the air only feature if available.

20. During the hot season, avoid stovetop cooking during the day and use an outside barbecue or serve cold foods.

21. Resist the temptation to peak into the oven. Depending upon how long it is open and the width of your oven, you can modestly reduce its temperature.

22. If you have two ovens, always use the smaller one when possible.

23. Turn off the oven before cooking is done. About three minutes before finishing your oven baking, it can be turned off with only a slight drop in temperature. Likewise, turn off the heat when boiling or frying a few minutes early because the water, the burner, and the pan retain heat. However, make sure the food is cooked.

24. Use toaster ovens and microwaves (unless you fear adverse health effects) for cooking and reheating whenever possible.

25. Use a small portable electric fry pan or grill.

26. Choose pans with tight fitting lids, flat bottoms, and straight sides that cover the whole flame or heating element. This reduces heat loss and damage to the pan and conserves energy.

27. If steaming, use only enough water to produce steam (be careful not to boil it all away). To retain more nutrients, put vegetables in a strainer instead of directly in the water. Cook at a slow boil to conserve and avoid humidity (unless wanted).

28. Unplug microwaves, toasters, coffee makers, and blenders when going on vacation. They use energy even when not turned on, and plugged in appliances are a small fire hazard.

29. Make soups with a pressure cooker. It takes less cooking time.

30. Run exhaust fans when you cook and shower, at least in the cooling season and always when cooking with gas or propane. During the heating season, depending upon humidity and mold problems and what you are cooking, you may not need to run the stove fan if using an electric range. The same is true for shower fans in dry climates.

31. Don't buy a bigger (or smaller) energy using copier than you need.

32. Buy new energy efficient equipment (such as grinders, generators, and waterfall, well, and sump pumps).

33. Use power strips for multiple appliances and electronic equip-

ment and shut the strips off when not in use. A single power strip could be employed for charging all portable devices like cell phones, re-chargeable batteries, and MP3 players. They won't be damaged by this process. **In an average home, 75% of the electricity used for home electronics is consumed while the products are turned off.**

34. Choose the smallest computer monitor that meets your needs.

35. Favor energy saving laptops over desk tops.

36. There is a false misconception that computers will last longer if never turned off.

37. Choose settings that automatically put the computer monitor in sleep mode when not in use. Shut the monitor and computer off when not used for long periods.

38. LCD TVs use about 40% less energy than a similar sized plasma TV.

39. Make sure children finish their electronic games and don't leave them switched on to continue playing later.

40. Encourage Congress to pass mandatory efficiency standards for electronic devices including usage on stand-by mode.

41. Put your dehumidifier on a timer or use one that has a moisture level sensor that will shut off when the desired humidity level is reached.

42. Try preparing extra foods on the week-end when utility demand is low and then reheating during the week.

43. Read the directions for swimming pool pumps to determine how long or how often to run them.

Building a New House

1. Early in the process, check out "green" certified buildings and practices. Consult with your builder, city or county building officials, utility company, your state energy department, and the various websites. There are many incentives. The worst scenario is to have building plans finished and then check the options. "Green" buildings have lower energy costs and higher resale values.

2. Many construction methods save energy. You should carefully look at concrete insulated blocks (instead of wood framing) which are super efficient. Outer walls can have studs spaced at 24 inches on center instead of 16 which is cheaper and more energy efficient. There are many other green options from which to choose including solar, wind, and a new geothermal heat pump which draws heat from the ground. With incentives, the net cost of many "green" options brings them closer to less energy efficient choices. As energy prices escalate, energy efficient green buildings will sell at a greater premium.

3. Make sure that cathedral ceilings and flat roofs are well insulated. Rigid foam insulation gives a high R value.

4. Recessed lights should be IC rated to allow insulation to be packed around them.

5. Consider putting some new construction partially underground. You will benefit by reduced heating and cooling.

6. Consider splitting your house in multiple climate zones. This optimizes the heating and cooling where most needed.

7. Design rooms for cross ventilation.

8. Expand up rather than out to be more energy and cost efficient.

9. Cathedral ceilings, while nice, add considerably to your energy use because heat rises. Possibly have a smaller "great room."

10. Match your kitchen, stove, and countertop size to your actual needs.

11. Avoid aluminum framed windows because of low "U" values.

Some of the ideas in this chapter came from the U.S. Department of Energy's Energy Savers program and PacificPower.net.

Help your Utilities

Do all of the above and these additional items to help your utility and other regions of the country when you travel.

1. Conserving water also saves energy and carbon emissions because water companies use lots of electricity to pump, delivery, and purify it.

2. When traveling, ask that your towels and sheets not be changed every day. Often, signs in the room give you an option of not changing the linen and reusing the towels. According to a university study of bacteria on towels, it is sufficient to change towels once per week.

3. Recycle cans, glass bottles, cardboard, plastic, and newspaper to cut down on manufacturer's electrical use.

4. Conserve as much as possible like you would at home.

CHAPTER 17

A Primer for Understanding and
Legally Minimizing Your Taxes

Most taxpayers are concerned about their taxes because for many, it represents their single biggest expense. According to the National Bureau of Economic Research, taxes take an average of 40% of income. This figure would include all types such as property, sales, income, and excise taxes.

There are volumes of information on taxes, much of it barely readable except to a commercial tax preparer. This chapter is meant to cover the needs of most taxpayers and small business owners, not in doing their taxes, but in making sure they are aware of the most common deductions, exemptions, and IRS policies. To start, I offer 12 suggestions for taxpayers:

- Buy a simple easy to read tax publication, not one of the 700 page tomes.

- Read this chapter carefully before you do the next suggestion.

- Make a list of your current assets, liabilities, expected future investment purchases and sales, and then talk with a tax accountant about them. Bring your last tax return. You will likely avoid missing some important deductions. Especially for real estate assets, there are some important things to consider before selling them. It is the old adage of being "penny-wise and pound foolish" (for the U.S. version it should be dollar foolish). Despite my experience and education and 43 years of doing my own tax returns, I still consult an accountant at least every year.

- You might miss some important deductions and credits by filing EZ tax forms.

- Itemizing may lower your taxes more than taking the standard deduction.

- Filing jointly is not always a good idea. Joint filers may lose medical deductions, not qualify for a lower capital gains rate, or become liable for all taxes in a divorce.

- Learn to use a computer for searching out tax tips and information. **All of the federal documents mentioned in this chapter are available on the internet at irs.gov or by calling 1-800-829-1040.**

- Never pay a tax preparer $150 an hour and up to organize your receipts. Either do it yourself or hire a bookkeeper for $15-50 an hour.

- Never believe that you know every tax rule. Even professionals that do hundreds of returns miss deductions or misinterpret the rules.

- Buy an expandable folder and file your receipts by category (such as charitable donations). This system simplifies tax return preparation and the answering of payment questions such as whether a donation was made. Always mark the payment date on receipts, if not obvious.

- Save important articles on tax reduction issues and look at them every few months. Many are applicable year after year. Of course, this book will cover many current ones.

- Make a list of every deadline for write-offs and give yourself a little leeway. For example, you can make charitable contributions up to December 31st. You can write checks dated on the last day of the year, but don't depend upon last minute credit card contributions to show up unless done on line. I once sent eight credit contributions by mail on Dec. 22nd, but only four were charged that year.

Other deadlines and dates to remember include:

- Corporation tax return due date- March 15th

- Filing for an extension- Due date of the return, (personal and LLC's are April 15th or the Monday following that if April 15th is on the week-end)

- Length of the automatic extension- 6 months from the original due date

- Quarterly tax payments due (see following pages)

- Opening an IRA- April 15th or as adjusted for the week-end

- Opening a SEP- Extended due date of the return

- Contributing to an IRA- April 15th or as adjusted for the week-end

- Contributing to a SEP or 401(k)- Extended due date of the return

Legal Deductions

Be on the look-out for **every legal deduction** including:

- Unreimbursed vehicle expenses, non-vehicle travel, equipment, professional fees, publications, and tools related to your business or profession.

- Charity expenses including materials and travel. The charity mileage allowance is lower than business travel.

- Home office space (depreciation on building and furnishings, interest, taxes, utilities, insurance, supplies, repairs, maid service, internet, and lawn care). Your deduction for the home office could be a few hundred or many thousands depending upon your building's cost, expenses and square footage used. The building depreciation must be recaptured when sold so you need to consider that. However, you can do a 1031 exchange on the home office portion by buying another commercial or rental property and defer the gain. Use of the home office does not dilute the $250,000 capital gains exclusion upon sale for a single flier or $500,000 for a married couple filing jointly. There are two advantages to the home office deduction. First, it eliminates the office percentage of real estate taxes from being added to your income for the Alternative Minimum Tax. In addition, if your first and second home acquisition mortgages collectively exceed $1,000,000 (the maximum allowed for the home interest deduction), you can allocate some of that debt to the home office which is not subject to that limitation. Also, a home office is allowed at more than one location, and the interest on $100,000 in home equity debt is deductible, but it is added back for the AMT.

- Certain educational expenses (not related to a new profession)

- Meals and entertainment expenses (limited to 50% for business related purposes)

- Advertising

- Investment expenses (like publications)

- Business use cell phones (best if put in the business name)

- FICA or health insurance (where applicable)

- Other expenses as listed in the following sections

Generally being self employed is better than being an employee when it comes to deductions. The former is not subject to the 2% threshold for deducting some expenses which can be more easily justified. However, employees should take legitimate write-offs.

Be Creative and Think Ahead

For example, suppose a professional (teacher, lawyer, artist, etc.) wanted to visit Las Vegas and expense much of the trip. One strategy is to attend a conference related to his field, even for one day. If you drive, deduct the mileage or actual expenses for the whole trip except personal mileage even though your spouse and kids came along. If the family shares one room, deduct the single rate. Then scrimp on meals and take the IRS allowed rate for meals and incidentals (see publication 1542 for allowed rates by cities). The lowest rate is $39 per day, with most larger cities above $50. If your conference is on Friday or Monday, the week-end expenses are deductible even though you aren't attending the conference.

The IRS considers a business day as any on which you travel to and from your business destination, have a pre-arranged business appointment, or spend at least four hours on business related activities.

If your association isn't planning a trip to a desirable location, look for other conferences. I checked the internet with the words "2009 conference, history teacher" and found conferences in Australia, Ohio, Indiana, Michigan, and Illinois. You could even take courses at sea and expense them in some cases. The rules for international travel are stricter than domestic travel. Check them before scheduling a trip.

My wife and I have attended tax deductible conferences in a variety of places including Las Vegas, Denver, Jackson Hole Wyoming, and a penthouse suite on a builder's/real estate conference cruise in the Caribbean. Since we were actively building apartments (for ourselves), 100% of the $15,000 cost was deductible.

Look for Easy to Read Tax Free Information

I have purchased income tax guides from J.K. Lasser and Ernst and Young. While comprehensive, they were a chore to read even for a finance Ph.D. like me.

There is some readable and basic information put out by the IRS at irs. gov. When you get to the site, enter the words "tax topic" in the search engine followed by the number of your desired choice as follows:

Information category	Number to enter
Which Forms to File	350
Should I itemize?	501
Medical and Dental Expenses	502
Deductible Taxes	503
Home Mortgage Points	504
Interest Expense	505
Contributions	506
Casualty and Theft Losses	507
Miscellaneous Expenses	508
Business Use of Home	509
Business Use of Car	510
Business Travel Expenses	511
Business Entertainment Expenses	512
Educational Expenses	513
Employee Business Expenses	514
Casualty, Disaster, and Theft losses	515

The topic also provides links to other free publications available for downloading. I have sometimes gotten a message that an upgraded Adobe Reader was needed to print the document, but I ignored that and it still printed.

Small business owners may want to view Publication 334, Tax Guide for Small Business. Also don't forget about the Section 179 expense deduction of personal property in lieu of depreciation. This is available to those filing Schedule C, but not real estate owners filing Schedule E.

Filing an Amended Return

Amended state and federal returns can be filed up to three years after the filing due date or two years after you pay your tax, whichever is later. Filing amended returns is fairly easy, though annoying just like all tax returns. Filing extends your audit deadline and all amended returns are looked at by an IRS agent.

The following information about tax credits and deductions **is subject to change each year** (including inflation adjustments) so check the current regulations or call your tax preparer.

Tax Payment Options

Even if you can't pay your taxes, file anyway. The penalties and interest are greater than most normal interest rates paid to borrow the funds. Sometimes people don't file because they are owed a refund and think it will be sent automatically. It won't.

If you can't pay immediately, go to irs.gov and click on "Online Payment Agreement Application." You can either pay on-line or send in a voucher. There are three payment options (other than paying immediately). If your total amount due including tax, interest, and penalties is no more than $25,000, you can use the next two options to pay on-line:

- Ask for a 120 day extension for which there is no fee, but you still owe interest and penalties. Call 1-800-829-1040.

- Pay monthly. You must have filed your tax returns and the fee is $105 (plus interest and penalties), but is reduced to $52 if deducted directly from a bank account, and $43 for certain low income individuals. File Form 9465 or do online.

- Get a six month extension for full payment using Form 1127. Most people don't use it because of difficult requirements.

Those struggling financially may qualify for "Currently Not Collectible" status, but this designation must be reapproved periodically and interest still accrues. Another cost cutting option is to partially pay and request one of the above for the reminder.

Two other possibilities are to get a loan from your lender or charge it on a credit card. Charging is usually the most expensive option, even if later paid in full. The processors who accept IRS tax payments charge a fee averaging 2.5%. If you finance the payments for four months at an annual rate of 20%, then your effective annual rate on both the fees and interest is over 27%.

Penalties

The penalties and interest charged for various infractions are:

Type of penalty	How Assessed
Late payment of tax	½ of 1% of the unpaid amount for each month or part of a month up to a maximum of 25%.
Late filing of return	5% of the unpaid amount for each month or part of a month up to 25%. Can be 15% per month up to 75% if the failure is fraudulent. Can be waived for a good reason such as hospitalization with traumatic injuries.
Frivolous returns	$5,000 for returns being substantially incorrect because a ridiculous position was taken like the government doesn't have the right to collect taxes plus penalties and interest.

Frivolous returns are usually filed by people opposing the government levying any taxes or using tax money for welfare, unemployment, and abortions. People have cited the Constitution or the Bill of Rights as giving them the moral authority to withhold tax payments. This approach is likely to create a lot of grief, time and penalties for those employing it. Ultimately, the IRS is likely to seize your assets for payment.

There are many other penalties as discussed on page 19-20 of IRS Publication #17. Most can likely be avoided by filing your returns on time. For example, there is a 20% penalty for underpayment due to negligence (defined as a failure to keep books or a reasonable attempt to comply with the tax laws), disregard of the rules, or underpaying your tax by 10% of the correct tax or $5,000 whichever is larger. Unless the underpayment is due to a tax shelter or fraud, the penalty might be waived by citing prior court cases, revenue rulings, and notices by the IRS.

Avoid repeating your mistakes. A first time offense might be forgiven if a reasonable explanation is given for the treatment of an item, and you acted in good faith. I once failed to file a partnership return, but all of the partners had included the income on their timely filed returns. The substantial penalty was waived for just this time.

Avoiding Audits

About 1.5% of returns are audited each year in which the taxpayer meets a real person. Your audit chances are about 1% if your return has income of $200,000 or less, 3% for $200,000 and above, and 6% for returns with $1 million or more in income. Your chances increase with a high DIF (Discriminate Function) score assigned to your return by a computer. A high DIF score indicates that more revenue will likely be produced by an audit. The higher is the score, the greater the revenue that is likely to be produced. Some things raise the DIF, e.g., if you have stock sales and no dividends or have no real estate taxes when a mortgage interest is declared.

Here are some tips to reduce the chances of an audit:

1. **Avoid lots of math errors.** You can do this by using a tax preparation computer program or double checking your math.

2. **Don't show crossed out numbers (if not using a computer).** Use a pencil and erase changes (erased changes don't show up when copied).

3. **File late.** About 20 years ago, a college finance professor named Amir Aczel was upset about a comprehensive audit. He assembled a large sample of 1,289 personal tax returns from accountants about evenly split between those audited and those not. He found two variables (in the form of ratios) that explained 90% of your likelihood of being audited. The first involves those filing Schedule A and the second is concerned with those filing a Schedule C. These ratios are as follows:

(Total deductions on Sch. A) divided by (Adjusted Gross Income).

Ratio	Likelihood of Being Audited
Less than .35	Slight
.35-.44	Relatively likely
.45 and up	Almost certain

The second ratio for Schedule C is (Total Expenses) divided by (Gross Income)

Ratio	Likelihood of Being Audited
Less than .52	Slight
.53-.67	Relatively likely
Over .67	Almost certain

He found two factors which dramatically reduced the chances for audit even for those with very high ratios. The first and best was to file for an extension and then file late. None of the 73 such returns, including 17 whose ratios made them likely to be audited, were flagged. Perhaps the IRS had reached its quota. The second was to include an explanation for the high ratios. If your tax returns have high ratios, file late, include an explanation, and claim valid deductions.

His study was done many years ago but may still apply today with some exceptions. The IRS seems more focused on inconsistencies like a home office with little income on Schedules C & E; no dependents, yet child care and educational expenses are claimed; and educational expenses for a new career. The IRS policies may also have changed.

If your ratio is due to one large item like charitable donations, it is not very likely to be audited according to a declassified IRS Audit Manual.

4. **Don't be greedy.** If one room is used for your home office, don't claim half of the house. However, if you have a large empty part not being used, then by all means, make your home office larger.

5. **Your tax return should fit your income.** For example, a clothing donation of $5,000 will look suspicious coupled with a $50,000 income.

6. **Be especially careful for hobby businesses.** If you raise horses or dogs, participate in bass tournaments, etc., be mindful that the IRS scrutinizes these businesses.

7. **Show balance.** If you have a small business that generates $20,000 in revenue, having $50,000 in costs might look okay for a new or closing business. However, if you lose $30,000 every year for five years, that would not.

8. **Never use round numbers like $500.** Make it $499 or $501. Round numbers sound made up and not supported by receipts.

9. **Never use the same number on adjacent columns such as multiple rental properties on Schedule E.** During an in office audit, an agent noticed the same number for legal bills on my adjacent properties. The properties were identical and the numbers were the result of my allocation method for common expenses.

10. **Remember both spouses need to sign the return and put their social security number(s) on it.**

11. **Make sure your state return matches your federal one.** The IRS has cooperative matching agreements with some states.

12. **Don't panic and forego legal deductions.** Some people will forego the home office deduction, for example, without realizing that Congress made it easier to qualify.

13. **Report all income from interest, dividends, and capital gains.** The IRS gets computerized reports on most of these sources of income. Some mortgages such as those providing owner financing don't report such income.

14. **Avoid excessive tax aggression and creativity.** Back in the 1970s, one of the big accounting firms advised its clients to call toilets "temporary comfort stations" and doors "movable partitions." The renamed assets could be written off in one year while the toilets and doors had to be depreciated over a long life.

15. **Consider the pros and cons of filing electronically.** On the pros, a trip to the post office and a certification request are avoided, saving time and money. Without certified mailing, there is no proof

of the return being sent until your check is cashed. Second, your return will have fewer errors since tax preparation software checks for mistakes and omitted information. Errors can trigger an audit. Of course, the software can be used without filing electronically. Third, you get an e-mail acknowledgement of receipt. Finally, refunds come more quickly, especially if direct deposit is used.

You have several options for filing electronically, including buying software and filing yourself. Because each state with an income tax requires a different form, the state options can sometimes be more expensive than the federal ones.

Some software options which include at least one free electronic filing are:
    Taxact.com - Ranges from free to $16.95 (last price includes state)
    Completetax.com- Ranges from $14.95 to $29.95 (excludes state)
    Taxbrain.com- Ranges from $14.95 to $69.95 (excludes state)
    Taxcut.com- Ranges from $29.95 to $89.95 (five free e-files, two most expensive options include state taxes)
    Turbotax.com- Ranges from free to $109.95 (excludes state)

Those taxpayers with income of $50,000 or less can use the Free File program, a partnership between 20 tax software companies and the IRS. All electronic taxpayers must go through these companies since their tax returns aren't file directly with the IRS.

Electronic filers are likely to get a sales pitch from these 20 companies or your tax preparer for refund anticipation loans (RAL). The RALs are very expensive, short term loans that allow people to spend their refund more quickly. The National Consumer Law Center and the Consumer Federation of America has estimated that when all bank and administrative fees and the size and length of the loan are considered, the annual interest rate can range from 70% to over 1700%.

You should avoid RALs because of the high rates. If your refund is denied or reduced, the loan must be repaid. RALs belong in the same avoidance class as payday loans (or even worse).

The first advantage to mailing your return is the availability of "float time" for raising the money to cover your IRS check. However, if your check bounces, you will incur bounced check charges from your bank and IRS penalties. Many businesses take advantage of float, but float time has been reduced over time due to computers. In the 1960s, it took seven days for my checks written in California to clear my bank in Pennsylvania.

The second is only a potential advantage. If the IRS enters your mailed return manually, it might possibly reduce your chances of an audit. With electronic filing, every number on your tax return can be sifted through their DIF program. It appears that only selected numbers are entered electronically from a mailed return. The offset is that they might enter your numbers incorrectly (which happened to me on a state return), also possibly producing an audit. On the other hand, if your mailed return is scanned, it would seem to make no difference.

A possible third advantage is that the IRS has likely compiled figures on whether electronic filers are less honest and more aggressive than those filing manual returns. The latter group **on average** likely has lower income, is less inclined to see a tax preparer, is less sophisticated about the tax laws, and will probably miss deductions. Thus, electronic filing may subject you to a larger chance of audit although the greater frequency of manual filers' mistakes may somewhat offset that tendency.

What to Do if Audited

The majority of IRS correspondence coming within the first six months of filing is simply generated by its computers which found something wrong with your return. Don't panic, but check your return for accuracy. The IRS isn't always correct.

The audit from Hell arises from the Taxpayer Compliance Measurement Program (TCMP) in which the IRS randomly selects tax returns and painstakingly does line by line audits. It uses this information to better target fraudulent or erroneous returns.

The IRS must generate money to support the government and their own jobs. During a recession, tax revenue falls and agents are under greater pressure to collect. IRS agents do have some flexibility and will most likely exercise adjustments in your favor when you provide supporting information. Do the following after receiving a notice:

1. **Take a deep breath.** Relax. Have a cup of coffee, tea, or maybe a beer. Many millions of IRS letters are sent out every month.

2. **As soon as you receive a notice of an audit, read Publication 1 of the IRS code entitled "Your Rights as a Taxpayer."** Delay the audit until you collect your records, do some research, and possibly consult a tax preparer.

3. **Respond promptly since penalties and interest accrue quickly, and the IRS will eventually garnish your wages or seize assets to pay unpaid assessments.** Employers often receive employee garnishment notices for back taxes, court judgments, and child support.

4. **Determine if your paid tax preparer has some guarantee for paying any penalty and representing you if due to his error.** Contact him immediately as he may be willing to look at the IRS notice for no charge.

5. **Make your work look organized.** Run a computer tape for a bunch of invoices and staple it on the front or have a computer print-out. Do this for each category like utilities, supplies, etc. If receipts are missing, substitute checking account, credit card statements, or other reliable information.

6. **Each category of receipts and depreciation expenses should contain the same number as used on your tax return.** The information should be neat. Use a depreciation spreadsheet or type or print the information. A session with an IRS auditor is like dressing for a job interview. A major factor in its focus and decision is the organization and thoroughness of our work. A sloppy dresser and a sloppy taxpayer both make a bad impression.

7. **Try to follow the rules.** For example, the IRS requires a log to record business use of a personal vehicle or computer. A 100% daily log isn't needed. A sample of every fourth week is sufficient, but it should be a contemporaneous vehicle log which would show worn pages, smudges, and different inks. To guard against computer crashes, use a hand log.

8. **Be persistent.** If you don't like an auditor's response, ask to speak with her supervisor. The next level after that is to the Appeals Office of the IRS. If the sum involved is no more than $25,000 per tax period, consider a "small case appeal." An appeal can oc-

cur by correspondence, phone, or in person. The Appeal Office is separate from the IRS office doing the audit. You can represent yourself or use a CPA, an attorney, or an "enrolled agent." See IRS Publication numbers 5 and 556 for details on appeals.

State and federal auditors can be very slow. In the meantime, penalties and interest may be piling up. Press for an IRS decision, and if necessary, file an appeal with a Taxpayer Advocate. Having advocate involvement may cause the IRS to be more careful that it is making the right decision.

9. **Become informed by reading and talking to you tax preparer and other taxpayers.** In some respects, an audit is an educational experience in which one learns about tax laws, record keeping, and procedures.

   Unless there is serious fraud, the worst that is likely to happen is that it will cost some money. Accept that fact and try to do better next time. Resolve to maintain better records, file your taxes on time, avoid penalties, think in advance of how to lower your taxes, check your math, schedule an appointment with a tax preparer, etc.

10. **Don't take anything to the audit not specifically requested except applicable reference material or cases.**

11. **Don't volunteer anything.** Only answer the questions asked.

12. **Don't allow the audit to be in your home under any circumstances.** The IRS might wonder about hidden income if you have a nice well furnished house and vehicles. They might question your home office deduction. It is your right to schedule it (within reason) at a suitable time and place.

13. **If all else fails, sue the IRS.** For claims (taxes, penalties, and interest) involving $50,000 or less per year, the Small Case Division of the Tax Court is available. Most cases settle before going to court with the majority of taxpayers getting some reduction. In fact, the IRS will ask you for a pre-trial meeting with its lawyers.

    The procedures are similar to most state's informal small claims courts. The IRS will send a lawyer and you can represent yourself or have a lawyer, enrolled agent, or accountant who is admitted to practice before the tax court represent you.

If you pay the IRS assessments in advance, you can go to the U.S. Claims Court or the U.S. District Court in which taxpayers have had more success than in the Tax Court.

14. **One accountant told me that an audit at an IRS office takes two hours, one for going through your records and another hour to write up and explain the results.** He suggested going there prepared with a series of questions, requests for verification on the law, and cases that your accountant or internet searches suggest may bear on your issues. The idea was to show that you are informed and thus deserve a carefully thought out outcome, to make sure the agent knew all relevant facts, and possibly to convince the agent to focus on fewer and more important items, particularly if time is running out.

15. **Show respect to IRS personnel.** They have a job to do.

16. **My last piece of advice here is to never, ever try to bribe an IRS agent. That tactic is likely to result in jail time.**

Tax Avoidance and Evasion

For tax evasion, individual taxpayers can be sent to prison for up to five years and/or be fined $250,000 ($500,000 for corporations). This would be in addition to any penalties and interest due. As a practical matter, most people never go to jail like Leona Helmsley, the New York hotel magnate, who was dubbed the "Queen of Mean" and who served 18 months for tax evasion, filing false returns, and mail fraud.

According to the IRS, "The distinction between avoidance and evasion is fine, yet definite. One who avoids tax does not conceal or misrepresent. He/she shapes events to reduce or eliminate tax liability and, upon happening of the events, makes complete disclosure. Evasion, on the other hand, involves deceit, subterfuge, camouflage, concealment, some attempt to color or obscure events or to make things seem other than they are." On a joint return, the fraud penalty does not apply to the spouse unless he/she was partly responsible for the fraud.

Unreported income would appear to fit criminal evasion, but rarely are such people so charged. The size of the crime, the knowledge of the individual, and the circumstances seem to be important. In the Helmsley case, she was reported to have coerced contractors and her own employees into falsely claiming that most of the $8,000,000 spent on remodeling her mansion was for her hotels. Then she was sued by the contractors for withholding payments. Finally, she reportedly told her housekeeper, "You must pay a lot of taxes. We don't pay taxes. Only the little people pay taxes."

There should be a Helmsley first "law" of being a tax cheat that says: "Don't tell anyone and don't involve anyone." The second Helmsley "law" is: "If you do involve anyone, don't cheap them or cheap on them." She seriously violated both laws.

Maybe we should add a third law called the "Hatch law." This refers to Richard Hatch, the first "Survivor" winner in 2000, who spent nearly four years in prison for not reporting his $1,000,000 won on the show. The Hatch law would say "High profile individuals are more likely to be caught for tax evasion than low profile cheaters."

Readers should be aware that the IRS (U.S. Treasury Department) has an Informant's Claims for Reward Program that encourages people such as spouses, significant others, accountants, bookkeepers, and business associates to "snitch." Harry Reid, Senate Majority Leader, has labeled the program as "rewards for rats." If the unreported tax liability is more than $2 million or the individual's gross is over $200,000, an informant can collect up to 30% of the IRS proceeds. Lesser amounts will generate 15% in rewards.

Tax evasion is now harder because of computers, data sharing, and the rewards program. In 1968, a colleague of mine at Hughes Aircraft Company told me about reporting only about one-third of his capital gains. He violated Helmsley's first law. In another violation of the same law, I overheard an individual bragging that his salary was paid from an offshore account so as to avoid taxes.

The IRS has recently been focusing on individuals with large undeclared foreign assets and unpaid taxes. In 2009, Swiss Bank UBS AG revealed the names of 4,450 such accounts of U.S. residents and another 14,700 turned themselves in under a partial amnesty program.

Because of the states' and the federal government's bad fiscal situation, expect more efforts to catch tax cheats. The typical evaders often claim many expenses but short change revenue, particularly those businesses receiving lots of cash. An IRS forensic accountant can usually find moderate to massive evasion. A fast food restaurant, for example, should have orders of food bags, drink cups, and pizza boxes that correspond to sales.

There are many ways that people skirt the law. For example, someone might list their formal address with a relative that lives in a low tax state or get a mailbox there. People often do that to avoid sales taxes on large purchases or income taxes. You could live in Washington with no income tax and shop in Oregon with no sales tax. Some jurisdictions have cooperative reporting laws to try and catch these people.

The IRS is starting to use mortgage interest payment data from banks to find non-filers and those who report less income than they pay paid in mortgage interest. Obviously, not all such people are evading taxes as some are making payments from their savings.

Keeping Tax Records

Tax records should be kept as long as needed. There is a three year statute of limitations (SOL) on most tax returns from the date of filing with some exceptions as follows:

- If you paid late, then the SOL is two years from the payment date or the three years whichever is greater.

- If the IRS suspects fraud, then the SOL is six years.

- There is no SOL for non-filers.

- Anything that might cause a capital gain (stocks, bonds, real estate, including your house beyond the tax free portion) needs the receipts from the date of purchase.

- Keep pension records indefinitely.

- Dispose of unused receipts (like medical records or miscellaneous deductions on Schedule A).

- If you have records on a hard drive, back them up for security.

Except for capital gains, keep everything for six years from the date of filing as a defense against an IRS fraud claim. This is particularly important for businesses because a disgruntled employee, vendor, subcontractor, ex-spouse, or ex-significant other may accuse a taxpayer of cheating on his taxes (whether true or not). Your receipts are your best defense against such a claim.

I have had two false allegations reported to Washington State's Labor and Industries, an agency that collects worker's compensation fees. One was by a disgruntled subcontractor and another by an unhappy tenant who happened to work for my building supply store. Both resulted in audits with no assessment. This was a reminder that even if your accounting is honest and accurate, an audit can be triggered by something outside the IRS's computer analysis.

Selecting a Tax Preparer

Because of the complexity of tax laws and the regularity of their changes, choose only experienced preparers, especially for complicated returns such as those involving 1031 exchanges, partnerships, C Corporations, and some confusing schedules. For additional help, go to irs.gov, type in "tax topic 254," and "How to Choose a Tax Return Preparer" comes up. Never use a preparer who promises to obtain a higher refund than anyone else or who charges a fee based upon your refund. Make sure you are given a complete copy of your tax return before signing it.

Like most other expenditures, shop around. The prices aren't uniform. Assuming your records are organized and this year's return is similar to last year's, request an estimate based upon the forms. There are currently no licensing requirements for tax preparers, but Congress seems ready to regulate them. Currently, a wide range of expertise exists. CPAs are likely to be better than non-CPAs, and those licensed to practice before the IRS are likely to be the best, but the greater the credentials, the higher the price. Tax accountants in smaller towns are also likely to be cheaper than their big city counterparts.

Should you have your taxes done by a big chain like H & R Block, Jackson Hewitt, or Liberty Tax Service to save money? There you will find seasonal employees whose advice **on average** is probably less reliable than a practicing tax accountant. For simpler returns, the trade-off may worth it.

In an undercover operation by the Government Accountability Office (*SmartMoney*) which submitted tax returns to the big chains, it found that "nearly all of the returns prepared for us were incorrect to some degree." To be somewhat balanced, the annual tax return contest conducted by *Money Magazine* for years, though likely much more complicated, found numerous mistakes by professional tax accountants.

In 2007, the U.S. Government sued five corporations and 24 individuals doing business as Jackson Hewitt franchises in four states alleging that they "created and fostered a business environment in which fraudulent tax return preparation is encouraged and flourishes" (*The Wall Street Journal*). This suit likely changed or at least caused a reexamination of business practices in such firms. When the IRS perceives more fraud or errors at certain tax preparation firms, it seems plausible that the audit rates of their clients will increase.

Tax preparers should be hired according to your time, expertise, and wallet. They could be hired every year to completely prepare your return, simply to review it, or only on special occasions. On average, tax preparers make more mistakes, and more costly ones, than people doing their own returns. However, the preparers likely had more complex returns involving more income.

For tax planning advice, go in the fall before the main tax season starts in early February. That way, a taxpayer can seek information for making decisions before most December 31st deadlines. During the "high season," tax preparers may charge higher rates or may not have time to see you.

Ask for a multi return discount for family members or businesses. Your request will be more favorably received before February or after April 15th. If an extension is filed, the estimated taxes must be paid. Also, some preparers may be reluctant to just review a taxpayer completed return, but that reluctance often goes away after April 15th. New tax preparers generally offer lower rates, but if you have a complex return, hire an experienced pro.

Some tax returns are being outsourced overseas which raises one's concern about identity theft. Also, be cautious about businesses that only appear during tax season, especially if they are unavailable during the off season when an IRS notices comes. Be leery of pitches to sell other products like extra guarantees and insurance products. These are often overpriced and should be carefully considered.

To find out if your accountant has been disciplined by the American Institute of Certified Public Accountants, go to aicpa.org/consumer information/disciplinary action. Many accountants don't belong to this organization, and the disciplinary process is slow.

Tax and Debt Resolution Services

A number of tax resolution services promise "to get the IRS off of your back." I went online and typed "tax resolution services" and checked the Better Business Bureau (BBB) rating of the first five that came up, including J K Harris and Company and TaxMasters. Their ratings ranged from A to F with some corporate offices having hundreds of unresolved complaints.

Some local offices are highly rated and independent of the parent so check their BBB ratings. An "F" rating can occur because the business failed to respond to one complaint, the nature of the industry, or the short time of operation. Other than ratings, my biggest concern is how they structure their fees. I would only pay a small fee in advance and would mainly pay based upon their performance.

An alternative to a tax resolution service and my preference would be to talk with an experienced tax accountant or preparer with at least 15 years of such experience for an hour or so. Using that information and any on-line research, I would negotiate with and/or persuade the IRS. If that is unsuccessful, then consider a tax resolution service, but be quick as the penalties and interest add up.

The IRS has a formal "offer in compromise" program where the IRS agrees to a substantial reduction in taxes, but only 12,000 such offers were accepted in 2007. Thus your "first line of defense" is to see if it is mistaken, you have made an error, or just more information is needed. Ask if there is an appeal process to reduce penalties.

Similar comments can be made about debt settlement services whose purpose is to reduce debts. There has been an explosion of such companies from 300 in 2005 to about 1,000 today so there are likely many dishonest firms (*The Washington Post*). Always check the BBB rating.

The biggest problem is the requirement for payment of advanced fees. Crooked companies can collect the fees, never make any attempt to settle the debts, and then close down. Prefer those with little advanced fees and a high BBB rating. Frankly, I would first try negotiations on my own.

Tax Burden by State

The most important factor regarding state taxes is the percentage of income taken rather than the absolute amount since high income states will have higher average tax burdens. One must also recognize that the tax burden falls differently depending upon your circumstances. If you live in a big house, then low property taxes are desirable. With high earnings, low income tax rates are important, but if most income is from a tax free Roth IRA or sheltered by depreciation write-offs, the opposite is true. For low spenders, sales taxes may be of little concern. We also have different concerns at different stages of life.

Readers should visit the non-partisan website TaxFoundation.org which has a wealth of information on taxes at the state, local, and federal level. The site can assist a person in deciding where to live or retire. Use its tax averages only as a guide and adjust for your individual circumstances.

The Tax Foundation has interesting tables including those showing the average state-local taxes, percentages of income taken, and the date of the tax holiday (how long someone must work to pay their taxes). One of the more interesting features is their "State Tax Climate Index Rankings" by state. The top ten best for 2009 are:

Ranking	State
1	Wyoming
2	South Dakota
3	Nevada
4	Alaska
5	Florida
6	Montana
7	Texas
8	New Hampshire
9	Oregon
10	Delaware

For more specific state information, go on-line and type in the state (like New York) followed by ".gov) to find an official government site. Then seek out "taxes" and identify them by type such as estate, sales, or personal or corporate income. Remember that many localities also have income or other taxes. Be aware that moving to a low tax state may not fully reduce your taxes. Some states where you have worked may try to tax your retirement income even if you move to a state with no income taxes. In addition, your income from property may be taxed in the state where it is located and/or your state of residence.

Free or Reduced Fee Tax Help

Some cities and organizations have volunteers that help persons with low and middle income file their income tax returns. For example, the AARP Tax-Aide program has 34,600 certified volunteers to assist from February 1st to April 15th each year. The emphasis is on those aged 60 and over and generally must be done at one of the 6,500 AARP sites. However, they do serve special needs persons who are homebound or confined to hospitals, assisted living sites, etc. Contact AARP at taxaide@aarp.org or call 1-888-AARP-NOW (1-888-227-7669). Help may also be available by contacting your city, county, state, some community groups, or church.

What's New

To assist in filing correct returns, check new tax information at a site like H & R Block's (HRBlock.com). Read their "Popular Articles" and "Breaking News" sections. In addition, go to irs.gov and download the "1040 Forms and Instructions." Look at the "What's New" section.

Tax Credits

Tax credits are better than deductions because you save $1 in taxes (if you owe them) for every $1 in credit. The savings from tax deductions are equal to the marginal tax rate multiplied by the deduction.

Since the qualifying criteria and size of any tax credit can change every year, consult your tax professional, the IRS, or one of their publications. The most common tax credits are as follows:

Child and Dependent Care Expense. This credit is only available to those with earned income. Earned income excludes capital gains, dividends, interest income, rental property income, and gifts. Wages and income from a business are okay. If social security taxes are not paid, the income doesn't qualify. In addition, you can't take this credit for any money paid from a Flexible Spending Account.

The qualifying expenses are those paid by you so that you or your spouse could work or look for work. The qualifying person must be a child under 13 or a disabled spouse or other person for whom you care. Reimbursed expenses can't be included.

The maximum 2009 credit for the care of one person is $1,050 and for two or more, it is $2,100. The size of the credit depends upon your adjusted gross income, but there is no income limit. However, the maximum credit drops down to $600 for one person and $1,200 for two after your adjusted gross income exceeds $43,000. File Form 2441.

Child Tax Credit. A maximum tax credit of $1,000 per dependent child is allowed through 2010. The child must be under 17 on December 31st of the filing year. You must have provided more than half of her support, and she must live with you for more than half of the year. The credit phases out at income levels from $55,000 to $110,000 depending upon filing status. A partial credit is allowed for those with little taxes. After completing the 1040, 1040A, or 1040NR Child Tax Credit Worksheet, fill out Form 8812, Additional Child Tax Credit.

Credit for the Low Income Elderly or the Disabled. The credit is up to $1125 (if both spouses qualify) for 2009 depending upon income, age, and disability. Attach Schedule R.

Education Credits. Every person who is paying for education for herself, a spouse, or a child should read IRS Publication 970 entitled "Tax Benefits for Education." The tuition and fees deduction and the Hope and Lifetime Credits are available even if the taxpayer does not file Schedule A. The following is a summary of this information.

Hope and Lifetime Learning Credits are available for you, your spouse, or a dependent claimed on your tax return for expenses at a qualified institution. File Form 8863 for both credits. The Hope credits are only available before the student has completed two years of college at the beginning of the tax year. For example, for tax year 2010, the Hope tax credit can only be taken if the student has not completed his sophomore year by January 1st, 2010. The Hope credits can't be taken for more than two years and are limited to $1,800 per year. They are only available to those married, filing jointly who make less than $116,000 and the other filing categories making less than $58,000. Only tuition and fees qualify.

The Hope and the Lifetime Learning Credits can't both be taken for the same student in the same year. The Lifetime Learning Credits are limited to $2,000 per year, regardless of the number of students who qualify. The Hope Credits do not have that restriction. Also, any tax free scholarships or grants are deducted from the educational costs when computing credits.

When your eligibility for the credits is depleted, consider filing Form 8917 for the Tuition and Fees Deduction. Of course, the deduction is less valuable than the credit so use the credits first. Forms 8917 and 8863 can't be filed at the same time for the same student. The 2009 income threshold for losing the deduction is higher ($160,000, if filing jointly or $80,000 for other filing statuses) than for the credits.

American Opportunity Tax Credit. This is really an expansion of the Hope scholarship tax credit. The credit now allows up to four years at $2,500 per year for a maximum of $10,000. The actual amount received will depend upon your income with those over $180,000 not qualifying. This credit is 40% refundable, which means that families not paying income taxes can receive a refund.

Retirement Savings Contribution Credit. For people with 2009 Adjusted Gross Income (line 38 of Form 1040) of less than $27,750 (single), $41,625 (head of household), and $55,500 (married filing jointly) and who have taxable income, there is a tax credit for contributions to a 401 (k), IRA, or other qualified retirement account.

The credit is limited to $2,000 ($1,000, if single or filing separately) and varies based upon income. The deduction drops as the above limits are approached. Eligibility is lost for being a full time student for any part of five different months, being under 18, or being claimed as a dependent on someone else's return. File Form 8880.

Earned Income Tax Credit. Persons with low income may qualify for the Earned Income Tax Credit. Call the IRS at 1-800-829-1040 to see if you qualify, get free publication 596, or use the EITC Assistant found at irs.gov. The maximum credit depends upon your filing status, income, and the number of qualifying children. Children have the biggest impact upon the EIC.

Energy Efficiency Tax Credits. Use Form 5695. This credit was discussed already.

Mortgage Tax Credit. Mortgage Credit Certificates (MCC) allow qualified low income, first time home buyers to take a credit of up to 20% of the mortgage interest payments. The MCCs must be issued by a state or local government agency under a qualified mortgage credit certification program. File form 8396. The credit is available every year that one lives in the house with the same mortgage.

Other Schedule A Deductions

Medical and Dental Costs. These costs must exceed 7.5% of your Adjusted Gross Income (AGI) to be deductible. They include medical insurance, parking fees, mileage, chiropractor, naturopathic doctor, prescription drugs, nonprescription drugs, therapy, eye glasses and contact lenses, hearing aids, crutches, wheel chair, canes, orthopedic shoes, acupuncture, drug or alcohol treatment, adding wheel chair ramps, grab bars, handrails, and a doctor recommended exercise pool. In some cases, business owners may be able to fully deduct medical insurance costs so check with your accountant.

State and Local Taxes. Schedule A filers are allowed to deduct **either** state and local sales taxes **or** state and local income taxes. If the former are deducted, taxpayers have the choice of using their actual sales tax or the "Optional State and Certain Local Sales Tax Tables."

It isn't clear how these tables were constructed as the 6% rate for Connecticut, Idaho, Kentucky, and Michigan all produce different deductions, possibly because some purchases like food are excluded.

The local sales taxes are added to the state tax amount and shown in "Optional Local Sales Tax Tables." However, Washington State has a local sales tax and it is not shown, possibly because every community can set its own tax. The tables are based upon the number of your exemptions and income. The sales tax numbers are quite conservative as they represent (even in high tax states) only about 1% for incomes above $50,000 (somewhat higher for lots of exemptions). Those taxpayers anticipating a large purchase, like a new car, should save all receipts and deduct their actual sales tax. If most purchases are made with credit cards, taxes could be estimated from the type of store.

If your local community or county's tax deduction is not shown, try the following. For example, assume the allowed deduction from the state sales table was $1,000 with a tax rate of 6%, but with local taxes, is 7.5%. Then a reasonable conclusion might be that your adjusted table deduction with local taxes could be 7.5%/6% X $1,000= $1,250. People from states with no income tax like Texas, Florida, and Washington need to remember to deduct sales taxes.

Points. A point is equal to 1% of the loan principal and is often charged by a lender on a new loan. The points are fully deductible on the original mortgage in the year of purchase but must be amortized over the life of the mortgage on a refinance. For a second refinance, the entire remaining points balance of the first refinance is deducted on that year's tax return.

Second Homes. The interest and taxes are deductible for itemizers. This includes any property with a bathroom, kitchen, and bedroom so RVs and houseboats are included. Those of you (luckily or unluckily) with a third personal home can only write off the taxes. Unfortunately, the taxes are added back to income for the AMT calculation. Special regulations apply if it is rented and you and your family use it more than 14 days per year or 10% of the rental days, whichever is larger.

Special Real Estate Tax Deduction. Those taxpayers not filing Schedule A can still deduct up to $500 in real estate taxes paid, if single, or $1,000, if filing jointly.

Job Hunting. Job hunting expenses and other costs such as an employment agency, advertising, resume preparation, etc. are deductible as long as you stay in the same profession and are employed at a new location at least 50 miles away.

Charitable Donations. Donations of clothing and household items must be in good used or better condition. However, this appears to be a somewhat unenforceable regulation because the items are not segregated by the recipient under the donor's name, the definition of condition is rather arbitrary and usually not noted on your receipt (make sure you get one), and most items are not held for the IRS to inspect.

To be safe, the donor should note the condition on the receipt after it is issued. A better alternative is to note on the receipt "see attached list," make your own itemization with condition and quantity, and take pictures (if it supports your case). The most likely IRS challenge would be that a person's income is too low for the size of the deduction. If many items were received as gifts (like from grandparents), be sure to list "gifts" as one source on IRS Form 8283.

You can use various valuation techniques including hiring a professional appraiser, going to Goodwill or a thrift shop to see prices, or using software like TurboTax or TaxCut. You can go to ItsDeductible. com and find free tracking and valuation software for deductibles from TurboTax. Most decent used clothing and house wares sell for 25-35% of the new cost. Don't use yard sale prices which are too low.

Donations must be made to a charity that qualifies for tax exempt status and a receipt is needed. Donations valued at $5,000 for any one type of item (e.g., clothes or house wares) and up require an appraisal though stocks with a verifiable market value don't.

Donating appreciated assets such as stocks or a building rather than selling them and paying a capital gain tax is preferable. This avoids not only the tax but also the transaction fees. Another tax saver is to donate funds directly from your non-Roth IRA.

Land Donations and Conservation Easements. A huge amount of land has been developed since World War II to the detriment of fish, wildlife, and open spaces. Congress and organizations like Ducks Unlimited and The Nature Conservancy have provided funding or assistance for the donation or purchase of undeveloped land or conservation easements.

A person or business can obtain a large tax write-off on federal and state tax returns for such donations. Conservation easements preserve the land, usually forever, and allow farming, logging, hunting, and fishing. The landowner is allowed to deduct the fair market value of a qualified easement, subject to an annual limit. Unused deductions can be carried forward.

Casualty Losses. These occur from storms, floods, earthquakes, and other such acts of nature. After subtracting $100 from your loss, you can deduct anything that exceeds 10% of your adjusted gross income. Attach Form 4684.

Miscellaneous Expenses- They must exceed 2% of your AGI. Valid expenses include union and professional fees, employee business expense, business/newsletter subscriptions, safe deposit box rental fees, tax accounting fees (except any business portion is not subject to the 2% threshold), separately paid IRA fees, uniforms not suitable for street wear, travel expenses away from home (meals, copying, travel, laundry, parking fees, phone calls, tips, and entertainment), and unreimbursed local transportation.

You can deduct educational expenses as long as they doesn't qualify you for a new profession (see IRS Publication 970). Those with previous business experience who receive an M.B.A. degree should look online at ustaxcourt.gov for the case of Lori Singleton-Clarke vs. the Commissioner of the Internal Revenue Service. She successfully sued the IRS and was able to deduct her M.B.A. educational costs. This case might be precedent for others pursuing advanced degrees in their same field.

Other Tax Issues

Low Capital Gains and Dividend Rates. Through 2010, persons in the 10 percent and 15 percent tax bracket have a zero capital gains and qualified dividend rate. Starting in 2011, unless Congress changes it, the capital gains rate for those above the 15% tax bracket will be 20% and below that 10%. Large capital gains or dividends may push taxpayers into higher tax brackets for a portion of that income.

Tax Managed Investing. Taxable capital gains notices from mutual funds often surprise investors who didn't sell their shares. The solution to this problem is to buy tax managed funds, ETFs, and index funds (all of which have smaller distributions) or to trade individual stocks so that you can decide when to realize capital gains. Shares in a retirement plan are not affected.

Special Tax Considerations. There may be special tax or delayed filing benefits for areas declared as a disaster area by the U.S. Federal Government.

Type of Business Entity. Filing your tax return as a sole proprietorship or a single member LLC (can include a husband and wife if sole owners) on Schedules C and E is definitely far superior to other entities for ease and cost of reporting. Check the regulations for qualifications.

Partnership returns are far more complex and generally require a tax preparer costing $1,000 and up, even with all records summarized into appropriate categories.

If audited, taxpayers filing the simpler Schedule C and E forms may also save on professional fees as they may feel more comfortable representing themselves. In addition, the dissolution of a business involving simpler organizations is easier. That being said, if you run a business that is risky like renting apartments, being a contractor, or having a restaurant, you will likely want to have a formal LLC or similar structure for liability protection. If you have a single member LLC, you can have the best of both worlds, protection and simplicity of filing.

An alternative to an LLC is to be a sole proprietor with a large umbrella insurance policy which is often relatively cheap. Umbrella policies are desirable for both personal and business reasons. Check with your lawyer and insurance agent.

Since the net profits of an LLC filed on Schedule C (up to the maximum) are subject to FICA (social security) taxes, consider applying for Subchapter S status which have both liability and tax advantages. You can split the profits between wages and distributions. The wage part is subject to FICA, but the other portion can be designated as a distribution not subject to FICA. That amount can be withdrawn and/or re-invested in the business. Be careful not to record too little as wages since this will encourage an audit and will reduce payments into retirement plans. Another reported advantage of Subchapter S status is substantially reduced audit rates.

To reduce required contributions to social security, a husband or wife could own a business separately instead of jointly. This only helps when the total net income exceeds the maximum base subject to FICA for that one person. For 2009, that was $106,800. Check with your legal advisers to ensure that the omitted spouse still gets her share of the business in a divorce or bankruptcy.

Some Other Tips

Loss Carry-forwards. People often forget about tax decisions made in prior years. Remember to carry losses forward and consider selling something with a gain to offset losses larger than $3,000. Capital losses can only be carried forward. Operating losses can be carried back to the extent of the profits.

Worthless Securities. Sell a worthless to someone for some nominal amount like one cent per share. If other investors have the same worthless security, agree to sell to each other.

Wash Sale Rule. A loss on a security sale is disallowed if a "substantially identical" security is purchased within 30 days of sale. It even applies if a security in your regular account is sold and repurchased in a retirement account.

The Hated Alternative Minimum Tax (AMT). The AMT was originally implemented to tax high cash flow individuals paying little tax. Unfortunately, it now hits much of the middle class. The AMT is added to your regular tax because of preference items that are allowed as deductions on your 1040 but are added back to your taxable income for AMT purposes. Anything beyond your exemption is taxed at the AMT tax rate.

Here are some "preference" items that can trigger it:

- Large itemized deductions for state and local taxes (includes property, sales, and income taxes). A deductible home office can help reduce this preference item.

- Dividends and capital gains. The effective rates go up for those subject to the AMT.

- Deductions for accelerated depreciation. For example, on personal property like furniture, using the 200% Declining Balance (DB) Depreciation method adds to AMT except that it reduces it when 200% DB becomes lower than straight line depreciation.

- Miscellaneous deductions like employee business and investment expenses.

- Incentive stock options that have been exercised even if the acquired stock hasn't been sold.

- Private activity bonds from some municipalities and states (estimated by the Securities Industry and Financial Markets Association to be 9% of the muni-bond market).

- Medical and dental.

- Many others that most people don't face.

To assess one's chances of being hit with the AMT, use the AMT Worksheet in the 1040 instructions (irs.gov) or the AMT Assistant, the electronic version (click on the Online Tools section).

Some strategies to reduce AMT are to delay payment of state, local, and some real estate taxes into a year where there is no AMT (after considering interest and penalties), move to a state with low or no state income tax, defer or accelerate income or expenses, retire, marry, divorce, etc. Some of the latter need explaining. For example, if a high AMT is expected, one can increase the non-preference business expenses so as to lower taxable income. Retiring would reduce income. Another strategy is to marry someone with a low AMT exposure and file a joint return. Dating just added a new AMT dimension. EHarmony.com are you listening?

Recovery of AMT. Remember to recapture the Alternative Minimum Taxes (AMT) paid in past years as a credit against current taxes. Such things as a drop in state income or real estate taxes might trigger a recapture opportunity. The AMT has been adjusted for inflation annually, but it might not increase in a given year or might drop down to the original $45,000 for married taxpayers and $33,750 for single and head of households. Congress has to authorize the new level each year.

Standard Deduction. Figure your taxes both with the standard deduction and itemizing on Schedule A, especially if you have real estate taxes and interest, medical deductions, state taxes, and/or employee business expenses. You might save hundreds or thousands of dollars. Any savings are tax free so $1 in tax savings is better than a $1 in taxable income. If your itemized deductions are close to the standard deduction, bunch your deductions and take the standard deduction one year and itemize the next. Delay or accelerate some elective surgery, property taxes, expenses, income, donations, etc.

Tax and Insurance Escrow Accounts. Avoid escrows accounts which simply give banks an interest free loan. Without escrowed funds, property tax and business insurance payments can, to some degree, be timed to minimize taxes as just discussed.

Automatic Payments. Automatic payments generally eliminate the risk of the bank not receiving your funds. One reason for not having them though is to be able to make your January payment in late December and be able to deduct almost 13 months of interest in a given year. That only works the first time, as after that, only 11-12 payments are possible. For automatic deductions, it isn't worth trying to make the January payment early since it means stopping and starting them, which creates the risks of double or no payments.

Section 179 Expense. Businesses (excluding rental real estate) with net profits can expense a certain amount of personal property such as equipment and furnishings instead of depreciating them.

Unfair Advantage. The IRS pays a lower interest rate on refunds than it charges on back taxes, the latter being higher than general market rates.

IRA Contributions. You have until April 15th (or on the following Monday if the 15th falls on a weekend) of each year to make them. Contribution limits are \$5,000 or \$6,000 for people at least 50 years old. Traditional IRA contributions are tax deductible for those with low **earned income** or for those taxpayers even with high earned income without a retirement plan at work. If money is withdrawn from an IRA before the age of 59 ½, it is subject to an early withdrawal penalty of 10% except in the following cases:

- Permanent disability

- Payment for non-reimbursed medical expenses

- Unemployed who is paying for medical expenses

- First time home buyer

- Back taxes

- Higher education costs

- Death

Roth IRAs and Conversion. Income taxes must be paid on the value of any regular IRAs converted to a Roth IRA and any new contributions to one. The two key advantages of a Roth IRA are that there is no required minimum distribution at age 70 ½ (as in a regular IRA), and all further income and appreciation in the account are tax free.

Two new 2010 features concern conversions of regular IRAs to Roth IRAs. The AGI and status requirements limiting those eligible are eliminated. You can also choose to include all of the taxable income caused by the conversion either in 2010 or in equal amounts in 2011 and 2012.

Retirement Income. Pull funds out of your taxable accounts first (unless you have lots of other taxable income), then your tax deferred, and lastly from your Roth. This strategy maximizes the time the funds grow tax free or tax deferred. If circumstances warrant, try to make taxable withdrawals more in years with low taxable income or high deductions.

SEP-IRA Contributions. Self employed individuals can open a SEP-IRA (which is similar to the regular IRA) for themselves or their employees. The advantage of these is the higher limit, which is 25% of your income up to a maximum of $49,000 for 2010. These retirement accounts require a fee to open and an annual maintenance fee of $300 and up. In addition, if the business is disbanded and you stop filing tax returns, then you need to transfer the assets to a personal IRA.

Forgiven Home Mortgage Debt. In the past, forgiven debt was considered income. This is a big issue now that many individuals are losing their homes. The law was changed so that singles and joint filers don't have to pay taxes on up to $2 million of forgiven debt on a principal residence from 2007 to 2012.

Extra Exemption for Age 65 and Being Blind. Besides the standard personal exemption(s), blind persons and those over 65 receive an extra exemption. For the 2010 return due on April 15th, 2011, you qualify if you turn 65 by Jan. 1, 2011. It seems curious that a person qualifies on January 1st. My take is that Congress felt sorry for those missing the prior year's tax exemption by being born on January 1st instead of December 31st.

Reduction in Personal Exemption Loss. People making above a certain income lose all or part of their personal exemption, but this loss is phased out in 2010 unless changed by Congress.

Reduction in Itemized Deductions. People making above a certain amount lose all or part of their itemized deductions, but the loss is phased out in 2010 unless changed by Congress.

Student Loan Defaulters. In 2005, the Supreme Court ruled that a portion of a person's social security payments could be garnished to pay student loans that are more than 10 years old.

Annual Gift Tax Exclusion. For 2009, you can give annual gifts to non-charities (usually individuals) totaling $13,000 and not affect your lifetime estate exclusion.

Kiddie Tax. The "kiddie tax" is applied to the investment income (like dividends and capital gains) of children as old as 23, depending upon whether they are full-time students, unmarried, and the amount of earned income. The tax rate of the parents is applied for investment income exceeding $1,800.

Alimony. It is tax deductible.

Social Security Taxes. With high income and two different employers, some people pay too much in FICA taxes. To apply for a refund of excess FICA, fill out page two of Form 1040.

Flexible Spending Accounts (FSA). Employers and employees can contribute to them and they are not taxable. The funds can be used for unreimbursed medical costs (prescription and non-prescription), insurance premiums (medical, dental, and long term care), childcare, and eldercare costs. Expenses paid from the FSA can't be deducted on Schedule A. If your marginal rate is 35% and $5,000 is spent from the FSA, then $1,750 in taxes is saved.

Health Savings Account. Payments for this account are used to pay medical bills. The employee contributions are tax deductible and the employer's are tax free.

Credit Card Rewards and Purchase Rebates. IRS Publication #17 says cash rebates are not taxable income but do reduce the basis (cost) for any item depreciated.

Teacher Deduction. Teachers can deduct up to $250 spent on classroom supplies without needing to itemize.

Capital Gains Rate for Collectibles. The maximum rate for art, stamps, coins, antiques, and other collectibles is higher than the regular capital gains and can be as high as 28%.

Capital Gain on the Sale of the Primary Residence. Normally, a primary residence must be lived in for two of the last five years in order to exclude up to $250,000 in gain for a single person and up to $500,000 for a married couple filing jointly. However, there are a number of exceptions to this requirement including moving more than 50 miles for a job, health reasons, divorce, and a number of "unforeseen circumstances" like losing your job, natural disasters, death, and multiple births. The owners receive a "reduced maximum exclusion" based upon the number of years lived there. The additional exceptions can be invoked even if they happen to other household residents who are relatives as distant as cousins (See Publication #23).

Don't forget to add capital improvements, title insurance, advertising, inspection fees, and any fix-up costs (like painting, wallpaper, and maintenance) completed within 90 days of the sale to your basis to reduce the capital gain.

Widowed homeowners now have two years following a spouse's death to sell their home and keep up to $500,000 in tax free profits. A divorcing spouse moving out of the home should consider a "use of residence" clause which allows him to declare the home as his principal place of residence. Then when it is sold by the ex-spouse, he can exclude $250,000 in capital gains.

Home Equity Loan Interest. The interest on up to $100,000 of home equity debt is deductible if filing jointly, but is added back to calculate AMT.

Unmarried Couples. One issue faced by couples is how to split deductions like taxes and interest. The biggest concern is an IRS audit. One person, possibly the person with the highest marginal tax rate, could take them all or they could be split. If the money is paid from a joint account, the IRS would probably accept a 50/50 split or one in proportion to the household expenses paid by each person. To be safe with another split, you might want to have a written agreement or write separate checks from an individual account with a note on the check and the ledger about the amount of interest, for example, to be allocated.

Like-Kind Exchanges. Like kind exchanges (also called 1031) allow you to defer taxes on the sale of business real property when it is exchanged into similar property. Before completing the sale of property, it is important to understand the rules. The basic rules are:

- The seller has 45 days to identify the new property after the closing date of the first sale and 180 days to complete the purchase transaction.

- The exchange must be into "like-kind" but not identical property. For example, residential real estate could be exchanged for commercial.

- A licensed exchange agent, who controls the funds, is required. The rates at which your funds are invested and the 1031 fees can vary enough that it is worth checking different agents.

- During the period when the funds are with the exchange agent, depreciation write-offs are lost. Only the interest on the account is received. Thus, reinvest as soon as possible since in most cases, the rate of return on the new investment will beat short term interest rates, especially when the tax shield is considered.

- There are specific other rules on the amount of debt, values of the properties, and cash involved. The details and filing your tax return are too complicated for most people so consult an accountant, both before and after the transaction.

- The rules about who can handle exchange transactions and how the money is invested vary by state. Some exchange agents have loaned the funds to real estate developers or made other risky investments and gone bankrupt. To be safe, obtain references and hire an attorney to insure that the funds are deposited at the exchanger's bank, possibly in your name and the exchanger.

- For a multi-million dollar transaction, negotiate with your exchange agent and several banks to place your funds there. Some exchange agents may insist upon their own banks, but others won't. The funds should be placed in the highest, but safe, yielding instrument that facilitates your purchase commitments. If the purchase will occur 100 days after the sale, a three month CD would be appropriate. For a series of spread out transactions, limit some commitments to varying lengths of time.

- You can also do a reverse exchange in which new property is purchased first and then the old one sold and still get the same tax benefits.

Exchanges are not always the best approach. In a community property state, the real estate assets are written up to market when a spouse dies so the survivor may simply want to sell them. Other persons not wanting an exchange include those in a zero or low tax bracket, those expecting big increases in the capital gains rate, and taxpayers having prior years' losses including passive losses to offset the gain.

Withholding and Quarterly Tax Payments. For some people, forecasting their annual taxes is a chore because of unforeseen occurrences like unemployment, accidents, and medical bills, and the nature of their employment.

However, it is not desirable to overpay and let the government have your money interest free (especially for persons with high interest credit card debt) nor underpay and owe a lot of interest and penalties. Furthermore, neither the interest nor the penalties are tax deductible. To determine your quarterly payment, download IRS Form 1040-ES.

The deadline for quarterly payments is:

First Quarter   April 15th of the tax year

Second Quarter   June 15th of the tax year

Third Quarter   September 15th of the tax year

Fourth Quarter   January 15th of the next year (Can be extended to Feb. 1st if the tax return is filed and the entire tax due is paid by then)

You can avoid penalties and interest if you pay the following:

- 90% of the current year's tax liability (some small businesses also can qualify) **or**

- 100% of the prior year's tax liability if your AGI is $150,000 or less ($75,000 for married filing separately), but is 110% for taxpayers with over $150,000 in AGI **or**

- 90% of the tax liability based upon the actual income received in a given quarter.

The first two situations assume that your income is received evenly throughout the year. The third option would be employed if the largest chunk of income occurs in the latter half of the year. Such events often occur with bonuses and investment sales.

The best way to figure taxes for the current year is to pull out last year's return, make a copy, and go line by line to estimate changes. Be sure to use appropriate schedules (like A, B, and D), your main tax form (like the 1040), and the AMT form.

From a taxpayer who is not self employed and who budgets well or who has alternative income, the best option for payments may be to have minimal amounts withheld, such as 2% of income from January to October. Then have most of your November and December paychecks devoted to taxes. The IRS treats funds withheld from a paycheck as being equally distributed throughout the year. Be sure to request the withholding changes (up or down) by your employer's deadline to avoid having almost no paycheck in January.

Write to your Congressional Representative. They often get action where others don't.

Forms 8275 and 8275-R. Don't file them as they basically admit that you are knowingly taking a position contrary to IRS regulations

Maximize Deductions. Take deductions, where possible, on the schedule that maximizes your write-off. Specifically, it is better to report them on Schedules C and E than Schedule A because deductions on the latter are often limited and/or subject to the AMT.

Changing Your Withholding Rate. Being unemployed may cause your income taxes due for the year to drop substantially, both from the loss in income and being shifted into a lower tax bracket. This obviously depends upon whether and when another job is found, its pay, and the size of your severance package and unemployment checks (both of which are taxed).

For quick cash, reduce the amount withheld for taxes by filing a new W4 for your last paychecks and any severance package. Withholding rates can always be quickly raised again.

Other Business Oriented Deductions

- Those eligible should take the research and development credit including salaries.

- Use the section 199 deduction for manufacturers, construction companies, design firms, and some others. The deduction is based upon a percentage of net income.

- Switch to LIFO (last in, first out) for inventories if prices are rising.

- Cash accounting- To increase expenses, pay as many bills as possible before year's end. Call vendors and ask for an early invoice. If your office is being carpeted in January, pre-pay for the carpet in December. (Note: the IRS might argue that it wasn't depreciable until placed in service). Likewise, submit December billings in January. Furthermore, when using the accrual method, income is billed when the sales or service occurs, regardless of when money is received.

- Accrual accounting. Get invoices and accrue before the end of the year if you want to increase expenses. Bonuses can be paid up to 2 ½ months after year end.

- Look at Form 3800 for 35 business credits. Many relate to alternative energy and energy efficiency activities, but there is a bizarre group of special interest "lollipop" credits for railroad track maintenance, mine rescue team training, agricultural chemicals security, Indian coal production, distilled spirits, orphan drugs, and new markets.

Real Estate Professional

A person spending more than half of her work hours on real estate business or more than 750 hours per year is considered a real estate professional and can deduct all of her real estate losses against her taxable income. File Form 8582 and include the following statement with your tax return:

"In accordance with Reg. 1.469-9(g)(3), the taxpayer hereby states that it is a qualifying real estate professional under IRC 469 (C)(7), and elects under IRC (C)(7)(A) to treat all interests in real estate as a single rental real estate activity."

Taxpayers who are not real estate professionals may have their losses limited depending upon their income, the size of their losses, whether they are a limited partner, and their level of participation. Running a business with real estate like a motel does not qualify one as a real estate professional.

Illegal Deductions

There are actually many that can trigger interest and penalties if audited, but I'll mention only some of the prominent illegal deductions.

1. Utilities in your home (except a portion related to an exclusive use of a home office)

2. Expenses for your guard dog that lives in your home. I knew an Amway salesman who deducted them. If one lives exclusively in a non-home business like a salvage yard, it could probably qualify.

3. Property taxes and insurance reserve payments on your house. Actual tax payments are deductible and a portion of insurance may be if related to a home office.

4. Non business use of a car that has business advertising

5. Losses on securities not sold or losses within IRAs, 401(k)s, and other retirement accounts

6. House hunting expenses and temporary living arrangements before a taxpayer moves into his new home. The cost of moving household goods and lodging while in transit is deductible. Employer paid temporary housing becomes income to the taxpayer.

7. Credit card interest and fees except for a business credit card

8. Boat and recreational property costs unless clearly used for business. Non-business use must be excluded. There are strict rules on this.

9. Broker's buying commissions. Some people try to deduct them as investment expense. The purchase costs are added to the cost and the sales' commission is deducted from the proceeds.

10. Gambling losses that exceed gains. Save your race track stubs, canceled checks, credit card bills, etc. to offset losses in a given year

in case you "score."

Big winners at casinos, lotteries, or tournaments will have 30% of their winnings withheld for federal taxes and possibly some for state taxes. Non U.S. residents may obtain a partial or full tax refund. Contact a professional refund service, available in many casinos.

11. Political contributions. Some states with an income tax allow a deduction.

12. The cost of entertaining friends

13. Commuting expenses. See Publication # 529.

14. Club dues

15. Travel and living expenses for employment away from home that exceeds one year

16. Legal expenses for personal matters that do not produce taxable income. Deductibility may depend on the wording on the bill. For example, an accounting bill for "estate advice" is more suspect than one for "accounting advice" or "tax advice."

17. Lost or misplaced cash or property

18. Travel as a form of education unless you are in the travel business or writing a book on travel

19. Expenses of attending a seminar, convention, or similar meeting unless related to your employment

20. Fines and penalties (including state tax)

21. Adoption expenses (but you might use Form 8839 for a tax credit)

22. Expenses of producing tax exempt income

23. Personal car rental expenses

24. Tax losses on the sale of your home (except for the home office portion)

25. Federal income and excise taxes

26. Social Security, Medicare, federal unemployment, and railroad retirement taxes

27. Customs duties

28. Federal estate and gift taxes

29. Gasoline tax, car inspection fees, sidewalk assessments, and most license fees

30. Improvements to your property except when selling or business related

31. Funeral expenses

32. Diet food

33. Medical expenses under 7.5% of AGI

34. Deducting all points at once on a refinance

35. Claiming 100% of food and entertainment expenses while traveling

36. Losses from insects or gradual wearing down of a building

37. Undocumented donations

CHAPTER 18

Understanding, Buying, and Needing Insurance

Understand Why You Need Insurance

Insurance is important for wealth building because the expense is modest but the consequences of not having any or insufficient insurance can be catastrophic. The cost of any insurance policy includes covering a company's loss payments, employee benefits, retirement plans, other benefits (like golf course memberships, retreats, etc.), sales commissions, asset purchases (like buildings), dividends, profits, corporate jets, travel, claims processing, and other overhead. Thus, don't buy insurance that is not needed, that has large mark-ups, or that is duplicated elsewhere. Also, don't forget about its existence, especially life insurance. Note the policy in your will and inform your will's executor, trusted friends, and/or family.

Examples of insurance that, in my opinion, are overpriced include insurance covering flights, baggage, car rentals (see comments later in this chapter), cancer, identity theft, appliances, car repairs, electronics, and credit life (offered for loans). An example of an unneeded policy is life insurance covering your kids. They don't support you and tragic as a death is, your expenses will actually go down. A small policy to cover funeral expenses, assuming you don't like the relatively cheap cremation, might make some sense. I also wouldn't buy life insurance for a self supporting significant other or spouse. It would be better to put the money saved into a retirement fund.

Lower your Rates With Comparison Shopping

Fast insurance quotes for a variety of different policies can be obtained quickly at Insurance.com or InsWeb.com. However, this action will trigger follow-on emails so you will need to hit "unsubscribe."

Be aware that different quotes may be obtained on-line than from an agent selling the same insurance policy. Progressive Insurance, for example, allows direct purchases from them or through an agent. If the agent price is about the same, always use an agent for advice and to "go to bat" for you in case of a difficult claim.

For flood insurance, go to Floodsmart.gov which provides details about the National Flood Insurance Program (NFIP) passed by Congress in 1968, floods zones, and insurance quotes. For an individual or business to qualify, your community needs to participate and pass certain building requirements.

Behavioral or Ownership Issues That Affect Rates

Certain things are likely to make your agent and insurance company nervous. They may result in a cancellation or a hike in premiums. Such things as ski diving, bungee jumping, hang gliding, smoking, owning a potentially dangerous animal (such as a Rottweiler or Pit Bull) or a motorcycle, frequent calls about what is covered in this situation and that (a few are okay), DUIs, being arrested, and owning a high powered sports car. A combination of them will put you on the "endangered species" list.

Redlining Raises Rates

An insurance company may charge higher premiums for certain areas and zip codes, e.g., in high crime areas, flood zones, and earthquake prone areas. This practice is known as "redlining," and sometimes it may be illegal. It is best to shop around as not all insurance companies will treat the perceived risk in the same way.

Policy Cancellations are Bad News

A cancellation of your insurance is bad news because it sends a signal to other companies that you are a poor risk. It is then difficult to find new insurance and you may be thrown into a "special" or "assigned risk" insurance pool. Your best bet may be to fight the cancellation by first contacting your insurance company. If not satisfied, then complain to your state's insurance commissioner or consult an attorney. Move swiftly so your insurance doesn't lapse.

The reasons for cancellation could include those just listed behavioral issues, a drop in your credit score, a lawsuit, an unkempt yard, a felony conviction, a perceived change in your risk, or even a late insurance payment. Staying with one company reduces your chances of being cancelled if you rarely file claims. A loyal and experienced insurance agent can assess the chances that a claim will cause cancellation, and he may be able to reverse a cancellation.

Your Claims Record and How it Affects You

1. The more claims filed, the higher will be your insurance rates. People carrying a low deductible, get hit twice. First, they pay more for the lower deductible and second, are put into a higher rate class for filing more claims. To reduce this double whammy, use high deductibles, usually $1,000 or more on a home and auto (collision), and $5,000 to $10,000 on apartment buildings. **Over the long term, I have saved probably twice as much in insurance premiums as I spent on actual repairs.** Have your agent quote several different deductibles to check the savings.

2. See your past insurance claims on personal property (like clothes, books, and diamonds) and auto losses by reading your CLUE (Comprehensive Loss Underwriting Exchange) report. The report can be found online at choicetrust.com and is free once every 12 months. Your date of birth and social security number must be provided, and five security questions are asked to reduce unauthorized use. If you are concerned about on line safety, order your report by phone at 1-866-312-8076. Choice Trust also will provide free copies of its Tenant History Report, Employment History Report, and Full File Report. The latter can be obtained by using their "Request for Full Disclosure" form (found at the website) and sending it along with two documents to:

> ChoicePoint Consumer Center
> Attn: Full File Disclosure
> P.O. Box 105108
> Atlanta, GA 30348-5108

One reason for checking your files is that many losses will affect your insurability and cost, and you want any errors deleted. Of course, if your insurance company has missed listing any claims, don't alert them. Choice Trust also sells your home insurance and auto insurance scores (for $12.95 each).

Insurance Scores

Most people are unaware of their insurance scores which are derived from their credit record, claims history, driving record, and other variables like age, sex, and miles driven. The insurance score is created by Fair Isaac and the three credit bureaus can produce them if requested by an insurance company. One important method for increasing your insurance score is to raise your credit rating. Information about how scores are calculated and used is available at InsuranceScores.com.

Avoid Low Rated and Unregulated Companies

1. Check with your library, the internet, or insurance agent for ratings. Insurance company ratings are determined by A.M. Best Company (ambest.com), Standard and Poor's Rating Information Services (standardandpoors.com), Moody's Investor Services (moodys.com), Fitch, Inc. (fitchratings.com), and TheStreet.com, Ratings, Inc. (weissratings.com). The first two sources are free with registration. Best only asks for your email while Standard and Poor asks for some additional information including your company. Stick with insurance companies rated at least A+.

Be cautious about buying insurance from a regional and lower rated company in areas prone to catastrophic losses like hurricanes, tornadoes, or earthquakes. If the company isn't broadly diversified, its capital could be wiped in one large loss. However, most states have some safety net or guaranty association to cover claims from insolvent insurance companies, but for off-shore or unregulated companies, the state will not generally cover insolvency.

For annuities, there may be stricter dollar limits because it has some elements of investment risk. Check to ensure that your policy doesn't exceed your state's limit, in case the insurance company fails.

2. Go to your state's insurance website for much information. It often has important information about filing complaints, the number of them against an individual insurer, rates, underwriting standards, types of coverage, minimum insurance requirements for auto insurance, filing a claim, and typical questions and answers. For this assistance, type "insurance division" and then your state in the search engine box. If a company has many complaints relative to the number of policies written, it is advisable to find another insurer. Such a company is portrayed to the extreme in the movie "The Rainmaker," starring Matt Damon and Danny Devito.

3. Don't buy insurance from any company not licensed in your state and only buy state licensed products. Check with your state's insurance division.

4. Report insurance fraud at naic.org (National Association of Insurance Commissioners). That website also has printable guides for auto, home, and life insurance.

5. If insurance is unusually cheap, read the fine print and investigate. In some cases, companies will offer cheap insurance for the following reasons: to penetrate a new market; the policy has many exclusions; the coverage isn't effective for some period; there are big price increase clauses; the company is not registered; or it is shady or undercapitalized.

Understand What Your Policy Covers

Read your policy and call your agent about confusing aspects of your policy's coverage. Be careful to understand your need for flood insurance in or near floodplains and coastal areas. In addition, check on coverage when traveling (especially out of the U.S.) and renting a car, and for special collections (like stamps, coins, and antique guns), cash, and jewelry. You likely need supplemental coverage. Ask your agent who is covered when working on your house or yard and when that contractor needs to be licensed?

Some Policies Require Prior Approval

Some medical procedures need prior approval or a second opinion. Read your insurance contract carefully. If the issue involves a lot of money, have them put the information in writing.

Getting Your Insurance Company to Pay Off

Sometimes, your insurance company doesn't want to pay a claim. Though the following suggestions are most applicable to medical claims, they apply to others as well. Here are the steps to take, and the first five should be done quickly:

1. Contact your insurance agent and obtain his opinion and help. Depending upon the size of the claim and her clout, she may be able to prod the insurer.

2. Keep a log of the dates and people contacted and their actions or reactions. Keep this log next to your phone so none is omitted.

3. Organize all contact information (letters, notes, and calls), bills, and payments in a folder. File them chronologically by category.

4. For a medical claim, ask your doctor's receptionist for notes and letters in your file.

5. Call the insurer's customer service department to see if a problem can be resolved. Request a key contact to avoid repeating information. Ask that a supervisor or a senior caseworker be assigned to your case if it involves a considerable amount of money.

6. Consider sending requests to the insurance company by certified mail with dates for it to respond.

7. Find out how to access your insurer on line and follow your claims. Having electronic access will spend up the whole process.

8. For medical claims, do research by going online to the major medical centers and the U.S. Government's sites that list on-going research. For complex and new approaches, you want evidence that some procedure works well, is the new standard of care, and/or is cost effective. Ask your doctor to incorporate this information into his letters. If you are comfortable with the information, consider writing a draft for him.

9. Check out blogs and support groups.

10. Go online and check complaints about the company and at the Better Business Bureau. This will help you determine if the case is more isolated or indicates a pattern of reimbursement problems.

11. For a group policy, contact the liaison to the insurer. He may be able to pressure the insurance company.

12. Provide copies of your letters sent to your insurer by "cc" to your boss and benefits department. You want the insurer to know about others in the loop.

13. Make sure your doctor is billing under the correct billing code.

14. Appeal any unfavorable decision. Determine the appeals process early and follow it carefully. There may be several levels of appeal and **deadlines.**

15. Enlist a patient advocate. Information can be found at sites such as patientnavigator.com, insurancenightmare.com, and everypatientadvocate.com.

16. Many states have a "Patient's Bill of Rights" that may help, especially for getting care from an out-of-network provider.

17. Contact your state legislator. Some insurance companies may not be meeting state requirements or possibly the requirements should be changed.

18. Contact the president or CEO of the insurer.

19. Write and call your state's insurance department and possibly your members of Congress. Insurers are often afraid that Congress will pass laws that raise their costs.

20. Write to various entities which may put pressure on an insurer such as a local newspaper, *AARP, Money Magazine, BusinessWeek, The Wall Street Journal, and Smart Money Magazine.* Be sure to send or email copies of your correspondence to the insurance company and your agent or company representative. Some contacts may do nothing, but the insurance company doesn't know that. Write individual letters by simply changing the heading rather than a "cc" with everyone listed. The "cc letters" have less impact.

21. Hire a lawyer.

Consider an Umbrella Policy to Safeguard Your Wealth

Persons with considerable net worth or who face unusually high risks should consider a personal and/or business umbrella policy for extra liability. The umbrella provides added insurance beyond your basic policy for relatively little money. Many basic policies have a basic liability of $1,000,000 per occurrence with a $2,000,000 limit. If the liability is lowered to $500,000/1,000,000 and a large umbrella ($3-5,000,000) put on top of that, the insured will have much greater protection for little extra money.

Building Insurance Issues

Insured Value. Buildings shouldn't be either over or under insured. If the amount of insurance is too low, the insurance may not cover your losses. For some older buildings, only "actual cash value" coverage (which replaces the damage minus depreciation) may be available. Depending upon the age and condition of the building, this may represent only 50% of its replacement cost.

If overvalued, then premiums are being wasted since the insurance company will not pay for more than the structure is worth. Insurance companies typically raise the insured value of a building by an inflation factor nearly every year. However, this value may not be accurate, especially during a deep recession. Your insurance agent should have access to a manual with standard building values with local area adjustments. Ask him for the dwelling square footage and the dollar values used by the insurance company for the basement, main floors, outbuildings, patios, etc. Then ask him to measure your house or do it yourself. The correct measurement would be from the outside walls, not the inside.

Lenders often require homeowners to buy building insurance that covers the whole mortgage even when that value is considerably higher than the building's replacement cost. Excessive insurance is ridiculous and a waste of money because the insurer won't pay more than the building's value.

Security Devices. Some equipment, such as a burglar alarm, safe, a fire alarm connected to a local fire department, and fire extinguishers may lower your premiums. It depends upon your insurance company and what is covered.

Remodeling. Remember to raise your insurance to cover expensive remodeling projects.

Special Risks. Those with a pool or trampoline, for example, should add extra liability protection. Just being friendly and inviting friends isn't enough to avoid being sued. Money often trumps "friendship."

Typically not Covered. People are often surprised about what isn't covered. This may include damage from termites or other infestations, floods, water line breaks, sewer back-up, mudslides, earthquakes, and stolen or damaged motorcycles (unless specifically insured), and boats.

Because of hurricanes, some insurance companies in coastal areas may not even cover wind damage. Especially hard hit with high insurance increases are states like Mississippi, Louisiana, and Florida, and even some surprising locations like New York City and Long Island. Because of their proximity to the ocean and elevation, these areas are thought to be increasingly vulnerable to rising waters and coastal storms in part due to global warming. The ocean has risen about two inches in the past 15 years with much more expected in the future.

Pet Insurance

In 2009, pet owners are expected to spend $12.2 billion for pet insurance (*The Wall Street Journal*). Premiums can vary from about $100 to $1,000 per year depending upon the age and breed of your pet, location, and policy features. As in my human policies, limits on what is paid may fall far short of covering the bill. Pet insurance is like that for people, namely, if you have it, you will spend more on care.

I personally wouldn't buy pet insurance unless there were preferred providers offering lower rates to policy holders. Instead, I would determine the insurance rates and every month put that money into a low expense index fund with perhaps 50% in stock and 50% in bonds. The problem with this investment approach for some people is that they would pay insurance premiums, but wouldn't invest the funds saved by not having a policy.

Identity Theft Insurance

This is a relatively new type of insurance which State Farm calls Identity Restoration Coverage. This insurance is often an add-on to dwelling coverage and is relatively cheap at $25 per year. Their policy provides up to $25,000 per year for covered expenses caused by identity theft. These include fees for credit reports, phone calls, postage, notary/filing (to correct credit reports), legal bills, lost wages, child/elder care, and financial institution charges. Since the rate is only $1 for every $1,000 in insurance, State Farm is likely counting on relatively few people needing it and the actual claims being very low or it is a starter rate to gain entry into a market..

Some Insurance Issues

1. Buy term life insurance. I only buy term life insurance which doesn't have a cash value. Whole life has an investment feature which accrues a "cash value" that includes a lot of insurance company overhead not included in an index fund. However, if you already have a whole life policy, then carefully evaluate whether to cancel it because of termination fees and income taxes on the net proceeds (surrender value minus premiums paid).

2. Get an appraisal of your life insurance policy. For $75-85 (the second appraisal is $55), EvaluateLifeInsurance.org will assess your current or a prospective whole life, universal life, or variable life policy. This service compares its true investment rate of return to an alternative of buying a term life policy and investing the proceeds into a hypothetical alternative investment such as a CD or a mutual fund. The analysis includes a print-out showing expected rates of return on your policy for holding periods for 5, 10, 15, and 20 years.

3. Determine your life insurance needs. To determine your life insurance needs, go to smartmoney.com/personal finance/insurance/life insurance and click "How much life insurance do you need?" Its personal calculator takes into account your surviving spouse/partner's and children's ages, income, current assets, debts, contingency fund, future educational expenses, child care, and funeral and estate expenses. The most underinsured are families with young children; and the most overinsured are secondary wage earners, non-working spouses, and people approaching retirement.

Other sites to consider are tiaa-cref.org and choosetosave.org. The latter has a two page worksheet called "Ballpark Estimate."

4. Avoid bottom of the barrel insurance policies. One type of life insurance to avoid is the cheap ($10-15,000) policies which advertise "You can't be turned down for any reason." It is not economical to sell insurance in small amounts so you are likely to see a "bait and switch" to more expensive policies, or there are many restrictions (like no payment if you die within a couple of years and no pre-existing illnesses). These policies, in fact, use the healthy to subsidize the unhealthy.

5. Update your insurance beneficiary list. Don't forget to change it as circumstances warrant like the death of a beneficiary, the birth of a baby, or a divorce. Also change your address when you move. Your insurance costs often adjust for a new location.

Health Insurance Issues

1. Look at your plan provisions carefully. When choosing a medical plan, the most important variables are: dollar limits and copayments per doctor visit or prescription, your lifetime maximum benefit, annual deductibles, the ability to see specialists, out-of network reimbursements, and out-of-pocket maximums. A high deductible and a bare bones plan is probably most appropriate for those who want to guard against a catastrophic bill, the young and healthy, and those who are risk tolerant.

A cheap plan is not very good if medical choices are highly limited, the insurer rejects many claims, and he doesn't return phone calls. The plan you want balances your ability to pay with your needs. You don't want to go bankrupt. If you have children and modest income (varies by state), check with your state about free or cheap medical care or insurance.

2. Never include anyone on your plan that doesn't qualify. It costs your employer money and could be grounds for disciplinary action. Also enroll your eligible family members as soon as possible to avoid problems should some emergency arise. Proving eligibility in a crisis may lead to delayed treatment and additional stress.

3. If an enrolled employee dies, the family members should contact the insurer and his employer as soon as possible. The insurance policy may be extended for some specified period with premium payments. There is usually a window of 60 days to apply for this extension so act quickly. Some policies allow the spouse (and in some cases, a domestic partner) to continue the insurance until death.

4. Continue your company's insurance. People who are laid off, fired (except for gross misconduct), or quit their job are usually eligible to continue their old health insurance for 18 months through COBRA (Consolidated Omnibus Budget Reconciliation Act). Check the information at the Department of Labor's site (dol.gov/ebsa/faqs) to find out if your company is subject to the requirements and the qualifying events that allow an employee to invoke COBRA. The law covers the worker, their spouse, and dependent children. If your employer is subsidizing the insurance rates, then your premiums will likely be higher. Your human resources department should be able to advise you on your eligibility.

5. One of the misconceptions that people under 65 have is that Medicare pays most of one's medical costs starting at 65. The Employee Benefit Research Institute (ebri.org) estimates that Medicare covers only 60% of heath care costs for Medicare beneficiaries aged 65 and older.

The additional lifetime health premiums, Medicare Part B, and out-of-pocket costs for those retiring at age 65 in 2009 are:

Men	Employer Subsidizes Premiums	No Employer Subsidy
*Median	$68,000	$111,000
*75th percentile	$104,000	$168,000
Women		
*Median	$98,000	$159,000
*75th percentile	$129,000	$209,000
Married couple		
*Median	$165,000	$268,000
*75th percentile	$214,000	$346,000

I am interpreting these figures to mean that these amounts are needed on the day of retirement at age 65 and that the funds are invested at some "average" rate of return instead of a savings account with low returns. The funds are then withdrawn as needed. The median number represents a 50% chance that your savings will cover the amounts needed and the 75th percentile refers to a 75% chance that your savings will cover your needs. Women live longer than men so they require more savings. Couples that pool resources benefit in their model so those at higher levels need somewhat fewer resources.

The dollar amounts understate the needs of those who retire prior to age 65, sicker people, or those in high cost areas. The figures also don't include funds for long term care or care insurance. At ebri.org, the rates for Medigap Plan F and Medicare Part D (instead of private insurance) are shown. Those who work beyond age 65 and have medical benefits will obviously need fewer funds.

During the period from 1975-2005, Medicare cost increases grew 2.4% faster than the economy. I believe the rate will accelerate because of the passage of the health care bill, and it will have a substantial compound effect on the taxpayers, the economy, and the burden of and for retirees. The taxpayer burden will increase because retirees only pay about 25% of the cost of Medicare Part B which covers doctors' services, outpatient care, and diagnostic tests.

It is likely that the funds needed are conservative. Tax revenue is projected to cover only 81% of the expected benefits of Medicare Part A in 2017. Congress will need to make a number of changes including most of the following: cut benefits and medical reimbursements, and raise the eligibility age, retiree premiums, the payroll tax rate, and the base. Congress has failed to address the funding problem because most members fear losing their Congressional seats. Putting off the corrections only means that the pain will be worse and be more shocking because of its severity.

Compounding all of this is that people are expected to live longer with new drugs and expensive new equipment coming out every day. The present value of the Medicare lifetime benefits is estimated at $376,000 for a husband and wife turning 65 in 2010.

6. Insurance Companies are Super Snoopers. The nation's biggest insurers analyze drug prescriptions to identify people with a dependency, hypochondria, or a serious illness. They could deny coverage, raise rates, or exclude conditions. It is less of a problem in group plans, but when new coverage is needed, your past prescription history may affect the cost and availability of coverage. Adopting a healthy lifestyle at the earliest possible age is the best way to reduce the need for drugs.

7. Caesarean births make it difficult and expensive for women to obtain private insurance. These births are rapidly rising and now account for over 30% of all births and the number of women with a previous one followed by a vaginal birth is down to less than 10%.

8. Check trade groups in your field for group insurance. It may be worthwhile to pay dues and join one. Be creative; a landlord, for example, may be able to join a builder's group.

9. Small businesses with one or two employees may be able to establish their own group health insurance plans.

10. Make sure the insurance company is licensed in your state.

Disability Insurance

These policies cover very sick or injured workers and are particularly important for sole wage earners and families with children. They can be relatively cheap but are complicated, and policy holders should understand what qualifies as a disability. Being too tired to work from chronic fatigue syndrome isn't likely to be covered.

The policy replaces 50% to 80% of lost income. Premiums will vary based upon one's income, coverage, age, waiting period, and medical condition. The best policies are likely to be offered by your employer. Individual plans will cost 15-20% more.

The policies vary considerably with some covering those persons unable to perform their current occupation; others cover any occupation; and some replace the difference between prior and replacement income. There are some new types for the self employed called "business overhead policies" which cover business operating expenses.

Long Term Care Insurance and Other Options

Being frail and weak and dependent upon others is something most people worry about as they age. However, the time for concern is early in your earning years so more money can be saved and invested. People are justly concerned about long term care since the average annual cost of a nursing home was $74,806 in 2007 (*Genworth Financial's Cost of Care Survey*). That figure should rise at least at the rate of inflation, if not more, so that in 2010, the figure is probably over $80,000. The cost of assisted living is over $30,000 per year while home health care averages $18 per hour (*MetLife's Mature Market Institute*)

1. Long Term Care Insurance Features. This type of insurance is intended to provide funds for those unable to care for themselves. However, it is complicated and the combination of possible features is large. The variables include:

- Inflation rate- This protects the insured from large increases in the cost of care. The higher the rate, the more expensive will be the monthly premium.

- Non forfeiture clause- Upon cancellation, a portion of the payments is refunded. This feature raises a premium.

- Daily rate for nursing or home care- Increasing it raises premiums. If the actual rate in your nursing home is less than the daily rate, typically the coverage period is extended.

- Shared care- Two partners both buy coverage but pool benefits so that any unused by one can be used by the other. This raises the premium.

- Activity of daily living (ADL)- These are normal activities that include dressing, continence, eating, using the toilet, moving back and forth from a bed to a chair, and bathing that a non-disabled person can do. Two disabilities are typically needed to qualify, but it can also be triggered by substantial cognitive impairment like Alzheimer's. Normally, a medical professional must testify that the condition will last 90 days or more. Two is the standard as outlined in the Health Insurance Portability and Accountability Act of 1996.

- Home care- An aide comes to your home to help with important activities. These might include shopping, bathing, and cleaning. The more activities listed the higher the premiums.

- Waiting period- Days required in a nursing home or being disabled at home before benefits start. This can be 0 to 180 days. Shorter delays raise the premiums.

- Exclusions- The exclusions may include alcoholism and drug addiction, illnesses related to war, treatment already paid by the government, self inflicted injuries (including attempted suicide), and mental and nervous disorders or diseases (except organic brain disorders). Fewer exclusions raise the premium.

This type of policy is difficult for the insurance companies to price accurately so there may be substantial variations in rates for similar policies. The five biggest issues are the cost uncertainty of future care, deciding which benefits to include, increases in your monthly premium, collecting from your insurance company, and the difficulty of changing insurers. An insurer may petition the state for rate increases if his investments haven't done well or because his payouts are greater than expected. He can't raise the rates for an individual but can for a class of policy holders. Because of these problems, some people opt for self insurance. That option means that they need to invest money that would have been paid in premiums.

2. Tax Advantages. One big advantage of this insurance is potentially being able to deduct premiums (assuming you have taxable income and itemize) and having tax free pay-outs. The premiums are deducted on Schedule A, but including other health care expenditures, must exceed 7.5% of your adjusted gross income to be deductible. In some cases, the premiums can be deducted as a business expense or by the self employed. Be aware that the allowed deduction varies by age. For example, in 2009, the most that a person aged 51-60 could deduct was $1,150.

3. Advice of the National Association of Insurance Commissioners (NAIC). It advises the following on long term care insurance (see naic. org/long term care):

- Those currently receiving Social Security or who expect to have minimal or no retirement savings will likely qualify for state aid and therefore, should not purchase long term care insurance.

- Match your long-term care needs with your need to protect assets and your ability to pay. Don't pay more than 5% of your income (some say 7%) on these premiums.

- Long term care may be reduced if you have a spouse, children, or friends who are willing to care for you.

- Women, because they live longer, will more likely need long term care.

- Research companies to determine if they have a history of raising rates.

- Check with a financial adviser or accountant to see if it is appropriate for you.

- Buy only from a licensed and reputable company in your state.

- Pre-existing conditions may be excluded from coverage.

- For many policies, age 60 is a trigger for a rate increase. Thus, you may want to purchase your policy before your late 50s. According to some information given by NAIC, the annual cost of insurance on a new policy can double from age 50 to 65 and then be six times as much by age 75 (compared to age 50). Starting early lowers premiums, but you will be paying longer.

- Don't rely on Medicare or Medicaid to cover long term needs. Medicare usually pays for only a small percentage of nursing home costs. Medicaid only pays for those meeting federal poverty guidelines, and the choice of facilities is limited.

- Don't divulge personal financial or medical information over the phone to insurance salesmen. If someone appears dishonest, contact your state insurance department.

- Don't trust advertising suggesting Medicare is associated with long-term care insurance. Medicare neither sells nor endorses insurance.

- For more information on Medicare and Medicaid services including enrollment and benefits, visit the U.S. Government's site at hhs.gov (Health and Human Services).

4. NAIC Recommended Policy Provisions.

- An "outline of coverage" that describes benefits, terms, limitations, pay-outs, and policyholder's out-of-pocket costs.

- Waiting or elimination period.

- A minimum of one year of nursing home or home healthcare coverage or both, including intermediate and custodial care.

- The right to cancel the policy for any reason within 30 days of purchase and receive a full refund.

- A guarantee that the policy can't be canceled or terminated because of the policyholder's age or physical or mental condition.

- Consider an inflation protection option that periodically increases the benefit level without the policyholder having to provide evidence of insurability.

5. A Typical Rate Quote. Allianz's annual premium for a person aged 50 with a $150 daily benefit for four years and 100% home health care, a 5% annual inflation factor, and a 90 day elimination period is $1843; at age 60, it would be $2300; and at age 70, $4515. The aged 70 group might be better off foregoing the inflation premium because they could raise the daily benefit to $250 per day and pay a lower premium.

6. Thoughts on Self Insurance. Self insurance makes the most sense for people with substantial assets, the non-obese, people with close family willing to care for them, possibly those with a family history of wellness (though old age or an accident can disable even the strongest people), and healthy habits. Self insurance works best if your investment fund is started early in life. It isn't necessary to have a fund labeled "self insurance-care fund," but designating one likely would cause more contributions to it.

One of the big advantages of self funding is that all funds belong to the owner even if he stops paying. The biggest disadvantage occurs if long term care is needed in the early stages of accumulation when the fund is small. Some people may not want to take that risk.

If your disability risk is relatively low, then you are subsidizing higher risk policyholders. According to Milliman, Inc., an actuarial firm, about 45% of individuals who reach age 65 will need some long term care (*Money*). However, about 68% of those spend less than 90 days there in any given year (*Smart Money*). Furthermore, only 9% will have a long term stay in a nursing home, but the average will be 2 ½ years. A total of 18% will need long term assisted living.

7. An Example of Self Insurance. Let's put this information into perspective with different assumptions. Using the 2010 average annual cost for annual assisted living of $80,000, the 2 ½ years average stay would cost $200,000. In 15 years (2025) and 25 years (2035) with inflation rates of 3% and 5%, the average 2 ½ year nursing home stay would cost:

	Inflation rate			Inflation rate	
	3%	5%		3%	5%
2025 cost	$311,593	415,786	**2035 cost**	418,756	677,271

Assuming an annual premium of $1,800 per year with an annual increase of 1% for the 15 and 25 years, the long term care premiums paid would be:

2010-25 premiums paid $28,974

2010-35 premiums paid $50,837

Instead of buying insurance, let's compare the investment returns from investing premiums as part of a self insurance plan. For simplicity, let's assume annual returns of 8%.

The invested premiums would grow as follow:

	8% return
Portfolio value in 2025	52,850
Portfolio value in 2035	152,462

Let us now summarize:

	2025	2035
Nursing home cost (ave. 4% annual inflation)	363,690	$548,013
All premiums	28,974	50,837
Investment value (ave. 8% annual return)	52,850	152,462

The above figures are based upon three assumptions, namely that inflation in care costs increases an average of 4% (range shows 3-5%), premiums rise by 1% a year, and investment returns by an average 8%. Changes of just a few percentage points can substantially change the results.

The above suggests that long term care insurance is a great bargain if care is needed. The projected nursing home costs are more than 10 times the premium and 3.6 times the investment value. However, if long term care isn't needed, the potential investment returns generated from investing the insurance premiums are lost. Finally, don't be "bummed" if it's not used. It means you were healthy to the end or had loved ones who cared for you.

One thing is certain though; a nursing home is a more likely option with long term care insurance than without it.

8. Ways to Reduce Premiums. The four biggest ways to cut the insurance premiums are to reduce the benefits by increasing the waiting period, cover fewer care days, pay less per day, and reduce the inflation rate. The latter two methods increase the chances of the nursing home room charges exceeding the allowed insurance rate. However, the solution is to find nursing homes with lower rates, especially in low cost states. Likewise, you may be a patient for much longer than planned. If benefits and assets are exhausted, the state will pay for care. This trade-offs may be acceptable for lower risk people who still want a policy.

9. Self Insurance Options. Here is my view of the following four options.

A. Live life to the fullest (as best you can) without much regard for saving. When you run out of assets, let the state take care of your long term needs. As a taxpayer, I don't care for this option. It also may be very risky. When looking at the new health care law, the aging population, and the obesity trend, it is easy to postulate substantial cuts in government funding. That safety net may not be safe.

B. Make a calculation of how long you and your significant other expect to live. Look at your nearest relatives, their diseases and age at death, and your own medical history. To supplement this information, use one of the life expectancy calculators, such as found at **livingto100. com** by Dr. Thomas Perls, one of the foremost experts in the field. If your spouse/significant other is likely to survive you in good health (to take care of the frail/sick one), the healthy spouse could be insured and the other self insured. Maintain conservative spending and a strong savings and investment strategy. This approach reduces the odds of having financially crippling bills.

C. Make a deal with friends or relatives to receive all or part of your estate if they take care of you. Put it in writing as to what they will do and what they will receive, but with some language that allows contractual changes if you are abandoned. If one of your children is the primary care giver, make sure the other(s) understand the deal. Some kids who don't pitch in to help parents still feel entitled to equal estate treatment.

D. Pay out part of your estate each year to your caregivers. Each beneficiary could be given an annual tax free gift (currently $13,000) or more using the lifetime gift exclusion.

Longevity Insurance

This insurance covers people who live well beyond expectations and deplete their assets. Basically, a fixed sum is paid now for the insurance and the policy holder receives a monthly income for the rest of his life starting at some advanced age, like 75, 80, or 85. The monthly pay-out increases with an earlier and larger payment and by delaying the payouts (at 85 instead of 75).

Let's assume you are 60 years old and buy $10,000 of insurance for an annuity starting at age 85. If you die early, the $10,000 is lost. Alternatively, if the money is invested in a broad based equity index fund that returns 8% per year, it would be worth $68,000 in 25 years. If you die prematurely, your heirs will have the funds. The following are less likely to benefit from longevity insurance: smokers, drug users, the obese, those with unhealthy life styles, sedentary individuals, diabetics, and people with unfavorable family histories, certain diseases, and uncontrolled high blood pressure (especially, with a combination of these).

Other Thoughts

Those people with children have invested considerable time and money in raising them. You don't owe them an inheritance, especially if it means a great personal sacrifice. There is an old joke that says, "People who spend wisely run out of money just as they die, and their check to the undertaker bounces." Life is a set of risks and whether to invest in care insurance is one of those risks.

No matter what we do, our bodies, reflexes, strength, senses, balance, confidence, and coordination decline with "old age." Bernard Baruch (statesman and financier) once said, "Old age is 15 years older than I am" so I will refuse to define "old age." Some people age more slowly than others. However, to reduce the personal risk of being disabled, you might want to consider the following:

- Move to a climate with little or no snow.

- Change from biking to walking.

- Eat a well balanced healthy diet.

- Drink in moderation.

- Wear proper shoes and avoid high heels and slippery conditions.

- Use the handrail on stairs.

- If you have great trouble with stairs, live at the ground level or use an elevator.

- Do strength training and aerobics, but don't overdo it.

- Quit smoking.

- Don't lug heavy objects, even your purse.

- Achieve a healthy weight.

- Lift with your legs, not your back.

- Drive vehicles that are at least midsized and only during good weather in daylight hours.

- Avoid climbing on ladders and roofs.

- Change risky sport habits.

- Reduce prescriptions that aren't helping you.

- Surround yourself with optimistic people.

- Make new friends and socialize.

- Exercise your mind.

- Don't ever give up.

- Get plenty of sleep.

Some of the aforementioned are appropriate for your entire life (like good habits). Others may be adaptations that become desirable at some point. For example, biking requires more alertness, coordination, and is more dangerous than walking. So it might be a good trade-off that reduces your risk of having a disabling accident.

When people are young, old age seems like something that happens to others, but it eventually hits all of us. I remember vividly my long time friend, Dr. Bob Wallace from Pullman, WA. We met when he was 64 years of age. Then, he could walk all day up and down mountains carrying a heavy back pack. He could wade to his chest in swift streams. He was the "greatest dog lover" imaginable with his big and powerful English pointers. In his early 90s, I went to see him with my much smaller Vizsla, and he was visibly afraid of her because of his frail body.

Qualifying for State Long Term Care Assistance

To qualify and leave money to heirs, people sometimes transfer assets to relatives. This must be done five years in advance of the need which is generally too long for people to give up their assets. States have their own requirements so check with your state for guidelines. In addition, make sure the long term care facility being considered is licensed as the insurance carrier likely requires that.

Auto Insurance

The Seven Types of Auto Insurance.

- Bodily injury liability- Pays for damages other people cause if you or someone you allow to drive your car causes an accident.

- Property damage- Covers damage to other people's property.

- Personal injury protection (PIP)- Pays for medical, childcare, funeral, lost earnings, etc. for you or your passengers, regardless of who caused the accident.

- Uninsured and underinsured motorist bodily injury- similar to PIP that covers you if the other driver has inadequate or no insurance.

- Uninsured motorist property damage- Often combined with the above but this covers damage to your property.

- Collision- Covers repairs to your vehicle in an accident.

- Comprehensive- Pays for damage resulting from theft, vandalism, windstorm, fire, hail, etc.

Don't make the mistake of buying the minimum required. You might end up being bankrupted by a large claim that exceeds your insurance limit.

Basis for Rates. Auto insurance rates are based upon car make and model, driving record, prior insurance coverage, and consumer credit history. To find the approximate average insurance costs, go to Edmunds.com and click on "True Cost to Own" for each make and model being considered.

Your credit score is directly related to the accident frequency of drivers. In 2003, Michael Miller and Richard Smith studied a random sample of

2.7 million records from the files of national insurers. They found that those individuals with the lowest credit scores had 2.5 times as many liability claims per car as those with the highest scores. In fact, the following factors are related to **higher accident** and **insurance rates:**

- Low credit score

- Living in a zip code area with low income

- Low educational level

- Buying the car on installments

- No prior insurance (often a young driver)

- Male (but men drive 63% more than women)

- Had an "at fault" accident

- Had a "non-fault" accident

Some states limit how credit scores can be used. They may forbid insurance companies from using them to cancel a policy or raise rates, but they may allow their use for issuing new policies.

Categories of Drivers. The insurance companies typically have three basic driver categories. The "preferred" drivers have the best driving records and receive the best rates. This category is followed by "standard" which are moderate risk drivers, and lastly, are the "nonstandard" drivers who pay the highest rates and include young drivers, those with several tickets or accidents, those with poor premium payment records, reckless driving convictions, and DUIs.

Proof of Insurance. Carry proof of insurance at all times with one in your car and another in your wallet. In addition, most states mandate a minimum insurance coverage, often consisting of bodily injury, property damage, uninsured and underinsured motorist, bodily injury, and PIP.

Auto Insurance Discounts. Use the following discount list as a checklist when contacting insurance companies (most companies do not have all of them):

- **Accident Free**. Make sure your company is applying the longest possible accident free period for which you qualify. If you switched insurance companies, see if the new one will include your accident free period from the old company. When replacing a vehicle, the new car should carry the accident free discount period as the vehicle traded or sold.

Be cautious about loaning your vehicle to anyone, but especially those with a history of consuming drugs or lots of alcohol, a suspended license or moving violations, a criminal record, or a propensity to drag race or excessively speed. Concern is also warranted for situations involving many teens in a car.

Although it varies by insurance company and some may forgive the first accident, the industry standard is to raise your rates by 40% after your first at fault accident. If your carrier's base rate is $500, then your rates would go up by $200 for at least three years. If the driver of your car doesn't have insurance, and the claim exceeds your policy limit, the injured party can sue you and your family (if you are a minor). If the "friend" did not have permission to drive the car, then you may need to file a stolen car report with the police to avoid liability.

- **Educational or good grades discount**. For getting a degree or good grades, especially your kids.

- **Multiple vehicles including motorcycles**

- **Bundling several insurance policies like home, auto, and/or life**

- **Large collision deductible.** Check on the cost for $500 and $1,000.

- **Low mileage or non-commuting.** Typically policies will offer some discounts for mileage not exceeding some amount like 7,500 miles per year. Drivers below that level should check with several companies. (If you are laid off and your mileage drops, immediately contact your insurance company about a rate reduction).

- **High credit score.** If you have recently had an increase in your score, tell your agent about that.

- **Long term client.** This applies to all types of insurance.

- **Defensive driving class discount.** AARP offers a class called "55 and Alive." Check with your insurance company to see qualifications needed. The discount is usually 5-10%.

• **Discount for factory installed antilock brakes, automatic seatbelts, and airbags.** This is an option in some cars so ask your agent if it applies.

• **Discount for moderate speed, braking, and acceleration** (tracking device in your vehicle monitors these factors). Progressive and GMAC Insurance offer it.

• **Anti-theft devices**

• **Hybrids.** Some insurance companies are offering discounts on hybrids because such owners apparently are safer drivers.

• **Specialty discounts.** Some insurers offer them to people belonging to certain professional groups, senior government officials, and the military. Farmer's, GMAC Insurance, and Geico offer them, with the latter having 275 affiliated groups. However, if the deals are offered to too many policyholder groups, the premiums for unaffiliated individuals increase. The discounts are offered because professional individuals are safer drivers.

• **Non-smoking discount**

• **Single payment discount if paid in one lump sum instead of monthly.** Discount varies considerably between companies.

• **New parent's discount.** Offered by Farmers to find new young customers.

• **Steer clear discounts.** Offered by State Farm for teen drivers. It requires them to log their trips for 30 days and watch a DVD with stories of their peers offering advice.

• **Country or small town discount.** People in large cities have higher claims.

• **Garage discount for cars parked in a garage**

• **Independent agent.** These have access to many insurance companies and may be able to save money or find insurance where others can't.

One danger is that he may sell you the policy giving him the highest commission rather than the best one for you.

Necessary Actions when you have an Auto Accident

• **Identify witnesses quickly.** They may be inclined to leave. If possible, run to the driver's window and ask them to stay. If they want to leave, get their name, phone number, and car license number. If there are two people in your car, one person should talk with the other driver while one seeks out witnesses. If you are at fault, then this strategy may not be the best.

• **Exchange information with the other driver(s).** Include his name, address, phone number, and his insurance carrier and its phone number.

• **File an accident report if required by your state (normally within 72 hours).** Usually there are some specific factors which trigger a required filing (includes injuries, death, and the amount of property damage). Ask your agent about that.

• **Notify your insurer as soon as possible.**

• **Don't sign a release waiving an insurer's liability until the repairs are okay, and any monetary settlement for injuries is acceptable.** For the latter, you may wish to consult an attorney.

• **Don't admit fault.** This admission can and will be used against you. Don't say "I'm sorry," "I made a mistake," or "It's not your fault." The other person may be on drugs or alcohol, severely depressed and therefore distracted, or is wanted by the police. If the police are involved, describe what happened. If you are not sure about the circumstances, let your insurance company and the police sort it out.

• **If your insurance company's offer for physical damages is too low, ask for an independent appraiser to review the claim.** One likely disagreement is a total loss claim. In such cases, request a copy of the valuation, check newspapers for dealer and private party sales, and go to Kelley Blue Book (kbb.com) or Edmunds.com for additional retail sales data. To get the best value, focus on dealer sales prices which are higher than private party sales.

The insurance companies have their own valuation techniques and software and usually don't rely on Kelley Blue Book or the National Association of Automobile Dealers' guide. To supplement your case before an accident, keep your maintenance records and take pictures of your vehicles after they are washed and waxed. This information can be used to persuade an insurance company that your car was in good condition and well maintained.

Also get several quotes for similar replacement cars from dealers and ask the insurance company to supply names of dealers within a reasonable driving distance who would sell your car for their price. If you still aren't satisfied, check your policy for binding arbitration or mediation procedures. You may also have the option of going to court including "small claims" court.

Another more expensive option is to hire a company that fights insurance companies regarding diminished value and total loss. One such group is Appraisal Group of America (autoloss.com or call them at 877-655-1661). For a fee of $250-400, this type of appraisers will do a total loss estimate which might persuade the insurance company to favorably settle or could be used in court.

Diminished Value. In a severe accident, your car likely has diminished value after it is repaired. Fourteen states (Florida, Georgia, Hawaii, Kansas, Louisiana, Maine, Maryland, Massachusetts, North Carolina, South Dakota, Texas, Virginia, Washington, and West Virginia) allow you to recover this diminished value, assuming the accident was not your fault. You can recover from the other driver or his or your insurance company and even after receiving reimbursement for repairs.

Aftermarket Parts. To find out whether your state allows them as compared to using only Original Equipment Manufacturer (OEM) parts, contact your state's department of motor vehicles or insurance regulator. Your insurance agent should also know the answer to that question. Where they are allowed, you most likely will need to pay the added cost of getting OEM parts. The aftermarket parts are definitely cheaper so the insurance rates in states that allow them should be lower.

Sales Tax Reimbursement. If you live in one of the 28 states requiring the insurer to pay the sales tax on replacements for totaled vehicles, make sure you request it. These states are Alaska, Arizona, Arkansas, California, Connecticut, Florida, Georgia, Hawaii, Illinois, Indiana,

Kansas, Kentucky, Maryland, Minnesota, Missouri, Nebraska, Nevada, New Jersey, New York, North Dakota, Ohio, Oklahoma, Oregon, South Dakota, Vermont, Washington, West Virginia, and Wisconsin. Some of these states don't have a sales tax so presumably it applies to residents purchasing a replacement in another state.

Stacking. When hit by an uninsured motorist, you may be able to collect from several of your automobile policies until all damages are covered. Nineteen states allow it or don't forbid it (*moneycentral.msn.com*).

Dangerous Foods and Other Driving Distractions. According to a study by the National Highway Traffic Safety Administration (NHTSA) and the Virginia Tech Transportation Institute, 80% of crashes and 65% of near crashes involve some form of driver distraction. This is particularly the case involving rear end collisions (in which the lead vehicle was stopped) and in single vehicle crashes. Eating food is especially a problem when something unexpected happens; such as a person or animal crossing the road, a turning car, ruts in the road, or a sharp turn. Many teens are fast food "junkies" and that combined with their lack of driving experience, causes more accidents.

The top ten worst consumables while driving involve hot, "drippy," "fizzy," and greasy foods and liquids. They tend to splash, ooze, and end up on your lap, shirt, and fingers, meanwhile distracting us. Apparently, 83% of us eat and/or drink while driving (*Exxon* report). The top ten worst foods (insurance.com) include coffee, hot soup, tacos, chili dogs, hamburgers, barbecued food, fried chicken, jelly/crème-filled donuts, soft drinks, and chocolate. Most of these can be purchased at a fast food drive-in so these distractions are readily available.

Other causes of inattentive driving accidents include:

- Reading

- Looking at a map

- Making out (happened to my brother)

- Reaching for or just seeing a moving object

- Insects and bees in the car

- Cell phone use (including those with a head set)

- Applying make-up

- Focusing on something outside the vehicle

- Playing games (including those where you look for some object along the road)

- Using a cell phone

Other Auto Insurance Tips

1. **Don't insure your teen until he gets a permit or a license.** If the teen isn't going to be driving for a while due to an injury, illness, or maybe being a foreign exchange student, drop her from the policy. Of course, don't forget to reinstate her when she is driving again. If you know the approximate date, write it on the calendar, and contact the insurance company. Ask for an email verifying the start date.

2. **Formally cancel your policy when you change insurers.** Finding a new insurer doesn't stop the billing or the obligation from the old company. Send it an email with the cancellation date. Also request that the new company notify the old insurer.

3. **Cancel your insurance as soon as you sell a vehicle.** The agent may be able to back date the cancellation with proof of sale.

4. **Always insist on a bill of sale and complete and sign the title's transfer section.** Then make a copy of the signed documents. You need this in case the buyer has an accident before transferring ownership.

5. **Never leave visible items in your car, even a small gym bag with clothes in it.** A thief will not realize that a gym bag contains no valuables. The best hiding places are first in a locked trunk, then in a covered cargo area, next under a blanket behind the front seat (it doesn't stick out as much there), then covered and under the passenger's side dash, and finally under a blanket in an uncovered cargo area. There is some added protection from tinted windows.

6. **Build trust and an honest relationship with your child so that he will do the following while driving; turn off the radio, not talk on the cell phone (except in an emergency), and limit the num-**

ber of passengers to one and have him sit in the front seat.

7. **Several more options to save money is to buy a "beater" that is safe but for which you don't need comprehensive or collision insurance.** Have the teen assigned to your cheaper, yet safe car. You will pay much more for liability in a small car and much of your gas savings will go toward higher premiums. Ask your agent about accident "forgiveness" so that if your child has one accident, the rates don't skyrocket.

8. **Switching your child's status to an "occasional driver" may reduce rates.** If she doesn't have a car at college, consider stopping her insurance as long as she isn't driving another car. If she has her own vehicle, ask about the aforementioned discounts.

Student Insurance

Find out if your child attending college will be covered by your medical insurance. Under current law, coverage is allowed for full time student up to age 26. An alternative is to acquire insurance through the college. Finally, if your child is healthy, consider a comprehensive policy with a high deductible.

Renter's Insurance

Renter's insurance, which is relatively cheap, covers such things as theft, but also someone being hurt in your apartment or a case in which you accidentally burn the place down. Always buy "replacement value" coverage. As for covering a child's possessions when living away at school, you have two choices. Obtain a rider on your homeowner's policy or a separate renter's policy. This category reminds me of my undergraduate days when all of my possessions were transported in two cardboard boxes.

CHAPTER 19

Getting the Best Loan and Real Estate Deals

Loyalty to One Financial Institution

All institutions use FICO scores and their own internal analysis in granting loans. Those individuals with less than stellar credit (below 720) and fewer assets will probably receive better treatment by being loyal to one institution. If you have checking, savings, and credit cards there, you may get better loan terms (or even a loan) if you have behaved responsibly. However, always shop around for deals.

I wouldn't ignore the small local banks as you may be able to develop a more personal relationship with them than with a big bank, and they may be less inclined to saddle you with paperwork. For example, for my real estate construction loans, one small local bank didn't insist on costly third party progress inspections, had a smaller fee, and required less documentation.

In another case, a large nation-wide bank changed its policy to my temporary detriment. Despite using them as my principal banker for many years and having a great credit history, it stopped giving me a line of credit and would not finance any commercial real estate projects where the loan was less than $3,000,000. Nevertheless, many other banks were willing to finance my projects and give me lines of credit. By the way, I still do a considerable amount of business with this bank because they have given me great rates on some loans, a home equity line, and CDs. I recognize that any business can change its business model so I didn't let my pride and annoyance stand in the way of a good deal.

Multiple Financial Institutions

As a person's assets expand or he starts one or more businesses, there is a greater likelihood that multiple institutions are desirable. There are a couple of reasons for that. First, banks in a given locality will often have different interest rates and terms for pricing identical CDs and loans and they often change. One bank might be trying to attract deposits by offering high CD rates because it needs to meet some government "capital requirements," or it wants to expand loans. Another might decide that it is too heavily into commercial mortgages, for example, so it requires a higher interest rate and more down payment than its competitors. Second, some banks won't do certain types of loans. Third, some won't lend money into some geographic areas. I am not talking about the illegal practice of red-lining where banks restricted loans in certain low income areas. Finally, banks don't view every person or business the same.

Having loans with multiple banks doesn't present any extra problem, but opening up more checking accounts does. Obviously, there is a trade-off when you have multiple accounts because you have to balance them and worry about minimum balances. Alternatively, you can adopt my time saving model. If all checks and deposits are accounted for correctly, I didn't bother to try to balance the checkbook as long as the account was within $250.

Selecting Your Financial Institutions for your Main Business Account

The U.S. Congress and the U. S. Government has, in my opinion, been lax in allowing too many mergers and acquisitions of financial institutions. In 1990, the 10 largest banks controlled 25% of the market. By 2007, it was about 50%. This pattern of concentration got a further boost during the severe 2007-09 downturn when many banks were taken over by others. While it helped the banks to become more profitable by allowing some cost cutting and economies of scale, it reduced competition and interest paid on deposits and raised fees for bad checks, overdrafts, check processing, etc.

Unless you place your real estate or business in some entity like a limited liability company or a corporation, your best deals for checking account costs will usually be with a personal checking account where the checks are made out to you personally and not a business name. However, in the long run, establishing a business name is desirable for advertising and brand identity. I would compare the fees and make my selection based upon price, services offered, and convenience to your home or your business. One service that is needed for many businesses is a coin counting machine, especially those with vending machines or washer/dryers.

Buying a Home

About 2/3 of Americans own a home with many benefits such as tax savings, a sense of community, friendships, and stability. However, it can be an albatross if you lose your job or are financially irresponsible. Though a mortgage can be obtained for as little as 3.5% down, it is advisable to pay at least 20% to reduce the mortgage payments. In many cases, your home mortgage will be sold by your lender to Fannie Mae or Freddie Mac.

Generally, with the 20% down payment (and my recommendation), you can avoid paying for over-priced mortgage insurance (which protects the lender in case of default) and required escrows for insurance and taxes, the latter simply being interest free loans to the bank. The mortgage insurance doesn't fully protect the bank, but may cover 20-30% of the mortgage amount.

Mortgage insurance can be purchased through government agencies such as the Veteran's Administration (VA), United States Department of Agriculture (USDA), or Federal Housing Administration (FHA) or through private insurers. In some cases, the insurance is included with the interest rate so it may not be visible.

Anyone can apply for a FHA insured loan, but you must be a veteran or rural inhabitant to qualify for the VA or USDA loans. The FHA loans may be associated with low appraisals or strict loan requirements. A relative of mine had to tear down a less than perfect, but still functional, garage to qualify. Another relative had a FHA appraisal in which a finished basement was given almost no value. Check with your lender about these issues. My advice in buying a home is as follows:

1. **If you have the time and skills, buy a fixer-upper in a decent neighborhood.** If the house is used as a principal residence for two years (see Chapter 17), your value added to the home will be tax free when sold up to the maximum allowed capital gain.

2. **Spend less than you can afford.** This is a cushion against bad times.

3. **Buy a house with curb appeal.**

4. **Don't buy one unless you expect to live there for three or more**

years. The exceptions would be if the housing market was appreciating in that area or your employer had some guaranteed buy-back program.

5. **Ask a realtor what locations and housing features are most in demand.** Then use that information to help in your buying decision. If houses with a home theatre or swimming pool are in low demand, for example, you might want to pass on those. Alternatively, a low ball offer might be accepted.

6. **Other cases for a low ball offer are when a house has been on the market for some time or when it is vacant.** Time on the market may be misleading because homes can be relisted, ask your realtor if it has been relisted.

7. **If you are unsure of your future plans, make an offer of renting with an option to buy.**

8. **Figure out how much you can afford before you "house" shop.** Choose the lender with the best rates to help you. You could get pre-approved for a loan.

9. **Always pay for a home inspection.** If there are previously unidentified problems, buyers can often use this information to negotiate a discount or have the seller pay part or all of the fix-up costs.

10. **Find out if municipal work is planned that would result in an assessment (such as new sidewalks and street paving).**

Obtaining the Best Mortgage Deal

Because a home mortgage is the largest debt for most people, show no loyalty to any financial institution. Home loans are available from commercial banks, mortgage companies, credit unions, and thrift institutions. Brokers, who charge a fee that is embedded in the interest rate or as points, can arrange for loans by contacting several lenders, but don't depend upon one broker for such assistance.

The main loan variables are the interest rate, down payment, closing costs, flood plain determination, escrow and credit life and mortgage insurance requirements (find out when can the latter be dropped?), prepayment penalties (if any), the appraisal, and the length and type of the mortgage. There are a number of good sites for mortgage information including zillow.com, pueblo.gsa.gov, hud.gov, consumer.gov, and homebuyinginstitute.com. It is important to raise your credit score as high as possible before applying for a loan. If your credit report contains unfavorable information, and there are good reasons why you are a good credit risk, explain that to the lender. I would not obtain any home mortgage with prepayment penalties.

Qualifying for a Mortgage. The normal standard is that your housing expenses of principal, interest, taxes, and insurance (PITI) shouldn't exceed 28% of your gross monthly income. Additionally, your total payments from all long term debt (defined as any that extends 11 months or more), including PITI, should not exceed 36% of your gross monthly income for conventional loans. Thus, if your monthly gross is $5,000, then your all of your debt payments shouldn't exceed $1800 per month. For FHA loans, the allowance is 41% or $2,050. To calculate your monthly payment on any debt, go to bankrate.com or mortgage-calc.com.

In getting interest rate quotes, provide your credit score to the lender to avoid lowering it from too many bank searches. At your meeting with the bank official, she will require proof of debts, payments, and income.

Appraisal. I have seen some horrible appraisals. Two appraisers hired for my properties grossly under-appraised two different duplexes with four bedroom units because they could only find two bedroom units nearby that had sold.

Your lender probably has an approved appraiser list and doesn't actually pick her. If you don't like an appraisal, there are two choices, namely, ask for a reconsideration (based upon other comparables) or go to another bank, who hopefully won't use the same appraiser. Changes in appraisals are rare, but both of my bad appraisers raised their values after I challenged them.

If you are selling the house or refinancing, always make a list of its great features and any improvements. By calling realtors, I have even found my own comparables to help the appraiser, a few of whom are lazy or incompetent. I usually offer my opinion of the approximate property value. In an era of high foreclosures, low valuations are likely to be the norm because lenders have lost much money from mortgage defaults. If an appraisal is low, ask for a second appraisal. If the lender refuses, consider another financial institution. Be cautious with FHA appraisals because they stay on record for six months even with a new buyer or lender.

Length and Types of Mortgages. Fixed rate loans of 15-20 years have lower rates than 30 year mortgages and allow a quicker pay-off, but also have higher monthly payments. Your decision should be driven by your likelihood of losing your job, the availability of other funds, and your feelings about reducing your debt.

Until the housing crisis hit, some personal finance writers had been advocating the cheaper adjustable rate mortgages. Now they have switched to recommending fixed rate mortgages. In a period of rising rates, it is risky to take on an adjustable rate mortgage. They are most desirable during stable or falling rates. Another problem is the fluctuating nature of your loan payment. Of course, no one objects to a falling payment. One advantage of this type of mortgage is that a borrower can qualify for a higher loan amount.

Also, be cautious about the terms of adjustable rate mortgages. To reduce risk, you may wish to fix the rates for 5-10 years, and you should understand the index to which the adjustable rate is tied, the percentage added to the index, how often it adjusts, and by how much. Most banks will use an index like LIBOR (a short term rate from London) or the U.S. prime rate.

Balloon mortgages have a fixed interest rate for a certain number of years, usually 7-10. This type of mortgage is often found as private seller financing. The rates can be fairly low, but the danger is that all the money is due at once. Balloon mortgages are most desirable if full pay-off is allowed at any time so that financing can be obtained when rates are low.

Jumbo mortgage loans are those above a certain size. In 2010, this level is $417,000, which is increased in some high cost housing areas. This sector of the market is less competitive than the smaller traditional loans and rates and down payments are higher. For non-jumbo loans, lender interest rate quotes generally don't vary by more than ¼%, but jumbos can vary by as much as 2%.

A buyer who puts less than 10% down may be forced into an FHA loan which allows as little as 3.5%. FHA loans often require things to get fixed, which if the seller agrees to provide some assistance, can be beneficial to the buyer. FHA loans do not have any maximum income cap to qualify for a loan.

Closing Costs and Other Issues. Closing costs (including the appraisal) are often negotiable. Some, like the application and appraisal fees, are paid when you apply for a loan. The rest are paid at closing. Ask for clarification of any costs you don't understand. Get a "good faith estimate" from each lender and ask for the annual percentage rate (APR) which includes the points, broker fees (if any), and certain other charges. Use the estimates to negotiate with the lenders and brokers who may quote different rates for the same loan to other similar borrowers. Sometimes a lock-in fee is charged to guarantee an interest rate. Get the lock-in and the expiration date, whether free or not, in writing.

Points are a fee, usually stated as a percentage of the loan. One point on a $100,000 loan would cost $1,000. The interest rate goes down with increases in the points paid. A ¼% reduction in the interest rate for a 1/2 point is a great deal, a ¾ point requirement would be a good deal, and one point would be a poor deal. Of course, avoid the points if the property is to be sold within two years.

After a banker has looked at your loan application, ask for a free appraisal, application fee, or perhaps a $500 credit at closing. Maybe the bank will allow a slightly lower interest rate for mortgage payments made through an account held there. Check to see if the financial institution will allow you to relock a lower interest rate after you have locked the first time. If rates drop 1/4% on a $200,000 loan, that saves about $500 per year initially.

If you have closed a mortgage loan on the same property within the past couple of years, ask the title company for discounted title fees. On my principal house, I refinanced twice within a six month period in 2009. I reused the appraisal, was charged no points or application fee, and received a discount on title insurance. For multiple loans closing near the same time, ask the closing agent to reduce its fees.

Energy Efficient Mortgages (EEM). There is new type of mortgage for energy efficient homes. It is federally recognized and allows the borrower to qualify for a larger loan with a higher debt to income ratio. The efficient house saves on utilities and has a higher resale value. A Home Energy Rating System (HERS) report, which is similar to a mpg rating on a car and costs $300-800, is needed. The FHA EEM covers upgrades for new and existing homes, is available in all 50 states, and doesn't require re-qualifying, a new appraisal, or additional down payments. Go to hud.gov for more details.

Reverse Mortgages. They are designed for seniors who don't want to sell or move out of their home and allows them to receive payments against the equity in their home. To look at non-governmental reverse mortgages, talk with your lender or type "reverse mortgages, conventional" in your browser. You will need to supply certain personal information like the value of your property, current mortgage, address, email, age, name, and phone number. The FHA's requirements for a Home Equity Conversion Mortgage (HECM) are shown at hud.gov. These include owning the property outright or having a small mortgage, being 62 years of age or older, occupying the property as your principal residence, and not being delinquent on any federal debt.

The mortgage amount is based upon the age of the youngest borrower, the current interest rate, and the lesser of the appraised value or the HECM FHA mortgage limit. Generally, the borrowed amount allowed is higher for more valuable properties, lower interest rates, and older people. There are no income, asset, or credit qualifications; no repayment as long as the property is your principal place of residence; and the closing costs may be financed in the mortgage. The property can be a single family or 2-4 units, HUD approved condominium, or manufactured home that meets FHA requirements.

The payments can be received in the following five different ways and can be changed later if desired:

A. Equal monthly payments for the life of one borrower living in the residence
B. Equal monthly payments but only for a fixed period of time
C. Line of credit so withdrawals are at the option of the borrower
D. Combination of A and C
E. Combination of B and C

There is a series of fees including a lender processing fee and closing costs. Lenders recover their principal and interest whenever the house is sold. If there is a loss, it is covered by the required insurance which costs 2% of the lesser of the home's value or the mortgage limit plus an annual fee of ½% of the mortgage balance. HECM are somewhat more expensive than regular loans.

Interest rates can be fixed or adjustable. The HECM must be repaid when you die, sell the house, move, don't pay property taxes or hazard insurance, fail to live there for 12 consecutive months, or fail to make repairs.

Special Home Buying Assistance. Some programs are available to help first time or low income home buyers. These may be federal, state, county, or local programs.

Refinancing. Refinancing a mortgage is always a difficult decision. Any points paid must be amortized over the life of the mortgage on your tax return, unlike the original home mortgage points which can be expensed in full in the year of purchase. I have refinanced my rentals and homes at least 75 times to take out equity or benefit from lower rates, mostly the latter.

The most important considerations are how long do you plan to keep a new mortgage, how much does refinancing cost, and what is the interest rate saving (if any). My refinancing decision rule (except for equity take-outs) is that the lower interest rate had to recover the costs within three years or less. Thus, if the costs for a $200,000 mortgage are $2,000, then the lower interest rate must save $2,000/3 or $667 per year. In a period of declining rates, some of my properties were refinanced several times and sometimes before recovering my earlier refinancing costs.

Home Equity Loan (HEL). I like them because the interest is tax deductible (up to $100,000 in debt) for itemizers, the HEL can be accessed or paid off whenever desired, there is no annual due date, and the net interest rates (after income taxes) are better than most other forms of credit. One main disadvantage is that rates can rise considerably during inflationary periods.

The tax deduction is particularly appealing. For example, the interest on a regular loan for a non-business use car is not tax deductible, but the HEL interest used to buy the same car is. People often use the HEL proceeds to pay-off credit cards, for home improvements, or to buy stuff. This is a great strategy because the after tax cost of a HEL loan is usually

50-80% **less** than credit cards. The only downsides are that a HEL lender can foreclose on your house while a credit card lender can't. In addition, this strategy is bad if you simply start running credit card debt again.

Fair Lending. The Equal Credit Opportunity Act and the Fair Housing Act prohibit lenders from discriminating based upon color, race, national origin, sex, marital status, religion, age, handicaps, whether any portion of an applicant's income is from public assistance, or she has in good faith exercised a right under the Consumer Credit Protection Act. The consumer can't be offered less favorable terms or refused a loan based upon these characteristics.

Selling Your Home and Retirement

The question often arises about whether retired people should sell their home or refinance it. There are a number of factors to consider including whether you want a yard or to live in a certain place, your income, health, marginal tax rate, and the size of your retirement funds. Many people want to downsize and selling their home and moving to a smaller less expensive one will allow them to reduce or eliminate debt.

You should also consider your investments and marginal tax rates. If you have a 6% mortgage and you are in the 40% marginal tax bracket, then the interest portion is only costing 3.6% after taxes. It may not be wise to give up the tax shelter, especially if your investments are doing well and you want the interest deduction. However, if your mortgage deduction is just barely greater than the standard deduction, it has little tax shelter value.

The advantages of paying off your mortgage are that it reduces your monthly expenses, your return on investment is guaranteed (it's the rate on the mortgage), and foreclosure is unlikely unless you have delinquent property taxes or some other obligations such as income taxes. Alternatively, if more cash is needed, you could refinance and withdraw equity. Another option is to refinance your current mortgage to lower your monthly payment. For example, the monthly payment on a 30 year $350,000 mortgage is $2098. If the mortgage has been reduced over time to $250,000, refinancing will lower your monthly payment almost $600 to $1499.

Foreclosure and Redemption

If you are facing the possibility of foreclosure, go to portal.hud.gov for a comprehensive list of options and assistance, including information for each state. This is the official site of the U.S. Department of Housing and Urban Development. Next visit the Federal Trade Commission's site (ftc.gov) and type in the search box "mortgage payments sending you reeling." This article has a great summary of the methods to avoid default and foreclosure.

After reading that information, call your lender ASAP and ask about refinancing options and prepayment penalties. You may qualify for loan modification from either HUD's Making Home Affordable Program or the FHA's Hope for Homeowners. If your house has been sold at a foreclosure sale, many states have a period of redemption in which the property can be repurchased by paying the mortgage and foreclosure costs. Check "state laws on foreclosure" on the internet.

The Rich Do Get Richer

The rich do get richer in a variety of ways. Banks have preferred client lists of important customers who do a lot of business with them or have substantial assets. These special clients are often given a personal banker. Preferred customers have higher credit scores because they are more reliable, financially strong, and less likely to default on a loan.

Ask your banker what qualifies a person for the list which may not be available in small banks.

When you put money into CDs, some banks will often give preferred customers an extra ¼% of interest or lower rates on loans. They are also more likely to waive extra charges like a bounced check, cover the bounced check temporarily with bank funds, offer lower transaction fees on foreign credit card transactions, and send newsletters. Bank of America and Wells Fargo both have very insightful free newsletters available. The same preferential treatment may happen at mutual fund or brokerage companies which give better rates on margin accounts, waive or reduce IRA fees, reduce commissions, or charge lower expenses. You may qualify with as little as $10,000 in an account for some benefits.

Other Comments

1. **Banks should not be charging overdraft fees on credit and debit card purchases.** The bank should just decline the charge. The Federal Reserve now requires you to "opt-in" for overdraft

protection for debit cards and ATM withdrawals. Don't do it. The cost is simply too great and some banks process the highest charge first so that your card is over the limit more quickly and hit more times. Bounced checks are exempt from the new rules so maintain a never used cushion of $100 or so in each checking account. A good alternative is to set up a small line of credit with your bank.

2. **Those concerned about the safety of their bank deposits can go to MortgageLoan.com, consumersunion.org, or fdic.gov (Federal Deposit Insurance Corporation for more information).**

3. **For the location of a local credit union and rates by state, go to CUlookup.com.** The site shows the interest rate advantage of credit unions. When I checked it, they had higher interest bearing accounts and CDs and lower **average** interest rates on all credit cards and loans than commercial banks except for 15 and 30 year mortgages. The information can be viewed by state. The differences were most pronounced for car, home equity, and unsecured loans.

4. **Arbitration clauses may mostly benefit the financial institutions.** To cut down on legal bills and thwart class action lawsuits, many financial institutions have such clauses in documents for financial products such as credit cards, mortgages, and auto and home equity loans. In California, where arbitration results are made public, 99.998% of the time creditors won when the National Arbitration Forum, a for profit company based in Minneapolis, handled the case according to a lawsuit filed several years ago (*BusinessWeek*). If the bank gets to pick the arbitrator, then it would naturally select one that favors itself. If a lot of money is involved, it is wise to consult an attorney.

CHAPTER 20

Maximizing Your Retirement and Surviving Bad Times

Fear of the unknown, including economic declines, causes a great deal of anxiety. The majority of our fears never materializes, but they are still responsible for many bad decisions. Fortunately, economic history has some comfort for us.

Expect Economic Recessions to Come Regularly

According to the National Bureau of Economic Research, there have been 12 recessions (defined as 2 quarters of negative economic growth) from 1945-2010. A recession, on average, occurs about every 5.5 years and is about 10-11 months in length. The U.S. stock market typically starts to decline about six months before the recession starts and bottoms out before a recovery begins (both patterns vary somewhat).

Recessions are not always easy to predict. There is an old joke that economists have predicted 11 of the past five recessions. **The regularity of recessions is one good reason to follow the advice in this book, have an emergency fund, keep debt levels within reason, pay off credit cards every month, and learn a craft or get a college education.** After periods of prolonged prosperity, some executives, politicians, consumers, and economists are typically lulled into thinking that the business cycle problem has been solved and good times will always be here. That will never happen.

Past Depressions

Depressions are much more severe than recessions (drop in economic activity of 10% or more) and last much longer (at least two years). These periods are characterized by high unemployment, bank failures, personal and business bankruptcies, and shrinking trade, investment, prices, and credit. Best known is the Great Depression from 1929-39, characterized at its depth by a 33% drop in economic activity and 25% unemployment. In addition, there were four depressions during 1800s. There have been regional depressions in Latin America, Russia, former Soviet Bloc nations, and Sub-Saharan Africa, some of which occurred in the 1980s and 1990s.

Future Depressions - Causes, Likelihood, and How to Prepare for Them

For the prudent, wise, and educated saver, regular recessions can usually be taken in stride, but depressions are another matter. To survive the latter, you would want considerably more savings, little debt, food storage, possibly a security system, and conservative investments like the debt of the U.S. government and AAA rated municipalities and corporations (that supply staple goods such as food and utilities).

The likelihood of a depression is much lower than in the past. The reason is that central bankers and economic policy advisers better understand their causes and how to counteract them. According to Liaquat Ahamed in *Lords of Finance: 1929 The Great Depression and the Bankers who Broke the World*, the primary cause of the Great Depression was the bad decisions of a few central bankers.

Possible Depression Causes. There are some events that might trigger a depression such as extremely high prices (known as asset bubbles) for energy, other commodities, and real estate. However, because of rapid information flows, flexible currencies (in much of the world), and government action, I doubt that these stressful, yet manageable, events will cause a depression.

Another possible, but remote, cause would be anarchy where disgruntled citizens rise up, overthrown the government, and paralyze the economy with regulations and the fostering of world-wide gloom and doom. The scenario is most likely in a totalitarian state with a highly privileged upper class, a huge and discriminated against lower class, a censored press, and an unarmed citizenry.

Another and more likely possibility is when the voters feel economic stimulus hasn't worked and elect politicians who not only cut spending, but simultaneously increase taxes. Their goal is to cut the deficit, but the increased taxes commensurately reduce private spending. Thus, we have spending cuts from both the public and private sectors. This is precisely what happened during the Great Depression of 1932 and 1936, and Ireland has recently done this with distrastrous effects.

There are some uncontrollable factors that might cause another depression. These include being hit with an extremely large asteroid or having prolonged massive volcanic eruptions causing global winters and chaos in our transportation, agricultural, and communications systems. Another depression trigger is several terrorist nuclear explosions in densely populated areas that cause widespread panic and paralyze the economy.

The Most and Least Likely Depression Causes. A combination of the following causes, and those previously discussed, could trigger a depression. Independently, the first most likely is the election of politicians who raise taxes and cut spending after a severe recession like that in 2007-09, especially if done worldwide. The other most likely is a nuclear explosion set off by terrorists. This would cause widespread fear and panic. Large scale volcanic eruptions seem the next most likely cause and with current technology and knowledge, are largely unpredictable. Even if we could predict them, doing anything to offset the effects would be difficult and expensive.

My last potential cause of depression, global warming, is both distant (in time) and controversial. Prolonged global warming, if it occurs, would cause great disruptions in agriculture, large increases in the size of deserts, squeezing the population into smaller areas, loss of massive coastal infrastructure from rising seas, possibly more severe weather, water shortages, and substantial fishery losses from the increasing ocean acidity (due to carbon absorption). This type of depression would occur gradually, but could persist for decades.

Most debate about global warming focuses on the amount of taxpayer money to be spent, the regulations and costs of compliance, limits on personal freedom, taxes, and whether or not it is happening, and if so, whether it is caused (at least partially) by man. Even if the threat is not severe, using alternative energy and conservation still offer the benefits of cleaner air and water (both of which are associated with substantial health benefits), smaller trade deficits, and greater energy independence (which is a national security issue).

The U. S. Government Stimulus Plan

The main criteria for stimulus money should have been to create the most jobs in the United States for each dollar spent. That approach would have favored some industries and groups over others. The funds should also have largely been channeled to the states with the highest unemployment. In fact, slightly more money per capita went to low unemployment states. Part of the problem is that funds were distributed based upon past formulas and that allocation process should have been altered. The Davis/Bacon Act, which required high prevailing wages for federal spending projects, should have been suspended. That would have created many more jobs. Common sense would suggest that only the most important projects would be funded. In fact, some bizarre and wasteful projects were approved. Earmarks should have been banned.

Another important reason for poor stimulus performance is that no country ramped up stimulus like the U.S. and much of our efforts benefitted other countries through our purchase of their exports. Of course, structural changes have likely played a role because stimulus spending provides a wide variety of benefits for most jobs including health and retirement benefits, unemployment, and social security.

Instead of the above approach, it was politics as usual with considerable emphasis on spending targeted to special interests who helped elect the members of Congress, pork barrel projects, and districts of key politicians. In addition, throwing that much government money quickly into the economy surely guaranteed sloppy government oversight. The result was that many fewer jobs were created than was predicted.

How we Got in this Economic Mess

Basically, the 2007-09 recession was largely triggered by the real estate meltdown. The drop in prices meant less demand for new housing (a big part of the economy), a decline in property and income taxes collected, foreclosures, a derivatives collapse, and toxic assets on bank balance sheets. This process weakened consumer demand, reduced lending, and kept repeating itself with a series of downward spirals. The recession would have certainly become a major depression without government intervention including bank saving policies, guarantees on some private debt, low interest rates, and a banking system flooded with reserves to lower interest rates. Even the stimulus initially had some positive effect because many consumers felt the government was doing something and jobs recovery was actually quicker than during the 2000-01 recession.

The source of this crisis goes back many several decades when Congress and various presidents wanted to encourage more home ownership, especially among the poorer groups of people. The practice of redlining (requiring higher lending standards for certain areas) which discriminated against some groups (particularly blacks) and others including single and gay persons, was outlawed by the Fair Housing Act of 1968. Over time the political desire to raise home ownership encouraged lax lending standards with the ability to buy property with little down and poor background checks. The resale of mortgages to Freddie Mac and Fannie Mae helped divorce the bank from liability as long as the rules were followed. If I were to name two individuals and two groups most responsible for the housing crisis, it would be George W. Bush who oversaw eight years of the problem, Alan Greenspan, Chairman of the Federal Reserve for 19 years, the U.S. Congress, and the lending institutions (including those making derivatives from the mortgages). Furthermore, the monetary incentives at many large banks were such that they were paid to take outsized risks.

The Current Economic Situation

Most economists, including me, are concerned about the massive federal deficits and potential problems created (inflation, higher taxes, loss of confidence in the government, and higher interest rates). The federal debt (including the social security trust fund) is currently about 89% of GDP, which is much lower than in 1945 (over 120%). Wars can add significantly to the debt as seen during and after the Civil War, World War I, and World War II.

Currently, a big part of this debt is IOUs to the social security trust fund. This debt occurs because Congress has used huge amounts of social security's surplus to reduce the fiscal deficit and used IOUs to represent that borrowing. I don't expect that to change so I don't view these IOUs as real debt. Subtracting them out means that current debt is closer to 60% of GDP. Since social security began in 1936, there weren't any IOUs in 1945 so public debt (excluding the IOUs) is now only about one-half as large as in 1945, as measured by GDP's percentage.

From 1945-70, the federal debt was reduced by more than three percentage points per year from over 120% of GDP to 40%. I would hope that we would eventually begin to reduce the annual deficit so that public debt doesn't exceed 80% and then declines by 1.5% or so per year to a more stable and lower level.

It appears likely that spending at all levels of government in the U.S. will decline in the latter half of 2010 and 2011. According to a recent Time magazine story, 67% of Americans oppose new stimulus and a

Wall Street Journal survey concluded that economists do too. A valid argument against new stimulus is that the debt load created is not worth the jobs created. I personally oppose it too because of the way the past one was handled and because other major foreign governments are cutting back and thus reducing their stimulus. To be successful, the world would need a large coordinated stimulus program (like WWII when most large economies were involved), unfettered by rules like the Davis/Bacon Act.

It is interesting to note that federal taxes went from 7.6% of GDP in 1941 to 20.4% in 1945. Obviously, what happened is that massive WW II spending occurred along with large tax increases. This might suggest that the Bush tax cuts could expire if strong stimulus is continued worldwide (not likely). However, the November elections may produce a U.S. Congress bent on spending cuts combined with the expiration of the Bush tax cuts (as Alan Greenspan is urging). If politicians removed the stimulus and simultaneously raised taxes, the odds of a double dip recession (which economists Blander and Zandi and Goldman Sachs both currently put at 25%) increase. A factor helping the economy is a weak dollar, which aids exports.

Meredith Whitney who, in 2007, warned of the banking sector problems, is projecting 1-2 million in local and state government job losses. If that happens and there is a sustained drop in real estate prices along with many additional foreclosures, that will almost guarantee a recession. Regardless of one's feelings about the stimulus funds, its removal will definitely slow the economy, at least temporarily. At some point, the debt from stimulus funding will create problems as interest rates rise and the principal must be repaid..

One economic area that must be addressed is this philosophy that the U.S. is the principal protector of the world. During the Vietnam, Gulf, Iraq, and Afghanistan wars, the U.S. supplied the bulk of the manpower and money and suffered most of the non-resident casualties. We will be paying for the last two wars far into the future with equipment replacement, pensions, disability pay, medical care, and financing the national debt. Essentially, all of the recent wars have been financed by borrowing money. If the democracies of the world perceive a major threat, they need to participate with large scale manpower, money, and equipment, and **the U.S. needs to insist on it before embarking on a new war.** Wars cause deaths and absorb lots of money. Why should the politicians of other countries risk election defeat if the U.S. is willing to fund and take the casualties of war?

Another area of concern is that nearly half of the U.S. households pay no federal income taxes. If you look at all of the tax credits in Chapter 17, you will see why. The Tax Foundation estimates that 60% of Americans get more income benefits from government than they pay to it. The trend is for an even greater percentage in the future. Economies that shift too far toward the welfare state grow at a much slower pace and with millions of illegal immigrants, slow growth will acerbate a reasonable solution to our immigration problem. This is especially true because illegal immigrants account for 4% of the population but for 8% of the births (Pew Foundation). Furthermore, as more voters become accustomed to more and more benefits, it will become difficult for a politician to vote against them, even in hard times.

When to Apply for Social Security Benefits

Now that the gloomy side has been covered, let us focus on the income and wealth maximizing side. In order to receive full social security benefits, you need 40 credits with a maximum of four earned in each year. In 2010, one credit was earned for each $1120 in wages. For past years, lower wages were required for each credit. If you were born during 1943-54, you can receive full benefits at age 66. Older people are eligible somewhat younger and younger people somewhat older.

Once a person reaches 62, his benefits receive cost of living increases even if they are not taken until age 70. If your normal full retirement age is 66, your benefits are reduced for each year of early retirement and increased for later retirement, as shown below. For persons in between, the reduction takes into account the extra months of age. For example, the reduction for a person aged 62 years and 6 months is 22.5%.

25% reduction at age 62	8% addition at age 67
20% reduction at age 63	16% addition at age 68
13.5% reduction at age 64	24% addition at age 69
6.67% reduction at age 65	32% addition at age 70 and beyond
0% reduction at age 66	

The three best reasons for drawing social security early and accepting lower monthly benefits are poor health, family history of early death, or shortage of money. The five advantages of delaying social security drawings are to increase the benefits for your family and survivors, enlarge your monthly benefits, draw down other funds easily gotten by creditors first, avoid the reduction in social security payments from working, and provide a measure of security if your investment nest egg takes a "hit." If you delay drawing benefits past your full retirement age, monthly benefits are increased by 6.5-8% per year (depending upon the year of birth) up to age 70.

The social security system was designed to provide a safety net for low wage workers so that the first $10,000 earned by minimum wage earners counts much more for the benefits calculation than the $10,000 earned at the top of the scale. I was unable to obtain the exact formula from the Social Security Administration, but I think that only 15% of the top of the wage scale counts compared to 100% at the bottom.

Thus, a high wage earner who is below the maximum for social security and Medicare payments (FICA) is better off to earn money by rents (on which FICA is not paid) instead of more wages. Then she can invest the avoided social security taxes. For example, a person could maintain and manage her own apartments and increase her taxable income by not hiring others to do the work.

Finally, two important points are worth noting. First, marriages must last at least 10 years for a spouse to qualify based upon the divorced spouse's work history. Secondly, garnishing social security and veteran's benefits is illegal in most cases.

How do People Increase Their Wealth and Save for Retirement?

This is done by following a series of principles as follows:

1. **Abide by the advice in this book so that more money is available for investing.**

   Strive for higher rates of return on investments because modest differences in returns can make a huge difference in accumulated wealth over the years. The following table shows the accumulated funds from a onetime initial investment of $100,000 and reinvestment of the annual returns for different rates of return and years:

Years Invested	Net Annual Rates of Return				
	2%	4%	6%	8%	10%
5	$110,408	121,665	133,823	146,933	161,051
10	121,899	148,024	179,085	215,893	259,374
15	134,587	180,094	239,656	317,217	417,725
20	148,595	219,112	320,714	466,096	672,750
25	164,061	266,584	429,187	684,848	1,083,471

Two obvious conclusions are apparent from this analysis; namely, high annual rates of return are better than low rates of return and longer periods of investment are better than shorter ones. For the five years of investment, the 10% rate shows an accumulated sum whose gains of $61,051 (after subtracting the initial investment of $100,000) are six times higher than the gain of $10,408 from a 2% rate of return. In 25 years, the 10% rate yields an investment gain that is 15 times as large. To achieve these better gains, investments must include stocks, bonds, and/ or other risky investments like real estate. The "net annual rates of return" assumes taxes are already paid or are deferred.

2. **Except for your emergency fund or saving for a major purchase, invest the maximum in a tax deferred or tax free fund like a 401(k), SEPA, or an IRA or a Roth IRA.** The idea behind this strategy is to accumulate untaxed funds and then either withdraw the funds tax free or pay taxes only as they are withdrawn. These tax savings depend upon a variety of factors including your current and future marginal tax rates, your investment types, and the frequency of trading. It is likely a safe bet that tax rates will increase in the future.

Here is an example of four investors who save $10,000 per year with an 8% annual return. One has all income tax deferred, another has a tax free Roth account, and the last two assume tax rates of 25% and 35% are paid on the 8% annual return. The summary of their wealth accumulations for various time intervals and tax assumptions is as follows:

	Years of Accumulation				
Investor Type	5	10	15	20	25
Tax Deferred	$58,666	144,866	271,521	457,620	731,059
Tax Free (Roth)	same as tax deferred				
25% Tax Rate	$56,370	131,808	232,760	367,856	548,645
35% Tax Rate	$54,478	126,959	219,062	337,736	490,644

As the reader can see, the difference between the accumulated amounts between the taxable and the non-taxable or tax deferred is sizable, especially for the longer periods. Of course, the tax deferred investor pays taxes on any withdrawals and the tax free Roth pays none. There are five advantages to having funds in tax deferred or tax free retirement accounts:

A. Most or all of your retirement funds are protected in a bankruptcy.

B. Most people have lower tax rates in retirement and the Roth IRA continues to grow tax free before & after retirement.

C. Because of early withdrawal penalties, most people withdraw funds only when needed.

D. Individuals are more likely to save with some formal retirement plans.

E. People who retire in a lower tax state than where they worked may be able to benefit from that.
The disadvantage of this strategy is that the money won't be available before your retirement for other needs or investments.

3. **Minimize your purchasing cost.** If you are confident about self investing, buy from a low cost broker such as Charles Schwab, TradeKing, Scottrade, etc. where the fees are as low as $4.95 per trade. If you want the ability to purchase some in-house mutual funds from your principal broker, Fidelity and Vanguard are great low cost options. However, some discount brokers pay very low interest rates on idle funds and charge high fees on their money market funds. Ask to have your idle money swept into a higher yielding account.

4. **Avoid "load" mutual funds that charge high commissions.** You can almost always find similar "no-load" funds that have low acquisition costs. However, many no-load funds have higher annual fees so check that out.

5. **Buy mutual funds or exchange traded funds (ETF) with low annual management fees.** The lowest are index (including some ETFs like Vanguard's) and bond funds. Before buying any funds, check the annual fees which can be quite high (1.5% or more). Index funds range from about .15-.6%.

6. **Consider tax sheltered or low tax investments outside your portfolio.** That means holding stocks over one year to receive the lower long term capital gains rate, trading less frequently, buying tax managed and index funds which have lower capital gains, and/ or investing in developed real estate which offers tremendous tax shelters. Residential real estate offers a better tax shelter per dollar of investment than commercial because of faster deprecation for structures.

7. **Avoid funds with permanent redemption fees.** Many have temporary ones that disappear in 2-12 months while others charge regardless of the duration held.

Can Ordinary Investors Beat Professional Investors?

It is difficult, but not impossible, for individual investors to beat professional money managers. The reasons are that the latter usually have a staff of economists and mathematicians (called quant jocks), attend high level professional seminars, network with other managers, do extensive research, buy in bulk, often have inside (possibly, illegal) information, work full-time, hire consultants, and have banks of computers that can slice and dice stock picking ideas at billions of bits per second.

How then do ordinary investors beat the pros? Most don't. Some will brag about their winners and not their losers. Of the ones who do perform better, most are lucky. If a coin is flipped 5 times, there is a 50% chance of it coming up heads three or more times. The average odds are 2.5 heads per five flips. All of the heads were due to chance and required no skill. Similarly, some investors could randomly choose stocks and just by chance, beat the market. This good luck also affects professionals who are lauded for their stock picking prowess, only to fall flat on their faces during their next predictions

Because thousands of people are sifting through mountains of historical data, the most successful investors are those who can spot trends, make forecasts, stay the course, and have the good judgment to make the right decisions before others do. It may be comforting (or maybe not) to know that big time, smart professionals make mistakes, including using sophisticated models that don't always work. Such was the case of the hedge fund Long Term Capital, whose board included two Nobel Prize winners in economics and which was liquidated in 2000 after barely avoiding bankruptcy.

Forecasting is not easy because of conflicting trends. You may have positive signs for the economy and the stock market like dropping interest rates, increasing net exports, and a rise in consumer confidence. At the same time, you could have negative signs like an increase in unemployment, a drop in consumer spending, and a decline in new housing starts.

Understand the Risks of Your Investments

Risks are inherent in our investments as follows:

1. **Interest rate risk.** When interest rates increase, the value of debt falls and the longer the maturity, the greater the drop. For example, 10 year bonds will fall much more in price than two year bonds. The price change works in the other direction too. When interest rates fall, debt prices increase. Therefore, when interest rates are rising, an investor should favor short term debt securities or buy Treasury Inflation Protected Securities (TIPS) whose principal and interest payments increase and decrease with changes in inflation. Unfortunately, the inflation driven increase in TIPS is taxable and investors may wish to put them only in tax sheltered accounts. TIPS can be purchased directly from the U.S. Treasury. Similar corporate funds are also available. Another option is I Bonds which don't fluctuate in price, have a guaranteed return above inflation, and the income isn't taxable until they are cashed in. Finally, during falling interest rates, investors should shift into long term debt. Stocks act somewhat differently. Interest rates usually increase after a recession, but stocks continue to rise until high interest rates cause investors to sell stocks and buy bonds. A further drag on

profits and stocks is that high rates discourage businesses and consumers from borrowing.

2. **Inflation risk.** This risk is the erosion of purchasing power and investment returns caused by price increases (often measured by the Consumer Price Index). If an investor buys a short term Treasury bill yielding 1.5% and inflation is 2%, the 1.5% return is not even keeping up with inflation and is even less if taxes are paid.

3. **Business risk.** This involves the basic nature of a firm's underlying assets and the possible loss of all or part of an investment caused by inadequate cash flows. Business risk is denoted by ratings such as Morningstar, Standard & Poor, Moody's, and Fitch. Another indicator is "beta" which compares an investment's risk to that for the broad market.

For example, the index fund for Turkey (symbol TUR) at ishares. com has a beta of 1.35 compared to its S & P 500 (large American companies) beta of 1.00. The higher beta for Turkey means that the price and returns of the Turkey fund move up and down much more than the broad based S & P 500 fund. The Turkey fund rose more than 200% in the 14 months from its low on March 9, 2009 to May, 2010. However, the fund trades at a much lower price to earnings ratio than the S & P fund which is an indicator of perceived risk. High beta stocks can be great investments when the stock market is going up and really bad on the way down. Risk adverse investors should check the beta of all stock investments.

Long Term Rates of Return on Investments

An important question is whether to buy mostly stocks, bonds, or short term securities like commercial paper and Treasury bills. The book "Stocks, Bonds, Bills, and Inflation" published by Morningstar contains the rates of return on the S & P 500 stocks, long term Treasury and corporate bonds, and Treasury bills from 1926 to 2009. Ignoring taxes (okay in a retirement fund) and buying and selling costs (not bad for a buy and hold strategy, ETFs, index funds, or low commission brokers), and reinvesting dividends, the accumulated value on December 31, 2009 of $1 invested on January 1, 1926 is as follows (Professor Aswath Damodaran, New York University; years 1926 and 1927 added by the author; inflation from bls.gov):

Large stocks (S & P 500)	$1518
Long term U.S. Treasury bonds	$56
Treasury bills (short term)	$20
U.S. Inflation	$12

The winner by a huge margin is large company stocks. In the 84 years from 1926-2009, stocks beat bonds 62% of the time. The only periods of two or more years in which bonds beat stocks in each year was from 1929-32, 1939-41, 1973-74, and 2000-02. By contrast, stocks beat bonds during some years of every decade and in each year of the following periods: 1926-28, 1935-36, 1942-45, 1947-52, 1954-56, 1958-59, 1963-65, 1967-68, 1971-2, 1975-6, 1978-80, 1987-89, 1994-99, and 2003-06. The average annual rates of return from 1926-2009 are:

Large stocks	11.59%
Long term U.S. Treasury Bonds	5.31%
U.S. Treasury bills	3.73%
U.S. inflation	3.09%

Though the annual long run rate of return on large stocks is 11.59%, returns can vary greatly by year and decade. From December 1999 to December 2009, the annual rate of return on the S & P 500 including dividends was 0.6% which was far short of the inflation rate (standardandpoors.com). If the prior two decades are included, the annual return jumps to 10.1%.

The annual distribution of large stock and U.S. Treasury bond returns from 1926-2009 by their size is interesting as follows:

Size of Annual Returns	Number of Years- Stocks	Number of Year- T Bonds
Over 30%	18	3
20.01 to 30%	14	3
10.01 to 20%	15	14
0 to10%	13	42
-.01 to -10%	14	22
-10.01 to -20%	4	0
-20.01 to -30%	3	0
Over -30%	3	0

You will note that there are only six years with big stock losses of over 20%, but there are 32 years with gains of over 20%. That is a compelling reason to bet fairly heavily on stocks, at least in your early years before retirement. By contrast, the bonds have only six years with returns over 20%, but have no losing years of over 10% which helps you sleep at night.

Stock Market Corrections

Since 1950, the Dow Jones Industrial Average has seen nine drops of 10% or more after an economic and stock market rebound (*The Wall Street Journal and Ned Davis Research*). These pullbacks lasted from 18-238 days and ranged from 10-32%. In a study of the S & P 500 from 1927-2009 by Bespoke Investment Group, it was found that 63% of declines of 10% resulted in a bear market of 20% or more. Some research indicates that horrible periods are often followed by strong recoveries. This was certainly true during the Great Depression and in 2009-10.

Annuities

An annuity is a retirement option that provides a monthly income that can be fixed or variable. An individual can make a onetime payment and receive income immediately or later or make a series of payments and then start later. Taxes on the annuity's income are deferred until paid. There are three types of annuities.

Fixed- The monthly payment is fixed and guaranteed by the insurance company.

Variable- Funds are placed in subaccounts, each with its own risk and rewards, so returns vary based upon the success of the underlying assets. This type has more risk, but offers potentially more rewards.

Equity-indexed- Similar to a fixed annuity with a small potential for upside based upon a stock index.

Only invest in annuities from a company with an AM Best rating of A+ or higher. Most states will protect annuity holders from default up to $100,000 based upon its current value. Before investing in an annuity, determine how much you have invested in IRAs, pension funds, mutual funds, and other investments. Because of high fees, I personally do not invest in them.

For information about annuities, go to sec.gov/publications/insurance or totalreturnannuities.com. The latter can provide quotes. For example, I plugged in my age, state, and sex and a onetime investment of $500,000 for the "single life income with no payments to beneficiaries." This investment provides $3,238 in monthly income for my life with no payments to beneficiaries. In other words, the $500,000 disappears. The annual payout rate is 7.77%. Whether this is a good deal depends upon my lifespan and how much risk I am willing to assume when investing the funds myself. If I live 30 more years and would have invested conservatively for a 6% return, this annuity is a good deal. For the "riverboat gambler optimist" who dies in 10 years, it would be terrible.

Other Investing Advice

1. **Avoid Day Trading.** The average day trader experiences a lower rate of return than an investor who holds longer term. Furthermore, if the day trader spent his time working at a job, he would really be ahead. Before becoming a day trader, try making trades without using real money.

2. **"Buy and hold" doesn't mean "buy and forget."** You still need to monitor your investments. It is desirable to rebalance your various investments periodically so your target proportions stay as desired. For example, if there is a big run-up in stock prices, and you want 50% in stocks and 50% in bonds, you will need to sell some stocks and buy bonds.

3. **Since 1971, the S & P 500 realized cumulative positive returns for an average of 12 months after the Federal Reserve first raised interest rates.** Thus, don't start selling stocks when interest rates begin rising.

4. **Investors who buy stocks or bonds should subscribe to *Smart Money* and *Kiplinger's* magazine and with the time and money, *The Wall Street Journal* and *BusinessWeek*.** Morningstar.com is also a great resource for investors with loads of information, including stock and mutual fund analysis and ratings. Some of their information is free. Interestingly, Morningstar just produced a study which showed that low fees was a better predictor of high returns than its own ratings. A number of financial newspapers and magazines can be purchased with frequent flier miles.

5. **Index funds and many ETFs, offered by many mutual funds,**

provide one of the best investment options because of their low management fees and their returns beat 70% of the managed funds. If you want to outperform the pros, this is consistently the most successful technique.

6. **Avoid financial planners that make their money by charging commissions on investments.** They are less likely to provide unbiased recommendations and more likely to suggest options that increase their income. The best planners are those with the CFP (certified financial planner) designation. Go to fpanet.org or napfa.org to find a planner near you. If the planner manages more than $25 million, find his 10 year disciplinary record at adviserinfo.sec.gov. He should listen to you and be willing to discuss how he personally invests. You may also wish to consult with a planner who can give some guidance with estate planning.

7. **The Financial Industry Regulatory Authority regulates brokers and they can't make false claims over the social media networks.** However, these rules don't apply to financial planners working independently of a fund or brokerage company.

8. **Forget dividend reinvestment plans unless you buy and hold for a long time.** Instead of receiving cash, the investor receives fractional shares which can be sold with whole shares. The problem occurs when an investor sells all shares after a dividend is declared, but before the fractional shares are received. These fractional shares may cost as much or more to sell than they are worth, causing the investor to lose the dividend. In addition, dividend reinvestment loses its appeal with the very low commission rates now available.

9. **Don't buy investments that are too complex for you to understand such as derivatives.** Indeed, many advisers, banking executives, money managers, and hedge funds were recommending these securities during the 2000s without understanding the risks or the factors influencing their prices. For the uninformed, speculating in commodities and currency is also very risky.

10. **Be cautious of short selling.** Investors make money on short sales when the price of the investment (including stocks) falls. An investor must pay the dividends on any stock being held in a short

position. Short selling makes sense at certain times. For example, during 2008, when the U.S. was in a recession and oil prices were above $130 a barrel, it was clear that RV makers were in for some tough times, and RV share prices plummeted. However, short selling goes against the long term upward trend in stock prices.

11. **Use leverage judiciously.** Though borrowing money to buy investments can magnify returns, it can be extremely positive as well as negative. It makes more sense in real estate where the interest rates are more fixed, and you usually don't experience immediate margin calls.

12. **Both timing stock market purchases and the selection of them are important.** Personally, I have more trouble with timing. If I could time stocks, I would simply buy a selection of high beta index funds, stocks, or ETFs and make a killing.

13. **Some diversification into foreign markets is desirable.** An investor can buy stocks in large American companies with foreign sales (like Coca Cola, IBM, Caterpillar, etc.) or a fund that owns S & P 500 companies or other large cap stocks. Alternatively, foreign shares can be purchased through funds or ETFs like those offered by ishares.com, Fidelity, or Vanguard and which can be purchased through any broker. The reason for adding foreign exposure is that it provides some diversification, reduces risk from a declining dollar, and the growth in sales and profits is expected to be greater in some markets than the U.S. and Western Europe. The diversification effect is less now than before because stock prices in all countries now move more closely together.

14. **Investments in emerging markets are desirable, but more risky.** Emerging markets are underdeveloped economies such as India, China, Russia, Brazil, South Africa, Malaysia, Singapore, Vietnam, and Turkey. These investments are riskier in part because of more fraud, corruption, and inadequate stockholder protection, laws, and accounting. The betas of their stocks are usually high so that when the U.S. market tanks, their stock prices will drop more than the U.S. When investing in emerging markets, most investors should only buy funds or ETFs.

15. **Commodities and precious metals are a legitimate type of**

investment for a diversified portfolio. Instead of owning the actual products, I buy the stocks, ETFs, or funds of companies producing them. As the commodity or metal value goes up, so normally do the profits and stock prices. However, the stocks are likely to be more volatile than the commodity. The theft risk and insurance costs are too high to store precious metals at home and if stored elsewhere, storage costs must be paid. These types of investments have sometimes been a good hedge against inflation (CPI) and precious metals can be a haven in troubled times. That statement depends upon the time interval as shown here for gold (data from Kitco.com and inflationdata.com).

Date	Actual Price	Price in Today's Dollars	Price (6/9/2010)
Jan. 1975	$175/oz	$731	$1234
Jan. 1980	$850	$2378	$1234

From January, 1975 to June 2010, the price of gold rose from $175 to $1234, considerably beating the inflation adjusted price of $731. However, when measured at gold's 1980 peak of $850, the June 2010 price of $1234 is about half of the inflation adjusted price. Over-reliance (more than 10-20%) on precious metals will subject a portfolio to substantial varying rates of return. Over long periods, the returns likely won't greatly exceed the rate of inflation unless central banks expand gold reserve holdings.

16. **People should invest in somewhat greater amounts of debt as they approach retirement.** Some advisors suggest using your age as a guide. For example, at age 55, an individual would hold 55% in debt. I don't believe in that approach because it depends upon one's risk tolerance, total net worth, expected life span, life style, extended family, current inflation and interest rates, desire to leave an inheritance, and annual cash flows. Most young people should invest heavily in risky assets. If your relatives live into their 90s, you may wish to continue an aggressive equity policy beyond your 50s to avoid outliving your nest egg.

The trade-off is clear. Conservative investing, like buying short term CDs, will produce a small retirement nest egg. If you save only $100,000 and receive a 4% return, that produces only $4,000 in income annually. If the entire $4,000 is used for living, the purchasing power of that $100,000 declines every year. With 5% inflation, its value drops by half in 15 years. A more aggressive investment in long term bonds, preferred and common stocks, and income producing real estate has more risk, especially business risk, but is more likely to provide a sizable retirement fund and annual income. This is especially true for time periods of over 10 years.

17. **Some employers have a retirement plan in which employee contributions are matched.** Always contribute at least to that matching amount.

18. **Always contribute to a retirement plan as soon as you are eligible and avoid withdrawing early.** Unfortunately, the average worker doesn't contribute 10% of his salary until age 55; 20% borrow from their 401(k)s; 15% withdraw funds early; and many far exceed the 4-6% recommended withdrawal rate (JPMorgan Chase study).

19. **In years when your marginal tax rate is low or zero, consider converting some regular IRAs to a Roth.** Tax rates are certain to rise in the future so conversions before then can make sense. Part of any IRA can be converted instead of all of it, and a big conversion may push you into a much higher tax bracket.

20. **Look for unusual investment opportunities.** In 2008, some tax exempt money market funds had considerably higher yields than taxable funds. Consider buying bond funds in currencies likely to appreciate. An investor benefits by higher yields and currency appreciation.

21. **Look for low annual fees on bond and money market funds (about .4%).**

22. **Check the internet for higher interest on savings, CDs, and checking accounts.** Competitive banks include EmigrantDirect. com, BankofInternet.com, and INGDirect.com. These banks have the same requirements as other banks. Check out their FDIC insurance status at fdic.gov.

23. **Link your savings account to your checking account and transfer funds online.**

24. **There is an old Wall Street saying, "Investors buy on rumors and then sell on news."** This could involve buying stocks in anticipation of Federal Reserve interest rate cuts or rising corporate earnings before they happen. Basically, the typical person waits until these events occur and thus misses much of the price increase.

25. **Ultrashort bond funds with average durations of one year or less may have higher yields than money market or short term funds.** They might also have somewhat higher risk.

26. **While more risky than bonds, high dividend stocks may offer some protection against interest rate increases.** The protection is likely to occur in the early stages of a recovery when the stock market and the high dividend stocks are rising even if interest rates are increasing (which depress bond prices).

27. **Another alternative to bonds, but less risky than common stocks and more than bonds, is preferred stocks.** The dividends are less likely to be cut than those on common stocks, but they act like bonds (when interest rates go up, they fall in price, and vice versa). However, some elements of common stocks can be realized by buying convertible preferred which can be converted into common stocks.

28. **Don't buy 10 year or longer bonds when the Federal Reserve first tightens interest rates because rates likely will keep going up.** Though recoveries differ, good buying opportunities are when the 10 year Treasury note hits 5.5-6%. The chart below gives the average annual 10 year Treasury bond rates (federalreserve.gov).

Rates	Years	Total # of Years
Under 3%	1953-55	3
3-3.99%	1956-8, 1961-2, 2008-09	7
4-4.99%	1959-60, 1963-6, 2002-07	12
5-5.99%	1967-8, 1993, 1998-9, 2001	6
6-6.99%	1969, 1971-3, 1995-7, 2000	8
7-7.99%	1970, 1974-77, 1986, 1991-2, 1994	9
8-8.99%	1978, 1987-90	5
9-9.00%	1979	1
10% & up	1980-85	6
	Total	57

About half of the years are 6% and above and half below that. When rates are high or low, they tend to persist for quite a time. Rates below 6% occurred every year from 1953-68. Rates above that had a similar pattern from 1969-1997 except for 1993. With the massive debt that the U.S. has (and it will get much larger), once rates get high, they seem likely to stay high in order to attract capital (barring a sharp recession).

29. **The biggest component of the inflation rate (CPI) is labor costs which make up 70% of it.** According to economists and the Congressional Budget Office, labor costs trigger inflation when the unemployment rate drops to 4.8%. Thus, inflation is likely to be muted for quite some time unless the prices of commodities skyrocket. Inflationary pressures are usually lower when unemployment is high. One exception is the early 1980s.

30. **Build a laddered portfolio of bonds with staggered maturities to provide some stable and predictable income that is not affected by changes in interest rates.**

31. **Roth IRAs have some advantages over traditional IRAs because there is no mandatory distribution age and the funds can be withdrawn at any time free of penalties and taxes.** Early withdrawal of earnings may be subject to taxes.

32. **Resist the pattern of most investors to sell stocks at the bottom of the bear market and buy them after substantial market gains.** The reverse strategy, namely, selling in market highs and buying in dips, is better.

33. **Check the track records for any mutual fund and whether the same managers who achieved the returns are still there.** Successful managers often start their own funds or are hired away by other mutual funds.

34. **Seventeen billion dollars of U.S. Savings Bonds no longer earn interest and should be redeemed.**

Figuring Retirement Savings Needed

Future retirees should assume that the government will help less than now. The group aged 65 and over is expected to increase from about

10% of the U.S. population now to about 20% in 30 years. The number of workers for each retiree has been steadily dropping as the following statistics show (ssa.gov):

Year	Worker per retiree
1940	159
1950	16.5
1960	5.1
1970	3.7
1980	3.2
1990	3.4
2000	3.4
2008	3.2
2020 (projected)	2.5
2040 (projected)	2.0

The current number of workers per retiree is expected to drop (under current law) by almost 40% by 2040, and this will cause substantial funding problems because social security is a "pay as you go" system in which current workers fund the retirees. The current situation of having excess revenue over expenditures is predicted to run out in 2016.

Adding to this problem, the taxpayers will be enormously burdened by the 2010 Patient Protection and Affordable Care Law which will add 33 million new patients to the medical system. Three other trends will add to this medical crush including the aging population, rising disability among the elderly (compared to the past), and greater obesity (1/3 of U.S. adults). Medical inflation will increase and cause medical costs to rise from 17% of GDP to 25%. The combined effects will mean later retirements, more working years, fewer benefits, and more taxes. This means that people still working should be saving a minimum of 10% of their gross income (preferably closer to 20%) and should invest heavily in risky assets.

Advisers often suggest that 4% (adjusted for inflation) of a retirement account be withdrawn annually. The problem with withdrawals is that we don't know how long a person will live, how his investments will perform, or his medical costs. However, most people would prefer to be left with too much money than run out so it is wise to be prudent.

My suggestion is that during down markets, consider reducing withdrawals to avoid depleting the principal. Furthermore, during high inflation, which often accompanies down or stagnant markets, don't increase your withdrawals as much as inflation.

There are two excellent "retirement calculators" at aarp.org and Kiplinger.com under their "tools" section. After you provide information about your family, the two models produce numbers for your "nest egg goal" and the required monthly savings. Kipling also has a "risk tolerance calculator" to determine what percentage to invest in stocks. AARP has a "retirement contributions calculator" that shows the effect of increasing your contributions to an employer sponsored retirement plan. Along with the other information in this section, you can estimate your retirement needs. Then invest aggressively. Remember my advice from Chapter 1:

- **You can almost never save too much or start too early.**

- **Save more in good times than bad times.**

CHAPTER 21

The Economic Effects of Bad Politics

It is no secret that the U.S. Congressional system is broken. **Hundreds of billions of dollars are wasted every year and is the direct result of two main factors:**

1. Campaign contributions that give an incumbent a sizable advantage in elections. Since many members of Congress want to be re-elected, they vote for legislation that benefits the contributors so the contributors will give more and not give to their opponents.

2. Career politicians who build up a power base, heavily influenced by large special interest groups.

The effects of this legalized vote buying will only get worse because of the 2010 U.S. Supreme Court's ruling in "Citizen's United v. Federal Elections Commission." The court basically gave First Amendment rights to large groups such as corporations, Indian tribes (the nation's second largest campaign donors in 2007 and 2008), professional groups, and labor unions to spend whatever they want to influence elections. The floodgates will open up to an avalanche of distorting and misleading ads. Campaign periods will increasingly be dominated by negative ads. The "Swift Boating" tactic done to discredit John Kerry in the 2004 presidential elections may become routine.

While this campaign finance problem is most evident at the national level, it also exists at the state and local levels. *The Wall Street Journal* ran a feature about money given to out-of-state candidates by law firms. In the past decade, the top 25 law firms specializing in shareholder litigation gave $21 million to these state and local officials and parties.

A Current Example of Bad Politics

The recently passed medical insurance bill is a classic example of the U.S. having the best political system that money can buy. It is clear that, at some time in the future, a fix to our health care system would be needed. Each year, the number of people not covered by a medical insurance plan increases, and this strains the whole health care system. The solution should have been a bipartisan effort to share the pain where the parties hammered out a plan in which no one was very happy. Unfortunately, no Republicans supported the health care bill, and it was laden with features influenced by campaign contributions, unsavory deals, and special interests.

Some provisions that would have dramatically reduced the cost of the plan and should have been considered include:

- Allow re-importation of drugs from countries where they are cheaper. Americans pay two or more times what people living elsewhere pay.

- Allow easier introduction of generics.

- Require doctors to use best practices. For example, recent studies show that many heart patients do as well on drugs as those with stents. Yet some doctors who make more money from stents will still recommend them unnecessarily.

- Fund massive U.S. Government studies to show the effectiveness and cost/benefits of treatments.

- Limit the number of medical tests based upon science of cost versus benefit. The mammogram recommendation was very controversial, but these hard decisions need to be made.

- Have a large public option. Seniors will eventually find that the new law is going to cripple their access to medical care. Medicaid and Medicare will be the main parts of the system that have controlled costs. The private plans will reimburse medical providers based upon cost plus the insurance company's mark-up. With doctors flooded by all of these new patients, they are going to choose the highest payers, i.e., those with private insurance. With a great supply of new patients and not a comparable increase in care givers, medical inflation will accelerate.

- Severely limit malpractice suits.

- Have binding arbitration for some malpractice cases before an impartial arbitrator.

- Limit experimental treatments until proven effective. Society can't pay for everything.

- Aggressively weed out fraud.

- Reduce incentives for doctors who over treat patients and those making frequent mistakes.

- Require members of panels who make recommendations to have no conflict of interest. Some panels receive funds from the groups benefitting from the guidelines.

- Limit future health expenditures to 20% of GDP. Currently, it is about 17.5%. Then implement strong measures to insure it doesn't exceed that level.

- Pay for what works. Many operations, medications, and procedures have little value. This would be controversial and hard to implement, but important.

- Have a massive campaign aimed at every age group to encourage healthy eating, drinking, and exercise habits and to discourage smoking.

- Introduce federal regulations to weed out bad doctors.

- Allow more qualified foreign doctors to become citizens.

- Have federal regulations to allow more nurse staffed clinics.

- Develop guidelines for end of life care. Massive amounts are spent to provide care in the final years of life. When my own mother was in her final years and very sick, her nursing home was aggressively trying to push care that was expensive, useless, and paid for by the government.

- Encourage "living wills." This often reduces end of life care since many people do not want expensive procedures done when they are terminally ill.

- No special deals for any group, with some exceptions, like low income.

- Widely publish the cost and frequency of procedures at different clinics and cities. Some medical facilities buy expensive equipment or develop medical specialties, and this usually results in more tests and operations. A limited amount of this information is available at Data.Medicare.gov.

- Severely restrict advertising for prescription drugs.

- Require the use of generic, older proven, and over-the-counter drugs where they work nearly as well as expensive drugs. A good example is the prescription drug Nexium. The over-the-counter drug Prilosec is very similar and others such as Pepsid AC are effective.

- Widely advertise the downside of drug reactions, complications, drug interaction, and side effects (to discourage overuse).

- Encourage more conservative use of medical facilities. Most people probably don't need annual physicals and many other tests.

- Allow all medical insurance providers that meet certain criteria to operate in every state.

- Be less aggressive about the number of people covered until the fiscal situation is better.

- Restrict premiums that medical providers can charge to "out of network patients".

Consider how many businesses would be affected by and opposed to any regulations implementing these policies. They include the majority of doctors, nurses, medical technicians, laboratories, hospitals, clinics, testing suppliers, medical equipment and supplies manufacturers, wholesalers, pharmaceutical companies, distributors, lawyers, insurers, and media outlets. Then think about how much money they can spend to influence legislation.

The solution to the Congressional gridlock is to do the following for all Congressional and presidential elections:

1. Eliminate all private financing except small contributions of $100 per person or business.

2. Severely limit outside spending on commercials.

3. Provide for large scale public funding for all Congressional and presidential races.

4. Shorten the period for campaigning during primary and general elections to 30-60 days each.

5. Establish term limits so Congress has the guts to make hard choices.

6. Ban earmarks.

7. Have secret ballots for chairmanships. Election should not be related to seniority.

8. Increase public access to decision-making.

9. Severely restrict former members of Congress from accepting any job with any firm over which his committee had jurisdiction.

10. Put greater restrictions on lobbyists. There are now 11,000 lobbyists in Washington, D.C., or more than 20 for each member of Congress.

11. Establish "open" primaries in which voters can vote for any candidate. Currently, to get elected, a politician has to appeal to the extreme wing of his party. The U.S. needs more moderates.

Without substantial changes, Congress will continue to waste the taxpayer's money and put off making decisions that bring fiscal responsibility. It is undesirable for an extreme segment of one party to be in control of the Presidency and both houses of Congress. If most of the eleven suggestions aren't passed, then the best option is to hope that voters will create a "do nothing" Congress by mixing control of the three bodies.

INDEX

WEBSITE INDEX (current at time of publication)

CPSIA information can be obtained at www.ICGtesting.com
Printed in the USA
LVOW041632220212

269957LV00005B/90/P